This book is dedicated to the more than one hundred thousand men and women, living and dead, who for a time, briefly or impressively long, contributed their talents to give The News a unique place in the history of journalism.

THE NEWS

The First Fifty Years of
New York's Picture Newspaper

220 East 42d Street, New York, N.Y. 10017

Library of Congress Catalog Card Number: 77-93225

First Edition—Second Printing

By LEO E. McGIVENA
and others

[Mr. McGivena, who watched the birth pangs of The News, wrote approximately the first half of this book before encountering insurmountable difficulties. The balance was put together by Warren Hall, who wrote portions of it. Other editorial assistance was provided by William J. White Jr. (retired), Joseph Martin, Phil Santora, Donald Singleton, Jack Metcalfe, Jack Smith, Kermit Jaediker, Phil Pepe and (especially) Clarence Woodbury, all of The News. Thomas J. DeSena, assistant purchasing agent, assisted ably in many ways. The project was in charge of Richard W. Clarke, retired editor.]

For his part of the book, Mr. McGivena wishes to thank Miss Sinclair Dakin, of Administration, Mrs. Marguerite A. Andrews and Miss Beatrice Kinn for invaluable help in research; Joseph F. McCarthy, Michael Rufolo, Nicholas Loprete and other members of The News library; Robert E. Wathey and the staff of The News personnel department; Edward F. Quinn, assistant to the executive editor; Randolph F. Paulson, advertising research supervisor; and all those who racked their memories to make the record more complete.

CONTENTS

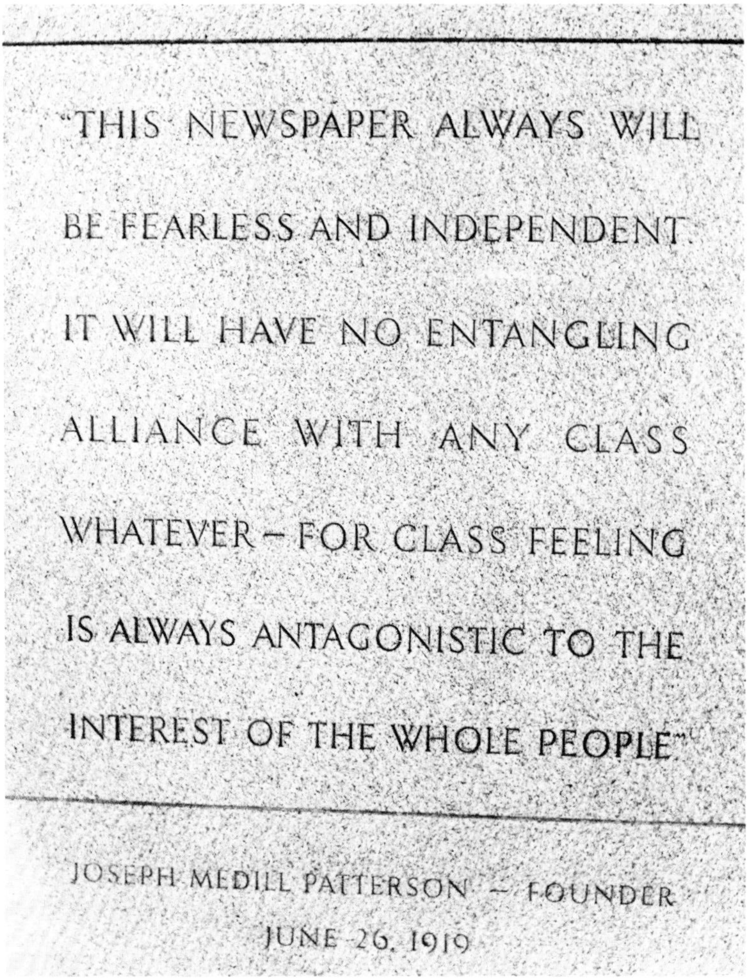

"THIS NEWSPAPER ALWAYS WILL
BE FEARLESS AND INDEPENDENT.
IT WILL HAVE NO ENTANGLING
ALLIANCE WITH ANY CLASS
WHATEVER—FOR CLASS FEELING
IS ALWAYS ANTAGONISTIC TO THE
INTEREST OF THE WHOLE PEOPLE."

JOSEPH MEDILL PATTERSON — FOUNDER
JUNE 26, 1919

The News credo as set forth in part of the paper's first editorial, June 26, 1919. It is engraved on a marble slab mounted on the west wall of the building at 220 East 42d St.

Part I

The Old Timer on the copy desk in Chicago told it this way:

"Joe Patterson and Bertie McCormick came back from the war full of vim and free enterprise, all set to show their muscle.

"Bill Field had cut out of his business manager's job on the Tribune, and was sort of standing by in New York. So they asked Bill to find them a New York paper. Why New York? Well, when you're top dog in Chicago, there isn't much kick in Keokuk.

"Field shopped the big town papers, and didn't find any bargains. Then he ran into this fellow Utassy who had been a big man with the Hearst magazines. Utassy was hot to start a tabloid in New York, but Hearst wouldn't buy it—then. So Field got Utassy together with Joe and Bert and Max Annenberg, and they started the Daily News in the old Evening Mail Building. On a shoestring, you might say. In about six months it caught on, and has been going like a house on fire ever since.

"After all, they gave New Yorkers a new paper with pictures and features, something they could read on the subway. It was as simple as that . . ."

Begging the Old Timer's pardon: It wasn't simple—as anything.

It wasn't simple at all.

INVOLUNTARY INVOLVEMENT

FIRST PERSON

It was nearly noon when Jim Cleary came back to the office. He stopped by my desk, and said casually "You better get ready to go to New York Monday. The colonel wants me to stick around next week."

The day was Saturday, June 21, 1919. The place was an eleventh floor office in the old Chicago Tribune Building at Dearborn and Madison Sts. James Mansfield Cleary, former reporter, had come back to the Tribune the year before to start a promotion department, although we didn't know it by that name. The colonel was Robert R. McCormick, co-publisher of the Tribune. I was a fledgling copywriter, five months out of the army; a disappointed flying cadet whose flight training had ended when the field was closed in January. I wasn't happy with civilian life, or my job, or Chicago.

The business taking me to New York was the Illustrated Daily News, the newspaper the Tribune was to start in New York the following week, on Thursday, June 26. We had been told about it some weeks earlier, and shown the dummy of the odd four-column page. It was to be a combination of newspaper and magazine, with lots of pictures and features, modeled after the London Mirror. It was called a tabloid.

Publication had originally been set for some time in August; then the date was advanced because of a rumor that Hearst was coming out with a tabloid in New York.

We were to do the initial promotion to advertisers. Max Annenberg, the Tribune's circulation manager, had planned a beauty contest, which was to be advertised in New York papers by the Tribune's agency, Burnett, Kuhn, and was not our concern.

Jim Cleary wrote three form letters, to go to a list of 4,000 advertisers and agencies; one for the day before The News appeared, the second for June 26, the third the day after. I devised a broadside which was to reproduce pages from the first issue. The accompanying copy was written, the text set and electroplated.

*　*　*

The weekend passed in mixed elation and apprehension; I was pleased that I had been picked to go to New York, and concerned that I might flop on the job.

So, Monday afternoon I was on the Century, the New York Central's 20-hour train, the fastest conveyance to New York. Tuesday morning I was in Grand Central. I checked into the Biltmore, and hurried down to the Tribune's eastern office at 251 Fifth Ave., on the northeast corner of 28th St. The office was a half floor above the street, in a made-over town house. The reception area on the Fifth Ave. end had a rack which held two weeks of Tribunes, and heavy black leather chairs and lounge. Behind the rail which shut off the rest of the office, a stubby girl, named Minnie, tended a small switchboard, fielded callers, sold Tribunes. A row of private offices ran along the 28th St. side.

I met Roy C. Holliss, broad-shouldered, tanned, athletic looking, the Tribune's eastern manager. He introduced me to William H. Field, whom I had seen around the Tribune but had never met before. He was tall, lank, thin, with a grave face and clipped gray mustache, a warm smile and low voice. I showed them the form letters and the dummy of the broadside. Field rather stunned me by thanking me for coming to New York to help the new paper.

Letterheads and the card lists had been shipped earlier, and were in a letter shop at 28th and Lexington, where I proceeded next. A harassed looking bald man presided over a large room of young typists who chattered like birds. He assured me the first form letters would be ready by 5 o'clock.

* * *

Following Holliss' direction, I went down into the 28th St. station, and had my first subway ride, always somewhat terrifying to the outlander. Off at the Brooklyn Bridge station, I came upstairs opposite City Hall Park.

The sun was bright that June morning, the grass in the park brilliant green; and City Hall as impressive as its early American builders intended it to be—although the gray barracks of the "temporary" Post Office south of City Hall was an eyesore. On the east side of the park was Park Row, dominated by Joseph Pulitzer's brownstone World Building with its gold dome, once the tallest building in New York.

The park was well patrolled by young policemen. One after another, when asked where City Hall Place was, jerked his thumb over his shoulder. I circled the park and eventually stumbled into it. (On a recent sentimental journey I couldn't find it; and learned from the Bureau of Streets that City Hall Place had been "abolished" in August, 1929.)

City Hall Place was a two block long street. Its tallest structure was the 12-story Mail Building, which looked old and tired, like the rest of the street. Opposite was a three-story public bath; a drain pipe out in front dribbled soapy water into the gutter during daylight hours. Adjoining the public bath was an Italian *groceria,* and next to that a bar which shortly became the street's first speakeasy.

* * *

In the Mail Building, the fifth floor was bleak and barren. Some small offices had been partitioned along one side. Some people sat at desks; and a group was clustered around a long table which held their typewriters.

There were two familiar faces. Harry Canfield, editor of the Sunday Tribune gravure section, had been brought East as picture editor. He was central casting's image of an editor: leonine head with close-cropped, iron-gray hair, and an impressive way of bellowing "Boy." The other was John Alcock, a tall, wispy, unhappy-looking Tribune sportswriter, who had been tapped as sports editor. The scene was a far cry from the big organized Tribune newsroom in Chicago. The small staff seemed uncertain and confused; and an unlikely lot to produce a newspaper the next day.

I looked up George von Utassy, the business manager; stocky, affable, confident. (He and the managing editor, Arthur Clarke, were the only bona fide New Yorkers in the bunch.) I explained I would need casts of pages from the first issue to be multigraphed for the broadside. He dictated a memo to somebody on the Mail, called a printer and sent me over to Varick St.

A bored service man gave me an indifferent reception. His first question was "Who's going to pay for this?" He was doubtful about finding the type of paper required for our broadside, coated stock, and seemed shocked at the idea of getting the job out in three days. (It took a full week.) Again, I was impressed with the fact that New York was not Chicago, where the Tribune's prestige always got action.

* * *

I went back to the Tribune office on Fifth Ave. which already seemed like home. Familiars were Chalmers Pancoast, an older man, transferred from Chicago the previous year and second in command in the New York office. Another import from Chicago was Tommy (Thomas J.) Cochrane, recently a 1st lieutenant in the 32d Division Cavalry headquarters troop, who would eventually become The News advertising director.

Not known to me previously were J. J. Evans Hessey, slight, dapper, with his red hair and mustache and his English speech, not long out of the Canadian forces, destined to become manager of the Tribune's

Paris Edition, and later the business manager of This Week. And there were two just hired cubs, Allison R. Leininger and Frank C. Cortright, ex-army, ex-Lafayette College; both over-six footers domiciled in a Pullman compartment room at the Brooklyn YMCA. Cortright later switched to real estate, and became executive director of the National Association of Home Builders, in Washington. Al Leininger had a distinguished career with magazines, was eventually president of Parents Magazine Enterprises.

At 4:45 that first day, I hurried over to the letter shop, where all was not well. Four thousand copies of the first letter had been multigraphed, but names and addresses had been filled in on only a thousand. We offered the girls double time to finish the job, but they laughed merrily and left at 5 o'clock. The thousand filled-in letters were sent out. Letter number two was revised to cover the rest of the list the next day. Letter three went out on schedule.

* * *

Chalmers Pancoast took a number of us to dinner. And I went willingly to bed at the Biltmore. My room on a lower floor was over a series of private rooms where riotous parties took place, in anticipation of National Prohibition which was to go into effect on July 1. After two such nights, I switched to the Hotel Prince George, across from the office on 28th St.

When No. 1, Volume 1, of the Illustrated Daily News appeared Thursday morning, I thought it was terrible—probably because it was not another Chicago Tribune.

The chores I was supposed to do in New York in four days took 10. On July 3, I had checked out of the Prince George, had my ticket on the Century, packed bag in the office, and was set to shake the dust of New York from my feet forever. But along toward noon, Field emerged from his office. He had been talking with Gene Parsons, advertising manager of the Tribune, he said; and it was all right with Parsons for me to stay the balance of the summer—if it was all right with me. Since I had done little but spend money and make mistakes, I had no very solid objections. I hustled back to the Prince George and reclaimed my room.

I managed to keep busy the rest of the summer but I don't remember at what. On Sept. 13, I was glad to go home to Chicago. I was back again for a week in April, 1920, and a week in October, to do promotion for classified at Field's request.

In January, '21, he asked for me to come with The News for keeps. I still didn't want to, but he convinced me that I could move ahead faster with a new organization than with the settled, stable Tribune. On Jan. 15, I was transferred to The News payroll.

SOME BACKGROUND WITHOUT MUSIC

The New York News was the end-product of the dissatisfaction of two dissimilar cousins with their status as heirs—Joseph Medill Patterson and Robert Rutherford McCormick. Both were grandsons of Joseph Medill.

* * *

Son of a Belfast shipwright, William Medill's marriage to an Espiscopalian girl so outraged his strict Presbyterian father that the young couple decided to emigrate. In 1819 they settled on a farm near St. John, New Brunswick, under the impression that they were in the United States; the territory was in dispute, and was later awarded to Canada. Joseph Medill was born on this farm on April 6, 1823.

Nine years later the family moved to a farm near Massillon, Ohio. Joseph attended the village academy, but family finances did not permit him to go to college. He was an omnivorous reader, walked miles to borrow a book. After school, he worked on the farm, and sold subscriptions to Horace Greeley's Weekly New York Tribune. In his late teens he taught in a district school in adjoining Tuscarawas County.

Like many young men of this period, Joseph aspired to a career in politics, via the law. He read law in the office of two Canton attorneys, was admitted to the bar in 1846. With George W. McIlvaine, later Chief Justice of Ohio, he practiced law in New Philadelphia.

His lean law practice left him with a lot of spare time, which he took to spending in the office of the Tuscarawas Chronicle, a weekly, where he learned to set type, and later compose editorials out of the type case. James Patrick, the Chronicle's publisher, was a local wheel—judge of common pleas, Indian agent, Presbyterian elder, and a potent figure in Whig politics. In his office Joseph Medill met politicians who became prominent in the Lincoln regime. An apt pupil, he studied Patrick's power structure, learned how politics and the press meshed; opted for newspapers instead of law.

In 1849, he bought the Conshocton (Ohio) Whig, renamed it The Republican. The paper prospered. Two years later, Medill moved on to Cleveland, founded the Forest City Daily; and shortly merged with a Free Soil paper, the Cleveland Free Democrat; the merged paper was titled the Cleveland Leader.

He also found time to marry Katharine Patrick in New Philadelphia on Sept. 2, 1852—against the opposition of her father. Miss Patrick was an experienced compositor, and a handy lass to have around a newspaper. She helped out on the Leader until a few days before her first child was born on July 11, 1853—Katharine Van Etta Medill. Her second daughter, Elinor Medill, was born June 30, 1855.

Horace Greeley, whose New York Tribune was the most influential journal in the East, urged Medill to start a penny paper in Chicago. Medill arrived in Chicago in the spring of 1855; studied the Chicago papers, and bought a third interest in the Tribune. He was joined a month later by Dr. Charles H. Ray, a physician who had given up medicine, and made a name for himself as editor of the Galena Jeffersonian. Ray bought a quarter interest in the Tribune and his editorials were to make it a power in the West.

The Chicago Tribune had been started in 1847, drifted through a succession of publishers and editors. In 1855, its daily circulation was 3,000; its weekly edition 4,500. The Tribune never drifted again.

In 1855, Medill was 32 years old, red-haired, handsome, a tireless worker. His brand of journalism was personal, political, partisan. He was opinionated, often extreme in his view, black and white in his judgments. Still a rigid Presbyterian, with a special animus against liquor, he never doubted that God was on his side.

Chicago in 1855 had a polyglot population of 85,000; would almost triple the figure within the next decade. An important Lake port and a rail terminal, it was a funnel for men and materials going east and west. Every train stopped in Chicago. Industry found the central location desirable, with ready access to men, materials, and markets. Chicago kept growing, making money. And the Tribune grew with it.

* * *

Slavery was the dark shadow on men's minds. As every new State applied for admission to the Union, the South tried to keep the ratio of slave states even; and the North wanted the new States free. For nine years Dr. Ray's editorials were anti-slavery, abolitionist. With Medill he gave substance to the new Republication party. They were the first to discern Abraham Lincoln as presidential timber, made him known outside Illinois, worked for his nomination and election, supported him through the Civil War. Ray, tired and in poor health, resigned in 1863.

* * *

Fires were common in the jerry-built town. The Great Fire of 1871 devastated square miles, destroyed much of the business district—including the Tribune's relatively new and presumably fireproof $150,000 building. Medill bought a small print shop on Canal St., a few blocks away; and two days later his paper was back on the streets.

After the fire, he ran for Mayor on the "Fireproof Ticket," won handily. And lost his popularity in 1873 when he tried to legislate the Sunday closing of saloons. He resigned office, and went to Europe for a few months. On his return the next year, he bought a majority control of the paper, borrowing money from Chicago's merchant prince, Marshall Field. And until he died in 1899, he was master of the Tribune.

* * *

The fire was followed by the Chicago Renaissance. The new millionaires proceeded to build on the near North Side and South Michigan Ave. pretentious town houses with lawns and stables. The boom brought architects, artists, artisans, art dealers and assorted adventurers; and sparked *grand tours* of Europe in quest of art objects, bijoux, English butlers, French chefs, and eventually titled husbands.

* * *

Medill's two older daughters were tall, handsome, red-haired, strong willed—and usually at odds with each other.

Katharine, the eldest, married Robert Sanderson McCormick on June 8, 1876. He was a nephew of Cyrus Hall McCormick, developer of the McCormick reaper, president of the Harvester Company and a power in Chicago; but a comparatively poor McCormick relative. Medill and Cyrus had been bitter enemies; Medill characterized the McCormicks Copperheads (Southern sympathizers) during the Civil War. So the marriage did not meet with his favor.

Robert had studied law at the University of Virginia, and started a brokerage and shipping business in Chicago. His first son, Joseph Medill McCormick was born in Chicago on May 16, 1877; and was promptly nominated by his mother as publisher-elect of the Tribune. A second son, Robert Rutherford McCormick, was born July 30, 1880.

In 1883, Robert S. McCormick speculated in wheat, lost his patrimony. Thereafter he was dependent on his wife, who was dependent on her father and the Tribune. He drifted for the next few years until the election of Benjamin Harrison in 1888 restored the Republicans to power. Joseph Medill secured for him a post as second secretary to Robert Todd Lincoln, son of the Great Emancipator and head of the Tribune's law firm, who was appointed Minister to Great Britain.

In his other son-in-law, Medill was fortunate in having an able lieutenant, and successor—Robert Wilson Patterson, Jr., son of an eminent divine who had been pastor of Chicago's Second Presbyterian Church for 32 years.

Chicago born, Patterson went to local schools, and entered Lake Forest College which his father had founded. He went on to Williams College, and was graduated with the class of 1871. He studied law for a while but after the fire worked as a reporter for the Chicago Times, and later for a religious weekly.

In 1873 he came to the Tribune as assistant night editor, subsequently served as Washington correspondent, editorial writer, and managing editor. In 1878, against the wishes of his own father and Medill (opposing parental wishes seemed to be standard with the Medill tribe), he eloped with Medill's second daughter, Elinor.

Their first child, Joseph Medill Patterson, was born in Chicago on Jan. 6, 1879. Their second was Elinor Medill Patterson (Cissy), born in Chicago Nov. 7, 1881. When she grew up she changed her first name to Eleanor.

Patterson was a better newsman than Medill, broadened the paper's coverage; adopted linotypes (again in opposition to Medill) and new machinery for more efficient production. He was mild-mannered, without color but not without character; and in time became the one man on the paper who could countermand a Medill order and make his decision stand. On Medill's death in 1899, he became the Tribune's publisher.

Robert Patterson's term as publisher was not too happy. His health began to fail in 1905, and his successor presented a problem.

Joseph Medill McCormick, who was generally known simply as Medill McCormick, was graduated from Yale in 1900, put in a stint as a reporter, and spent a year as a correspondent in the Philippines. In 1903 he married Ruth Hanna, daughter of the Cleveland industrialist and senator from Ohio. Thereafter politics overshadowed publishing in his interest. Patterson came to distrust him, and he was deposed by the directors in 1910.

Joseph Medill Patterson, Yale '01, had worked as a reporter for a while, found the paper dull, and left. Robert Rutherford McCormick, Yale '03, came back to Chicago to study law at Northwestern, and he too was early involved in politics. In 1909, Publisher Patterson persuaded him to serve as the Tribune's treasurer, at no salary.

On March 1, 1910, one month before Robert Patterson's death, the paper's directors appointed James Keeley as general manager "with absolute authority in all departments."

Keeley was London born, had emigrated to this country in 1883 while not yet 16. He settled in Kansas, supported himself with odd jobs. While living in Wyandotte, he began to send brightly written items to the Kansas City Journal, was hired as a reporter. He subsequently worked in Memphis and Louisville, came to the Tribune in the summer of 1889. By 1895, he was city editor, and three years later as managing editor he proceeded to revitalize the paper.

Keeley gave the directors some uneasy times. A series against Mayor Carter Harrison brought three $100,000 libel suits; Keeley tried to wriggle out but finally had to run full retractions. And an expose of Sen. William Lorimer's activities threatened to turn sour, but three years later the Senator was expelled and the Tribune vindicated.

By 1914, McCormick and Patterson had grown in influence, and Keeley sensed the decline of his position. On May 11, he left the Tribune to take over the management of the Record-Herald, backed by Kohlsaat, Insull and some other money men. The paper was a failure, went to Hearst Jan. 1, 1918. Keeley for the rest of his life was a publicist for the Pullman Company.

NOT A NICE PLACE TO VISIT

In 1919, living was simpler, poorer, less varied. Foods were fewer, and prepared foods rare. Vegetables came in season, not from a frozen food cabinet; you ate strawberries when strawberries were ripe in New Jersey rather than Florida. A cake-mix was something a housewife did, not bought. Refrigeration meant an ice box. Coal was used in most dwellings for heat and cooking. Drug stores sold drugs and had soda fountains.

Of the 9,000,000 cars in use, most had open bodies; and the majority were Model T Fords.

Health was much more precarious. Tuberculosis took a high toll; if it was discovered early enough, the patient might recover in two years with treatment. Pneumonia was a killer. Diabetes was slow death. The vitamin was still a laboratory curiosity. The average height of men in World War I was 5 feet 7½ inches—two inches below the World War II average.

Prices by present standards were laughably low. So were wages and salaries. A stenographer earned $15 a week, a bookkeeper $25; and $75 was junior executive scale. Factories worked six days a week; though most offices closed at 1 p.m. Saturday.

* * *

In the last week of June, 1919, New York was a mad place, with too many people, too much going on.

The American Expeditionary Force was coming home. Troop transports arrived in bunches, debarking men on both sides of the Hudson, in Brooklyn, on Long Island. Officer casuals, sweating in trench coats and laden with kit bags, went cursing from hotel to hotel to find rooms. Bands played and parades marched somewhere during the daylight hours. Home town delegations arrived by chartered trains to welcome the returning heroes. The heroes, on pass from the camps, roved the town in small groups, uncomfortable in their high-collared winter issue uniforms.

The weather was New York tropical. It rained some time every day. The heat and humidity were facts of life from which there was no escape. Most businessmen wore vests; the working girls in their dark skirts and white shirtwaists fared better. Hostesses placed a block of ice before an open window and played electric fans on it to cool their guests. On the lower East Side, life went on with open windows; and at night people swarmed out of doors. Passengers on the elevated trains in summer observed the domestic rites of unabashed flat dwellers. A decade would go by before you could catch cold in the primitively air-conditioned Broadway movie houses.

Traffic was agonizingly slow, clogged by horse drawn vehicles and pre-war trucks that broke down frequently. On the principal streets, policemen at the intersections tried to maintain some control of traffic.

Prohibition was to take effect the end of the month. At night the town was awash with parties, celebrating the demise of John Barleycorn. From 5 o'clock until well into the night, a crew of doormen tenderly steered fuddled celebrants from the broad granite steps of the old Belmont Hotel across from Grand Central Terminal into waiting cabs. Brewers had been hopeful that the Volstead Act would be amended to permit 3.5% beer; lost hope as Congress refused to act, and in the closing days of June began to give away their beer. On Friday and Saturday nights of that last week, the original Madison Square Garden, which actually was quite close to Madison Square, was the scene of an enormous free beer bash. Bands showed up every 20 minutes. East 27th St. was crowded with would-be participants.

What the well-intentioned drys could not foresee was that Prohibition would launch the speakeasy, give drinking social status, bring on the Jazz Decade of the '20s.

* * *

Housing was scarce, vacant apartments nonexistent. Some unscrupulous landlords raised rents; and tenants unwilling to pay the increase could be evicted after 30 days. City marshals and their deputies worked overtime. In poor neighborhoods, the possessions of some families were piled up on the sidewalks for days, exposed to the elements, simply because the evicted tenants couldn't find other places to live.

Merchandise of all types was in short supply. A buyer would order the same item from a half dozen sources; when one filled the order, the others got cancellations. Manufacturers and distributors coasted along with phony backlogs of orders until mid-1920 when the inevitable deflation began.

Prices were high, often exorbitant. The humble pre-war 10-cent hamburger had doubled in price. One hotel distinguished itself adversely by charging 30 cents for coffee *and* 20 cents for cream. Apparel of all kinds was in short supply and almost double pre-war prices.

A burly lieutenant of engineers landed at the Battery, stopped at a fruit stand; took a banana off a stalk, peeled it, started to eat it, and asked the vendor "How much?" When the man said "fifteen cents," the lieutenant floored him with a single punch. Police had to be called to calm down both parties.

Fortunately the federal government acted with unwonted speed, arrested profiteering merchants; and courts handed down stiff jail sentences.

New York with its 5,000,000 plus inhabitants was not so much a city as an assemblage of neighborhoods. Some Brooklynites lived and died without ever setting foot outside the borough. And a large number of Manhattanites had never been in Brooklyn. There were open spaces in all five boroughs, and even farms on the northern end of Manhattan.

This was the hot, crowded, unhappy town where the emigres from Chicago had elected to bring out a novel newspaper. Yet, as events proved, the timing was near perfect.

* * *

What made 1919 notable was the existence of a vast euphoria unprecedented in our past. Millions of young men shed their uniforms with the conviction that the world had seen its last war; and most Americans shared their belief. Of course we would need a small army and navy and some marines for policing trouble spots. But war among nations was a thing of the past. The relief that swept this country and the world was much like that we might experience today if the atom bomb could be abrogated or abolished.

It was a time "to make no little plans." Even the conservative president of the United States Steel Corporation, Judge Elbert H. Gary, who held that 12-hour shifts were essential to make steel, proclaimed that this country was on the threshold of unbounded opportunities.

This optimism survived the strikes, shortages and deflation of the next three years, the sharp business decline of 1922, and tripped off the enormous industrial expansion and widespread prosperity of the '20s. The Dow Jones average in 1919 reached a new high of 120, and sparked the wave of fantastic speculation that ended ignominiously with the market crash and the Depression.

The Chicago Tribune was fortunate in this period of great post-war opportunity to have great resources in talent and men. Patterson and McCormick had reached the full vigor of early middle age and neither had known failure. Field was available, and invaluable. And there were many others whose dedication and intense individual effort made the collective success that is The News.

Costs were a fraction of what they are today.

Even more remarkable, in a city where 17 English language papers were published, there was no competition, no pressure tactics such as had marked the course of newspapers in Chicago.

The last two big wars were not good for newspapers. During a major conflict the news is the war—the most important story the casualty list. Staffs are depleted, and have to be replenished. The normal business of the newspaper is interrupted.

In 1919, the New York newspapers were not only disorganized by World War I, they were old and tired. Joseph Pulitzer, Whitelaw Reid, the senior Scripps, the Bennetts were gone. William Randolph Hearst was 56 years old. Frank Munsey was soon to get into stride as a buyer and seller of newspapers but he trafficked in them without talent or understanding. Adolph Ochs was the most active and purposeful publisher in New York, building to his particular pattern the empire that is the Times.

When The News came along, the other publishers didn't put out "welcome" mats or send floral horseshoes. They simply ignored it.

Another factor that must be noted is that in 1919 the newspaper occupied a more important place in the lives of Americans than it does today. As Arthur Rudd, of Columbia's School of Journalism, was to point out in a master's thesis on tabloids in 1925, the newspaper had become an anodyne. It informed, amused, distracted; gave people something to do with their time in the morning, and filled the void between dinner and bed—without the competition in spot news and entertainment that came later with radio and television.

The year 1919 was a good time, and New York was a garden spot for something new in newspapers.

This is not a mystery story so it is needless to turn to the last chapter—although a reasonable denouement is there. Few will be surprised. Much water has gone over the dam between the musings of the Old Timer and the 50th birthday of The News, and some of it flashed into foam and was swept away and some iridesced excitingly in the sun and some flowed steadily onward through light and shadow. The course was never placid. This needs describing but first a word from our sponsors. (They are interesting too.)

THE PRIME MOVERS

Patterson wanted a newspaper in New York. McCormick was not particularly interested, but agreed to cooperate. Field couldn't find one worth buying. Utassy proposed a tabloid. These four were the prime movers. Patterson comes first.

Joseph Medill Patterson

Joseph Medill Patterson was 40 years old. He didn't get along too well with his father, then managing editor of the Tribune, but in his later years he was proud of him and of his grandfather, the eminent clergyman and founder of Lake Forest College.

Patterson attended private schools in Chicago and in France for a year. He was sent to Groton in 1891, spent six years there. He entered Yale in 1897, but skipped a year in 1900, served as an assistant to Hearst correspondents covering the Boxer Rebellion in China; and was graduated in 1901. The next year he married Alice Higginbotham.

In the following decade, he was a young man in a hurry. He worked as a reporter on the Tribune for two years, found it unexciting. Like his grandfather, he took an early interest in politics. He was elected in 1903 to the Illinois House of Representatives, had a brief and stormy career in Springfield. His advocacy of municipal ownership of street railways brought him into conflict with his father; then he learned that his election had resulted from a deal with the State Republican Committee, made by his father. He resigned at once, allied himself with the Democrats, campaigned for Edward F. Dunne as mayor.

With Dunne in office, he was appointed Commissioner of Public Works in 1905. He promptly proceeded to bring suit against Marshall Field & Company (of which his father-in-law was president), for using space under Chicago streets. He also tried to force Chicago newspapers to pay higher taxes. But the support of the Dunne administration was lukewarm and laggard, and once again he resigned office.

Disillusioned with both Republicans and Democrats, he declared himself a Socialist; and in 1908 served as campaign manager for Eugene V. Debs, the Socialist candidate for the Presidency. His activities alienated his father. The young firebrand retired to a farm in Libertyville, Ill., to become a part-time dairy farmer and the successful author of socialistic tracts, plays and novels.

His opening shocker was "The Confessions of a Drone" published in 1906 in the Independent, a Socialist periodical. This was followed in 1908 by "A Little Brother of the Rich," a novel later turned into a play with the collaboration of Harriet Ford. Next came another play, "The Fourth Estate," also with the collaboration of Harriet Ford. It opened in Wallack's Theater in New York on Oct. 6, 1909; and was subsequently revised with a happy ending for stock companies.

A one act play titled "Dope" became a popular feature in vaudeville for years. A third play "Rebellion" opened at the Maxine Elliot Theater in New York on Oct. 3, 1911. It was also published as a novel; reprinted in London.

Intermittently, his articles appeared in Collier's. The fact that he realized a sizeable income from his authorship was a source of wonderment and irritation to his family.

In time, Patterson became as disillusioned with the Socialists as he had been before with Republicans and Democrats. In 1912, when his cousin Robert McCormick urged him to come back to the Tribune, he was amenable; and began a new editorial apprenticeship on the Sunday Tribune. He experimented widely with features and articles, and in inducing readers to relate their experiences for small money prizes.

Not the least of his triumphs was the Sunday Tribune's participation in the first of the movie serials, "The Adventures of Kathlyn." The first installment of the story was published Jan. 4, 1914, in the Sunday Tribune, and ran for 26 weeks. The film version was shown the week after. The star was Kathlyn Williams; the hero, Thomas Santschi; the villain, Charles Clary; the producer, Selig Polyscope Company; the author, Harold MacGrath; scenario, Gilson Willets. (These nuggets of information are from the Lincoln Center of Performing Arts Library.)

The motion picture was then in its infancy. After 1908, a rash of nickelodeons swept the country, offering this new type of entertainment for five or ten cents a head. The big feature was a two-reeler, which produced the first crop of movie stars. It was supplemented by single reel showings, plus a popular song on movie slides.

The films were silent, with printed captions; and in the higher class houses a pianist provided an appropriate musical accompaniment. The drama was ultra-dramatic; the hero extra-heroic; the heroines beautiful and innocent beyond belief; the villain consistently black-hearted; the comedy slapstick; and the action so fast it was frequently jerky. And the enraptured audience saw strange scenes such as Paris, France; and wide open spaces where the wagon wheels ran backwards in the Westerns.

The Tribune's tie with Kathlyn was extraordinarily successful. Out in the hinterlands, Tribune circulation men increased the news agents' orders by hundreds of copies each week. When the serial was finished, the Sunday Tribune had upped its circulation approximately 100,000 copies, a phenomenal increase for the times.

This experience probably was responsible for Patterson's life-long love affair with motion pictures. He sensed the width of their appeal, the universality of their interest, and their power as a popular attraction. (Hollywood later reciprocated by making The News required reading in the writers' offices.)

* * *

In 1914, Patterson gained his first experience as a war correspondent. A revolution brewing in Mexico had erupted in Tampico, and killed 27 Americans. This assignment was cut short when James Keeley's switch to the Record-Herald brought Patterson back to Chicago.

The second experience came in 1915, when he set out to see at first hand the war in Europe. He spent three months in England, France, Belgium and Germany. During his return on a slow steamer, the S.S. Cymric, he wrote a series of articles for the Tribune that were reprinted in a small volume, "The Note Book of a Neutral."

He observed that Europe, in many respects, was superior to the United States; in art, music, literature, medicine and medical education, colonial government, military prowess, and the social sciences. "There aren't as many slum dwellings in all Germany as in Chicago alone."

He admired German efficiency; and said that Germany could be beaten only if England and France adopted German principles and methods. (These opinions caused both Patterson and McCormick later to be labelled pro-German in many quarters.) He stressed the point that sympathy for Belgium and France and hereditary ties to the old countries were not valid reasons for entering the war; that the United States should help the Allies in every way possible, without expecting gratitude from them; and that the interests of America should be paramount. He also emphasized a need for military preparedness, and universal service, policies he held with the rest of his life.

* * *

In accordance with his conviction about military training, Patterson enlisted in Battery B, Field Artillery, Illinois National Guard in June, 1915. The battery had its own armory on the near North Side, met one night a week for drill. Horses used by it could be rented for riding at other times.

A year later President Wilson issued the call for service on the Mexican border. On June 21, Battery B entrained for Camp Lincoln at Springfield,

Ill.; on July 4 left for Camp Wilson at San Antonio, Tex; moved again on Aug. 16 to Leon Springs, an artillery practice range. On a hike to Camp Mabry at Austin, Battery B covered 124 miles in seven days; marched back to Fort Sam Houston a week later. After it became obvious that there was no longer a need for the guard on the border, the battery was shipped back to Fort Sheridan, Ill., and on Oct. 31, was mustered out of federal service, and returned to guard status. Patterson seemed to enjoy the experience, made sergeant while in Texas.

He was offered a commission as 2d lieutenant on Sept. 23, 1916; but for some reason delayed acceptance until Feb. 27, 1917. On July 9, after the United States had entered World War I, the battery was mobilized at Fort Sheridan, and redesignated as the 149th Field Artillery of the 42d or Rainbow Division, which contained units from all states and was the first National Guard division to get to France. While at Sheridan, on July, 1917, Patterson was moved up to 1st lieutenant.

A period at Camp Mills, Long Island, followed. The 149th was shipped out Oct. 17, on the S.S. President Lincoln, reached St. Nazaire two weeks later; on Nov. 18 arrived at Camp Coetquidan, a French School of Artillery. After three months of hard training, it took its place on the Lorraine front. During this period Patterson was promoted to captain, in command of B Battery. Four more campaigns followed; Champagne, second battle of Marne (during which a meeting with McCormick at Mareuil-en-Dole took place); elimination of the San Mihiel salient, and the month-long bitter battle of the Argonne. In 13 months overseas, the 149th Field Artillery was in line service about 200 days, with relatively little relief. And Illinois' summer soldiers had become hardened combat veterans.

Much of the above information comes from a rare book titled "Men of the Rainbow" whose author was Leslie Langille, a member of Battery B. Published 15 years later in 1933, the book is innocent of literary pretense. But the author does convey the feeling of men at war; the initial enthusiasm and high spirits, the rumors and alarms, the hangups and gripes, the inevitable hurry-up-and-wait, the exhilaration of adventure and the foreign scene; the hardships of field service, forced marches, rainy nights in muddy gun emplacements; and finally the sobering effect of the deaths of comrades, the slaughter of enemies, and fields of rotting dead.

Artilleryman Langille has much to say of Captain Pat, and all of it good. Old enough, important and wealthy enough to have secured a State-side or staff post, he was a volunteer among volunteers. Under fire he showed little concern for his own safety. He went on dangerous patrols when he might have ordered others to go. He gained the respect of his men by explaining fully orders and objectives. And he won the affectionate

Robert R. McCormick
1880–1955
Co-founder of The News.

William H. Field
1877–1935
General manager of The News from 1919 to 1927.

Joseph Medill Patterson
1879–1946

Founder of The News and its publisher for 27 years. This photograph was preferred by him to all others made in his later life. He presented copies to his executives in December, 1939.

nickname of "Aunt Josie" because of his often extreme consideration for his men. Somewhere in the five major actions in which he took part, he was gassed, spent some time in a field hospital, and qualified for a wound stripe.

On Nov. 15, four days after the Armistice, Patterson was relieved from the 149th, which moved on to Germany in the Army of Occupation, and given a leave of absence.

In early December, he saw Lord Northcliffe in London, whom he had met before while on furlough, told him of his ambition to start a paper in New York. Northcliffe urged him to start a tabloid.

Patterson left Europe for Camp Meade, Md., Dec. 20; and was discharged at Camp Grant, Rockford, Ill., January 8, 1919.

In many respects, his World War service was one of the most satisfactory periods of his life. He returned to the Tribune to face a new crisis; Field wanted to retire.

* * *

Much has been made of the fact that Patterson, child of an affluent family, product of Groton and Yale, could become the editor of the newspaper that was to have the largest circulation in this country. Some observers seemed to believe that he underwent a particular personal metamorphosis, as if he had become a Buddhist monk; or somehow acquired a peculiar ESP of the interest of ordinary people. Actually, Patterson was one of the ordinary people. His conflicts with the cornfed politicos at Springfield, his relationships with the Democratic machine managers and office holders in Chicago, his association with the blue-shirted proletariat and parlor pinks of his Socialist period, his acceptance as a popular free-lancer and playwright, his Mexican border sojourn as an enlisted man, his success as an editor of the Sunday Tribune, and his experience in commanding a unit of a citizen army—established his identification with ordinary people, made him aware of their aspirations, motivations, likes and dislikes.

Patterson was a natural like his grandfather Medill; only 50 years separated the Massillon schoolboy from the Groton student. And he had more and better tutelage than Medill.

If your father is an atomic physicist, microbiologist, or a mining engineer, you are not likely to learn much about his business. But if your father works for a newspaper which comes into the home every day, it is almost impossible not to learn a good deal about newspapers.

With a grandfather and father who were editors and publishers, Patterson had a head start. He seemed to know Pulitzer's principles and practices, whether or not he ever had access to Pulitzer's epistles to his editors. In his 10 years at Groton and Yale he became familiar with the New York papers—Joseph Pulitzer's Worlds, Whitelaw Reid's Tribune, Dana's Sun, Bennett's Herald; and watched the rise of the Hearst papers. He met Brisbane while he was still young, and admired him greatly. (When Brisbane died in 1936, his obituary in the editorial column exceeded in volume and praise any tribute to an editor ever to appear there, including the one published in 1946 honoring Patterson himself.)

An editor is largely a creature of instinct—an instinct that assesses and calibrates the degree of public interest and response to a topic or event. He is often a hunch player, sometimes prophetic. He may sense a need to know, a groundswell of opinion or sentiment. He is part detective; an out-of-character act or utterance by a prominent person may indicate or predicate newsworthy consequences.

Invariably he is an innovator. Greeley, Medill, Bennett, Pulitzer, Hearst brought something new to newspapers. George Horace Lorimer, Edward Bok, Harold Ross, Henry Luce, DeWitt Wallace were innovators in magazines.

Some editors are brief-blooming, do not outlast their early period. Patterson carried The News through the frivolous 1920s, the serious depressed '30s, the crucial War II years, without ever losing the perspective of the public, or its patronage.

As his personal project, The News became the proving ground for his ideas. Whatever worked (i.e. sold papers) was repeated; whatever failed was dropped.

As an editor, Patterson put a high premium on brevity, and the short, telling, clever caption. He had an artilleryman's appreciation of maps. He rarely ordered; his approach was "Don't you think that . . . ?" If you didn't think so, and could advance good reasons, he could be persuaded to change his mind. He liked perceptive writing; in the early months of The News he wrote managing editor Arthur L. Clarke to give Ralph Armstrong a $10 bonus, for one paragraph about a line of strikers standing in the rain. He admired, and rewarded initiative. He rarely called anybody in the editorial department to his office; instead he wandered down to the newsroom, talked with individuals at their desks.

He was not apt at visualization; a page layout marked off in sections with numbered photographs to fit the sections, seemed to give him trouble; so when time permitted, the editors and layout men photostated the pictures to the proper sizes, and pasted them in place.

* * *

In his personal life, he was a loner; believed that a publisher could not have many close friends, or his feelings would distort his judgments.

Five feet eleven and a half, square shouldered, physically active and in good trim, he was indifferent about his appearance. And just about as indifferent as to what and where he ate.

On occasion he showed a shyness that seemed not in keeping with his character. Elsie Janis, whom he had met in France during the war and greatly admired, once phoned and invited him to a party. He accepted with pleasure. The head-hunting hostess then proceeded to catalog her guest list. Patterson became more and more uncomfortable and finally told Miss Janis he wasn't coming. "I'd be out of place among all those brilliant people."

He had almost a dread of ostentation and show. In the late 1920s, after he had moved to New York, he often visited newsdealers with Joseph Goldstein, then a circulation inspector, later superintendent of delivery. One day he asked Goldstein to help him buy a car. The following afternoon, Goldstein took him to the showrooms of Isotta Fraschini, Cadillac, Lincoln, to Patterson's increasing unease. They ended up on Broadway where he bought a Studebaker for $540. (Later he acquired a Packard limousine, and another car.)

* * *

It must also be remembered that in New York Patterson was aided by a succession of able editors who not only improved and supplemented his ideas, but executed them better than he could have done. And as The News grew, it acquired a large and competent staff, whose abilities and dedication notably improved the paper's coverage, impact and interest.

Robert Rutherford McCormick

Robert Rutherford McCormick in 1919 was a handsome, 6-foot-4, 38-year-old, Bond Street tailored individual, fastidious, and considered by most people as somewhat aloof. But he had a considerable record of accomplishment behind him.

When his father and mother went to London in 1889 with Todd Lincoln, he and his brother, Medill, had accompanied them and spent some time at Ludgrove, a preparatory school in Middlesex. He was reasonably happy there, acquired an English accent, learned to play cricket, visited the Paris Fair, spent some months at Versailles, where he was tutored in French. Later, when his father returned to Europe as Ambassador to Russia, he lived with his grandfather Medill most of the time.

He was enrolled at Groton in 1894, but never liked the school. He thought the teaching provincial, and resented being snooted by the Eastern kids. His attendance was irregular. In his first winter he developed pneumonia, and was shipped to Thomasville, Ga., where his grandfather sought warmer weather and relief of his arthritis. He was with him again at San Antonio, Tex., when Medill died on March 16, 1899.

He entered Yale in 1899, was graduated in the class of 1903. He lost some of his shyness, made friends, enjoyed himself, and finished in the middle of his class.

Graduation was followed by a trip to Costa Rica and Panama, where he walked over the isthmus where the United States was taking over the unfinished canal from the French.

He was in his first year of law study at Northwestern University when he was catapulted into politics. The local Democratic machine had come apart. Fred A. Busse, coal dealer and Republican boss (and later one of Chicago's outstanding mayors) knew young McCormick; the Tribune was one of his customers. He persuaded him to run for alderman of the 21st Ward, a slummy North Side neighborhood. To McCormick's own surprise he was elected.

Later, Busse and others persuaded McCormick to accept the presidency of the Chicago Sanitary Commission. The commission had been established to build the Drainage Canal, then 10 years under construction and not completed; and redolent of graft, corruption, inefficiency. McCormick steered clear of the politicians, hired and used technicians. He familiarized himself on riparian rights, and operations and costs. He found he had a bent for machinery, planning and construction; that he could manage men. Even his critics have agreed that his contribution to Chicago's future and welfare was sizable. However, when his term of office expired in 1910, the Democrats were back in the saddle and he was not reelected.

Meanwhile he had been plugging away at the law, was graduated in 1906, admitted to the Illinois bar in 1908, and formed his own law firm.

In 1909, McCormick was drawn back to the Tribune when Robert Patterson appointed him treasurer without salary.

In April, 1910, when Robert Patterson died, McCormick learned that the directors intended to sell the paper to Victor Lawson for $10,000,000. Patterson, in poor health, had been depressed by the strong opposition of Hearst's American and Examiner; and Lawson's morning and evening News. Among the city's eight newspapers, the Tribune was third in circulation and advertising.

McCormick called in his cousins, Joe and Cissy Patterson, persuaded the directors not to sell. He stalled Lawson by telling him that he had to get the consent of his mother and aunt who were in Europe. He made a trip abroad ostensibly to consult them and on his return he told Lawson the deal was off. The News reduced its price to one cent; the Tribune followed. But circulation director Annenberg held off Lawson in the struggle for readers and the Tribune emerged stronger than before.

* * *

By 1912, McCormick was strong enough to persuade the directors (and his mother and aunt) to allot $1,000,000 for the construction of a paper mill, to meet the price advantage Hearst enjoyed as a larger buyer of newsprint.

Warren S. Curtis, an engineer and something of a genius in his own right, built the first integrated paper mill, from tree chunks to newsprint in one continuous operation. The site was Thorold, Ontario, north of Niagara Falls.

It was also in 1912 that McCormick persuaded his cousin Joe Patterson to come back to the paper as Sunday editor; and both were made directors of the Tribune Company.

In August, 1914, McCormick was in Newport, talking to James Gordon Bennett, Jr., about buying the New York Herald. World War I started that month, and McCormick hustled home without making any commitments. Shortly thereafter he got himself a commission as a major in the Illinois National Guard—which worked to his advantage the following year in the war zones. To Europeans a "major of the guards" is a professional soldier of high social status and McCormick was treated as such. He met the notables of several countries; toured the Arras front, and had his first experience under fire.

In London on March 10, 1915, he married Mrs. Amie De Houle Irwin Adams, whom he had known in Chicago. Later that spring, he had an audience with the tsar and visited the Russian front. He paired off with an American cameraman, Donald F. Thompson, who took the first motion pictures of the war, later shown to packed houses in Chicago. He sent back stories as transmission permitted. In London, he made another round of official and social visits, and then returned home. On shipboard he dictated his first book "With the Russian Army."

McCormick's first military experience was similar to that of his cousin, Joe Patterson. It came in 1916, when the national guard, 150,000 strong, was sent to the Mexican border, with poor equipment and too little training. The experience convinced him that military preparedness was imperative.

He reported for World War I service June 13, 1917, and was shortly in Paris where he served with Gen. Pershing's staff from June to September, when he was assigned to the 5th Field Artillery. In December, he made lieutenant colonel, commanded the 1st Battalion to May, 1918. His next assignment was the 122d Field Artillery, 58th Field Artillery Brigade. He saw action in the defensive sectors of Ansauville and Cantigny. Then he was sent home to train a new command, the 61st Field Artillery at Camp Jackson, S.C. He was discharged a full colonel, Dec. 31, 1918.

At a New York News dinner on Feb. 2, 1947, McCormick told how in August, 1918, when he was ordered home, he detoured from Valadon Artillery School to see Patterson at Mareuil-en-Dole where the latter's battery was engaged in the second battle of the Marne. Patterson told him of having seen Northcliffe in London; and of his ambition, if he lived through the war, to start a picture newspaper in New York. McCormick pledged his support of the project.

The colonel does not figure much further in The News story. He has his biographers, and his own monuments in the huge development of Baie Comeau, Quebec, with its model towns, dams, power stations, paper mill and shipping line.

William Henry Field

William Henry Field, who had been such an able business manager of the Chicago Tribune, was a remarkable man, by any measure. He had a pragmatic intelligence of a high order; the ability to realize and define a problem, determine its solution, and find somebody to effect it—usually in the shortest time, and simplest and most economical manner. Yet he was not without imagination, and would inaugurate programs which required a long time for fulfillment.

He was always approachable. If you proposed an idea he did not favor, he would advance objections A to Z. Later, if you thought of reasons which seemed to outweigh his objections, you could always go back and resume discussion.

And he had an active sense of humor. World War I brought a sharp reduction in national advertising. Once in early 1918, Walter Bloeser, a salesman in the national department, produced a 70-page plan for a Tribune-sponsored automobile excursion to California. Walt estimated the Tribune's cut of the gasoline, oil, tires, housing and repairs required, and the extra linage that could be secured by tying in with certain brands. Field returned the plan with the following note: "Dear Mr. Bloeser: We are having so much trouble running a newspaper these days that I hesitate to undertake anything really big. (signed) W. H. Field."

With Patterson based in Chicago, Field was often the buffer or filter of impulsive orders relating to The News. He was also the one man in the organization who could make Patterson change his mind.

One afternoon in New York, Field was at his desk talking with a visitor. Patterson stormed in, furious because something had not been done.

"McDonald Dewitt (the attorney for The News) says it's against State law," said Field mildly.

Patterson insisted that nevertheless he wanted it done.

Field, very stern, pulled a sheet of paper out of his desk, picked up a pencil, and said coldly: "All right, Joe, just what is it you want?"

Patterson told him the first step. Field made a note. Patterson mentioned item two. Field made a note. Then Patterson shrugged, said "Have it your way !" and stalked out.

Field crumpled up the sheet of paper, dropped it into the wastebasket, turned to his visitor. "As you were saying when we were so rudely interrupted . . ."

He was tall, thin, angular; a light eater who was always trying to hold his weight; and a light sleeper. His hair and trimmed mustache were iron gray, and he wore gray suits. Although he was only 43 when The News was started, most of the staff thought him far older than he was. He set an office example by paying for the postage on his personal letters; made the switchboard report charges on personal calls. He rolled his own Bull Durham cigarettes. And it seemed that there wasn't anything he didn't know about running a newspaper.

* * *

Field was born April 18, 1877, in Rutland, Vt. His father was a banker and had been State Treasurer of Vermont. He attended Phillips Andover and then Yale, where he was graduated in 1889. At Yale he came to know the McCormick brothers and Patterson; more important, as it later turned out, their mothers came to know Field and apparently thought well of him.

During his first few months out of college, he worked as a salesman in Charles Scribner's Sons bookstore in New York. Next came an apprenticeship in the advertising department of the Munsey magazines. Much to the surprise of people who knew him, Field with his quiet, low key attitude, proved to be a good salesman. However, in July 1901, Field broke with Munsey; the legend is that Munsey wanted him to go to Chicago and Field didn't want to go. He went back to Rutland, worked with his uncle Fred A. Field in his real estate business. Seven months later, Munsey sent an emissary to Rutland to heal the breach, and Field returned. He apparently felt sure enough of his future to marry Ethel Scovil Clement, daughter of Percival Clement, former governor of Vermont, on Sept. 8, 1903. Field had known his bride since childhood.

Not much later Field was made advertising manager of the Munsey magazines, and apparently was a good one. The majority of the Munsey magazines had pulp insides which carried little advertising. Their principal space revenues came from the second, third and back covers, in color. Field attained a reputation in the business as always able to find a needed cover ad when a closing date was near.

* * *

During his decade in New York, Field saw something of McCormick and Patterson on their trips east. Medill McCormick was probably responsible for his coming to the Tribune.

Field went to Chicago in October 1909. Legend again has it that one of his reasons for the move was that he was fed up with being thought of as "Gov. Clement's son-in-law" by his Vermont neighbors.

He had no previous newspaper experience. It is true that his father-in-law owned the Rutland (Vt.) Herald; but whatever he may have known about the Herald had little application to the needs of the Tribune. In 1927, when Field bought the Herald, he had difficulty accustoming himself to the operation of a small newspaper.

* * *

By the time Field went to Chicago, the Tribune had probably the best advertising department of any newspaper in this country. It was developed by Marshall Parker. Thomas A. Lowery had established a code for financial advertising that became the model for most newspapers. Wilbur E. Macfarlane had developed classified by dividing the city in districts, promoting his men to better districts as they were able to show gains. Classified familiarized a man with the city, and was constant and convincing proof that advertising sells.

After Christmas, a crew of young salesmen fanned out through the wintry environs of Michigan, Wisconsin, and Minnesota, signed up proprietors or resorts, camps, hotels, transportation lines; and gave the summertime reader the largest selection of vacation opportunities.

The national salesmen were assigned territories; and the Tribune probably started more national advertisers than any other medium except the Saturday Evening Post.

Parker, however, had other business interests, and was unwilling to limit his efforts to the paper. So 26-year-old Eugene W. Parsons was made advertising manager; and 21-year-old Roy Holliss went to New York as Eastern manager.

Like many another newspaper, the Tribune was dependent for retail advertising on a few large department stores. Parsons started a copy and art service to serve local advertisers. William E. Donahue, retail manager, started a drive on small local accounts. The small local accounts in 10 years grew to many times the volume of the department stores, and removed the threat of a department store's defection.

Circulation as well as advertising grew during Field's tenure, and the Tribune was a very prosperous paper.

With the war, and McCormick and Patterson in the army, Field's responsibilities grew; and included editorial. He took over Patterson's office, and posted on the wall behind him the lettered legend: "This is Joe Patterson's office. /He is fighting in France. /I am sitting in his chair /For a little while /Until he comes back."

As the war went on, he became grimmer, more taciturn, more tired. He later said that by the summer of 1918, he felt he was on a treadmill he couldn't get off; and that after the Armistice, he dreaded coming to the office every day. When Patterson and McCormick returned, he announced that he was quitting.

Both were disconcerted, and dismayed. A strong bond had grown among them; they signed even routine business letters to each other "Affectionately." A long vacation was suggested. Field made it clear that he did not wish to hold his old status.

Field, Patterson and McCormick had earlier obtained from the directors of the Tribune a contract that gave the three of them (and possibly two other key men) a percentage of the profits. Field's earnings in 1918 were probably around $70,000. He had saved enough, he thought, to permit him to live comfortably in Vermont the rest of his life.

After much discussion, it was decided that Field would stay in the company, move to New York with the title of eastern vice president, and be available if anything important came up.

He moved into the University Club in New York in January, 1919, and was hardly settled in his new office when something important did come up; the Tribune opened negotiations with the Canadian government for extensive timber grants, to assure future paper requirements. Field went to Ottawa, Quebec, Washington, Chicago, handling the negotiations.

He was not back in New York very long when Patterson again brought up the idea of a New York paper. Field started looking, but New York at the time was hardly a buyer's market.

Adolph Ochs was in no mood to sell his top morning circulation Times (341,589). The World (334,698) was bringing prestige, and the Evening World (335,862) profits to the Pulitzers. The morning Tribune (120,559) was the fief of the Reid family. The morning Herald (103,957), and the evening Telegram (189,717) were involved in the complicated settlement of James Gordon Bennett, Jr.'s estate, and not immediately available. Both were bought by Frank Munsey a year later. Munsey, who owned the Sun (137,171) and the Evening Sun (199,320) had been ill in the fall of 1918 and was minded to sell his papers; but changed his mind when he recovered the following spring. The American (304, 240) was Hearst's editorial mouthpiece; the Journal, with the largest evening circulation in New York (637,624), was his most profitable paper. Jason Rogers, crusading publisher of the Globe (190,074), was hopeful of better times, as was Henry Stoddard of the Evening Mail (103,235). And the evening Post (30,439) after many vicissitudes was cozily subsidized by Thomas Lamont. (The figures are from ABC statements, of Sept. 30, 1919.)

In Field's own words, the good papers cost too much, and the poor papers cost too much. While Field was wondering what to do, another solution appeared.

On the evening of March 19, 1919, Field was having dinner at the University Club. George von Utassy, whom he had known in his Munsey period, came over and started to talk to him. Utassy knew about his newspaper shopping and proposed a tabloid.

George von Utassy

George von Utassy was also a remarkable man of many accomplishments, and well known in his day. His biography has been pieced together from Who's Who, Phillips Exeter Academy records, his Harvard class yearbooks, the recollections of his son, Maj. Chapman d'Utassy (Retired) and Richard E. Berlin, president of the Hearst Corporation.

He was born Nov. 5, 1870, of a well-to-do family in Germantown, Pa. His secondary schooling was delayed by a teenage injury; during this period he worked in a family-owned lumber business at Elizabeth City, N.C. In 1891 he was enrolled at Phillips Exeter as a member of the class of 1895; entered Harvard that year, and was graduated with the class of 1898; a Big Man on Campus, editor of the Lampoon and Crimson, officer or member of almost every student organization, excluding the Prohibition and Sound Money Clubs.

His first job was with Harper's Magazine as an advertising salesman. Later he was with Collier's Weekly. His first tie with Hearst seems to date from 1903; he may have been instrumental in starting Motor, first of the Hearst magazines. In the decennial issue of his class yearbook, he reported that he was manager of Cosmopolitan and Motor. In his first listing in the 1914–1915 Who's Who, his position is described as general manager of a group of Hearst magazines, and secretary of the International Magazine Company. John W. Clements, public relations manager of the Hearst Corporation, reported that he was never on the magazine's payroll; which may be accounted for by the fact that he had a personal contract with William Randolph Hearst. With salary and overriding commissions on advertising volume, his annual income was more than $40,000—a spectacular income before World War I.

In 1913, he took flying lessons at the Curtiss School at Hammondsport, N.Y., obtained a pilot's license, flew his own plane a year later, and was an aviation enthusiast the rest of his life.

When Hearst acquired Nash's Magazine early in 1912, Utassy moved his family to London for six months. He watched with interest the progress of Northcliffe's Mirror, and became convinced that a tabloid newspaper would do well in New York. Hearst, with the American and Journal in New York, was not interested.

Some time around 1916, he parted with Hearst (apparently amicably, as he later returned to the Hearst organization) and for a brief period was general manager of the Conde Nast magazines. The Nast publications have no record of him.

In 1917 his age precluded military service. Utassy bought a fleet of White trucks which were equipped as ambulances; and offered his rolling stock and himself to the Norton Harjes Corps, an American volunteer ambulance group. He was an ambulance driver with the French Army at Verdun from July to October 1917. On Oct. 12 of that year his unit was taken into the American Red Cross Ambulance Service; and in February, 1918, he received the equivalent rank of captain. (During this period he had so much trouble with the "von" that he changed it to "d' "; although his signature on business documents was usually "Utassy.") In 1918 his unit crossed from France to Italy at Vingtimillia, and served with the Italian Army on the Piave and Austrian fronts. His service ended on Dec. 8. He was awarded the Ordine della Corona d'Italia, and the Croce al Merito di Guerra.

Back in the States, he and some business associates tried to buy the old weekly Life, but negotiations lagged. And on March 19, he met Field.

A meeting with McCormick and Annenberg (who knew him from his own period with Hearst) followed. Then Utassy went to Chicago, met Patterson. Eventually a contract was worked out; he did not get the title of publisher, but agreed to serve as the new paper's business manager.

In 1919 he was stocky, balding, wore a *pince nez;* was always available, easily approachable, affable, and helpful to everybody, particularly the strangers from Chicago.

* * *

By this time, it was well into April. Field found office space on the fifth floor of the Evening Mail Building at 25 City Hall Place, for a rental of $166.67 a month; and made arrangements to use the Mail composing room and pressroom, to be paid for on a production basis.

The new paper was financed by demand notes payable to the Tribune Company; and through the rest of 1919 operated at a deficit of around $40,000 a month.

Field started looking around for an editor, and found one in Clarke, then city editor of the Evening World. Clarke's selection was determined by two factors; he was a former Chicago Tribune man; and a tabloid enthusiast who had tried to find capital to start one.

THE ORIGINAL CAST

Arthur L. Clarke had had a rich and rounded career on the editorial side before Field first talked to him about the new tabloid in April, 1919.

Born in Connersville, Ind., Feb. 5, 1869, he had begun as a cub reporter on the Springfield (Ohio) Globe; moved on to the Omaha Bee as a general assignment reporter and sports writer. Some time in the mid-1890's, he was on the staff of the San Francisco Chronicle (and later its editor-in-chief after he left The News).

In 1898, Clarke was London correspondent for the Chicago Tribune during part of the Boer War; back home he served as the paper's city editor. In Chicago he came to the attention of William Randolph Hearst and for a dozen years thereafter was shuttled around the Hearst circuit; city editor of the Chicago Examiner in 1902; one of the founders of the Los Angeles Examiner a year later, and its managing editor.

His next move was to New York, as managing editor of the New York American, and later in the same capacity on the Journal. He put in a hitch as managing editor on the Boston American.

When James Keeley became publisher of the Chicago Record-Herald in 1914, he brought back Clarke as its city editor. He remained in Chicago until the Record-Herald was merged with the Examiner on Jan. 1, 1918. Back in New York once more, he succeeded the notorious Charles Chapin (who was convicted of murdering his wife, and served a long prison term) as city editor on the Evening World. It was there that Field found him.

Clarke was then 50 years old, but plunged into the new enterprise with the energy and enthusiasm of a youngster. He started to assemble a staff; and with the often nebulous and frequently changing ideas of Patterson, began to shape a tabloid.

The new paper had Chicago Tribune news service and features, United Press service, and little else. In the beginning, the optimistic expectancy was that the pictures needed would come from the picture services. This failed to happen, but throughout the early months, Clarke was always sanguine, never admitted the possiblity of failure, and tried to bolster Patterson's courage.

A rift with Patterson developed early, however. Clarke, accustomed to the daytime work schedules of the Evening World, did not want to work nights. But Patterson insisted that his managing editor be on hand until the second edition was put to bed.

Merton E. Burke was Clarke's first selection as assistant managing editor; he had known Burke during the latter's long service with Hearst, and particularly valued his skill at makeup.

Burke was a boyish-looking, cocky little bantam of a man. He was good natured, generally imperturbable, and a thorough cynic. "If one good story will sell the paper, why fuss around with a lot of reporters?" He was 48 at the time, and his years with Hearst had left him impervious to surprises and changing orders.

There is little to be learned about him. The Boston American files contain some of his post-war reports on the Peace Conference and conditions in Europe; but the UPI files (International News Service was merged with United Press in 1958) show nothing.

It is known, however, that he was born and brought up in Boston; and cut his editorial eyeteeth on the Rockland Free Press. Back in Boston he spent four years as a reporter and rewrite man on the Boston Post; then switched to the American where he remained for 12 years, as reporter, rewrite man, makeup editor, city editor, and Sunday editor. In 1916 he went to the Mexican border as a correspondent.

In the spring of 1917, International News sent him to Rome. According to his own account, Italian officialdom ignored the American press. Burke sought out the Duke d'Aosta, King Vittorio Emanuele III's cousin and chamberlain, and told him the government was making a mistake; that in the United States there were millions of native Italians, and more millions of Italian descent, who wanted to know how the war was going in Italy. The duke promised to take up the matter with the king. A few days later he called Burke and said the government wanted to be as helpful as possible to the American press—if Burke would be responsible for press relations.

After the Armistice, he was sent to Paris as an accredited correspondent to cover the Peace Treaty negotiations. And on Feb. 28, 1919, d'Aosta presented him with the Italian Third Army medal and another decoration (which Burke said were helpful in getting service in Italian restaurants in New York).

Back in Boston he received a telephone call from Clarke, came down to New York and was persuaded to take a chance with the new paper. His title was assistant managing editor.

* * *

Sumner Blossom was Clarke's next acquisition.

Blossom was born in Kansas City, Mo., June 25, 1892. After high school, he spent two years as clerk and timekeeper in copper mines in

Arizona and Sonora, Mexico. He attended the University of Missouri Journalism School for a year, when his money ran out; and found a job on the Kansas City Star. After four years as reporter, copyreader, and assistant telegraph editor, his salary had advanced to $100 a month. Then Associated Press offered him $40 a week as night editor in its Kansas City office. Subsequently he opened AP bureaus in Topeka and other Midwest points. In 1915 he was made night city editor in Chicago.

The following year, assigned to the Pershing Expedition into Mexico, he set up an AP bureau in El Paso and supervised news coverage. When the national guard was released from duty, Blos returned to his job in Chicago.

During his spell in Texas, he had made a friend of Capt. William A. Moffatt, USN (later admiral, and first commandant of Naval Aviation). When the war came, Moffatt was in command of the 9th, 10th and 11th Naval Districts, with headquarters at Great Lakes Naval Station, Ill. Moffatt persuaded Blos to join the navy, set up a daily newspaper and monthly magazine for the station; and to give his editor some status, commissioned him as ensign and aide to the commandant. He was allowed to take the 90-day course and qualify as a deck officer. Application for sea duty approved, in December 1917 he was assigned to the U.S.S. Sierra, a troop transport. During the next year he made several round trips to France. In the spring of 1919, he was transferred to the U.S.S. Philippines, a captured German liner, then being refitted in Hoboken. Lt. (j.g.) Blossom was given leave.

Wandering around New York, he ran into Clarke, whom he had known on the Chicago Record-Herald. Clarke invited him to join the little group of serious thinkers who were trying to formulate the "daily magazine" contemplated for New York. For three weeks Blos worked with the group, suggesting ideas, writing stories, making page layouts, while awaiting his discharge. The discharge did not come through. He was ordered to report for duty on the morning of June 7. On the night of June 6, he bade goodby to his coworkers. The next morning, two hours before the ship was due to sail, the discharge arrived. By noon Blos was back on the job, and back on the staff.

His first title was feature editor, soon changed to city editor; and the whilom expert on Kansas City, Chicago and points west had to do a lot of heavy homework, getting acquainted with the geography and demographics of his new territory.

Blos was serious, thin, younger looking than his age; the women in the office immediately christened him "the boy editor." He had one eccentricity that was astonishing on first sight; he stood like a stork, making or revising a page layout—with one foot on the table!

Edward H. Miner was a horse fancier. He had spent 14 years as art director of the Telegraph, the racing paper; and sketching and painting horses on his days off. Two years earlier he had quit the Telegraph, started as a free lance artist. In May, 1917, he had just finished a long and arduous advertising assignment and was planning a lazy summer in Maine, when he got a phone call from Clarke—and an offer of a job.

He thought it over for a week, and took the job; with the private notion that the new paper might not last long enough to interfere too much with his vacation. The vacation was a long time coming.

Miner made one early and important innovation after the paper started. He devised a system of coding photographs for reproduction: 1a, 2b, etc.; the figure for column width, and the letter for depth in inches. The system speeded up the preparation of the photographs, and the reproduction. Metal bases were cut to fit the standardized halftones, another time-saving step in makeup.

* * *

This foursome—Clarke, Burke, Blossom, Miner—worked at first at 251 Fifth Ave., largely in Field's office. Blossom complained that a leather lounge made a poor layout table.

A 16-page dummy was set, plated, and a few dozen copies run off. Nobody liked it very much.

A second trial run was made June 4, copies of which are still extant. It was more magazine than anything else, not very striking or interesting. It was hoped that this dummy would help the advertising salesmen. It didn't.

A lot of work and changes preceded the actual first issue, which was more professional looking, more orderly, and a better newspaper—if not a very good picture newspaper.

* * *

Some of the other June 26, 1919, originals were:

Harry Canfield, previously mentioned former editor of the Chicago Tribune's Sunday gravure section; and an authority on pictures and picture sources. He returned to Chicago a year later, and was subsequently managing editor of the Chicago American.

Mabel McElliott, transferred from the Tribune's Sunday department, covered both theater and movies.

James J. Montague, editorial writer, had worked on a number of newspapers in New York. He had developed a short verse feature "More Truth Than Poetry" which was syndicated by the World. He wrote simply, clearly, forcefully, and really started the tradition of News editorials worth reading. He had the respect of Field and Patterson, who "suggested" editorials and rarely ordered one, except to repeat something run in the Tribune.

Ruth Boyle, feature reporter, was a graduate of the University of Wilson School of Journalism, served in France during the war with the Y.M.C.A.; and probably had some New York newspaper experience before Clarke hired her. She did special assignments under the Investigator byline, and in 1920 became movie and play reviewer, jointly with Mabel McElliott. She left in 1922, to join McCall's Magazine as an editor; and subsequently spent 25 years as associate editor of Good Housekeeping.

Edward Brandt was the first full-time man in the art department, and stayed with the paper a long time. The next man hired was Bernard Corvinus, but his stay apparently was brief. A Vincent Liddane is listed as office boy. Peter T. Levins, classified as "picture clerk," went back to college, and later was a long-time member of the Sunday staff.

One J. L. Burns is listed as a clerk, and Augustin Lardy and E. Levick, occupations not given, were also on the original staff.

In July, Blossom hired Philip A. Payne, who had been born in Ontario, grown up around Jersey City, spent some years with the Hoboken Observer. He was its city editor when the war came. His poor sight kept him out of the armed forces, but he went abroad with the army as a field representative of the Knights of Columbus. After the war he was hired by Hearst, toured with Eamon de Valera who was in this country to enlist sympathy and support for the Sinn Fein and Irish rebels. Then he was assigned to covering returning troopships for the Chicago American.

Payne was of moderate height, broad shoulders, with a round face topped by a brush pompadour, and brown eyes peering behind spectacles. He had a quirky imagination, the naivete of a child coupled with considerable ingenuity, all of which made him a good editor.

Another arrival in August was a tall, grave young man who was originally hired as a "picture chaser" whose function was to get existing pictures of people in the news. He was Frank J. Hause. Born in New York, Hause had attended City College and Penn State, worked at the printing business in Albany, had some brief experience as a reporter on the Evening World. He enlisted in 1917, was made a sergeant in the 59th Pioneer Infantry, and sustained serious shrapnel wounds in his head and body. Hause, who was called "colonel" by The News staff because his name sounded like that of Col. Edward M. House, Woodrow Wilson's adviser, began to keep a file of Times clippings which the whole staff used. He was shortly assigned to the city desk.

The paper was not very old when Blossom brought in another Clarke—Richard W., Arthur's son—as an assistant on the city desk. His father was less than enthusiastic.

The junior Clarke had attended the universities of Munich and Grenoble, got his B.A. at Harvard, and was headed for a career in the State Department when the war changed his mind. He was accepted for the first officers training course at Fort Sheridan, won his commission and assignment to a machine gun company. He was a just returned 1st lieutenant, after five months as adjutant in the base camp at Le Mans and a semester at the University of Grenoble.

He had held vacation jobs on the Hearst papers in Chicago, and shortly settled down as a picture caption writer.

In December Eugene McHugh, a recently discharged 1st lieutenant of infantry and still in uniform, came to the office and asked for a job. He had been graduated from the College of St. Thomas in Scranton, worked on a number of Pennsylvania papers, and had been press agent for the evangelist Billy Sunday. McHugh came in every day hopefully. On Christmas day, he was hired "temporarily" as a rewrite man; and spent the rest of his life with the paper. McHugh had the small town boy's interest in celebrities, Broadway, the stage; and was a walking encyclopedia on theater and movie people.

EVOLUTION OF A NEWSPAPER

The first issue of the Illustrated Daily News on June 26, 1919, had the "What is it?" aspect of the wholly unfamiliar. It wasn't a newspaper. It wasn't a magazine. And not by the wildest imagining would anybody have suspected a demand for it.

The front page carried a photograph of the Prince of Wales astride a horse. (His highness was due to visit us shortly.) It was outlined by a border that looked archaic even in 1919.

The inside pages had four columns, each two and one-half inches wide and 14 inches deep. Page 2 carried a John T. McCutcheon cartoon on Prohibition (from the Chicago Tribune); a column of Washington stories without display heads, signed "By Henning" (chief of the Tribune's Washington bureau); and a small box on weather (Probable showers).

Page 3 had pen and ink sketches of the judge, defendant, and courtroom visitors at the trial of Dr. Walter K. Wilkins, accused of the murder of his wife. (The doctor was convicted, and hanged himself in the Mineola jail a few days later.) There were short stories on naval officers organizing a union, a murder in Italy, a jewel robbery at the Biltmore, and nine other short items; three strike stories—telephone operators, produce teamsters, papermakers. Strikes were epidemic that summer; Samuel Gompers, president of the American Federation of Labor, back from the Peace Treaty conference in Paris, had 66 of them to settle!

Page 4 carried pictures of estates in Newport (where the Prince would be a visitor), some of their occupants, the story "By Van Rensselaer"; and a small boxed notice offered cash awards for useable snapshots.

Page 5 was editorial, topped by a strip of Carey Orr cartoons. The editorial, titled "Who We Are," promised a newspaper of interesting pictures, brief news stories, convenient size, larger text type; and dedication to the interest of the country and New York City. The opening paragraph advised "It will not be a competitor of other New York morning newspapers, for it will cover a field they do not attempt to cover." If this assurance was intended to lull other morning newspapers, it apparently was successful. Bert Leston Taylor's "A Line O' Type or Two," a column of verse and humorous items; and Dr. W. A. Evans "How to Keep Well" (Chicago Tribune features) occupied two columns. "Most Embarrassing Moment Of My Life," reader contributions which earned a dollar apiece; "People's Voice," letters from readers. (One was a note of welcome from

Walter Pulitzer, whose family owned the New York World). The paper's masthead filled column four, listed R. R. McCormick and J. M. Patterson as editors and publishers; William H. Field, general manager; George Utassy, business manager; Arthur L. Clarke, managing editor.

Page 6 had a half page advertisement for United States Tires; photographs of Mrs. Rogers B. Pratt, and her fiance Preston Gibson, author and playwright; two other society items; and "Our Daily Pattern" of a one-piece dress; available to readers for 12 cents in stamps or coin.

Page 7 was topped with a photograph of the "bullfight number, funniest scene in the Ziegfeld Follies." This page was the province of Mabel McElliott. Under the heading "A Guide To The Theaters," she reported on 13 musical comedies, four dramas and seven comedies, in five to seven line notices; and had the unenviable job of rewriting the notices every day. From July 9 on, she was also the theater reviewer. In an editorial on July 14, Patterson explained that McElliott was not a drama critic but a stenographer, whose attitudes would be those of the ordinary theatergoer. This pronouncement broke Miss McElliott's heart; and also made it harder for her to get first night tickets.

The center spread, pages 8 and 9, was pictures; Capt. Roy Francis USA, standing by the army bomber with which he hoped to make a transcontinental flight with only one stop (he didn't); the winner of the Los Angeles Bathing Costume Parade; Villa's reputed successor in Mexico; the winner of the London Daily Mirror Beauty Award; Miss Ditmars of the Bronx Zoo, coyly cuddling a pair of snakes around her neck; Capt. G. C. Martin and bride Barbara Judd, having a "congenial smoke" with their wedding attendants before leaving for the honeymoon; and the recent launching of the submarine R-26 at Bridgeport, Conn. By present standards, the pictures were drab and static.

Page 10 consisted of two half page advertisements; one for Lord Salisbury Turkish Cigarettes (15 to 20 cents, because they were packed in inexpensive machine-made paper packages, instead of expensive, handmade cardboard boxes); and an odd message from "Railway and Industrial Engineers" offering its services as industrial and engineering consultants.

Page 11 carried a story on the paper's first subscriber, Louis A. Coolidge of Boston, who used to be a newspaperman himself before he went into public life; he wished the paper well. There were also two items of foreign news, a story about successful business women; "Real Love Stories" and "Bright Sayings of Children," two more reader dollar contributions, and "Fashion's Blue Book" by Corinne Lowe—all Chicago Tribune staples. A column end of "Aero Notes" disclosed the fascinating item: "The fully-equipped American flying machine is made up of 35,000 distinct parts."

But the big item on page 11 was the announcement of the Illustrated

Daily News Beauty Contest—$10,000 first prize, $2,500 second prize, $1,000 third prize. Entrants were asked to send in their photographs taken "by one of New York's most noted photographers" at the paper's expense. "Lest you fear undue publicity" only the last name initial, occupation and street (but not number) would be printed.

Pictures could be sent to 25 City Hall Place or 251 Fifth Ave. Many of the entrants came with their pictures, probably with some idea that an in-person appearance might enhance their chances. They brightened the day for Iggy, the youth who ran the one elevator at 251 Fifth, who discoursed delightedly about the "bimboes" who came in that day. The advertising staff were convinced that few would interest Florenz Ziegfeld.

Arthur Clarke, with persistence, had succeeded in getting as judges David Wark Griffith of the movies, George M. Cohan of the theater, and Harrison Fisher, popular illustrator specializing in beautiful girls.

Page 12 was the paper's first full page ad—appropriately enough for D. W. Griffith's "art sensation" Broken Blossoms, "still playing to absolute capacity at George M. Cohan's Theatre" two showings a day. There was no vulgar mention of admission prices.

Page 13 led off with a boxed heading: "The Illustrated Daily News is going to specialize in first-class, first rights, never-before-printed fiction. Here's a sample—" and below the announcement began the first installment of "The Whimsical Three" by E. Phillips Oppenheim, popular mystery writer at that time.

Page 14 had a half-page photo of Jack Dempsey with three children, and his trainer Jimmy De Forest. The lower part of the page was an advertisement for Sloan's Liniment.

Page 15, topped by The Gumps comic strip, was devoted to sports. Americans were ahead at Wimbledon, had won the Inter-Allied track and field meet in Paris. Golf tournaments were under way at New Britain, Conn., and New Orleans. Yesterday's baseball scores, today's games, standing of the teams, were duly noted; as were yesterday's winners and today's selections at Aqueduct. "Sportographs" by Alcock packed ten stories in a single column.

Page 16 showed five beauty contest entrants, each with chaste captions such as "Miss W—148th St. Employed at Lord & Taylor's." And a bottom caption promised a full page of candidates every day. The beauty contest ran for 65 days.

* * *

This initial issue was obviously a tentative effort on a modest scale, and about as sensational as the Christian Science Monitor. The formula and makeup were fairly uniform during the first year. The paper published two editions; and Sumner Blossom admits that the first edition of the New York Times was helpful in filling his second. Curiously enough, the streamer head on the front page had no relevance to the front page pictures, which lagged days behind the news. Photographs of the Inter-Allied field and track meet in Paris appeared 10 and 12 days after the event. During the dog days of July and August, the paper continued relatively unexciting.

Its first beat occurred Monday, July 7, with eight pictures of the signing of the Peace Treaty in Paris. The pictures had been bought by Clarke for $500, and arrived on the British dirigible, the R-34, which left England at 2:40 a.m. July 2. It landed at 9:54 a.m. July 6 at Roosevelt Field, Mineola, L.I., closest airfield to New York City. The pictures occupied the center spread in the Monday issue.

Dempsey won a decision over Willard in three rounds on July 4. President Wilson arrived from Paris on the 8th, and began his losing fight to sell the Senate and the country the League of Nations. Race riots in Washington, reportedly started by soldiers on leave, were promptly suppressed by calling out the army. Later in the month Chicago had its first race riots, without benefit of the army; the city was in a state of siege for a week, with 32 fatalities.

The paper published occasional pages of $5 snapshots; the captions identified the sender, but not the subject or scene. An ice famine threatened. Silly season pictures of bathing girls, well sheathed and stockinged, filled many a page.

In August, the government started selling war surplus foods. The first contingent of French war brides arrived. The BMT subway was struck on Aug. 7 and the IRT on Aug. 9. Both strikes were settled shortly with sizeable pay increases.

On Aug. 8, an actors' strike darkened 12 Broadway theaters for almost three weeks. McElliott covered the strike. News photographers supplied a steady fare of pictures of strikers, all female, of course. The strike led to the establishment of Equity.

Ponzi, financial wizard of Boston who paid stockholders fantastic dividends from new sales of stock, came to grief; was accused of $7,000,000 fraud. A News editorial on the 13th sagely commented "You can get Nothing for Nothing."

The News held a girls swim meet, later one for boys; with plenty of pictures of advance entrants, none at all of the action. Frank King's "Gasoline Alley," Carl Ed's "The Love Life of Harold Teen," a new vertical strip titled "If You Couldn't Tell A Lie" by Llanza, were added; as were other Chicago Tribune features on cooking, beauty, and "Poems You Ought To Know."

The first rum ring murder was reported. Americans scored high at the Olympic Games in Antwerp, and The News claimed "First Olympic Pix." Terence MacSwiney, lord mayor of Cork, on a hunger strike to protest British misrule, roused sympathizers in this country.

During the summer, "Mrs. Homemaker" (probably Ruth Boyle) tried to find apartments for New Yorkers, learned that most of them were reluctant to leave the city. Miss Boyle also hired herself out as a domestic, and reported why hired girls were so hard to find and keep—too much work, too little privacy, loneliness, and $40 a month.

* * *

From the very beginning, pictures were a major problem. There were scores of pictures services but they were geared to supply Sunday newspaper gravure sections which were printed days in advance, and did not require topical material. The commercial photographers of the time regarded three days as rush job.

On July 22, 1919, a stocky Army Signal Corps captain, still in uniform, appeared in the City Hall Place office, and was promptly hired as The News first photographer.

Edward N. Jackson started to learn his craft in 1900 in a Philadelphia studio; later worked as a portrait photographer on the Atlantic City boardwalk. In 1910 he came to New York with the American Press Association.

In 1917 he attended a signal corps officers school; was commissioned a 2d lieutenant, and went overseas with the 27th Division (New York National Guard) as a photographer. He covered 10 division actions, received three citations and a battlefield promotion to captain. After the Armistice, he was picked by President Wilson to head a photographic unit to cover the Peace Conference at Versailles. On his return to the States, he was assigned to the White House, but found the job dull. He heard about the new picture newspaper in New York and, on his day off, came to the city to look at it.

The next photographer hired was Henry Olen. Louis Walker, a friend of Jackson's was fired by the World; and Jackson persuaded him to join the staff. These three were far from run-of-the-mill cameramen. Within the next year, their enterprise and contributions began to affect the content and character of the paper; and the calibre of the staff they eventually assembled.

* * *

The tensions of that first summer are exposed in yellowing correspondence. Patterson in Chicago was under many pressures. His contemporaries were either amused or indignant over "that funny newspaper Joe is getting out in New York." Tribune directors were concerned over the expense.

Patterson was a good customer of Western Union that summer. (Long distance phone calls, routed through many circuits, were neither satisfactory nor dependable.) Letters were frequent, to Clarke, Utassy, Field. He railed steadily about the printing. Curtis came down from the Thorold paper mill, suggested trying the gravure stock used by the Tribune. A better finish could be secured by running the paper-making machines at half speed; McCormick said no, the Tribune needed all the stock it could get. Halftones were reduced to 55 screen. A blue-black ink that cost four times as much as carbon black seemed to promise better impression; but Mail pressmen didn't clean the carbon black out of the press fountains. An expensive "bumping" process on halftones was tried, without results.

Patterson considered a colored cover. "Not yellow, yellow journalism. Not pink, Police Gazette," cautioned Utassy.

On Aug. 3, Patterson wrote Utassy to increase the size of the paper to 20 pages. There wasn't paper enough on hand in New York, until Curtis increased shipment from the mill. The first 20-page issue appeared Aug. 20, had no effect on circulation.

On Aug. 8, both News and Chicago Tribune principals were upset by a rumor that the New York Evening Mail had been bought by—of all people—Henry Ford. Utassy promptly obtained a denial from the Mail's publisher, Henry Stoddard; and everybody breathed easier.

The cause for concern was the Ford suit against the Tribune, under way for six months in Mount Clemens, Mich. In 1916 when President Wilson called the National Guard for service on the Mexican border, a Ford official let it be known Ford workers in the guard would not get back their jobs. The Tribune called Ford an "anarchist," among other things. The suit was delayed by the war; and had been a cliff-hanging headache for McCormick, Patterson and the Tribune directors. It was settled Aug. 15. Ford won a Pyrrhic victory, and 6 cents damages.

* * *

Patterson was unhappy about the name, considered "Mirror" and then turned sour on "Illustrated Daily." Field learned that "New York News" was copyrighted by a Harlem newspaper, arranged to buy a release. (The name was changed to "The News" on Nov. 20, 1919.)

Patterson was worried about a rail strike. Paper shipments from Thorold were stepped up, and Field leased a basement on Murray St. for paper storage.

Illustrated Daily News

No. 1 | Copyright, 1919, by News Syndicate Co., Inc. | New York | Thursday, June 26, 1919. | 2 Cents

GERMANS BLOCK SIGNING OF TREATY

Newport to Entertain Prince of Wales in August

A war-made democrat is the Prince of Wales. He reviews the Naval Division and, in another intimate photograph, borrows a light from Lord Reading.

(By Marshall)

The first circulated front page: June 26, 1919.

Illustrated Daily News

No. 33. Copyright, 1919, by News Syndicate Co., Inc. New York Saturday, August 2, 1919. 2 Cents

R. R. FOOD STRIKE BEGINS

YORK GANGSTER FRIENDS OF THE LATE "TANNER" SMITH VISIT HOBOKEN. (See Page 3)

THE Illustrated Daily NEWS

No. 104. Copyright, 1919, by News Syndicate Co., Inc. New York, Friday, October 24, 1919. 20 Pages. Trade-mark registered U. S. Patent Office. 2 Cents

STRIKEBREAKERS FOR THE PIERS

German Opera Sung; Audience "Scattering," Mostly

EXCLUSIVE PICTURES SHOWING

THE NEWS

No. 143. Copyright, 1919 by News Syndicate Co., Inc. 8 New York, Tuesday, December 9, 1919. 20 Pages. Trade-mark registered U. S. Patent Office. 2 Cents

STRIKE OVER; COAL PINCH BEGINS

Decides to Wait

Treaty Sleeps, Hitchcock Says; Dead, Says Lodge

SEE PAGE 2. See Page 2

THE BEST FICTION OF ANY DAILY NEWSPAPER IN AMERICA

THE NEWS

Vol. 2. No. 72. Copyright, 1920, by News Syndicate Co., Inc. 20 Pages. NEW YORK'S PICTURE NEWSPAPER

New York, Friday, September 17, 1920. Daily Except Sunday. 2 Cents

WALL ST. IGNORED WARNING

Evolution of a logotype. During its first year, The News front page logotype underwent many changes. The top three of these samples were used between August and October, 1919. At the bottom, Sept. 17, 1920, the legend "New York's Picture Newspaper" appears. It has been there ever since.

"Must have more pictures. Hire picture chasers," urged Patterson. The picture chaser was a journalistic institution in Chicago, but apparently not known in New York. His function was to get to the homes or families of people in the news, and cajole, borrow, beg or even steal pictures. Picture chasing was also considered an apprenticeship for reporters.

Field was busy as the proverbial bird dog. He read all the New York papers, sent clips of all stories missed by the News, which were many at the time. He pinch hit with editorials when Montague was on vacation. He wrote the house ads (promotion advertisements run in the paper). He shopped for a new location for the paper. When the professional photographer did not show up to take pictures of the second and third winners of the beauty contest, in a room reserved in the Hotel Knickerbocker, Field took the pictures.

He hired a pressroom foreman named Lambert from the Herald, and slowly, irregularly, the printing improved. "September third the best yet," Patterson wired Clarke. Unfortunately future editions did not adhere to the Sept. 3 standards. A printing expert, Charles Kietel, sent on from Chicago on Sept. 12, offered little encouragement of better printing from the Mail presses.

* * *

On Aug. 30, the beauty contest ended. Clarke had trouble getting his judges together. Griffith was delayed on the West Coast. When a meeting was arranged, Griffith and Fisher showed up. Cohan came later. On Oct. 10, the judges announced their decisions: First prize, Alice Louise Secker, a Manhattan girl who worked in a corset factory; second, Hazel Yopp; third, Mary O'Brien. Their portraits in gravure were supplements in early issues of the paper.

Miss Secker professed no stage or screen ambition. She figured in the news three more times. She bought a farm in New Jersey for her father. She got a $100 a week job as a cosmetics demonstrator, came down with flu in Milwaukee, and in alarm wired the new husband she had married secretly in New York on Jan. 2. The bridegroom's mother was desolated. "People will think he married her for her money," she said. In November, 1920, she sued for a separation, claimed her groom was enamored of another!

Pershing arrived on Sept. 8, 1919, and paraded with the First Division on Fifth Ave. the next day. A gravure portrait of the general was a supplement in The News of Sept. 9; "helped a little," circulation manager James S. Sullivan thought.

That first summer, too, circulation was the concern of everybody on The News.

The first day's print order of 150,000 copies disappeared off the stands. For the five days of June, the average net paid was 115,888 copies. Since papers were returnable by the dealers, it took some time to arrive at the net sale. July dropped to 27,120; August to 26,635—with one black day of about 11,000 sales.

On Aug. 28 an advertising series was started in the other New York papers; 50 lines on two columns, with a big logotype and a few bold lines about the paper. Copy emphasis after four weeks was changed to the first-run fiction. The advertising was prepared by Roy Durstine, of the new agency of Barton & Durstine (which later grew to the giant Batten, Barton, Durstine & Osborn.)

September brought the first lift, to 32,524. October was better with 41,268—justifying Sullivan's faith in the appeal of the paper.

The end of November brought that near-miracle, the limerick contest.

* * *

At Field's request, after it was all over, one Victor G. Whittier made a full report. He signed himself "Limerick Editor" and his name does not appear again in News' annals.

Whittier was vague about the origin of the contest; said the idea came "out of the business office."

Four lines of a limerick were published. A daily prize of $100 was offered for the best last line. The last lines had to be in The News office by 4 p.m. of the third day following. Judging and elimination started the fourth day. The winning line and winner were announced seven days after the incomplete limerick was printed.

The first incomplete limerick was:

> A princess from far off Cathay
> Found a dressmaking pattern one day.
> Said she "If I could
> Get the dress goods I would . . .

The winning line, published Dec. 1 was:

> Have Cal-cutta dress right away."

The winner was James F. Murphy, 23, a railway revenue clerk and resident of the Bronx.

In this inflated, entertainment-sated era, it seems inconceivable that a $100 prize and a last line to a limerick could generate as much excitement, entertainment and response as this contest did. The money value, however, may be estimated by the fact that the five to 15 girls hired to read the last-line entries were paid $3 a day; and two who operated an automatic letter opener were paid $2.50 a day.

At social gatherings in New York during the winter of 1919–1920, somebody would produce a clipping of an incomplete limerick from The News and those present would devise last lines. Thus thousands of people who had never seen The News before became acquainted with it; and many bought the paper to keep up with the limericks.

The first limerick brought 10,497 entries. The lowest day was 3,393. Seven days exceeded 20,000. The contest ran 100 days, with a total response of 1,213,378—a record for any newspaper with the then limited circulation of The News. It was copied by 20 other papers.

Circulation showed the impetus of the contest: November, 60,101, and December, 98,906. But the real effect was apparent in the first quarter 1920 figures.

* * *

The contest also established the structure of a circulation stimulant; an artificial attraction, plus money prizes, induced non-readers to try the paper. Some years of experience also established the fact that three weeks on the average were enough to form the reading habit—probably the shortest term required by any publication. And contests contributed to the unprecedented growth of The News to the largest circulation in America.

The effect of the limerick contest on Patterson and The News management was positive and encouraging. In November negotiations had begun to buy the Staats Zeitung, a German language daily, to get its publishing plant. The decision rested with the Tribune's directors. Then Patterson wrote Field that he was not going ahead with the transaction. Field asked if that was not a matter for the directors to determine. And Patterson answered: "The directors are not one of my worries. If we reach 100,000 by the end of the year, nobody is going to interfere with this paper." So the fateful year of 1919 ended on a note of triumph!

* * *

December, 1919, also provided a bit of *opera bouffe,* with Hearst's editorial poobah, Arthur Brisbane, playing the heavy. He invited Field to dinner one night and condescendingly told him that he was willing to take over The News from Patterson and McCormick "for a nominal consideration." He considered the paper too British, and too serious. Under his direction, it would be published for the ignorant and illiterate. While it would be his personal venture, he was sure he could get the Hearst circulation department to push it by threatening to withhold Hearst papers from dealers who would not cooperate.

He further proposed that he and Field jointly should buy from Munsey the Morning Herald and Evening Telegram, either with Chicago Tribune backing or financial support that Brisbane could command. Field, who was not even remotely interested in any association with Brisbane, passed along the proposal to Patterson and McCormick. They were unable to determine whether Brisbane was acting on his own or as a front for Hearst. Patterson urged Field to stall Brisbane, and await further developments. There were none. And it would be five years before Hearst finally did start a tabloid in New York, and then not at the instigation of Brisbane.

* * *

While 1919 ended well for The News, the country was not so fortunate. Food prices were 91% over those of 1913. In New York a dozen eggs sold for $1.16.

When war production stopped, so did the demand for coal. Marginal mines closed, others laid off workers. By midsummer 1919, families in the mill towns were starving. Sporadic strikes spread, eventually involving 600,000 men. President Wilson threatened to nationalize the mines. John L. Lewis, young president of the miners union, pleaded for a six-hour day and five-day week to spread the work; mine operators wouldn't listen. Attorney General Palmer called the strike illegal. On Nov. 1, the President appointed a tribune to arbitrate wages; the miners wouldn't listen. The First Division of the army, which two months earlier had paraded on Fifth Ave., was ordered into West Virginia to prevent sabotage.

The mines reopened Dec. 2; no miners showed up. A 20% wage increase finally ended the strike Dec. 9. But six weeks production had been lost, and the pinch was on. Working hours were cut in factories, stores, schools. Electricity was rationed in many communities. Broadway marquees were dark; New York subway cars were heatless. The first zero weather on Dec. 18 added to the misery.

A railway strike threatened. A hurriedly summoned Presidential commission proposed a pay increase which was indignantly rejected by congress. The ailing President put pressure on congress; got a fat raise for the railroad workers.

THE WAR THAT WASN'T

Max Annenberg, the Tribune's circulation manager, had come to Chicago at the age of 10, when his parents emigrated from Germany. He had been newsboy, delivery man, foreman, gang fighter, and finally circulation manager of the Hearst papers in Chicago. James Keeley persuaded him to switch to the Tribune; later was unable to get him to switch to the Record-Herald.

Max had a doglike devotion to Patterson, listened to him as if to an oracle; and rarely listened to anybody else. In his more effusive moments, he referred to himself as a genius, with some justice if not modesty.

Max came to New York prepared for conflict, and couldn't find any. If a new newspaper invaded Chicago, it would meet with plenty of headaches, mostly supplied by Max.

He made an early call on Joe Bannon, whose ambivalent role was Hearst's circulation chief in New York *and* president of the Newspaper Delivery Union. The roly-poly Bannon was affable as ice cream. He welcomed any venture that would make more jobs for his union. That these mavericks from Chicago could possibly affect the New York American or the Journal apparently never crossed his mind.

Morning newspaper delivery in New York was then a joint operation, through the American News Company. Its only merit was that it was cheaper than independent delivery. But as one circulation manager stated at the time, forcibly, if irreverently, "If Christ came back to earth tonight, there was no way of selling an extra copy except by padding." ("Padding" means adding extra copies to dealers' orders, hoping they would accept and sell more.)

The other New York publishers had no objection to the Illustrated Daily News using their delivery system; another paper would share the expense, save money for everybody.

Max didn't like the system, looked about for some leverage, some extra advantage. He learned that there was a Newsdealers Association, introduced himself to its president, painted a glowing word picture of how much money dealers would make with the new paper. He also intimated that the new paper would like to do something for the dealers. The president graciously accepted a donation of $900, certainly not for a stained glass window. Then Max learned that the association was a splinter group, with a small membership and no influence.

He didn't like the new paper, emerged from the Mail pressroom the first night of publication with a copy held at arms length, the thumb and forefinger of his other hand clutching his nose.

He quickly realized that his beauty contest, which had been successful in the Tribune in Chicago, was a flop—despite the $10,000 first prize and the $42,000 in advertising that had launched it. You don't send a picture of your best girl or your daughter to an odd-looking newspaper you know nothing about, he said.

By the third week Max had worried himself into a state of desperation, and stormed into Field's office.

"Boss, we're licked. We better pick up the marbles and go home."

Field did not lose his calm. He called in Jim Sullivan, whose title was circulation manager. To Max's surprise, Sullivan did not agree with him that The News was licked. He stated quietly, confidently, that if it were given a year, he was certain he could get 100,000 circulation.

Field bought Sullivan's judgment. Max climbed on the Century and went home. He did not get on The News bandwagon until the end of the year, when everybody else was on it.

* * *

Jim Sullivan was an authentic genius, but never tagged himself such. He was short, stocky, low-voiced; and handled his circulation crew, who were not Emily Post characters, with a velvet glove. And he could sell a newspaper feature or special edition with all the charm, persuasiveness and confidence of Franklin Delano Roosevelt in a Fireside Talk.

Sullivan grew up in Kerry Patch, a district in St. Louis that despite its label was liberally populated with Germans, Swedes, Poles, Russians, etc.; and spawned prize fighters, ballplayers, cops, and crooks.

When he attained long pants, he got a job as a subscription solicitor with the Globe Democrat. It was the heyday of the premium—the free cuckoo clock or set of dishes with an 18-month subscription. The solicitor's life was not a particularly happy one; if his customers stopped paying the paper boy, he had to call back and reclaim the clock or dishes, if any. But Sullivan made good, and learned what sells newspapers.

In time he met Annenberg, who had an eye for talent, and was hired. He defected from the Tribune once, spent two unhappy years with the Examiner and selling books for Collier's. Max called him back, made him a subscription crew manager; then an inspector calling on news agencies from Rockford to St. Louis.

Sullivan traveled by train. One day Max noticed that orders from Sullivan came from towns not on his itinerary. Max phoned Sullivan, wanted an explanation of the funny business. Sullivan said that after making his local calls, he phoned news agencies in surrounding towns and got orders. The flabbergasted Max kept him in Chicago for a month, teaching other inspectors to sell by phone. The year was 1912 or thereabouts.

* * *

Sullivan on the telephone was high dramatic art.

He places a call for an out-of-town distributor.

"Sullivan, New York News. How's business, Mr. Aronson?"

By Mr. Aronson, business is never good.

"Have I got something to change that!" He launches on a description of a new Sunday feature that is the nonesuch, an allure to fair women and strong men, candy for the children, educational, inspirational, sensational! And an ad in the local paper the Friday before will let all your dealers and their customers know about it. How much of an increase does Mr. Aronson want?

Mr. Aronson wants not any.

Sullivan gives him a replay. Mr. Aronson still says no.

Sullivan, very stern: "All right, Mr. Aronson. But when your dealers are on the phone Sunday morning yelling for more papers, don't call me. It'll be too late to do anything about it then!"

Mr. Aronson gives a little. Okay, add a hundred.

Sullivan, hurt: "Mr. Aronson, do you think I'd make a long distance call to such an important distributor as you for a hundred copy increase? How many dealers are you serving?"

Mr. Aronson tells him, reluctantly. Sullivan points out the inadequacy of an extra hundred copies among so many dealers. And like a fisherman tugging a lethargic whale, he finally brings Mr. Aronson up to the increase he thinks is adequate.

Finale: "Okay, Mr. Aronson, you won't be sorry."

And that was the secret of Sullivan's salesmanship. Nine times out of ten, his judgement was right. Distributors and dealers would sell more papers, be willing to order more. Sullivan reasoned that dealers couldn't sell papers if they didn't have them. He made money for them, which is the ultimate in salesmanship.

On the other hand, if Mr. Aronson was consistently uncooperative, one day a News inspector showed up in his town and transferred the distribution to a more optimistic agency.

Sullivan was picked for the New York job because of his spectacular performance in France two years earlier.

The Tribune began publication of an army edition in Paris on July 4, 1917. A few correspondents had such a tough time getting out the paper that they gave no thought to its distribution. About 6,000 copies were printed daily, and few got outside of Paris. Cable tolls and other expenses were enormous.

Annenberg was ordered to go to Paris to close down the operation. For some reason not known, he picked Sullivan to go with him. However, the French consul in New York refused Max a visa. That was because Max had been in Europe when the war broke; and on his return told reporters that the war was in the bag for Germany, would be over in a week. Sullivan was okay. Max told him to go ahead, and went to Washington, saw the French ambassador, and got nowhere.

So Sullivan, who had never been east of Columbus, Ohio, before, landed alone in Paris. He was shocked to learn that nobody on the paper had effected any liaison with the army. Sullivan thought the army should be consulted before the paper was discontinued. (He may also have conferred with Patterson or McCormick, both in France with the army at that time.)

He hired a car and driver and went to Chaumont where Gen. John J. Pershing was ensconced in a chateau. His office was in the *grande salle*. His desk had bronze ormolu legs and molding around the top. In the molding on the general's side were a dozen pearl buttons.

The general was puzzled by his civilian caller.

Sullivan explained what the Tribune wanted to do with the army edition. If the army wanted the paper, it would have to lend a hand.

The general said nothing, ran his thumb down the row of pearl buttons. The room filled with generals, colonels, majors.

"Tell them what you've told me," said Pershing.

Jim did. When he finished, the general said "Give Mr. Sullivan all the help you can, gentlemen."

In an incredibly short time, Sullivan had 150,000 circulation. Army supply trucks and ambulances, the Red Cross, YMCA and other services were his delivery department. The men who fought at Chateau Thierry read about the battle the next day in army editions dropped from American planes.

Aside from phoning the office once a day to raise the print order, Sullivan stayed out of Paris—so he could say later he never saw the peremptory cables from Chicago telling him to stop publication and come home. When Chicago learned about his performance, it was too late to stop the paper.

Field figured that anybody who could get circulation in France ought to do well in New York, and tapped Sullivan for the job.

In his first months in New York, Sullivan studied his territory, talked to newsdealers, tried to learn. He called on suburban distributors and out-of-town news agencies, who were balking at paying $1.40 per hundred for a paper that sold at 2 cents a copy. Shortly he raised the out-of-town price to 3 cents, gave distributors and The News more margin.

The rapid rise in circulation when the limerick contest started justified his faith in the paper; and he had his first 100,000 by the end of the year.

* * *

Sam Steiger was part of Sullivan's luck.

In the spring of 1919, Steiger was trying to distribute a predate (night) edition of the New York Tribune, and not doing well. Sullivan hired him two weeks before The News came out.

Steiger was young, short, slim, black haired, with the face of an elfin altar boy. He had been a newsboy, worked in the circulation department of the Mail, was a junior tycoon; with his family, he owned a half-dozen newsstands; and distributed papers in the suburbs with a small fleet of cars.

Steiger never provoked a fight, but never ducked one; when the occasion required, he could be hard as nails. Joe Blossner, another early bird in circulation, recalls how Steiger handled dealers who wouldn't display The News. Some morning he would show up with a pair of "hustlers" who carried all morning papers. They would stand in front of the uncooperative dealer's stand, sell papers to approaching customers—and cost the dealer sales.

During the first summer when News circulation was at its ebb, Steiger used a dozen men at traffic points to pass out sample copies.

He knew New York intimately, as Sullivan in his early years did not; was as familiar with neighborhood problems and peculiarities as a social worker. And he shortly developed an amazing judgment of the value of news.

Arthur G. Ells, who had previously worked with Hearst papers in New York, was hired as assistant circulation manager. And Dorothy Miller came in as Sullivan's secretary. This foursome pretty much ran the circulation department in its first summer.

STENOGRAPHER'S GAZETTE

Advertising in The News began with Roy Holliss.

Roy Coleman Holliss had grown up in Chicago, was graduated from Hyde Park High School in 1908, and immediately went to work in Tribune classified. He did well and was shortly moved to the national department. In 1911, he was married on his 21st birthday, and with his bride went on to New York as the paper's eastern advertising manager.

He did a good job for the Tribune in New York. He was a good salesman; but beyond that, his common sense and good judgment, his honesty and friendliness, in the next eight years gave him a status larger than his job.

When the decision was made to publish The News in New York, Holliss got wide encouragement from agency people and national advertisers; many of them were from the Middlewest, and welcomed the advent of The News in New York. Their subsequent disappointment when the paper appeared negated much of the initial promise.

Holliss' main problem, however, was that he had no experience in retail. His reception in the department stores was not reassuring.

The first rate card specified: Page $200, three-quarter page $150, half-page $100, quarter-page (minimum) $50. No distinction was made between national and retail.

The rate structure was foreign to the retailers. The competition for department store advertising was so intense that many New York papers carried it at rates that barely paid for the cost of composition. The big stores rarely paid card rates; were accustomed to secret lower rates, fixed positions, and from some papers, supporting publicity. They thought the tabloid page was too small, resented the arbitrary space requirements. And they had no reason to support a pioneering venture; their attitude was wait and see.

Field called on John Appel, Wanamaker's advertising manager whom he knew, met with only polite interest. In September, Field had a nibble from McCreery's, who offered a full page five days a week, but asked for a 12.5 cents per line rate, and a fixed position on page 5. Field and Patterson were unwilling to commit themselves to the rate and position.

Unfortunately, there was nobody else in the eastern office with retail experience except Tommy Cochrane, the first full-time advertising employe hired for The News. Cochrane was ex-Tribune, had gone through classified and advanced to retail, but his experience was with small accounts. A 2d lieutenant in the Illinois First Cavalry, he had served on the Mexican border; and was hardly settled back in civilian life before his outfit was called into federal service in July, 1917, and subsequently saw service with the 32d Division. Cochrane was one of the few Tribunites willing to move to New York. One reason was that he had become engaged to a New York girl, Paula Richards, an actress who had been in France with a YMCA troupe of entertainers.

Another Tribune man who arrived on The News scene early was Wilton R. Blend. He had attended the University of Chicago, gone through classified and advanced to national; and had gone to the navy officer school at Pelham, N.Y. He became acquainted with Holliss, and saw him during his brief stays in New York during the war. Holliss and he liked each other, and Blend agreed to transfer to the eastern office. So Blend was one of the staff who started beating the bushes for ads for the new paper. With the argument that any new paper, good, bad or indifferent, got a lot of extra attention just because it was new, he got a schedule of half pages on tires from the United States Rubber Company.

News advertising that first summer was a mixed bag, and a lean one at that. Bloomingdale's ran two columns on a sale in its drug department in the first Saturday issue; probably because it was a leased department and didn't have to have official store sanction. There were ads from small retailers, dress shops, jewelry and shoe stores. Someone dubbed the paper "The Stenographer's Gazette." In August, Brill Brothers, one of the better men's wear stores, ran some small space offering chauffeur's outfits, uniform and overcoat, at $89.50. But there were few gamblers to take a chance in New York's first tabloid.

In early fall, Cochrane ran into Miss Teresa Hinz on Fifth Ave. Miss Hinz had been an ad-taker (phone solicitor) on the Tribune before the war; had enlisted in the navy as a yeomanette and been assigned to navy communications in the Whitehall Building downtown. She was pretty, popular, and liked New York. Cochrane proposed that she come with The News and try to develop some classified. She agreed and spent weeks in fruitless telephone solicitations, but kept at it.

The Tribune national men gradually lost interest and began to devote themselves to their proper jobs. Cochrane had a bad time; he started each morning with youthful enthusiasm, endured a day of rebuffs and insults, came back to the office after 5 o'clock discouraged and downcast.

Emmett Gordon, who had worked for Utassy before the war, went to France with the 42d Division, and had a rough time; his platoon was trapped in Belleau Woods for several days until relieved. At Utassy's invitation he had come with The News, ostensibly as advertising makeup man. With so little advertising to makeup, Gordon did odd jobs.

One day Cochrane persuaded Arthur's, a photographer, to run an ad in the paper. He helped prepare it, 75 lines on two columns. It was set, and the proofs were passed around and duly admired; and the ad was ordered in for the next day. But that night, some Mail compositor who knew that The News never carried any ads, shifted the Arthur's copy to the Mail bank; and the paper appeared the next morning without it.

Many of the early birds found themselves doing chores they hadn't been hired for. John Herman Schwarz, engaged as a cashier, found himself running errands, sweeping the floor, answering phones and interviewing job applicants. When the limerick contest got under way, he was pressed into service opening envelopes, and found himself working from 7:30 a.m. to 1:30 a.m. seven days a week.

The paper's first advertising success was in amusement ads; theater ads mounted to seven in July, increased to 28 by fall; and declined correspondingly when the coal shortage forced many shows to close.

In late summer, there was a rather sudden advance in classified. On Aug. 15, the New York Telephone Company ran a piece of copy 40 lines deep on two columns. Four days later, with the telephone ad were four others: a candy factory in Brooklyn wanted dippers and packers, at $12 a week, Saturday half day, bonus promised for continued service; a baking company on Long Island wanted wrappers, 48-hour week; a restaurant chain had openings for waitresses; and a garment maker wanted bright girls to learn the trade. On Nov. 12, the first Male Help Wanted ad appeared; the Submarine Boat Corporation called for riveters, steamfitters, shipwrights, in its Port Newark yard.

With the rise in classified, Miss Hinz added two helpers. By December, classified was filling four pages some days.

By August, 1919, the eastern advertising offices of the Tribune at 251 Fifth Ave. were so crowded that Holliss looked around for more space; and on Sept. 1, the move was made to 512 Fifth Ave., at 43d St.

Blend, meanwhile, was wearing several hats. He carried one business card for his Tribune territory, Philadelphia and the South; and three News cards—manager automotive advertising, manager national advertising, and manager classified advertising. Before the end of the year, he elected to stay with the Tribune and began to give his neglected territory closer coverage.

In late September, Harold B. Sherwood joined the staff.

Sherry was stocky, athletic, and a fighter. He was another Chicago Tribune career man, had started in classified; and in 1917 was in charge of the paper's movie directory (theater advertising). With the 7th Regiment, Illinois National Guard, he served on the Mexican border. When the war came, he was put in charge of the Signal Corps school in the Board of Trade Building, and was later made captain, in command of the 416th Railway-Telegraph battalion. An injury to his hand delayed his return and discharge until the summer of 1919.

His new job demanded all his optimism and combativeness.

By fall, Holliss felt he was torn between his Tribune and News jobs, and not doing full justice to either. So in November, advertising manager Parsons in Chicago picked Arthur W. Myhrum as advertising manager of the New York paper. Myhrum had had some retail experience; but like Cochrane he was not long finding out that a News salesman in New York was a far cry from a Tribune representative in Chicago, and that he had to start all over again.

* * *

By the end of 1919, the growing circulation began to attract some advertisers. The American Magazine and Woman's Home Companion ventured full pages. Curiously enough, the New York Times became a fairly frequent advertiser on Fridays, reminding News readers that its Sunday issues carried lots of pictures in gravure!

The stock market broke sharply on Nov. 13 with call money at 20%, and the usual wails of the speculators. In the next few months, four brokerage firms ran small space in the paper, endorsing Liberty Bonds, French Republic 5½s, and such stalwarts at AT&T, New York Central, etc. Apparently there was no overwhelming response, as their invitations to investors dropped off.

* * *

News linage in 1919 was approximately 83,000 agate lines.

Part II

The 1920s were the season of hope, growth, expansion; of rising living standards; public and private building, better roads, the automobile, the spread of the suburbs; of emigration West and the Florida boom; of successively broken flight records, and the first ventures of the small airlines; of Prohibition, speakeasies, rum-runners, gangs, organized crime and lawlessness; of messy murders, protracted trials, breach of promise suits; of feverish interest in amateur and professional sports; of vaudeville, road companies, huge movie palaces, star worship, Hollywood scandals, and talking pictures as the decade ended; of flaming youth, flappers, cake-eaters, pocket flasks and the moral indignation of the elders; of industrial strife and the emergence of unions; of free-wheeling banking, unbridled speculation, "two cars in every garage," the market crash and the oncoming Depression that seemed to negate the American Dream.

The News reflected the spirit of the times. It was frivolous, irreverent, often outrageous, but it won intense reader interest and loyalty, did more to serve readers personally than other papers. It originated brief, concise news presentation, and a trenchant editorial style that affected all newspapers, and was gradually adopted by many. Virtually by itself, it developed the photograph as a major news medium. In its fourth year it attained the largest daily circulation in this country; in its seventh the largest Sunday circulation. For many years it has had more than twice the daily circulation of any other paper in America.

THE PARK PLACE COCOON

In the early spring of 1920 Field began to shop for new quarters to house the staff and provide production facilities.

John W. Barnhart, then purchasing agent of the Tribune, came to New York to help him. When Utassy resigned in April, Barnhart succeeded him as business manager.

The News was fortunate in having somebody with his background and experience. Born in Logan, Iowa, in 1878, he learned the printer's trade as a boy; and after high school worked on a country newspaper. In 1895, he moved to Chicago, got a job in the auditing department of Chicago North Western Railway, and studied accounting at night.

By 1903, Barnhart was back in the newspaper field as business manager of the Indianapolis Star. There were two other Star newspapers in Muncie and Terre Haute, Ind. The group had been purchased by Daniel Reed, the Republican state boss. His job gave Barnhart the unusual opportunity of learning the operation of both large and small newspapers. However, the Star group got itself involved in litigation that threatened to last for years; and in 1909, Barnhart went back to Chicago with the Tribune. His 11 years as purchasing agent made him familiar with all the paper's departments.

Moreover, he had spent the past year supervising the erection and equipment of the new Tribune plant, then one of the country's largest and best equippped. (The five-story plant was later topped by the Tribune Tower in 1924.)

Lower Manhattan offered little selection; there had been no business building for the past three years. The eventual selection was 23–25 Park Place. Park Place is a three-block long street that runs west from Broadway to West St. At the corner of Broadway and obliquely across the street from the site picked for The News was the Woolworth Building, at that time the world's tallest building.

The site was on the north side of Park Place, removed from Church St. by a single structure which held Suerken's restaurant on its ground floor. The building ran through the block to Murray St., had a depth of 152 feet, a frontage of 58 feet, was five stories high and about 40 years old. The lease was for 21 years. Basement and sub-basement had to be entirely rebuilt to accommodate the weight of presses; upper floors were reinforced, all the wiring reinstalled, with fans and ducts for ventilation. Alterations took 11 months, and cost more than $200,000. John Gow, stereotype foreman on the Mail, was hired as mechanical superintendent to speed the renovation. Operations at Park Place started April 16, 1921.

The building had splintery floors, and on the Park Place side an agonizingly slow elevator, operated by a cable grip. Elmer Flagler, a wisecraking youngster who was later to hold executive positions in the advertising department, observed that The News had the fastest growing circulation and the slowest elevator of any newspaper in America. In December, '22, the elevator was shut down for a few days; new controls were installed. Thereafter it moved faster.

The building had several tenants, and as leases expired, News departments moved in. The musical chairs game went on steadily during the nine years of occupancy, and there was rarely a time when carpenters, electricians and masons were not holding forth somewhere.

In 1923, the fire department insisted on a sprinkler system. One 7,000-gallon and one 10,000-gallon tank were placed on the roof and 1,200 sprinkler leads installed. Every few months parts of the new presses were lowered to the basement by the outside street elevator; linotypes lifted by a crane on the roof and squeezed through third story windows. The mechanical departments were augmented repeatedly.

Circulation occupied the first floor on Park Place for almost a year, then moved back to the Murray St. side. Adverising took the space vacated by circulation on Washington's Birthday, 1922; subsequently moved to the third floor, then the fifth, and by 1928 had cut through the walls into the building over Suerken's. Tess Hinz and her three telephone solicitors found themselves smack in the newsroom on the third floor, were later reunited with advertising. Editorial went from three to five, eventually to two, with 20 darkrooms for the camera staff. The composing room was in the back half of the third floor, eventually took over the whole floor; desks and chairs were easier to move than linotypes.

As a matter of fact, 23–25 Park Place was inadequate by the time the building was occupied. Nobody could have foreseen the unprecedented growth of the paper.

The Wise Wood press, speed king in 1920, was taken out in October, 1923, replaced by faster Goss units. The basement eventually held three lines of Gosses, with aisles barely wide enough to bring in the paper rolls. The Sunday paper was started two weeks after moving into the building, and had 250,000 circulation in a month. At the end of 1923, the plant had a peak capacity of 900,000 32-page papers; but the paper size soon increased; and the first 40-page product was run Nov. 7, 1924. The Sunday Brooklyn section in January '24 added another load. After the move to Park Place, Evening Mail presses were still used for a time. As late as 1925, some of the Evening Telegram's presses had to be rented on big nights. Barnhart and the mechanical department heads had some sleepless nights; a fire or breakdown could have wiped out large chunks of circulation.

Finally in May, '25, a site was obtained for a second plant in Brooklyn on Pacific St. between Carlton and Fifth Aves., and work was rushed on a factory type building. Five press units were installed, followed by 10 more in the next three years. A stereotype department was included; motorcycle couriers carried mats from Park Place for casting in Brooklyn. A branch studio was included, with Ted Dalton, studio boy in 1921, in charge, and a few cameramen based there.

When color comics were added to the Sunday paper, March 11, 1923, they were printed on Tribune presses in Chicago. Later a Brooklyn printer was used. Then an electrotype plant was established over the garage at Washington and Morton Sts., and early in 1925 moved to the Brooklyn plant, where color presses were installed.

The gravure section, started in 1926, was printed by Art Gravure Corporation; later a battery of gravure presses were added to the color comics plant.

By 1928, The News had two printing plants, a garage, and three rented stables. Park Place was bursting at the seams. The editorial department, with nine people in June, 1919, had grown to 190; and every department had expanded. It was time to find a new home.

* * *

The News was as fortunate in its early mechanical personnel as it was in the people who came to work for it in other departments. Compositors, pressmen and mailers on the paper in the Mail plant stayed with The News.

Ed Duffy, a 14-year veteran of the Times, came from a foreign language paper, and was the first press foreman.

Duffy was a big man, extremely competent; there wasn't any job in the pressroom he couldn't do, and he was a good teacher. In September '23, there was a wildcat strike of pressmen, not supported by the other crafts. With some men from the advertising department helping out, Duffy kept the presses running for the two weeks the strike lasted. But the strike cost The News circulation. On the average it sold 87,000 fewer copies daily in September than in August.

William G. McGuinness, another Mail veteran, was the first composing room foreman; and in October '23 he stepped down for A. C. (Gus) Smith, who grew up on Midwest newspapers and had been composing room foreman at the Herald for fifteen years. The competent and unflappable Charley Reber headed stereotype.

Until February, '24, the paper's engravings were made by the Powers Engraving Company, which kept a covey of messengers shuttling back and forth between its plant and The News. That month The News started its own engraving department on the Murray St. end of the fifth floor; Thomas S. Fuller was borrowed from the Chicago Tribune as its foreman. He went back to Chicago two years later, and was succeeded by Charles Hohmann. The latest in cameras and other equipment produced better plates, and faster.

The Sunday gravure section began in October, 1926, with Gustave H. Friess in charge of production. Friess had come to this country from Germany as the technical representative of Mertens, press manufacturer; had installed gravure plants all over the country, and earlier spent 10 years with the Chicago Tribune.

* * *

One morning in September, 1921, a tall, thin, young man in overalls stalked up to Barnhart's desk and told him that the News' handling of paper was lousy—with explicit details. He was James J. Brown, then driving a paper truck for Emergency Trucking Company. Barnhart was impressed enough to hire him on the spot.

Brown was born in New York City. His family had been in the stevedoring business for generations. He had friends among the police, the politicians, and the unions. He had spent 12 years as a brakeman on 15 railroads in the Northeastern part of the country. He knew routes, freight schedules; and more important, yardmasters and road officials. When the war come, he enlisted in a railroad battalion intended to operate railroads in France. After six months, however, the army decided the men were needed more over here, and they were released.

Shortly after coming to The News, Brown visited the Thorold paper plant in Ontario, made a good impression on its presiding genius, Warren Curtis, and got his complete cooperation. Brown's first consideration was adequate storage, at that time in a nearby basement on Murray St. He spread shipments over three or four railroads, so regardless of wrecks, storms or delays, there was always paper stock en route to New York.

When deliveries began to be made by ship, he devised the quickest and most efficient handling and transport.

At another time, when circulation had passed the million marks, Brown began to suspect that the circulation department's figures of copies, sold and unsold, with normal pressroom waste, were lower than they should be for the quantities of newsprint used. He showed the figures to Bill

Denhart, then assistant circulation manager, who was unwilling to show them to Sullivan. So Brown showed them to Sullivan himself. Sullivan was shocked. This episode led to months of investigation that eventually disclosed a major pilferage.

There was another amusing, and enlightening, incident about Brown. When he was hired, he didn't mention salary, and neither did Barnhart. When he saw his first weekly pay check, he was indignant, told Herman Schwartz, the cashier, that he wasn't working for that kind of dough. He refused to accept the check, or checks for the following weeks, to Schwartz's consternation. Near the end of the year Schwartz took the accumulated pay checks to Barnhart. By that time Barnhart thought enough of Brown to pay him a year-end bonus to bring his compensation up to what he wanted.

* * *

April, 1921, brought another important event. Patterson, fearful of Field's frail health, suddenly appointed Roy Holliss assistant general manager. Holliss, although he might have hoped for the position eventually, was taken by surprise. The change was difficult for him because all his experience had been in advertising, and he knew little about other departments. He moved downtown, had a desk facing Field's in an open space surrounded by a rail in the front of the fourth floor; and began to learn his new responsibilities.

* * *

In 1922, Barnhart and The News got another exceptional break, in the person of John J. (Jack) Murphy, a baby-faced, reddish-blond young Irishman who had had an adventurous life. Born in Waterford, Ireland, Murphy had attended Trinity College in Dublin. His father had been an accountant with the Irish Railways for years, and Murphy became an accountant and worked at a variety of jobs in London.

Bored with accounting, he emigrated to Canada in 1913 and served as a teacher in an Indian school in Vancouver. When the war came in 1914, he enlisted in the Princess Pats, a Canadian regiment that bore more than its share of fighting and was virtually wiped out three times. At Paschendale, Murphy got a bullet in his throat, and was invalided back to England. After his release from hospital he was sent to an officers school at Oxford, commissioned a subaltern, and sent back to his battalion.

One time in a high moment, he told how his battalion had jumped off one day at 4 a.m. on a planned push, and attained its objective, the second German trench. But something went wrong; the rest of the line did not move up, and they were exposed on both flanks. The Germans shelled the trench mercilessly, and by sundown only 20 men were on their feet, with Lieut. Murphy the senior officer. After dark a ration party found them and left food and a double issue of rum for 140 men. The survivors ignored the food, went to work on the rum—"and in a little while, it wasn't a half-bad war at all. But the poor Heinies were ill advised enough to pick that night for a raid, and our fellows were simply few-reeous! They leaped up over the parapet without their guns and engaged in wrestling matches with the Huns who were utterly confused by their unorthodox reception. I jumped up on the parapet with the rest of them, slipped and fell on my face in a pool of muddy water. When I got the mud out of my eyes, there were eleven prisoners in the trench, and that's how I got the Military Cross."

Both his eardrums were broken during the second battle of the Somme, and he was deaf the rest of his life. Discharged from the army, he went back to Canada, got a government job as an inspector of Indian villages. In January, '21, he came to New York, his only avowed intention to see the Dempsey-Carpentier fight.

A brother in the import business in New York knew Holliss and asked him to get Murphy a job. The only job available for an unknown was night clerk at The News advertising publication desk; receiving orders and retailers' copy, sending them to the composing room, dispatching proofs—$25 a week. Murphy took the job, which he described as "pasting little bits of paper together" and was quite happy at it. He found a Manhattan room, spent his days walking around New York, reading books from the Public Library, smoking his pipe. He was companionable, a good bridge player, interested in sports, and soon found friends.

His main problem was the telephone; when he couldn't hear, he hung up. One furious advertiser so treated called Myhrum, who came down to bawl out Murphy personally. "I couldn't hear the fellow," he explained, "and I knew if it was important he would call somebody else"—which left Myhrum speechless.

The paper had an auditor who had probably signed on for a routine job, but soon found himself riding a whirlwind. Receipts, expenses, and transaction escalated every month. The monthly statement, due in Chicago on the tenth of the month following got farther and farther behind. One day in mid-'22 he threw up his hands and quit. Barnhart brought in a crew from a firm of professional accountants to review the books from the beginning. Somehow he had learned that Murphy had been an accountant, and asked him if he would like to help out. Murphy was glad to get a daytime job for a while.

He reported next morning, was given a ledger and assigned a desk. As he turned pages, he snorted, chortled, guffawed. Barnhart went over

GROWING
THE EVENING MAIL
THE
EVENING MAIL
"THE
FASTEST
GROWING
NEWSPAPER
IN
NEW YORK"

The News' birthplace was one floor in the Evening Mail building at 25 City Hall Place, a street which no longer exists. In two years the paper moved to a converted loft building at 25 Park Place, where it operated until 1930, under difficult conditions.

QUIET
TUDOR
CLEANING
TAILORING
LAUNDRY
Whelan
DRUGS
SODA LUNCH
BAR
AUTOMAT

Present home of The News (at left) as it apeared when it was occupied in 1930. To satisfy space requirements an annex was added, completed in 1960.

to find out why. Murphy showed him so many things wrong in the one ledger that Barnhart immediately made him acting auditor, in charge of straightening out the books. He resigned once a month for six months, eventually decided that he liked the job. In a few months, the ex-clerk was an important figure in the company.

Murphy had the intuition and imagination that distinguish the accountant from a mere bookkeeper. He became a great favorite of Patterson's, who used to write for explanations of items in the statements he didn't understand. For an accountant Murphy had a wonderful bedside manner; he left you confident that he knew what he was doing, and everything was all right.

One time when a CPA firm was making an annual audit, Murphy took two of its young men to the garage to inventory the paper. Rolls were stacked on end, several rows wide. The young accountants scrambled around on planks piled on top of the rolls, stood on step ladders, and counted. At last they reported "962 (or whatever) rolls."

"Rolls," said Murphy. "Very nice. Now how do you know they're paper?"

Murphy was soon joined by Michael Feerick as his number two man. Feerick had been auditor for two book publishers and some British newspaper (in New York) until his war service in the army. Three years later, he was assigned to the editorial department and moved his desk there, to cope with the imaginative expense accounts of reporters. Here his sense of humor, often tried hard, stood him in good stead.

From the News Distributing Company, after its year of existence, Murphy inherited Charles Peer who became a stalwart in the department. Another young bookkeeper, Henry Lahm, stayed long and became important.

The paper had at the time a credit manager whom Holliss thought highly of, because he kept advertising bad debts down to less than 2%. Murphy soon discovered that his operation was to charge off all but 2%! He was succeeded by the youthful Edward Roche, who held the job until his retirement in 1968.

* * *

An employees' magazine, NewsPix, made its first appearance in May, 1922. Its policy was formulated by Field: "This paper is not for the brass. It is for the men and women workers who have never seen their names or pictures in print; and is to be largely concerned with their activities." This policy was followed closely while the paper was small.

NewsPix first editor was Kenneth B. Johnson, recently graduated from Dartmouth. Johnson left after a year to study accountancy.

His successor was Sinclair Dakin. She became the best known person on the paper, the repository of all sorts of confidences, and a personal problem solver. After three years, with the increase of her responsibilities in the publicity (advertising promotion) department, NewsPix passed on to a succession of editors.

Among its departmental reporters, NewsPix found its own gossip columnist in Bill Bessette, composing room day foreman. His "Pickups for Pix" was one of its most popular features.

NewsPix eventually ended up in the personnel department. The number of employees today prohibits many personals.

In the spring of 1926, Patterson moved to New York. The News' daily circulation passed the million mark in April of that year, and the Sunday was running 1,250,000. He had an additional reason: Liberty, the weekly magazine which he and McCormick had founded in May, 1924. It was printed in the Tribune gravure plant in Chicago, but its advertising headquarters were in New York at 247 Park Ave., and for a brief period its small editorial staff was housed at 25 Park Place. A small cubbyhole of an office was provided for Patterson on the fourth floor. Most of the time he spent at The News plant was in the news room. His presence prevented many of the frictions and delays that occurred while he was based in Chicago.

* * *

A number of people were transferred to Liberty: William Flynn, as makeup editor, Grace Robinson, George Carroll and Ed Doherty as feature writers. Tess Hinz joined its advertising staff. When Liberty was sold to Bernard Macfadden in 1929, all come back to The News, with the exception of Flynn. As part of the Liberty transaction, Patterson and McCormick acquired from Macfadden Publications the Detroit Daily which they published from April 1, 1931, until Aug. 6, 1932, as the Detroit Mirror.

In January, 1927, Field sent a long letter to Patterson, and said he wanted to resign. His reasons were: that he was still getting most of his income from the Chicago Tribune and contributing nothing to the Tribune; that he was not well, and neither was Mrs. Field.

On Sept. 15 Patterson issued a bulletin reluctantly accepting the resignation; but stating that Field would continue as second vice president of the company and maintain contact with The News in a supervisory capacity. "He has promised to spend not less than three months of the year with this newspaper, the success of which is so largely due to him."

Field did spend short periods in New York during the next year. However, in the fall of 1928, his doctors advised him that he had tuberculosis.

The diagnosis apparently was wrong. He went to the West Coast, by ship via the Panama Canal, spent three months in California, three months in Arizona, and no further trace of it was found. However, he had suffered a detached retina, and underwent a series of not entirely successful eye operations. The News saw little of him from then on.

John Gow, mechanical superintendent, resigned in December '28 because of ill health. The job was split. Ed Boisseau, the plant's first electrician, took charge of the Brooklyn plant; and the popular Ed Duffy was given the responsibility for Park Place, and later the uptown plant. In 1931, Duffy was found to have tuberculosis, and took a long leave. He died July 23, 1934. In April 1935, a bronze plaque with a perpetual light was mounted on the pressroom wall. This memorial to Duffy was contributed by the men with whom he had worked.

During Duffy's absence, Boisseau acted as superintendent of both plants. He also helped plan the wiring and power installations for The News building.

* * *

While the uptown building was under construction, Barnhart hired an assistant to act as liaison between the architects and contractors—youthful Francis M. (Jack) Flynn. Flynn had grown up in Mt. Ayr, Iowa; and was a 1924 graduate of the University of Missouri School of Journalism. While still in college he acted as local correspondent for United Press and the St. Louis Star. After graduation he stayed on in Columbia, Mo., as advertising manager of the E. W. Stephens Publishing Company. In early 1926 he went to Tokyo as manager of the American-owned Japan Advertiser Press; and also served as Tokyo correspondent for the London Daily Express, and represented Wide World Photos, a subsidiary of the New York Times. He returned to this country in February, '29, and joined The News March 18. When Patterson and McCormick started publishing the Detroit Mirror in 1930, he became business manager of that paper and remained with it until it ceased publication in 1932 when he returned to The News. On Barnhart's retirement in the summer of 1938, Flynn succeeded him as business manager. Early in 1930, three weeks before the move to the new News building, Philip B. Stephens was hired as manager of the publication (advertising) department. He too was a journalism graduate of the University of Missouri, and went to work in the family firm, the E. W. Stephens Publishing Company as production manager. He had learned to operate a linotype machine during his boyhood, and his next job was in the Government Printing Office in Washington, D.C. Subsequently he was advertising manager of a chemical company, and did advertising and promotion for the Vacuum Oil Co. In 1931 he was appointed assistant to the business manager of The News; later was business manager and general manager until his retirement in 1966.

In the fall of 1926, Sullivan started to extend his direct delivery. Staten Island was first covered; then Long Island, Westchester, and the nearby New Jersey counties. For the first few weeks the delivery men taken off city routes drove around in the darkness, got lost; but dealer complaints were remarkably few. By the end of the year, more than 1,000 suburban dealers were being served. Eventually, the dealer list expanded to more than 12,000.

Ben (Bunky) Lewis, first circulation inspector, was made the first city circulator; he left at the end of '27 and bought an interest in an out-of-town news agency. He was succeeded by Alexander B. McLean, who left in 1929 to become circulation manager of the Telegram, and the World Telegram in 1931. Morris Schiffman, one of the first delivery men, was made assistant delivery foreman; and in time became city circulator, and held the post until his retirement in August, 1940. Morton House was made country circulation manager; he too, late in the thirties, bought an out-of-town news agency and retired.

When Sullivan retired in 1932, he was succeeded by Annenberg, ex-circulation manager of the Chicago Tribune and ex-publisher of Liberty.

A very young man, Joe Goldstein, had started as a routeman in 1925. He later was put in charge of the campaign to force itinerant boys and dealers to stick to the established prices of the paper. To him the police department assigned two detectives, Johnny Broderick, and Johnny Cordes, both famous for courage and ability with their fists. The three cruised the city at nights; and when the identities of the scalpers became known, their supplies were shut off. This determined and successful effort undoubtedly was effective in fostering circulation growth. Goldstein, for some years past, has been superintendent of delivery.

THE DYNAMIC DECADE: 1920-'29

The year 1920 started off grimly enough. The first snow came Jan. 15, followed by a second storm a week later, a third on Jan. 28, with freezing rain that froze streetcars to their tracks; and the fourth and worst storm Feb. 3. Fifth Ave. was snowbound, the rivers frozen, the subways short of coal.

Influenza caused 30 deaths, pneumonia claimed 75 victims. Stores, offices, factories closed at 4:30. Theater openings were staggered 15 minutes from 7 to 9 p.m. In late February the policemen and firemen had dug out most of the city, and were acclaimed in a News editorial as the best in the country.

January brought one serious defection—Arthur Clarke, whose health had been deteriorating steadily. Coming home one morning after a very busy night, he had fainted in his apartment. At another time he spent three days with bandaged eyes, to recover from eyestrain. Patterson, however, insisted that his managing editor work nights. Clarke left at the end of January, for a vacation in California, resumed with the Evening World on his return. Subsequently he went back to San Francisco as managing editor of the Chronicle. He was succeeded by Merton Burke. Blossom became day managing editor, Payne city editor.

On Jan. 13, a house ad announced that The News had passed 100,000 circulation in December. Another on Jan. 26 gave the circulation as 150,000. A third on Feb. 16 reported circulation the past week above 175,000.

In February, paper became a problem again. Field wrote Patterson on the 7th that the Railroad Administration routed cars from the Thorold paper mill to New Jersey terminals; and with the Hudson full of ice floes, it was impossible for barges to ferry paper rolls across the river. The other New York papers were similarly affected, cut the size of their issues. The News went back to 16 pages. And one night was forced to borrow newsprint from the Mail. The paper supply did not improve until late in the month.

On March 13, News pages were changed from four columns to five, each two inches wide; with the exception of the editorial page which held its four-column format until six months later. Small two deck headlines of light Gothic type were used above short items, giving the pages a spotty appearance. It took some time for the staff to become accustomed to the new dimensions.

Later in the year, there were negotiations with the Mail for a joint publishing company, which came to nothing. But the decision was made to buy a Wise Wood press, which had been ordered for the New York Herald by Bennett, before his death; and was offered for sale by his executor, the Guaranty Trust Company. The capacity of the press was 200,000 32-page issues an hour, and it seemed to be the solution of The News production problems. It could not be used, however, until a year later when the paper had its own building.

On March 18, the limerick contest ended. The average monthly circulation was 141,238 in January; 184,399 in February, 209,499 in March—more than six times the September figure. New Yorkers were taking to the paper with unprecedented speed.

Another $100 a day contest was started; "What Does This Picture Mean?", with a different illustration every day. It was not effective. The meaning of a picture depended on the viewer; the awards usually went to the cleverest caption writers. The paper continued to grow nevertheless.

A proposal to award $100 a month "to a heroic policeman, fireman, or life guard" met with a rough reception. The first selection was a fireman. The fire commissioner threatened to fire the man if he took the award. Mayor John F. (Red Mike) Hylan took over, then reneged. Finally the fireman's wife was brought to the office and given a $100 check. Since then monthly awards to policemen and firemen (the amount was raised to $250 a month in May, 1953) have always been paid to the wife, widow or closest relative of the hero and have won the paper goodwill and cooperation of both departments.

An outlaw rail strike hurt New York, but was quickly quelled by Congress. The first rent strike, by tenants in Brownsville, made news. Overall clubs were formed in protest against high clothing prices. The New York Evening Journal advanced its price to 3 cents "for those who prefer merit to cheapness." News circulation passed 225,000 in April. A hasty News campaign raised $4,000 for Memorial Day flowers for the graves of American soldiers buried in France. And the paper began to issue three editions.

George Utassy resigned April 30; he and two of his associates had succeeded in buying Life (pre-Luce). A few months later he became a vice president of International Films, a Hearst production company.

* * *

On June 11, Joseph B. Elwell was found murdered in his apartment at 344 W. 17th St. Elwell, bridge expert, tournament player and teacher, had hundreds of friends, pupils, acquaintances. The district attorney summoned a few every day, kept the case going for weeks—and got nowhere.

Julia Harpman covered the story for The News as "Investigator," and met a young United Press reporter, Westbrook Pegler, whom she married two years later.

The News ran swim contests for boys and girls, with numerous pictures of entrants before; and not any of the actual events. Sir Thomas Lipton's challenger for the America cup, the Shamrock, lost to the defender Resolute in seven not very interesting races. Man O' War was the horse of the year. The civil war in Ireland worsened. The News celebrated its first birthday with a dinner at the Astor; the entertainment was Eddie Cantor; the toastmaster was Richard W. Clarke, "generally called Dick."

Ruby Ayres, an English author of cloying romances, became almost steady fare in the paper. The Inquiring Fotographer column started by asking three boys and three girls of 15 how long they wanted to live. The column was dropped after a month, later revived.

The Democrats held their convention in Chicago and nominated James M. Cox; the Republicans held their convention in Chicago and nominated Warren G. Harding. Circulation exceeded 275,000 in August. The "Black Sox" scandal broke; and eight White Sox players were indicted for bribery.

On the afternoon of the Wall Street explosion (Sept. 16) when The News scored its first big picture beat, as will be related in another chapter, Ralph Armstrong, who had just resigned as a reporter on the New York American, came in to ask for a job. He found a frantic Payne in an almost empty office where half the phones were ringing. "Hell, yes!" said Payne. "Start answering those phones." Armstrong became the paper's "Industrialist" specializing in labor and strike news.

* * *

On Sept. 29 State Sen. Charles C. Lockwood obtained passage of a bill compelling landlords to get a judgment before increasing rents; prohibiting arbitrary rent increases and then serving dispossess notices. More than 40,000 tenants were involved. And on moving day, Oct 1, many landlords were embarrassed by the arrival of tenants who could not be given the apartments previously rented to them.

In October, circulation passed 325,000. And The News ran an editorial, "We Make Some Money"—announced its first profit in September.

Brooklyn lost the World Series to Cleveland. Investigator Julia Harpman covered the series from the woman's angle, on a cool, windy day. (She lost interest in the game after she found out that hot dogs and coffee were available.) Lou Walker, with his new wide lens camera, took "panorama" pictures of the series games, showing action on three bases.

"Winnie Winkle, the Breadwinner," by Martin Branner, joined The News family of comics. Terence MacSwiney, the Irish patriot, died Oct. 24, after a three months' hunger strike, and considerable Irish agitation in New York.

Phil Payne for a month had assigned a reporter and photographer to every meeting of Irish sympathizers. On Thanksgiving Day, Nov. 25, after a memorial service for MacSwiney in St. Patrick's Cathedral, his hunch paid off. Outraged by a British flag flying in front of the Union Club at Fifth and 53d St., Irish adherents heaved rocks through the club windows; and Payne got his story and pictures, exclusive.

A few days later, the revived Inquiring Fotographer asked five people "What makes you maddest about the Daily News?" Three women: poor paper, poor printing, scandal, too many ads. Two men: the society column, too many ads.

In The News movie poll Norma Talmadge outpulled Mary Pickford; Wallace Reid beat Douglas Fairbanks. News editorial urged an immigration curb; 15,000,000 Europeans wanted to come to this country, and too many of our own people lacked jobs. Garment workers went out on a costly strike that led to unionization. Police declared a deadline against criminals. Area between 32d St. and 57th, Broadway and Madison, was proclaimed out of bounds for known lawbreakers; a midnight curfew was set and cops carried machine guns; but burglaries continued.

* * *

The assured continuance of the paper in 1920 brought a considerable increase in editorial staff.

George Ringler, police reporter, had worked on other New York papers, knew policemen, city hall officeholders, judges, lawyers, and assorted characters on the shady side of the law. He was strictly a legman, passed on his reports to rewrite; working like a detective, he would be on several stories at the same time.

Alex Orban, night law student, energetic and ambitious, covered the supreme court, was a favorite of lawyers and judges. On Friday, when undefended divorce pleas were heard, Orban would decide if any of the freshly freed females were picture worthy, and call for a cameraman. When the court was not in session, Orban had other assignments. One was The News "Queen Of The Beach" contest, and later he married one of the queens. He was with the paper until 1929.

William J. White, Jr., grew up in Brooklyn, and after high school worked in an insurance office and a bank. When the war broke, his efforts to enlist were thwarted by his 116 pounds. Later he managed to be drafted, with some mild collusion with his family doctor who was on the draft board. He became headquarters company clerk, 305th Infantry, 77th

Division, at Camp Upton. He was transferred at his own request to a signal platoon, which sailed April 18, 1918, and disembarked at Perth, Scotland. Brigaded with the British, his outfit served in the British sector of Lorraine, and relieved the 42d Division after Chateau Thierry.

The Argonne Battle began Sept. 26. White's outfit had been moved to the sector some days before, was occupying a trench on one side of a road. Across the road, on a rising slope of second growth woods, a cluster of German pillboxes effectively discouraged crossing the road. White volunteered to crawl through the underbrush across the road, and drag a wire up to a point near the nearest pillbox. The wire was to be used to direct artillery fire on the slope. It was not very effective; the second salvo it directed fell on the wrong side of the road on White's outfit. But this action earned him the Silver Star.

Back home, he worked briefly as a reporter for the Brooklyn section of the American, then was hired by Phil Payne on a $6 a day basis. His first assignment was to find a daily human interest story. By July he was on the regular payroll at $35 a week, and beginning a 44-year career on the paper.

Ray Binder, formerly with the Hudson Dispatch (Jersey City), started as assistant news editor, later became a stalwart of the Sunday edition. He was a fast, fluent writer, and had a bubbling humor, and he brightened up many a story until his death in 1941.

The very young Ted Dalton started as a studio boy, was soon a staff cameraman, and in five years headed the Brooklyn plant studio.

George Kivel was an experienced police reporter, ex-Fire Marshal of New York City, and had been an inspector in the intelligence branch of the army during the war. Kivel was generally on the night staff. A few months later, his brother Maurice (Moe) Kivel, just out of City College, came as a reporter. In time he moved on to the city desk where he functioned as assistant city editor until his retirement in May, 1969.

Edward H. McCloskey, a graduate of Boston College, had worked on Boston newspapers. During the war he was a chief petty officer on the liner Leviathan, which served as a troop transport, was later commissioned. After his discharge he worked on the Philadelphia Ledger, came to The News on the copy desk, and was shortly night editor.

George Schmidt, a five-year veteran of Underwood & Underwood, a picture service, was hired as a cameraman and later became picture assignment editor.

* * *

Robert Chase, a little man right out of Damon Runyon, came from the Brooklyn Eagle as a reporter. He professed to know who was who in every New York City department—or at least knew a man who knew the man you wanted to reach. Chase had unlimited gall; once prevailed on a general passenger agent to hold an express train to Washington 17 minutes for Burke on the plea that Burke had an appointment with the President. As contests and contributions from readers increased, Chase became the paper's first editorial promotion manager. No idea was too grandiose or spectacular for his scope; and he was prolific in inspiring imaginative projects, most of which were never carried out.

A girl reporter, Irene Del Mar, who had come to the paper from the American, became Chase's assistant, and the paper's first Sally Joy Brown. She ran the "Friend In Need" column, which tried to help readers in need and solve their problems. She also arranged trips to beaches, parks and Coney Island for poor children in the summer; movies and other entertainments in the winter.

To the art department, on a part-time basis, came Gabe Kinn. Born in Paris in 1893, he had come to this country with his parents in 1904, grew up in Tarrytown. Proficiency as a mechanical draftsman in high school encouraged him to seek an art job, part time, with the Evening World. When the war came, he was rejected as an alien by both the army and the navy. Drafted in the summer of 1917, he was assigned to the 302d Engineers at Camp Upton; and immediately found himself teaching French to officers and enlisted men. In France he was a sergeant in army intelligence, and was not discharged until 1920. He resumed his part-time job with the World, got another with the Globe. Art department manager Eddie Miner advised him to drop the second job when he came to The News. He first appeared on the permanent payroll about the time the paper moved to 25 Park Place. He subsequently became manager of the department, a job he held until his retirement in 1959. He died in 1968.

Kinn recalled that after the move to Park Place there were frequent fire alarms turned in on Murray St.—on which The News building backed up—invariably on Saturday nights when The News trucks and wagons were trying to get away with the first Sunday edition. These Saturday evening annoyances were attributed to Hearst circulation people. This was one of the first indications that other papers recognized The News as a real rival.

* * *

To the assorted cast of The News newsroom in the Mail Building was added a little elderly man with a white mustache, D. V. L. Sheppard, as editorial receptionist and usher. He was born in New Jersey May 31, 1843, had served in the Union Army and fought at Chancellorsville, cast his first vote for A. Lincoln. If any personnel standards existed at the time they were most lenient to permit the hiring of a 77-year-old man. Despite his age, Sheppard was competent and conscientious. He ejected more than one gate crasher from the newsroom with surprising vigor and virility. He was a regular and conscientious marcher in the G.A.R. Decoration Day parades. And on his birthday always walked across the Brooklyn Bridge; though his time of 17 minutes gradually crept up to 19 minutes. DVLS held his job until after the paper moved uptown, died of pneumonia at the age of 89 in 1932.

* * *

There was little physical change in the paper in 1921 and 1922. The light Card Gothic cap heads were replaced by bolder, more contrasty Chelt Bold Condensed heads.

The right-hand column of page 2 contained brief Washington items, bylined "Henning." Foreign news items occupied the right-hand column on page 3. When the news was important, boxes well forward in the paper gave the latest details and often the chronology. Major events such as the famine in Russia, Soviet-Polish conflict, the Irish rebellion, civil strife in Germany, and other important foreign stories were covered by the Chicago Tribune staff. Pictures were published as they became available. Asia and the Far East were little noticed, except for major cataclysms such as the Japanese earthquake in 1923. Routine foreign correspondence consisted of government handouts, personalities and scandals.

Public interest in foreign affairs was minimal. World War I was followed by a backlash of isolationism. The prevailing attitude was that we had saved Europe once, and from now on it could look after itself.

The News Shoes and Stockings Fund for children who needed them staged a long campaign, finally raised a total of $15,000. The first zero weather came Dec. 26, first snow Dec. 27. A dry New Year's Eve was forecast. And News circulation for December averaged 317,868!

* * *

1921

Jan. 1, 1921, was a near-zero Saturday, with no news. The back page carried the 1921 calendar, a pet idea of Patterson's. But Monday, Jan. 3, was a day to mark in red on any calendar.

On Dec. 13, 1920, three ballons manned by navy lieutenants, had taken off from Lakehurst, N.J. in a snowstorm, and were feared lost at sea.

Then on Sunday, Jan. 2, a telegram from Mattice, Ontario, brought word that the balloonists had been lost four days before they had been found by an Indian; were safe and well at a Hudson's Bay Company post at Moose Factory, Ontario. Storms had delayed getting the message to Mattice.

The News announced this in a story of the purest Rover Boy fantasy by Phil Payne, selected because "he had been born in Canada." He described the deep snows, silent forests, freezing cold, perils from wild animals; and conjectured that the balloonists had kept alive by eating squirrels and porcupines. The paper also announced that it was sending special correspondent James Whittaker and photographer Eddie Jackson to Canada to meet the returning heroes.

Whittaker's first story, on Thursday, was an account of his hard time getting to Clute, Ontario, where he thought the balloonists would arrive first. His next was an interview with two Indian guides. His third advised that the heroes would go to Mattice first; and had eaten two pigeons while lost. Meanwhile, every day the paper ran stock pictures of snowy forests, sledge dogs, Indian guides, trappers' cabins.

The next Monday brought the first Jackson photo, of correspondent Whittaker setting bravely forth for Mattice in a snowstorm. Tuesday's report was laconic; balloonists delayed by storms. The front page carried a dusky photo—Jackson in profile with outstretched right hand, stiff as a totem pole. A center figure was putting something on Jackson's protruding palm. A third figure looked on. Caption: Capt. Jackson getting instructions from the home office!

Then Whittaker did send some news. One of the balloonists had written his wife that a member of the trio wanted to commit suicide when lost. The wife gave the letter to the newspapers. When clippings reached Mattice, the would-be suicide slugged the letter writer.

Finally on Wednesday the 14th the paper had pictures of the balloonists returning, two in a sled, one on foot; with shots of assorted Indians and *habitants.*

Secretary of the Navy Edwin Denby was pained by the unbecoming conduct of the slugger and the letter writer, and announced a court of inquiry would be held. In a caustic editorial, The News suggested that the court find out who was responsible for sending the trio aloft with little food, no water, and poor equipment.

Back in New York on Jan. 19, Whittaker was appointed the paper's drama critic, probably because of his dramatic stories from Canada.

* * *

James Whittaker was 28, of moderate height, blond and personable, unfailingly articulate, with an irreverent wit. He had been a teenage prodigy of the piano, made concert tours in this country and Europe. Later he launched into musical criticism, then general reporting for the Chicago News. Patterson hired him for New York.

As a critic Whittaker was ahead of his time. The *cognoscenti* who quoted Alexander Woollcott a decade later never even noticed him; yet he was better informed, and as good a phrasemaker, without Woollcott's malice.

Knowing the theater from backstage, he was intolerant of sham and pretense. He dissected a formula musical comedy by pointing out the parts that came from previous hits. Of an Earl Carroll dramatic effort, he wrote that the scenery was better than the play or the cast. He fell out of grace with the Shuberts early, by calling their Century Theater on Central Park West a "mausoleum," and was officially barred from Shubert houses; but managed to review their shows as usual. He could be warm and enthusiastic when he thought a production worthwhile and well done. His reviews were never dull reading. His reviewing was often interrupted by reporting assignments.

* * *

In February, 1921, Burke hired a tall young woman just out of Ohio Wesleyan, Roberta Yates, who had worked summers on the Cincinnati Post. She did general assignments for two months, and then Patterson had a role for her—Martha, so called after the pragmatic sister in the Scriptures who worried about so many things. She became the paper's official worrier—about the American girl, school lunches, Chinese dance halls, hot dancing in Harlem, pushcart prices, unsafe excursion boats, divorce laws, inadequate fire protection; but more about the school shortage than anything else. She once advocated sex education in high schools—which was considered scandalous and made an uproar. When Miss Yates was assigned to the Sunday paper in 1922, her successor as worrier was Martha Harris, another Cincinnati girl, ex-Radcliffe, who had Brooklyn Eagle experience.

July brought Clifford Laube, for 10 years editor of a country weekly in Rico, Colo., when he was elected to the state assembly for one year. He saved most of his $2,000 salary to try his luck in the big city, which happened to be Denver; put in three years on the Denver Post before he came to New York. Hired by Burke for the copy desk, he was shortly assistant city editor; later editor of the Brooklyn section.

Another broth of a boy was Frank J. (Red) Dolan, Boston bred, who ran away from home at 16, served in the army on the Mexican border, saw a lot of the world as a seaman, and had some prior experience on Philadelphia papers. Dolan was red-haired, an imaginative writer with unlimited gall. His expense accounts were fictional masterpieces.

Alva Taylor, daughter of Bert Leston Taylor, conductor of the Chicago Tribune's column "A Line-O-Type Or Two," had eloped with Paul Gallico and come to New York. Patterson started her on a three-times-a-week column on men's fashion, which she carried on until her retirement.

Another young reporter who graced the newsroom at the time was James Vincent Sheehan, who took off for Paris the following year. He later attained some repute as an author (without the James). However, in "Personal History," his autobiography, he fails to mention his year with The News.

* * *

"Wanted: Man to work Sundays. $8."

The want ad in The News was answered by Lt. James Jemail, still in uniform, and on active duty with the 23d Fleet Division of the Naval Reserve. The job was watchman in the editorial department. The time was April, just before the start of the Sunday edition.

Jemail had been picked for Annapolis, was injured in his plebe year, and had switched to Brown, played in the first Rose Bowl game in 1916. He served in the navy, went back to Brown, and was a much publicized halfback. He was not much taller than he was wide and they called him "Iron-man Jemail."

On his first Sunday, the celebrity-conscious Payne offered him a permanent job—as inquiring photographer of The News. "You will be rebuffed and insulted, and some people won't even talk to you," explained Payne.

Jemail made his debut in the first issue of the Sunday News, May 1. The question: "Should a wife believe the things she hears her husband say in his sleep?" A staff cameraman went with him the first weeks; then Jemail took a course in photography and was soon able to use a camera.

He was rebuffed often in the early years, usually by people who didn't know The News or the feature. One day in Jersey City, his question was "How do you know you are sane?" He had no difficulty in getting answers from five people. The sixth man, however, objected violently, accused Jemail of persecuting him; and to settle the matter of his sanity, exhibited a discharge from a mental asylum! A policeman who had observed the commotion made a phone call. An ambulance drew up shortly, and the protesting Jemail was taken to the city's psychiatric center. Jemail insisted that he was a reporter carrying out an assignment. He was held several hours until the city desk obtained his release.

When he was ahead on his quota of columns, he covered assignments, sat in as a copyreader, did feature articles. For years he asked for a byline for his column, to give identification to the people he interviewed; and was told that traditionally the editorial page (where his column appears) never had bylines or signed articles. By 1935, however, "By Jimmy Jemail" appeared below the column heading.

During the Columbus Day parade in 1962, he pushed his way through to the President's box, much to the annoyance of the Secret Service men; and asked President John F. Kennedy "What is the height of your ambition?" The President replied "To do well whatever I am doing. Incidentally, Jimmy, I've followed your column for years, and I'm glad to catch up with you. My wife used to have your job on the Washington Times Herald, and I used to suggest questions for her."

Jemail has averaged about 2,000 interviews and photographs a year since 1921, and is one of the best known men in New York. People he interviewed years ago stop him on the street and reintroduce themselves. His column probably has as high readership as any other feature in the paper. And his close to 100,000 contacts have caused thousands to become aware of The News and start reading it.

The questions asked by the Inquiring Fotographer (a News spelling of the word) are submitted by readers. Originally $5 was paid for each question used; 15 years ago the amount was increased to $10. Questions are selected and replies reviewed by the editors of the editorial page.

* * *

On March 11, 1921, the Stillman divorce case broke, and made headlines for years. Patterson thought it was one of the great stories of all time—involving money, power, social position, sex and infidelity.

James A. Stillman brought action against his wife of 20 years, Mrs. Anne Urquhart Stillman, claiming that her fifth child, Guy, was illegitimate, fathered by Fred Beauvais, an Indian guide who worked at the Stillman's summer home in Quebec. Stillman was president of the National City Bank, which his father founded; and was the reputed heir of $10,500,000. He was obtuse, headstrong, wholly intolerant of public opinion.

Mrs. Stillman's attorneys countered with evidence that Stillman had supported and lived with a former show girl, Mrs. Flo Leeds, and had three children by her, two stillborn, one boy living. Early in the case The News published some letters alleged to have been written to Mrs.

Stillman by Beauvais. The American and Journal promptly pirated them; the more ethical Times bought them from the Chicago Tribune. Special correspondent Whittaker took off to Three Rivers, Quebec, to find Beauvais, who wasn't there. Whittaker interviewed the station agent and other locals, who thought Beauvais a fine fellow. After three days of nothing stories he came home.

Meanwhile The News printed dozens of pictures of Mrs. Stillman, from the cradle on; and one original photograph of the locked gates of the Stillman estate in Westchester.

The divorce was denied Stillman, on the grounds that he had not come into court with clean hands; a separation was granted Mrs. Stillman, with alimony of $7,500 a month.

The following year Stillman appealed the case, and lost in the Appellate Division. He fought the alimony.

In two editorials, The News called for Stillman's resignation as president of the bank! He offered it and it was at first refused by the board of directors, accepted a month later; but he still remained on the board.

In the spring of 1923 he went to Paris, abandoning Mrs. Leeds, who had her field day in the newspapers as the woman wronged. Various other characters cropped up from time to time, with claims against Stillman.

In 1925 the Stillmans were reconciled, bought a new house on Park Ave. Then in June, 1931, Mrs. Stillman obtained a very secret divorce in White Plains; and the next day married Fowler McCormick, 18 years her junior.

Stillman died in January, 1944. Two years later, his will came to probate, and the estate was largely worthless stock certificates, and technically $200,000 in debt! The Stillman case kept a number of News reporters busy, in fact it was the making of several of them.

* * *

In June, '21, James Montague resigned as editorial writer, with regrets on both sides. He was unhappy with the World Syndicate, which handled his verse feature "More Truth Than Poetry," and switched to the Tribune. Joining the Tribune editorial page staff was part of the deal. A trio of Payne, Blossom and McGivena were picked to write editorials; the honorarium was $10 per editorial, later cut to $5. The editors monopolized the assignments; McGivena got a few crumbs.

This arrangement ended Dec. 1, when Robert M. Peattie took over the editorial page. Peattie, a long time New York correspondent of the Chicago Tribune, with quarters and a leased wire in the Times office, had retired in December, 1920. He was able, and well liked by News people, but had specified that his editorial chore was for one year only. On Dec. 1, '22, he was given another retirement dinner; and boasted that he was the only Chicago Tribune man to get two retirement watches!

Peattie was followed by Roscoe E. McGowen, whom Patterson found on the Rock Island (Ill.) Argus. Roscoe was known for his memory. In the daily discussion with Patterson, he never took notes, feared that note-taking might make Patterson nervous. McGowen was not well, and gave up editorials in December, '24. He was assigned to sports, and went to Florida in January, '25, to cover the Dodgers spring training. His successor was William Randall, who had been night city editor. Various other incumbents occupied the post briefly, until the advent of Reuben Maury.

Maury was born and grew up in Butte, Mont. He got his L.L.B. from the University of Virginia in 1925, and started the practice of law in his father's office in Butte. He tried his hand at writing, sold some short stories to Redbook, Blue Book and Scribner's magazines. In an issue of American Mercury, H. L. Mencken remarked rashly that he never encountered a piece of good prose that came out of Montana. Maury obliged with a good one, a frank and full delineation of his native city, and what made it tick. He wisely used a nom de plume. The story appeared in the Mercury for October, '25. Patterson read it, liked it, and wrote Maury (care the Mercury) offering him a job.

He came to The News Jan. 2, '26, spent three months as a reporter and movie critic, to get acquainted with the paper. And on April 1, '26, began the job he was hired for—and a remarkable association lasting 20 years. Patterson once said that Maury could express his (Patterson's) ideas better than he could himself.

They met every morning at 11. Sometimes Patterson talked about a specific idea. Sometimes he advanced several he thought worthy of comment. Sometimes he professed to have nothing in mind. Maury rarely spoke at these sessions. But at 4 o'clock he came back, usually with one long and one short editorial. Often Patterson approved them without changes.

Maury's legal training showed in his writing. He outlined a situation quickly (unless it was so well known as to need no elucidation) and then made his point or points clearly, simply, forcibly. He often used slang or colloquialisms. His versatility was evident in producing regularly editorials on the same theme, such as "A Seat For Every Child" on the shortage of school facilities; or "Two Ships For One" (Patterson's idea) in the paper's pre-World War II campaign for a larger navy and military preparedness.

His editorials from the very first got close attention from politicians and office holders; often prompted or speeded action on certain measures. Lawyers and writers were perhaps the next group to follow them closely. Businessmen came next; many got the paper just to read the editorials and nothing else. Maury set a standard of lively style and interest, made News editorials the most and best read of any published.

Also in Maury's charge was "Voice of the People," the collection of letters from readers on the editorial page. In the '20s, these ran well over 100 per day. (Later they ran much heavier than that.) He made a selection, often briefed the original letter; and was careful to include different points of view.

Particular attention was given to beefs, complaints, and disagreements with the paper's policy. In the first few months, Patterson was insistent that knocks and kicks be published; and once sent a batch of complaints and disparaging letters to be used if too few came in. His rationale was that the complainer is gratified to see his letter in print, shows it around to others; and watches the paper to see any reflection of his views, or to find something else to be dissatisfied about. Patterson knew that a man's name in print is good insurance of his continued readership.

* * *

In September, 1921, Bromley Gray, a New York veteran, joined the copy desk, later was assistant picture editor, and filled a number of jobs for the next 21 years.

Charles A. Lovett came as New York correspondent of the Chicago Tribune News Service. With him was Harry Bolig, telegrapher. This pair was not on The News payroll, but was generally regarded as staff. Lovett held his post until his retirement in 1968.

Two youngsters were hired as copy boys, Osmund (Ossie) Leviness and Everett Breuer. They became inseparable, and News people found it hard to tell them apart. Both pursued the same careers; studio boy to cameraman, with long lists of credits. Breuer is still with the paper as studio production manager. Leviness died in 1966.

* * *

September also brought the first of the Hollywood scandals. Fatty Arbuckle, a popular comedian, was tried for the murder of Virginia Rappe, a movie extra girl. A hung jury released him. At a second trial he was acquitted, but dropped by the movies.

The end of the year 1921 brought a flurry of excitement. In Chicago, the Hearst papers started a lottery—gave away numbered certificates; drawings were held, and holders of winnning numbers got cash prizes. The American and Journal in New York took on the project, followed by The News which offered double the amount of prizes. "Gift certificates" were printed by the million; merchants and newsdealers stood in line for hours to get them to dispense to their customers.

The first News drawing was held Saturday, Nov. 29, in Battery Park, with a parade of clowns, mounted police, and the Sanitation Department Band, and $5,2000 was awarded to the winners.

As soon as the project started in New York, the management of the three papers looked for some way to stop it. Ralph Armstrong went to Washington to persuade Will Hays, Postmaster General, to bar the papers from the mails as lotteries. Hays was amused, saw nothing wrong in giving away money. By the time three drawings had been held, The News was out $16,280. Field and Brisbane agreed to a halt.

And The News invited all its readers and friends to sing Christmas carols (and even printed the carols) in Battery Park at 4:45 p.m. the Saturday before Christmas—a small-town touch that was never tried again!

* * *

May 1, '21, marked the start of the Sunday News, a 28-page paper selling for 5 cents. The initial press run was 200,000 copies. Blossom was appointed editor, and was not very happy about it as he regarded himself primarily a news man.

A mystery story, "Poor Rich Babies" by Lauchlin James, was the base for a contest—$10,000 offered for the best solution in 100 words. Four pages of the story ran in the first six issues. The winner, announced Sept. 1, was Mrs. Ilse Mohr, of Brooklyn.

There was a page of pictures of current movies, another page of pictures of scenes in plays. "The Potters," an illustrated episode written as a play-script, was new; its author J. P. McEvoy, a well-known humorist. "Angela" had a page of society. There was a page for children, and another on science. Radio newscasts were listed.

On Aug. 28, another limerick contest started with a $200 first prize, $50 second, $25 third, and 45 prizes of $5. Another contest for school children, for the best essay on Washington, ran for months.

By the time it was a year old, circulation of the Sunday News was running a little over 300,000.

A serial story by a big name author was a fixture. The appeal of fiction was very strong. "The World Outside," by Harold McGrath, which started Aug. 27, 1922, brought an increase of 50,000 circulation.

An eight-page section of color comics, first included in the Feb. 12, '23, edition, jumped sales 65,000; and the crowd of newsboys on Murray St. on Saturday nights required the police to maintain order. The sale of the Sunday paper by that time was running over 500,000. The Saturday night crowd of boys grew unmanageable; and the Saturday night sale was stopped after the Oct. 7 issue.

In December, '22, Blossom resigned to become editor of Popular Science. Patterson made Roberta Yates Sunday editor; she was all of 23 years old at the time. Bill Flynn was shifted from the copy desk as her assistant.

Another acquisition at the time was George Fry, a veteran of the American and the World. Not the least of his assets was the access he had to the World's morgue. Fry started what was to be a long time feature, "What Has Happened to Justice?" a review of unsolved murder cases. After the first two appeared, Patterson sent Fry a note of congratulation and a bonus, whereupon Fry disappeared for a few days; and editor Yates had to hastily finish his script for the next justice story.

After 1927, Fry went with some magazine and disappeared from the scene.

Another Sunday staff member was Peter Levins, the "picture clerk" of the original 1919 staff. He went back to school after that first summer, returned in 1922. For some years the "What Has Happened to Justice?" stories were his special province.

* * *

On Feb. 3, 1924, the Brooklyn section was begun. By this time, the Sunday edition was running 64 pages.

On Oct. 10, '26, the gravure section was started, under the editorship of Earl Overholt who had started on the copy desk five years before. It was printed in sepia monotone by the Art Gravure Corporation, and by present day standards seems quiet and prosaic. But three issues in October pushed circulation up to 1,180,350; and by December it was 1,222,391.

Another unexpected occurrence was a fantastic growth outside city and suburban zones. By 1930, this so-called country circulation was running over 400,000. To meet the demand of dealers, a predate or "pup" was printed the week before and sent to distant points. The "pup" had little hard news in it, covered amusements and sports, with the regular Sunday features. It was the lowbrow New Yorker, something read by people who had once visited the big city, or wanted to; and apparently imparted some sophistication.

Roberta Yates, who cherished ambitions to write the great American novel, resigned on Jan. 1, '27. Her successor was Ray Binder.

* * *

1922

The year 1922 promised to be lively.

Princess Mary married Viscount Lascelles; and the Boston Post spent $1,500 for a special train to bring the wedding pictures from New York. Railroad shopmen, 400,000 of them, went on strike, took other railroad workers with them; Government intervention and two months were required to work out a settlement. The civil war in Ireland worsened. The Roma, third of the Navy's dirigibles, burned and crashed at Hampton Roads, and there were some stunning photographs. Home and apartment building picked up, brought the first rent reductions. The Rev. Theodore Maynard, flying parson and the first man to walk on plane wings in flight, died in a crash. Later in the year, the Turks invaded Smyrna, killed 2,500 and left 180,000 homeless. The end of the big war had not stopped the little ones.

On Jan. 9, under the aegis of Doris Blake, The News started a lucky name contest, based on horoscopes, with a $1,000 prize weekly. The contest ended April 16. Isabel Cecelia Nelson, deemed by the astrologers to have the very luckiest name, was luckier by $5,000. This contest drew more than 1,500,000 entries—or better than three times the daily circulation, which reached 450,000 in February. The 10-month-old Sunday issue had passed 300,000.

In February, the much-married soldier of fortune Hollywood director, William Desmond Taylor, was shot in his study. The prosecution interviewed film celebrities for months, and got nowhere. Eddie Doherty, Chicago Tribune and News correspondent in residence, resolutely followed the hue and cry. The Taylor murder uncorked a series of Hollywood scandals that continued for years.

The Washington essay contest came to a close, with a $1,000 prize for the winner, Berenice Bucklin, of Staten Island, who told how she did it (determination, mostly); and she was photographed in appropriate domestic poses.

In April, Whittaker wrote a series on how theatrical managers and producers try to manipulate and coerce the press, with the Shuberts as horrible examples. Later he did an expose of Atlantic City, headquarters for rum-runners, gamblers and vice lords. Atlantic City was quite upset about it, and cried foul. Later in the year, at a typographic union convention in that fair city, The News delegate, tagged with his identification, was roughed up by some of his Atlantic City fellow craftsmen.

In May, the paper had another sensational series on Letchworth Village, the state reform school for girls. Bernadine Szold, an exotic looking young woman of Hungarian descent, had grown up in Gary, Ind.; put in her apprenticeship on local papers, attended Barnard for a year, been a reporter on the Chicago Evening Post before she was hired by Payne. Miss Szold got a job as an attendant in Letchworth, held it for three weeks. She was never in any danger, but was horrified by the quarreling that went on among the girls, and their criminal ambitions. The series caused parents of Letchworth inmates to protest, and led to the inevitable investigation.

In July, Mabel McElliott, who had become Mrs. Richard W. Clarke in January, asked for a leave of absence; and Patterson started looking for a new movie reviewer. He offered the job by telegram to Alva Gallico, then on vacation at Nantucket. She suggested her husband, Paul Gallico, who was then with the National Board of Review of Motion Pictures. After Patterson satisfied himself that the board had no commercial connections, Gallico got the job. In the announcement of his appointment in News Pix, he said that "most pictures were as bad as people said they were."

Gallico was not *simpatico* with the silver screen; his reviews tended to be cool when not downright unfavorable. In a letter to Patterson, Burke asked plaintively "Can't you stop Gallico from clobbering Marion Davies in every picture?" That summer Miss Davies brought suit for libel against Burke and Payne; and luckily for The News, lost. Gallico lasted a year as movie reviewer, and was succeeded by Irene Thirer, a youngster who had come on the paper the year before, fresh out of high school. She started as a clerk in editorial promotion; and in a few months moved to the newsroom, writing picture captions.

Patterson told Payne to "lose" Gallico. Payne knew Gallico had been on the Columbia crew, and transferred him to sports, where Gallico soon found himself. Later Patterson, always on the lookout for possible managing editors, assigned Gallico to the Sunday "pup," and he filled in as managing editor on certain occasions.

* * *

A young reporter, William E. Hutches, formerly with the Telegram, had heard of a "King of the Beggars," a mendicant who took in $80 a day. Hutches donned old clothes, bought a crutch, was able to throw his right leg out of joint, and spent two weeks as a street beggar. He reported on the value of various locations; subway entrances were the best. He spent nights with bums and drifters in Bryant Park. And he had the hard luck to be recognized by his hometown schoolgirl sweetheart, who cut him dead. Conclusion: Never say "poor" beggar; and the pencils they offered weren't worth taking!

* * *

Relations between Burke and Patterson had been deteriorating. Burke was ruffled by the constant flow of criticism from Chicago. The break came over the Atlantic City beauty contest, of which The News was the New York newspaper sponsor. Burke had arranged for free costumes and lodging for the four New York girl entrants, and publicized the contributors liberally. Patterson resented the publicity. On Sept. 9, Burke resigned, and was succeeded by Payne.

Payne did not hold with Burke's "one big story" philosophy, began to offer a larger assortment of news, made a better newspaper. And he was ingenious in ferreting out stories.

* * *

"What's Wrong In This Picture?" was an etiquette feature started that year, 1922. A situation was shown in a scratchy one-column sketch, described in the caption. The proper thing was described at the bottom of the column. The feature was widely parodied, became a catchword and standard gag in vaudeville. In time the art improved, was later followed by photographs.

And Walter Berndt began on Nov. 23 his strip of Smitty, the ageless office boy who has virtually outlived the occupation.

* * *

The big story of 1922 was the Hall-Mills murder, which might have been copied from a third-rate British thriller, except there was no Scotland Yard inspector to tie up the loose ends and lead the lawbreakers to the lockup.

The Rev. Edward Wheeler Hall was the pastor of the Church of St. John the Evangelist, in New Brunswick, N.J.. and the husband of a very wealthy woman. Mrs. Eleanor Rheinhardt Mills sang in the church choir. Some time on the night of Thursday, Sept. 14, both were shot to death. Their bodies were found almost 48 hours later, under a crabapple tree in De Russey lane, just outside Somerset County in which New Brunswick is located. The lone constable hesitated to call for help from either the New Brunswick or state police; and a curious Saturday night crowd wandered all over the place and possibly destroyed evidence. When the police were called, there was little they could find.

Mysterious strangers popped up with clues, most of them worthless. Witnesses claimed to have seen Mrs. Hall and her brother Willie Stevens outside the church and in De Russey lane on the night of the murder. A grand jury refused to indict Mrs. Hall. Julia Harpman tramped around with the reporter wolf pack, followed every clue and rumor; reported events and conjectures daily under her "Investigator" byline, although her own name was twice signed to the stories for no discernible reason.

* * *

Bootlegging was well on its way to becoming a national industry. There were periodic rumors of "rum rows"—clusters of ships bringing in liquor—along the New Jersey and Long Island coasts. News reporters in chartered planes were never able to find "rum row."

In November, Red Dolan went to Nassau, wore old clothes and stopped shaving, and some days later was signed on as a seaman on a vessel that had been landing liquor in the States. Nothing much happened; the boat was waiting for the next shipment from abroad. After 10 days, its skipper became suspicious of Red, and he was forcibly separated from the crew. Red wrote an interesting account of his adventures among the outlaws. The Literary Digest reprinted much of Dolan's story.

* * *

Irene Del Mar, the original Sally Joy Brown, had left the paper. Her successor was the small blonde Mildred Lee Shaw, who had come to the big city from Victoria, Tex., to study voice. By this time her mail was running 300 letters a day. An offer of a puppy drew 10,000 letters. Sally Joy Brown made more and more personal contacts, increased the personal relationships with readers, and gained influence for the paper.

* * *

Joseph M. Cowan's byline first appeared on Albany stories of the Ward-Peters case. His background was politics and police. A huge man, he once leaned over from a subway car platform and picked up a track-walker who was about to be caught between two trains. And in 1924, he conducted the first News poll in advance of national and state elections.

* * *

Edgar R. Bean was already a veteran newsman before he came to The News. Born in Fairfield, Iowa, he had been graduated from Parsons

College in 1911, worked on papers in Des Moines, St. Paul and Oklahoma City. During his army service he was stationed at the Port of Embarkation in Hoboken, and learned his way around New York. After the Armistice he spent a year with the St. Louis Post Dispatch, then more than two years with the New York Sun. He started with The News as a copyreader, soon headed the copy desk, later was makeup editor and news editor.

That year Pacific & Atlantic Photos, Inc., a picture gathering and distributing service founded by Patterson and McCormick, hired a young man, Harry Nichols, as mat editor who was to have a long and outstanding career with The News. He had started on the American as a copy boy, subsequently was secretary to the managing editor, and then a reporter. During the war he served in France as an artilleryman with the 26th Division (New England National Guard). In 1924, Payne hired him for the lobster trick on the city desk, the lonesome 1 to 9 a.m. shift. A few years later he became assistant city editor, and in 1947 he was appointed city editor, a position he still holds.

Herbert M. Berg, another newspaper veteran, joined the copy desk in July. He was shortly made feature editor, responsible for fitting into the paper the considerable number of features, from the weather report to fiction. He was the best raconteur on the staff and died literally with his boots on at his desk.

On Friday, Sept. 1, The News started a service feature on rent regulations, the rights of tenants and landlords. The paper was fortunate enough to get Junius Pendleton Wilson, chief counsel of the Mayor's Committee On Rent Profiteering. His column was kept up for almost two years; and by 1924 new apartment construction had relieved the housing shortage and reduced exorbitant rents.

And in October, Burns Mantle became the paper's drama critic. Mantle had started as a linotyper on a Denver paper, and first reviewed stock and repertory company productions for free tickets. He spent seven years in Chicago on the Sunday Tribune, and in 1912 came to New York as drama critic for the Mail. From New York he contributed a weekly drama letter to the Chicago Tribune. He was a student of the theater, edited an annual yearbook of the season's best plays, was widely known and liked in the profession. Mantle was always a kindly critic where actors were concerned, generally limited his disapproval to the play and its producers; viewed a production from the standpoint of the ticket buyer, and advised whether it was worth seeing or not. He was an old, old friend of Patterson and one of the very few News employes who addressed him as "Joe."

On Nov. 11, 1922, Richard W. Clarke, then picture editor, resigned.

He went to the World as editor of its gravure section and assistant Sunday editor.

There had been a succession of makeup editors. In early 1924, James A. Speirs, a Scottish compositor who had come March, '21, as makeup man, was transferred to editorial as makeup editor. He held the job until his death in November, '42.

* * *

A former Carnegie Tech art student, C. Warren (Kliney) Klinefelter moved from the World in March, '22, and did general art assignments. He became night art department manager shortly; later served as art director of the Sunday gravure magazine until his retirement in 1967.

Later in 1922, The News acquired another artist for whom greatness waited. The Yale Alumni Weekly reported it thus: "Reginald Marsh, '20, has signed a three-year contract to draw exclusively for the New York Daily News on the editorial page and to cover vaudeville circuits for them. He is also studying painting at the Art Students League and is designing sets for John Murray Anderson's new musical production."

Marsh, who had been a cartoonist for the Yale Record, was born in Paris. His father and mother were both artists and he was said to have taken his first steps "balancing precariously between his father's and mother's easels." He became one of America's leading artists, known mainly for his paintings of New York scenes, and in 1956, when The News Coloroto carried two pages of his work, it noted that he was an O. Henry of the canvas . . . "He dipped his brush in the juice of life itself and across his easel paraded millionaire and bum, Park Avenue and the Bowery, a night at the opera and the garbage of mean streets." He died a few months later.

* * *

In December, the daily circulation was 514,336; the Sunday circulation 388,007.

* * *

1923

By 1923, there were indications that The News was getting better as a newspaper. The coverage was wider, more inclusive. The tabloid pattern was shaping up. There was less routine writing, more character, color and brevity. Editors and copyreaders were learning to say something in fewer words. The heads were shorter and sharper; there was more significant detail and point in the picture captions.

The pictures were better, with more life and contrast. The cameramen were becoming more news conscious, showing more imagination and ingenuity, more awareness of light and angles. There was less time taken in transmission. On one occasion Harry Warnecke left Park Place on a Chinatown assignment; got his picture, was back in the office and had a wet print to show in 38 minutes. With its own engraving plant, The News lost less time in converting picture to halftone, and the plates were sharper and more even in quality.

Another factor, of which News people themselves were not quite aware, was confidence, with some pride and cockiness. No newspaper had ever grown so fast before. Every circulation increase was further indication that the product was pleasing the public, regardless of what other newspapers and newspapermen thought of it. The daily passed 600,000 in March, and the Sunday was only 100,000 behind.

* * *

Contests were still used. An offer of 50 walking, talking dolls every week for the best color treatment of the outlines printed in the Sunday edition, had been started the previous October; and 20,000 entries were coming in each week. Tongue Twisters, with a $100 prize every day, started in January; these were sentences with every word starting with the same letter, "Peter Piper picked a peck of pickled peppers" sort of thing.

One day the judges innocently gave the daily prize to an entry that came inscribed on an egg. For days afterwards entries arrived on bread, bricks, toy animals, spelled out on blocks, carved in soap, written on baseballs. Editorial promotion began to look like a rummage sale, and in self defense limited entries to those on paper.

F. Scott Fitzgerald's "The Beautiful and Damned" was run serially in April; and was so popular that his first 1920 book, "This Side of Paradise," followed it.

On Sunday, May 20, the first (and only) News sponsored marathon, with 52 entries, was run at the new Yankee Stadium. It was regarded as an unofficial trial for the 1924 Olympics. A 400-yard circular track had been laid down; the marathon distance of 26 miles and 385 yards called for 115 laps, plus. A crowd of 30,000 turned out. The winner was A. M. (Whitey) Michaelson, of the Cygnet Athletic Club of East Port Chester, N.Y., whose time of 2 hours, 48 minutes, 23⅘ seconds, was more than 6 minutes faster than the previous record. (The circular track probably helped.) Suitable trophies were provided by The News.

In May, too, Bernadine Szold ran a series on her adventures in movie schools, which had sprung up in numbers, and promised to train aspiring starlets for motion picture careers. Most of them, she found, were intent on getting the largest possible advance fees out of the aspirants. A couple were suspected of recruiting girls for other pursuits than movie acting. One honest (or flattering) proprietor told Bernadine that she didn't need training to be an actress, and his school could do nothing for her.

On Saturday, March 17, another murder case broke, and made headlines for the next two months. Dot King, showgirl, was found murdered in her E. 57th St. apartment. Her murderer had used surplus army chloroform. She had been the mistress of a married male member of a wealthy and socially prominent Philadelphia family. And she in turn had supported a boy friend whose record was far from lily white. The police grabbed wildly for clues, pulled in scores of characters for questioning by the district attorney; promised imminent arrests, and got nowhere. The murder has never been solved.

* * *

This was the year, too, when The News first showed its muscle, made two important contributions to the public welfare.

The United States Steel Corporation had been under fire for some years for its 12-hour shift, which the company claimed was necessary to complete a "heat"—the fusion of ore, coke and limestone to make steel. Then early in 1923, the corporation's chairman, Judge Gary, announced that the 12-hour shift had been abolished. However, newsmen were not permitted to inspect the plants or talk to the workers.

Armstrong, writing under his "Industrialist" byline, expressed doubts about the sincerity of U.S. Steel's intentions and gave himself an assignment that few reporters would have had the courage or stamina to carry out. He went to Homestead, Pa., in old clothes, and under an assumed name got a job in the U.S. Steel mill there, as a laborer at 40.5 cents an hour. He held the job for three weeks, lived in a boarding house with other mill workers, saw the situation from the inside.

He learned that a considerable number of men still worked 12-hour nights on alternate weeks. The work week was seven days; refusal to work, or not showing up on Sunday, brought a 10-day suspension. Physical examination for mill workers was a farce. Men with families were the worst off, were unable to save enough to move elsewhere. Company store prices were higher than those in ordinary stores.

Since cheap European labor was no longer available as it had been before the war, company recruiters went South, signed up Negro workers, who started in hock to the company for their transportation North. Field hands wilted in the heat of the mills, were unable to do the heavy labor. After a 10-hour day, supervisors could arbitrarily order the men under them to work overtime, without extra pay. Any complaints brought suspension or firing.

Homestead was a company town. Many of the town officials were company employees. The police took their orders from the company, checked in workers at the plant gates. Brothels and blind pigs were plentiful, to the despair of local clergymen and teachers. Of all the men Armstrong talked to, only one liked his job; he was a stolid Slav bachelor, who dreamed of going home rich.

A series about these conditions ran for six days in The News under the "Industrialist" byline; but each was prefaced by a paragraph which identified Armstrong as the author. He made no attempt to be lurid or sensational; the facts were sensational enough.

The series got the attention of a number of congressmen and senators. Judge Gary's reputation as an enlightened industrialist, and the company's "Corporation With A Heart" image lost their lustre. Pennsylvania state officials started to clean up Homestead. Six weeks after The News series was published, the company announced eight-hour shifts for all its mill workers. Armstrong's report was apparently the final push needed to end the 12-hour shift.

The second instance of The News' use of muscle had more immediate consequence for the paper.

On May 16, 1922, the body of a young man who had been shot to death was found on Chappaqua Road near Kensico Lake, in Westchester County. Two days later he was identified as Clarence M. Peters, 19, of Haverhill, Mass., recently in the navy.

The next day, attorneys for Walter S. Ward, 31-year-old son of George S. Ward, millionaire head of a large baking company, informed Westchester District Attorney Weeks that Ward had killed Peters in self-defense, and would be surrendered. He was on May 22, and was released by Supreme Court Justice Seeger on $10,000 bail. The News quoted Ward's testimony that Peters was associated with blackmailers to whom he had paid $30,000; and who demanded $75,000 more. Peters had called on Ward one evening at his home in New Rochelle, and was driven by Ward to meet two other members of the group. As they approached an oncoming car, Peters drew a gun. Ward said he had shot him in self-defense. The approaching car vanished.

On May 25, bail was withdrawn and Ward was committed to jail in White Plains. Two days later he was again freed in bail of $50,000.

On June 15, Ward was indicted for first degree murder, put back in jail without bail. Two days later, he was again freed in $50,000 bail by the same Justice Seeger, who held there was no evidence of murder.

The basis for blackmail was presumed to be wild parties held by Ward in a New York City apartment the summer of 1921. The News obtained confirmation of the parties from the building superintendent and rental agent who had asked Ward to leave. Ward's brother had been in communication by cable with their father in England. The prosecution wanted copies of the cables; the cable company refused to provide them and a long legal scuffle followed.

Meanwhile, Ward found allies in the Jones family of Haverhill, Mass., with whom Peters had stayed. Joseph M. Jones, a British-born butcher, his wife and divorced daughter, testified that Peters was a degenerate, and generally unwholesome character.

The case quieted down. Then on Jan. 2, 1923, the indictment against Ward was dismissed by Justice Seeger. The News went into action. The first step was an editorial, titled "How About It, Governor?" And every day thereafter the editorial column carried two lines of bold type: "Can a rich man kill a poor man in New York, and not be tried for it?" Twenty-two editorials, some addressed to Gov. Alfred E. Smith, some to Seeger and the prosecution, appeared between January and September.

Meanwhile, the Jones family disappeared. The News found that Jones had sold his house in Haverhill, and that the family had lived at three New York hotels for various periods before sailing to England—all at the expense of Ward's attorneys. The prosecution claimed that the Joneses could not be found. The Pacific & Atlantic picture agency found them in London, sent back a picture of mother and daughter. The prosecution said it had no funds to bring them back, which drew more editorial blasts. The climax was reached when The News received a letter from Jones, who wrote that he had sold his house, given up his job, and gone to England on promises which Ward had not kept! Then Peters' mother sent a petition to Gov. Smith. The badgered Governor finally called for an extraordinary grand jury to investigate.

The jury was impanelled. Justice Robert F. Wagner (later a U.S. Senator and father of a future New York City Mayor) was designated to preside over the hearing; and Attorney General Carl Sherman was assigned to conduct it.

The jury heard 72 witnesses, reindicted Ward on the charge of first degree murder. On Sept. 12, Ward went on trial before Justice Wagner.

The trial was covered for The News by Cowan. Westchester officials, and Attorney General Sherman, were openly hostile to the paper. On the first day of the trial, Sherman announced that the minutes of the trial would be available to all reporters except those from The News—a dubious ruling which probably could have been reversed in court if time permitted.

However, on the opening day of the trial, a husky, dark-complexioned individual appeared who gave an Italian name and said he represented an Italian newspaper. To establish his authenticity, he telephoned his editor and conversed with him in Italian. The new reporter was very co-operative, and offered to type the excerpts from the court minutes so everybody in the group could have a carbon.

Much to the annoyance of Sherman, and the consternation of the other reporters, The News carried a full account of the trial every day.

The trial ended Sept. 28; and the not too enthusiastic efforts of the prosecution resulted in an acquittal for Ward.

The "Italian" reporter was George Ringler, court reporter for The News. Anticipating resistance on Sherman's part, Payne had devised the subterfuge. Luckily Ringler was not known to other reporters covering the trial.

The News ran a final editorial; its objectives had been to bring a rich man to trial, and it had succeeded. No comment was made on the result.

J. J. (Jack) Gordon, long time circulation representative of The News, holds that the Ward-Peters case was a turning point for the paper. "By 1923, a lot of people were reading the paper. After the Ward-Peters case, they believed in it."

In addition to the laurels he won in that case, Reporter Ringler was credited with bringing to an end a long standing tong war in Chinatown. The feuding tongs decided Ringler was somebody they could trust; and eventually he brought them to negotiation. When the war was ended, the tongs presented him with a gaudy gold medal which only a general in dress uniform could have worn properly!

* * *

Industrialist Armstrong turned out another effective series in August, on the school situation. One of Mayor Hylan's strong planks which led to his election in 1917 had called for the enlargement and improvement of the school system. The war and material shortages had prevented any progress in his first term. Appropriations had been voted for new schools, but sites had not been cleared; labor shortages and the big contractors' preference for speculative building had further slowed up the program. Funds supposed to go for new schools had been diverted to other purposes.

Armstrong's August series hammered at the point that when the schools reopened in September, 1923, at least 250,000 children would be on part-time instruction and demanded "A Seat For Every Child." The stories led to changes in school board officials, the engagement of a special architect, and some speeding up on the school building program. And "A Seat For Every Child" continued to be a regular subject of editorials in The News for some years afterward.

* * *

Martin Sommers with his blond mane, glasses, serious expression and lisp, came in February. He finished high school in St. Louis, just in time to enlist in the army, but his poor eyes put him in the medical corps; he spent the war ingloriously at Jefferson Barracks, a half hour from home. He finished his freshman year at the University of Missouri, worked on two small town Ohio papers, and at the advanced age of 19 was city editor of the Cincinnati Commercial. Like many another war veteran, disappointed because he never got to France, he drifted over to Paris, and worked for little more than a year on the Chicago Tribune's Paris edition.

Sommers could do almost everything in the newsroom. He was reporter, rewrite man, pinch hitter as editorial writer, and in February, '24, was made night city editor. In 1925, however, he elected to go back to Paris as sports editor on the Paris Times. He returned to The News the following year.

In April, Lou Walker resigned after a series of clashes with Payne. He announced that he was going to Havana to work on an invention. He was succeeded as studio head by Frank Ryberg.

On a "Hands Of Death" chart kept through '23, bad liquor claimed about three-quarters as many lives as automobiles. In an editorial on Tuesday, Oct. 2, comment was made on how Prohibition was increasing the number of invalids in the country; in 12 months, doctors had written 17,000,000 prescriptions for 500,000 patients!

* * *

Another colorful individual who came on the scene in '23 was Mark Hellinger. Hellinger was a native New Yorker. His father had a prosperous real estate business, and wanted Mark to succeed him. Hellinger attended the Townsend Harris High School in New York, lingered briefly in two private prep schools. He left home, found a room in Greenwich Village, and for a while had a job as a cashier in a restaurant, free meals and $1 a day. He started sending items to Zit's Weekly, a then competitor of Variety, and he was hired as a reporter at $15 a week. In the next year he met Payne who was impressed with Hellinger's familiarity with Broadway and amusement circles; Payne hired him at $60 a week.

Hellinger started on general assignments but after a few months was given his own Broadway column. He set out to be a celebrity himself. He was good looking, somewhat in the Rudolph Valentino manner; had pallid white skin and dark hair. His dressed well in what was then the latest Broadway manner, often wore a dark blue shirt and white satin tie. He was extremely likable, made friends with everybody, and had no illusions about himself. In a book of his Broadway columns, he wrote in the preface that a year earlier when he was a reporter, he had been given the bum's rush every time he appeared in a restaurant or supper club. After his column started, he got the big hello; it wasn't Hellinger they liked, but sweet publicity.

He became a notorious check grabber, and a soft touch. Jim Bishop, in a piece written after Hellinger's death, told how much Hellinger helped him when he was a copy boy on The News in 1929. Bishop got $12 a week, he said, and usually had some money but Hellinger, who made many times that much, never had any.

(Other famous News columnists, past and present, have included Sidney Skolsky, John Chapman, Ed Sullivan, Danton Walker, Robert Sylvester, Charles McHarry and Robert Wahls.)

* * *

In August, Eugene McNerny, Jr., ex-Philadelphia Record and an instructor in the Penn School of Industrial Arts, joined the art staff. He illustrated the Daily Story for several years.

* * *

On Sunday, Oct. 7, the 64-page paper was the largest yet. And a house page advertisement announced that The News now had the largest daily circulation in America—633,578 net paid for the six months period ending Sept. 30, 1923. In the same issue, notice was served that the Saturday night sale to newsboys was being discontinued, because many of them were selling the paper for 10 cents. This was a first step in a long campaign to maintain the 2-cent daily and 5-cent Sunday prices.

* * *

And the November issue of National Geographic carried a 24-page supplement in full color on the evolution of the horse. The paintings represented a full year of spare time work by Ed Miner, who headed The News art department.

* * *

1924

The big story of 1924, and for some years thereafter, was the Teapot Dome scandal. The presidents of five oil companies founded a composite company, and secretly secured a lease on the Elk Hills, Mont. (Teapot Dome) oil fields, which had been set aside as a navy reserve. The composite company took 33,000,000 barrels of oil from these fields and sold it to its own companies.

President Coolidge appointed a senate committee which held hearings for the next three years. Albert Bacon Fall, Harding's Secretary of the Interior, defended the lease on the ground that military secrecy was involved. It was established that he had received around $300,000; and Fall was sentenced to a year in jail. The others escaped jail sentences, but 10 years later the estate of one settled a $6,000,000 claim by the government for $3,000,000.

The News carried the succession of stories, but the coverage came from the Chicago Tribune's Washington Bureau, and there was no participation by The News staff, and no opportunity for pictures.

Meanwhile, the Globe had ceased publication in '22; Munsey merged the Mail with the Telegram in '24 and that same year sold the Herald to Ogden Reid, who merged it with the Tribune.

* * *

Exciting competition developed for The News during the year as two new tabloids came into being.

George Utassy had been trying to interest Hearst in a tabloid, and finally succeeded. In June Brisbane asked Walter Howey to form a staff, and the first issue of the Mirror appeared June 24, the first day of the long drawn out Democratic National Convention. Brisbane's formula was 10% news, 90% entertainment. The Mirror attained a 300,000 circulation within a year, but that apparently did not hamper the growth of The News. The early Mirror was smudgy and poorly printed. The paper eventually established a following among racing fans; and Dan Parker's sports column earned an audience. Hearst apparently lost interest after the first few years, and Brisbane became the Mirror's principal supporter.

And on Sept. 15 appeared the Evening Graphic published by Bernarr Macfadden. No newspaper was launched with more pious pronouncements; it was to be a family newspaper, full of sweetness and light, educational for children and a mighty moral force. And no newspaper ever more thoroughly belied its publisher's promises.

Emile Gauvreau, the Graphic's first editior, was a thorough cynic, and from the start sought circulation with the rankest sensationalism. He was the inventor of the "cosmograph," which consisted of photographs posed by professional models, with the heads of principals of the story pasted on. For example, Edward Browning, a wealthy middleaged real estate man with an appetite for publicity, married an overblown young girl; and the adventures of Daddy and Peaches Browning were favorite subjects of Graphic cosmographs for months. In 1925, when Leonard Kip Rhinelander, scion of a wealthy New York family, sought a divorce from his wife of six years by claiming that she was part Negro, the Graphic ran a picture of a partly disrobed woman appearing before the jury to disprove the allegation of color. It showed the head of Mrs. Rhinelander on the disrobed woman. John S. Sumner, secretary of the New York Society for the Suppression of Vice, brought suit against the Graphic. Justice Ellsworth Healy of the Court of Special Sessions ruled that the paper "may be disgusting but doesn't violate the law."

Within two years the Graphic had 340,000 circulation, however, and eventually reached 400,000. Its most lasting contributions to journalism were Walter Winchell, who later went to Hearst; and a young sports writer, Ed Sullivan, who was to become the Broadway columnist of The News.

The principal effect of the two new papers was to deepen a prejudice against tabloids. The News was often pilloried for failings not its own.

In April, Max Lief was made radio editor; and radio thereafter was considered important enough to be given a daily column.

In June, James Crusinberry elected to return to the Chicago Tribune and was succeeded by Paul Gallico as sports editor. And on Dec. 16, Gallico was given his own column on the sports page. Illustrated with spot drawings by Grant Powers, it became one of the most popular features. Gallico's attitude from the first was that of the amateur. He professed to know none of the fine points of any sport, which sometimes enraged the knowledgeable fans but pleased many readers. He promptly invented the 98% Wrong Club, making outrageous forecasts of the scores of college football games; and being surpassed in prophesy by everybody on the sports staff.

As he gained confidence, he often let his column wander far afield from sports and indulged his sense of humor. One column was a letter to the New Haven Railroad, about his dog which liked to take naps on the tracks at Cos Cob, Conn. He suggested the train be stopped until the dog awakened; New Haven passengers were so accustomed to delays that one more wouldn't matter. Or they might switch the train to the express track and bypass the dog without waking it.

The News swimming meets one year were to be held in the lake in Central Park. Gallico wanted somebody to make the lake six feet deeper for the diving events, and a number of contractors told him it couldn't be done. Surely in the great city of New York, he maintained, there must be somebody who could move six feet of mud under eight feet of water. If he wasn't so busy he'd do it himself; his plea was answered; a contractor sucked up the mud through hoses for $600.

The column started Gallico on his career as a magazine writer. He met Frank Crowninshield, editor of Vanity Fair, with a low editorial budget and a questing eye for new talent. Robert Benchley and Dorothy Parker had come up through Vanity Fair. Crowninshield encouraged Gallico, who sometimes had more than one article in an issue of Vanity Fair. Liberty used a number of his articles on sports. Finally he made the Saturday Evening Post, a major objective of every ambitious writer in the '20s—first with articles and then fiction.

Gallico brought in Harry Schumacher, a veteran sports writer who had worked on other New York papers; Schumacher held down the desk for sports, gave out assignments, put the pages to bed.

On July 12, Tess Hinz, in charge of classified advertising, turned reporter. On her way home to Port Washington, her Long Island train was halted in the Sunnyside yards, behind another train. Miss Hinz left the train, walked forward, and found a wreck had occurred. She got the basic facts and phoned Frank Hause on the city desk. Hause wrote her a letter of commendation. Anybody on The News would have done it, said Miss Hinz, and became the heroine of the advertising department.

* * *

Among the 1924 staff additions was Lowell Limpus, who was to spend the rest of his life with the paper. Born in Indiana, he grew up in Oklahoma, went through high school there, spent some time in Southwestern College, and held a variety of jobs—cowhand, machinist, etc. He enlisted in the army when World War I broke, and afterwards was managing editor of the Army & Navy Journal. He won an appointment to West Point in the class of 1924, but dropped out after two years. Many of his classmates were generals in World War II, a fact which helped him as a correspondent. He was a reserve officer at the time he joined The News. In April, 1927, he was to be a member of a group planning to fly the Atlantic; the project dissolved after Lindbergh's successful crossing.

Limpus was tall, impressive looking and sounding, and an indefatigable reporter. From time to time he affected a goatee, which occasioned considerable ribbing from his coworkers. He was subsequently responsible for many major stories. In the 1930s he became a confidant of Mayor La Guardia, helped run his campaign, and refused to accept public office after La Guardia was elected. He was also the author of half a dozen books.

Rufus F. Cranston started as a photographer on the Brooklyn section, was later on general assignments. Cranston was a student of photography, set up a workroom in his own home and for some years experimented with color.

In January John Chapman left for Paris, to head the P&A Photos office there. Chapman didn't like the climate, came home two years later, and continued his dual role as cameraman and reporter.

Edward Doherty, a Chicago Tribune veteran who had been covering Hollywood, joined The News. With him came his wife, Mildred Spain, who was for some time movie reviewer. In 1925, Doherty was assigned to Liberty and did a number of outstanding stories. For one on the Mafia, he visited Sicily where Cosa Nostra originated. After Liberty stopped publication, he came back to The News, did feature stories for some years, and resigned to write books. His principal claim to fame, however, was the inception of the Medill School of Journalism at Northwestern University. Concerned about elderly reporters who had neither status nor substance, Doherty wrote a memo to Patterson, suggested that journalism deserved a professional status and special training. Patterson told him to go ahead. He made the alliance with Northwestern University at Evanston, Ill., helped assemble the first faculty of the Medill School.

In October, The News made its first poll of Presidential and Gubernatorial candidates. The idea was Joseph Cowan's, the political reporter. W. R. Fritzinger who made some of the later polls always insisted that the 1924 poll was not scientific. That may have been true, but Cowan crammed more excitement into his daily stories than any of his more scientific successors. He hired a gang of college students at $3 a day and covered every city precinct. In the opening days, the findings indicated that Robert M. LaFollette, Progressive Party candidate, would sweep New York City in the Presidential race. By the time the city was polled, Al Smith seemed to have the edge in the Gubernatorial contest.

Cowan then paid some of his students $4 a day and expenses and sent them upstate. In traditionally Republican counties, President Coolidge was so strong that Cowan figured he might carry Col. Theodore Roosevelt Jr. with him as Governor. But before the show was over, he predicted that Smith would win the Governorship by a large majority; Coolidge would be reelected President, and the early favorite, LaFollette, would lag behind the Democratic candidate John W. Davis. And that's the way it turned out.

* * *

In November, Harry Warnecke played detective. He had been assigned with Herbert R. Mayer, a reporter a short time with the paper, to cover the story of the missing 12-year-old Ernest Schwer, who was presumed lost in Cowkill Swamp, Richmond Hill, L.I. His playmates said he had disappeared in the swamp, but the boys contradicted each other as to the direction young Schwer had gone. Warnecke was suspicious and began to ask questions in the neighborhood. He heard that the Schwer boy had bought ammunition for a .22 rifle. He called at the house of one of the boys, met his older brother, and asked bluntly, "Where's the gun?" The brother, assuming that the truth had come out, told him it was in the possession of one of the boys. Young Schwer had been accidentally shot, and his body hidden in the swamp. The other boys confessed and led the police to the body. Four boys were held by the police and later freed because of their youth. Mayer wrote the story of Warnecke's solution.

* * *

On Monday, Oct. 10, The News began the publication of an afternoon edition, which appeared on the stands at 4 p.m., three hours earlier than the previous first edition, the Pink. The idea was that the extra exposure ought to increase sales.

The afternoon had a different type dress on pages 1, 2 and 3, but otherwise was little different from later editions. Gene McHugh was its editor, and with a couple of helpers started coming to work at 7 a.m., no easy assignment for McHugh, who was a night owl.

The circulation did continue to rise, but no faster than it had previously. The afternoon edition appeared until Saturday June 25, 1925, when it was dropped. The additional expense of mechanical crews brought in earlier wasn't justified. McHugh and his crew went back to normal morning paper hours.

* * *

On Monday Sept. 7, the paper started carrying two columns of closing prices on the New York Stock Exchange—the first step towards the present business page.

On Dec. 7, in the Sunday edition, Bernadine Szold began what was probably the first Broadway column, "About Town." Unlike her successors, she did not strive for a lot of items. Nor were her subjects limited to people on the stage and screen. They included artists, writers, and other people in the public eye. Started in three columns, the feature was immediately popular and soon filled a full page. When Miss Szold left, it was taken over by Mark Hellinger.

* * *

The average circulations for the six months period ending September 1924 were: daily 786,398; Sunday 807,279.

* * *

1925

On Jan. 23, there was an eclipse of the sun. Payne prepared to cover it as if it were the only eclipse of all time. Ryberg in the studio experimented for two weeks before, making test pictures in the late afternoon light, determining exposures and the type of film which gave the best results. Payne had a dozen cameramen stationed between Park Place and New Haven, with Jackson on a boat in the harbor and Tresilian aloft in a plane. Of course, the pictures that appeared in the Saturday, Jan. 24 afternoon edition were those taken in the immediate locality and earliest available. The quantity of photographs would have done credit to a Smithsonian expedition. Unfortunately, New Yorkers were not as interested as Payne, and paper sales for the day were normal.

The lucky name (horoscopes) contest was revived Jan. 19, and drew more than 900,000 entries within a week. A presidents contest started Sunday, Jan. 25. Four pictures were shown on a page, with segments of the faces mismatched; the contest was to match the proper sections. Prizes of $15,000 were offered, with first prize $1,000. That Sunday The News passed the million mark for the first time.

A handwriting contest was held in February. In March, $100 a day was offered for the best Didjever. Samples: Did you ever see a chocolate float? Didjever see a transfer point?

Lucky Bucks was a September attraction. Two photographs of $1 bills were printed daily. The holder of any of the bills had three days to show his winning bill, and collect $100.

On Saturday night, Feb. 28, New York had a very mild earthquake that barely rattled window panes. Payne with his overactive imagination dramatized the tremor with a Sunday front page showing the Woolworth Building shedding its skin; the caption explained that it *might* happen with a severe earthquake. But the picture caused considerable alarm out of town, and other newspapers castigated The News for its alarming picture.

* * *

On Feb. 5, a story broke that became a cliff-hanger for the entire country. Floyd Collins, a young man of Cave City, Ky., was caught in a cave and couldn't get out. He was imprisoned 35 hours before he attracted attention. A rescue was attempted but the rescuers were blocked by falling rock. After 135 hours underground, Collins was assumed to be dead. Somebody got a telephone to him and it was learned that he was alive. A massive new attempt was started, and people waited for hourly bulletins. Each day the rescuers hoped to reach Collins tomorrow, and were always delayed. On Feb. 16, rain slides again slowed the work. Collins was reached the next day, and found dead. A hardy News cameraman was lowered down the rescue shaft, and took a dim photograph through a lateral split of rock of the recumbent body. As credits for photographs were not given at that time it is not known now who took the picture.

* * *

In May, Phil Payne resigned. William Randolph Hearst had sought him out the year before. Payne went to The Mirror. Frank Hause, who had been made city editor when Payne stepped up, became managing editor.

Payne insisted on accompanying Lloyd Bertaud and James Hill on the Hearst-sponsored flight of the Fokker plane "Old Glory" from Old Orchard, Me., on Sept. 6, 1928. The destination was to be Rome. No trace of the plane or the three men was ever found.

* * *

On Sunday, July 6, Mark Hellinger started his "About Broadway" column. The next day the Monday paper carried Harry Warnecke's famous picture: a policeman holding up traffic while a mother cat crossed the street holding her kitten by her mouth. Warnecke heard about the cat moving her family one by one, but the move had been completed before he arrived. He picked one of the kittens, brought it back across the street.

Like an actor doing a retake, mama cat obliged; and the policeman held up traffic again. This picture has been reproduced all over the world, and appears again and again.

* * *

On July 10, 1925, in 100 degree heat, the Scopes trial started in Dayton, Tenn., a mining town of 1,800 population. George W. Rappelyea, mining engineer employed by a local company, and F. E. Robinson, the local druggist, planned the trial "to put Dayton on the map." The Butler law, prohibiting the teaching of evolution, had been passed that spring. Rappelyea and Robinson persuaded John T. Scopes, a diffident, 24-year-old biology teacher in the local high school, to be arrested and tried for violation of the law.

Rappelyea wired the American Civil Liberties Union, which assigned Arthur Garfield Hays and Dudley Field Malone for the defense. William Jennings Bryan, three-time candidate for the Presidency, Secretary of State in the Wilson administration, silver-tongued orator, and at the time in the real estate business in Miami, volunteered for the prosecution. Clarence Darrow, an eminent Chicago attorney, then volunteered; he said he had waited for years to cut Bryan down to size.

The trial lasted six days. Darrow called Bryan as a witness, and questioned him about his beliefs concerning Jonah and the whale and other Biblical matters until Bryan lost his temper. WGN, the Chicago Tribune's radio station, broadcast the trial from the courtroom. Bryan was set to make one of his famous addresses; Darrow prevented him, by asking for a directed verdict of guilty. Scopes was fined $100. Dayton was jammed the week of the trial, and the whole country was stirred by it. Bryan stayed on in the town; and the following Sunday night died in bed of a heart attack. The State Supreme Court two years later sustained the law, but held the trial was unfair; reduced the fine, *nolle prossed* the case to prevent an appeal to the U.S. Supreme Court. Dayton grew to 6,000 population. Scopes quit teaching, became an oil geologist.

Some of The News stories were bylined Hank Potts, probably a pseudonym, as it does not appear again.

* * *

September brought another cliff-hanger in The News. Two navy seaplanes left San Diego Aug. 30, attempted destination Hawaii. One dropped into the sea 100 miles off the California coast. At 4:12 p.m., Sept. 1, a radio message came from the other plane the PN 9-1 reporting that it was out of gas 150 miles from the Hawaiian island of Maui. Three days later, no trace of the plane or its crew had been found. But Friday, Sept. 10, the crew was picked up by a submarine, Comdr. John Rodgers, an old Annapolis man, had rigged a sail for the seaplane and was beating his way to Maui.

* * *

In 1922, Payne first took cognizance of radio, had a set installed in a telephone booth; he thought it could be used for listening to speeches, and save assignments. Two years later, more stations were on the air, and Red Dolan became the paper's first radio columnist. The effervescent Dolan didn't care to be chained to earphones; and an operation for appendicitis relieved him of the job. Terry Dixon was his successor, and resigned after a year.

Ben Gross, a slight, short, young man, had been hired as a reporter in March, to cover courts, labor and strikes. He had grown up in Birmingham, Ala., attended Tulane and the University of Alabama, and had worked on the Birmingham News. He went overseas with the 348th Infantry, 87th Division, and edited army publications while in France.

Out of the service, Gross came to New York; and as so many tyros did, started with City News, a cooperative news gathering service supported by all New York papers. City News had a dingy office in Hudson Terminal, with a long bench in the reception room, often occupied by drunks or derelicts. A switchboard operator looked out of a small window, and called or pointed to the next applicant to come in and see the editor.

There were scores of dinners to be covered every night. The City News man got a free dinner and $3. The standard dinner was a broiled half chicken, limp French Fried potatoes, an anemic salad with watery French dressing, and always spumoni or biscuit tortoni for dessert. Because Gross was dependable, he got assignments every night. After a month, the editor, asked how he was doing. "All right, I guess. But I'm awfully tired of chicken dinners." The editor produced a red ticket, promised him a different dinner that night. It was a Tammany Club affair, with corned beef, cabbage and beer. Never before or since, said Gross, had he eaten a more delicious dinner.

Later, he worked on the Bronx Home News, the American and Telegraph before coming to The News. When Dixon decamped, Hause assigned Gross temporarily as radio columnist. Gross didn't know how to turn on the primitive battery set. Neither did Hause or anybody in the city room. Gross went downstairs, found Eddie Boisseau, the plant electrician, who was able to make the essential connection. The temporary job has lasted 44 years!

In 1926, he got in trouble. It was the heydey of Rudy Vallee, the Vagabond Lover, and radio idol of American women. One outraged male wrote that he had a hound dog which could sing better than Vallee. As a gag, Gross offered a ticket to last year's World Series for the best singing dog.

Next morning when he came in, the city room, halls and corridors were jammed with dogs and their owners. Outside on Park Place, two policemen were trying to keep yapping, fighting dogs and owners in line. Hause was furious. Gross spent most of the day turning away dogs and owners. But "The Great Rudy Vallee Hound Dog Controversy" did prove that his column had readers.

He was an early crusader for better programs and less noisy commercials. "I Looked And I Listened," his 1956 book, won the Newspaper Guild Front Page Citation, and he has been awarded many honors.

* * *

Early in 1926, Helena Marsh, a veteran newspaperwoman who was filling in temporarily as society editor, covered a social highlight of the winter season—the marriage of Consuelo Vanderbilt to Earle E. T. Smith on Jan. 7. The wedding was held in the Vanderbilt mansion, then at 58th St. and Fifth Ave. The guest list was limited and the press definitely was not invited or admitted. One reporter attempted to gain entrance as a waiter; another posed as an altar boy; both were detected and heaved out.

An elderly woman with white hair, black dress, black hat with ostrich plumes, and "all the heirloom jewelry I could scrape up" came to the Vanderbilt doors. She explained to the social secretary that she was Mrs. Ward McCourt (Helena's married name), an old friend of the groom's family, and just returned from Europe two days earlier. The invitations had been sent out three weeks before. The secretary hadn't time to check the list, and let her in.

She bowed to three elderly gentlemen, who bowed back. Minutes later, one of the trio passed her, and she bowed again. He stopped. She explained that she was the Countess Pizzini, and had met him 20 years ago on the Riviera. He brought her some champagne.

She congratulated the groom, told the bride she was beautiful; and was beginning to enjoy herself when she remembered that she had a deadline to meet, and quietly made her departure. The News story of the wedding was an exclusive, of course. They don't make reporters like Mrs. McCourt these days.

* * *

1926

1926 was a year of growth and progress. The staff was bigger and better. News cameramen were becoming more sophisticated, more inventive, more determined to get pictures that were not conventional and ordinary. Daily circulation, which had reached a million copies the previous December, declined a little in January, but passed the million mark again in February, and kept rising; while Sunday was above 1,200,000.

In February, a nasty protracted strike occurred in the Passaic (N.J.) silk mills, triggered by a wage cut. The Passaic cops were strictly establishment, regarded pickets, reporters and cameramen as their pigeons. There were four clashes with strikers in February. On March 3, 3,000 strikers were attacked and beaten by mounted and motorcycle police and some 100 patrolmen. The 30 cameramen on hand were attacked by the police who did not want visual evidence of their conduct. They wrecked a $2,500 movie camera belonging to Pathe News, and clubbed the operator. Harry Warnecke and Nicholas Petersen of The News staff were photographing the incident when a policeman's club knocked the camera from Warnecke's hands. Broken cameras were rushed off scene by the police.

Meanwhile, on the roof of a nearby loft building, Larry Froeber of The News had photographed the Warnecke attack. When he was noticed, he and two friends left the roof, entered an office with a passkey, and hid the camera in a stove. The police broke in, and found three guys looking out the dirty windows. The cops locked them in. The passkey was used again to get Froeber out, and his pictures appeared in the editions of March 4. Gov. A. Harry Moore was asked to mediate by the chamber of commerce.

On March 18, photographers were again attacked. The News man on duty that day was the burly Martin McEvilly, who had presence of mind enough to copy down four police badge numbers. He immediately went to a local judge, and the four policemen were arraigned. The cases against the police dragged on for months after the strike was over.

* * *

The following month brought the big story of the year—and one The News was responsible for.

Gertrude Ederle, a New York City girl, was a promising young swimmer who had broken a number of records. She made the 1924 Olympic team but did poorly because of illness. In the summer of 1925 she tried to swim the English Channel but seasickness stopped her after six hours.

Gallico knew Miss Ederle, and sympathized with her ambition to swim the channel. He told Patterson about it, who decided that The News would finance a new trial for her.

The party sailed on the Berengaria in mid-May; Miss Ederle, Julia Harpman, as her chaperone, and Art Sorenson of P&A Photos to handle pictures. Westbrook Pegler, Julia's husband, was recuperating from an illness and went along. Quarters were obtained at Cape Gris Nez on the French coast and a trainer, Bill Burgess, was hired. Julia cabled occasional stories.

At 2:05 a.m. New York time, Aug. 2, word came to The News wire room that Miss Ederle had started. Her position was checked on a previously prepared chart of the channel, and news of her progress was relayed across the country by the wire room. Sorenson was in the launch that accompanied the swimmer. All went well until the seventh hour when the tides turned southwesterly; she spent seven more hours covering the last third of the course, and landed at Kingsdown at 4:05 p.m. English time; first woman to swim the channel, in 14 hours 31 minutes, better time than the five men who had already made the swim. Pictures by Bartlane came through the night; and on the morning of Aug. 3 Americans were reading of her feat.

Pictures were shipped on seven steamers. The Empress of Scotland, due to land first at Quebec, was delayed by storms. A seaplane intercepted the ship off Anticosti Island in the St. Lawrence, flew through 250 miles of fog to Rimouski, where Wurzel and McFarlane of P&A Photos were waiting, with Harry Schumacher of the sports department. The time was 5:30 p.m. Friday the 13th. McFarlane took off by seaplane, followed the St. Lawrence five feet above the water to Quebec. Wurzel, in a land plane, was forced by fog to land in a town called St. Eloi, and had to stay there until he could take off at 9:00 a.m. Saturday. McFarlane, still in the seaplane, left at dawn, reached Plattsburgh at 9:30 a.m.; picked up the fourth plane and landed in Jersey City at 2:30 p.m. Wurzel came in four hours later. There were plenty of pictures for the Sunday News.

Ederle, Harpman and Sorenson arrived on the Berengaria Aug. 27, 1926. Fire department boats sent streams of water aloft. The craft in the harbor hooted and whistled. The party was transferred to the City's Macom. Grover Whalen, New York City's official greeter, was on hand. So was Paul Gallico, driving the red roadster Patterson had promised to Miss Ederle if she was successful. And Gertrude Ederle, now known to the whole world as Trudy, made history with the first ticker tape parade ever held in New York City, while hundreds of thousands cheered her.

* * *

The 1926 staff additions included a notable number who stayed for a long period; and some are still here.

Anthony Marino started as a copy boy, and after two years was assigned as night reporter at Police Headquarters. He is still on the staff as assistant city editor; and married to Kay Gardella, who started as a copy girl, joined the radio television staff in 1955, became radio-TV editor in 1968.

Joseph J. Bera started as a reporter on the Brooklyn section, was later on rewrite, and is now an editor on the suburban sections.

Munson Pardee and Horace P. Thurlow, two veteran newspapermen of long New York experience, joined the copy desk and were employed there for the rest of their lives.

Jerry Rose got an after-school job as a copy boy while he was attending City College; became a full time reporter in 1929, and is still on the paper—the editor of Brooklyn, Queens and Long Island sections.

When the gravure section was started in October, its editor was Earl Overholt, who had joined the Sunday staff two years earlier. John Neumaier, who had started in the art department of the Herald, was later a layout man on the gravure section of the Times, was employed in the same capacity on The News gravure section until his retirement in 1959. He died the following year.

Another newcomer was Clarence Woodbury who described himself as an incorrigible in-and-outer. A veteran of World War I and the Sun and Telegram, he first went to work on The News copy desk in 1926, left in 1927, returned in 1928, "retired" to Europe in 1930 to write fiction. He returned to the fold in 1931, however, and stayed put until 1937 when he resigned once more and spent most of the next 22 years as an article writer for Crowell-Collier magazines. After those magazines folded, he again returned to The News and has been a member of the suburban staff since 1959.

A very young Jimmy Cannon started as a copy boy; worked on lobster shift, was promoted to sports reporter three years later. His lively writing and air of authority shortly brought him a better offer from The Telegram. Later he did a sports column for the Journal American.

* * *

In December, 1926, the average circulations were: Daily 1,129,653; Sunday 1,427,928.

* * *

1927

On Jan. 1, 1927, The News secured an Associated Press franchise by purchase from the New York Commercial Bulletin, a business daily. The price was $500,000. AP service started Jan. 23.

The paper already had United Press, City News (a cooperative), Standard News (suburban coverage) and the Chicago Tribune News Service; the most complete assortment of press services in New York, with the possible exception of the Times.

On Jan. 1, The News also acquired a new city editor—Harvey Deuell, a tall, serious-looking young man. Deuell had his first newspaper experience in Denver before going to the Chicago Tribune. He was assistant city editor when Liberty Weekly was started, and was made the magazine's managing editor.

Deuell was responsible for marked changes in the paper. He was concerned with the quality of the writing, and gradually built up a rewrite staff; insisted on better written picture captions, and demanded better performance from the copy desk. He also introduced the double byline of reporter and rewrite man. And on a complicated story there were sometimes as many as six bylines, as reporters fed items by phone to the man who actually wrote the story.

Deuell made lively leads on stories his own particular chore, and kept writing new leads for later editions.

When Hause retired in July, 1935, because of ill health, Deuell succeeded him as managing editor. Deuell died of a heart attack while driving his car on Oct. 29, 1939, and was succeeded by Clarke.

* * *

The automobile show opened Jan. 8 at Grand Central Palace. Visitors had a choice of 44 makes of cars, and the Sunday News motor section of Jan. 9 ran 24 pages. But the startling feature of the show was the absence of Ford. After more than 15 years, the famous Model T (any color as long as it's black) had outlived its popularity. The new Model A came on the market the following December, and was a national event, breathlessly reported by the press. Police had to regulate the crowds that came to see it. The Model A never matched the appeal of the Model T; but 40 years later some of them are still in use.

* * *

On Friday, April 8, The News had its first 80-page edition; of which 16 pages were Brooklyn section.

* * *

The big story of '27 was the Lindbergh flight.

In this day of 600-mile-an-hour jets, and six-hour transatlantic crossings, it is difficult to imagine the excitement and wonder caused by one man flying the Atlantic.

Aviation was still primitive. Lighted beacons and radio communication were still to come. Most airports were open fields. Ford trimotors, the first real transport planes, cruised at 90 miles an hour. In 1934, in his book "Record Flights," Clarence Chamberlin thought the best hope of the future was the Bellanca—with a speed of 172 miles an hour! The fastest transcontinental trips were made by train and plane; night train to Cleveland or Canton, Ohio; plane to the eastern edge of the Rockies; another night on a train; and the last leg by plane. In this way the U.S. could be crossed in 48 hours, as against five days by train. Full transcontinental airline service did not reach New York until October, 1931. The metropolitan airport was Newark, until La Guardia opened in 1939.

In 1927, flying the Atlantic was as much in the news as the moon flights have been recently. The craze was sparked by the offer of a $25,000 prize by Raymond C. Orteig, a New York hotel man, for the first flight, United States to France or vice versa.

The French made the first try. Capt. Charles Nungesser, a leading ace of World War I, and Maj. Francois Coli took off from Le Bourget (Paris) on May 8 in a big biplane. They estimated the flight would take 35 hours, had fuel for 40 hours. A rumor that they had landed in New York set off a wild celebration in France; when the rumor was not confirmed, the French blamed Americans.

Then a report that the French fliers had landed on the Labrador Coast sent a contingent of reporters and cameramen there. The News representative was Red Dolan, who was away two weeks, sent some no-news stories. No trace of the plane or fliers was ever found.

Dolan came back to the office with a monumental expense account. One item caught the eye of the editorial auditor, Mike Feerick—"Two interpreters, $14 a day."

"Why two interpreters, Mr. Dolan?"

Dolan put on an injured look. "One French, one Indian," he said. Feerick smiled sadly, shook his head, and approved the swindle sheet.

* * *

Among others aspiring to fly the Atlantic was Lt. Cmdr. Richard E. Byrd, who had flown over the North Pole the year before. His plane, the America, was built by Tony Fokker. On a test flight on April 20 a poor landing caused the plane to turn over, crumpled the nose and fuselage, left Byrd with a broken wrist, Floyd Bennett with a cracked thigh, and Lt. George O. Noville with an injured pelvis. Byrd's flight was delayed while the plane was rebuilt.

Joseph Levine, a New York businessman, bought a Bellanca and en-

HIGH JINKS AT THE MET

Opening night of the Metropolitan Opera House season was for years a major social event in New York. It still is. Some of the more prominent members of the city's upper crust were inspired by the event to indulge in unusual antics. Here are examples recorded by News photographers.

Mrs. Frank C. Henderson was the central figure in this picture, titled "Cheesecake and Champagne," which won a prize in the Editor & Publisher photo contest in 1948. It had been published in The News Nov. 11, 1947. Photographer, Walter Kelleher.

Mrs. Henry L. Doherty, widow of the public utilities magnate, expressed her wordless opinion of the cameraman in this Met opening scene published Nov. 23, 1943. Photographer, Walter Engels.

Richard A. Knight, society lawyer and clubman, was ejected from the Met opening in 1939. On the street, he performed this headstand to demonstrate his skill as a gymnast. Publication date was Nov. 28. Photographer, Walter Engels.

gaged Floyd Bertaud, a well-known pilot, to fly with him. Later he broke with Bertaud, and engaged Chamberlin.

Then an unknown entered the lists. Capt. Charles A. Lindbergh left San Diego one evening, arrived in St. Louis the next morning; and flew to New York the next day—total air time 21 hours, 20 minutes, a new transcontinental record.

Lindbergh had grown up in Little Falls, Minn., the son of an ex-Congressman. His widowed mother taught chemistry in a Detroit high school. Lindbergh had spent a year in chemical engineering at the University of Wisconsin, learned to fly at a private school in Nebraska. He joined the army, spent two years at Kelly Field training, and a year as a pilot. The army had so little money and so few planes that its pilots were relegated quickly to the reserve.

Lindbergh got a job flying the mail between Chicago and St. Louis for the Robertson Air Service, and obtained a commission as captain in the Missouri National Guard. He had parachuted to the ground twice, lost two planes in storms. Other pilots thought him yellow—which may have been the motive for his transatlantic flight.

He saved $2,000 of his pay, got the backing of some St. Louis business men. The Ryan Aeronautical Company of San Diego built his plane, "The Spirit of St. Louis," and Lindbergh spent two months in the factory while his plane was built. It had the newest Wright radial 220 h.p. engine, and a new earth induction compass. It had to be flown blind, with a periscope for forward vision.

Lindbergh ducked publicity and entertaining. John Chapman got pictures of his arrival, and Lloyd Acuff wrote the stories for The News. Lindbergh spent one day in the Wright factory in New Jersey, learning more about his engine.

On May 19, the forecast for weather over the Atlantic was unfavorable. Levine and Chamberlin locked the hangar doors and went home. Byrd was giving a dinner for the press that night.

The evening forecasts were better, and about 11 p.m. that night, Lindbergh decided to take off. After a couple hours sleep, he went to Curtiss Field and supervised the fueling and last-minute preparations of his plane. With two sandwiches, two army canteens of water and a rubber life raft, he took off at 7:52 a.m. The overloaded plane did not leave the rain-soaked runway until he was almost at the end of it, and barely cleared a ditch, tractor and some trees. At Montauk, 100 miles away he still had only 50 feet altitude. A News plane flew with him, and Herb McCory photographed Lindbergh's plane from above as he passed Montauk out to sea.

It took him 11 hours to reach St. Johns, Newfoundland,. his last point of land on the Great Circle route. The evening was uneventful but towards morning he ran into turbulence and a cold rain, had difficulty in keeping his plane flying. By mid-afternoon he was seen over Ireland, and the news spread around the world. He crossed England and the Channel, followed the Seine to Paris, and landed at Le Bourget in the darkening summer evening at 10:24 o'clock—33 hours and 29 minutes, 3,600 miles after takeoff.

Crowds swarmed over the field. A French pilot wrapped Lindbergh in his flying coat, got him off the field to the American Club where Ambassador Myron Herrick and French officials were waiting. He spent the night in the embassy.

The French idolized Lindbergh. He modestly gave his plane and equipment the credit for the flight. Early in his stay he visited Nungesser's mother and sympathized with her. A wealthy Frenchwoman donated 150,000 francs for a commemorative cup; Lindbergh insisted that the money go to the families of dead French pilots. President Domergue decorated him before a cheering crowd in the Chamber of Deputies. Two days later Lindbergh flew to Brussels, acquired another decoration from King Albert. The next day he flew to London. A mob of 100,000 people overran Croydon. Lindbergh made two attempts to land but couldn't until the police cleared the field.

President Coolidge received congratulatory messages from heads of states all over the world. The cruiser Memphis was sent to bring Lindbergh and the "Spirit of St. Louis" back.

The Memphis edged up the Potomac early one morning, landed Lindbergh at the Washington Navy Yard where his mother was waiting. They were driven up Pennsylvania Ave. lined by cheering crowds. At the Washington Monument, the President conferred the Distinguished Service Cross, and a commission as colonel in the army reserve. Lindbergh replied with a seven sentence speech, conveying the friendship of the French. That night he slept in the White House. Two days later he landed in an amphibian in New York Harbor, drove through a delirious ticker tape parade; was given the New York City Medal of Honor, and the State Medal of Honor by Gov. Al Smith, while a crowd of 250,000 people thronged Central Park. There were dinners, receptions, crowds.

Tall, blond, boyish-looking, Lindbergh had an infectious smile before he made the flight. Under the pressures of fame, the smiling boy was lost forever to a harassed-looking man.

In December he made a flight to Mexico City, at the invitation of Mexico's president, lost his way in the fog over the mountains, failed to arrive mid-morning as expected; and both countries waited gloomily. He did arrive four hours later, and all was well. In Mexico City he met Anne Morrow, daughter of the U.S. Ambassador Dwight Morrow; and later married her.

He was deluged with offers from the movies, vaudeville, companies that wanted him to make product endorsements, and turned them all down. He did accept the Orteig prize, made some money with his account of his trip which was syndicated by the New York Times; and a year later brought out his book "We." He also served as a technical consultant to an airline. Lindbergh did his best to back out of the limelight, and live a normal life. No American who remembers May, 1927, could ever forget him.

* * *

Byrd made his try on June 29 with Lts. George Noville and Bernt Balchen, and Bert Acosta, a former automobile racing driver. His earth induction compass failed to work. After flying around in the fog over France for five hours, they saw a lighthouse, ditched in the sea, and paddled two hundred yards to the fishing village of Ver-Sur-Mer. Fishermen helped pull in the plane. Two days later, in Paris, Acosta learned he had a broken collar bone.

Chamberlin and Levine took off on June 4, landed two days later at Eilsieben, Germany. In the next two years, a number of pilots made the flight, and some were lost at sea. But Lindbergh's achievement made ocean flying old hat.

* * *

Joe Costa had gone from copy boy to cameraman with the World, came with The News and stayed 20 years. As president of the National Press Photographers Association, he led a crusade for many years to permit photographs to be taken in courtrooms. His career on The News is covered in other chapters.

Lester Rose followed the footsteps of his brother, Jerry. He worked as a night copy boy in sports until he finished college; then became a sports writer. He is still on the sports staff.

John A. Crosson had attended Fordham, and his first job on The News was night switchboard operator while he attended law school. Later, on leave, he served as legal advisor to the narcotics division of the Southern Federal Division of New York. On his return, his assignments were largely on the courts and politics. He started a Sunday column "City Hall" and in the early years of WPIX, television station of The News, he conducted a panel program also called City Hall. He was president of the Inner Circle, the city political writers association, at the time of his death in 1953.

* * *

Robert Conway was born in Rome where his father, an American artist and sculptor, was living at the time; and first came to this country when he was two. His experience prior to The News had been on the New York American. After early assignments in New York he probably covered more stories abroad than anybody on The News staff. He covered the Greek civil war, the first Palestine war, the terror campaigns in Poland, where he was arrested as a spy. In 1941, he unearthed a fantastic plot on the part of Communistic and Falangist groups to start revolutions and diversions in Canada, Mexico and Latin American states. The story was denied by Communist states, but later confirmed by the State Department. He was also president of the Newspaper Guild in New York for one term. He retired in 1964.

* * *

Martin Sommers returned from Paris, served as assistant city editor and in other capacities. In 1931 he asked for a year's leave to go to China; and walked into the civil war going on there. Four weeks after his departure, his first story from China was bylined on page three. In 1935 he left The News to go to the Saturday Evening Post as foreign editor; later served on Eisenhower's press staff during World War II. On his death in 1963, the Post carried a full-page obituary.

* * *

1928

1928 opened with a cold wave, icy streets, transportation tie-ups. Bad liquor on New Year's eve took a toll of 36 lives. In conflict with the rebel Sandino in Nicaragua, United States Marines were being killed and wounded. The country was shocked by the unexplained sinking of the submarine S-4 off Provincetown with a crew of 40. RCA announced the invention of Radio Television, with a small picture panel in a radio cabinet. Lindbergh demonstrated his abilities as a navigator by a 1,600 mile flight to the Virgin Isles. In March stocks skyrocketed when call money dropped to 4¼%; the New York Stock Exchange had a mammoth 3,800,000 share day. And The News was engaged in the most important campaign in its history up to then.

Coal had been a sick industry since World War I. Bituminous coal miners had been on strike in the area around Pittsburgh since 1925. In the fall of 1927, mine operators in other parts of Pennsylvania announced a wage cut of one-third, and 85,000 miners in the area went on strike. Ugly rumors of fantastic conditions came out of the area. In November, The News sent reporter Lowell Limpus, and cameraman Herbert McCory, into the mining towns to check.

They started in Pittsburgh, interviewed Philip Murray, vice president of the United Mine Workers of America. Murray coolly told them of the oppression, destitution, abrogation of citizen's rights, and police brutality in the mine towns. Limpus didn't believe him, thought the conditions he described couldn't exist at the time.

With McCory he visited more than 20 towns, all largely inaccessible because of poor roads. Miners had been evicted from company houses, and the union was building as rapidly as possible barracks for the strikers. Household belongings were seized for unpaid rents. In some instances where the rents had not been paid, the roofs had been lifted from the houses, the interiors opened to rain and cold. The strike benefit was $3.50 a week. Children were fed on crackers soaked in tea. The universal villains were the Coal and Iron Police, paid by the companies but deputized by the state.

In Coverdale, Limpus and McCory were arrested by a police sergeant who took them to his headquarters and after some difficulty reached a company vice president on the phone. When the New York Daily News was mentioned, the vice president had something to say to the sergeant that caused him to completely change his attitude. He became friendly and offered to show Limpus and McCory around. Strikebreakers, they learned, were largely young Negroes imported from the South, and their lot was little better than that of the strikers. The state police took the side of the strikers.

In the companies' offices in Pittsburgh, the officials for the most part were not aware of the actions of their subordinates on the scene. And Limpus discovered the companies hated each other more than the strikers; blamed the Mellon companies for ordering the wage cut, and forcing the other companies to follow.

After a month of investigation, Limpus started his series, illustrated with McCory's pictures. Other newspapers were offered the series but wouldn't publish it. Many of the situations were beyond belief. In the town of Rossiter, the singing of hymns in a church on Sunday was prohibited by an injunction issued by a local judge, on the ground that the singing broke the strikebreakers' rest.

Sen. Royal S. Copeland of New York read the series in the Senate on Jan. 4, but accomplished nothing. Most of the senators considered the strike a local matter. Finally Sen. Hiram Johnson of California was persuaded to introduce a resolution calling for an investigation. But there was little hope of getting action during that session.

Back in the strike towns rioting started. Limpus and McCory found radical agitators from New York urging anarchy and revolution. The Pittsburgh newspapers and the Hearst chain began to cover the strike. Finally Sen. Johnson was aroused enough to phone Limpus and ask him to show him around the mining towns. Congressman Fiorello H. La Guardia of New York had preceded him. Sens. Robert F. Wagner of New York and Burton K. Wheeler of Montana backed the demand for an investigation. Johnson forced a hearing before the Interstate Commerce Commission. After a lot of jockeying, hard work by Sen. Johnson eventually brought the resolution to a vote. It passed unanimously.

A senate subcommittee then made its own inspection trip to the mining towns and at last, on March 7, 1928, the hearings began. Limpus spent the whole of March 19 on the stand, and was followed by McCory the next day. New legislation for federal control of the mines got under way. The Democratic party put a coal plank in its platform. The coal companies announced a return to the old wage scale, and began to close unproductive mines. The News received the credit for bringing the situation to light. And Limpus became a well known figure in Washington.

This News campaign, of course, did not settle the unemployment problem in the coal fields. The Depression and John L. Lewis eventually cut down the work force, and brought wages to a level with other occupations.

* * *

Late in 1928, there was a murder that had reverberations in many quarters.

Arnold Rothstein was a big time gambler with an astonishing lot of interests. On the night of Nov. 4, about 10:30, he dropped in at Lindy's the Broadway restaurant. The cashier gave him a message. Rothstein told a friend, Jimmy Meehan, "McManus wants to see me," and left a revolver with Meehan. McManus was another big time gambler, then occupying Room 394 in a hotel at Seventh Ave. and 56th St., registered as George Richards.

At 11:07 Rothstein emerged from the service entrance of the hotel, clutching his side. A taxi driver parked in front of the hotel saw a revolver fall in the gutter; one cartridge had been fired and five were unexploded.

Rothstein collapsed on the street. Two policemen tried to make him comfortable while waiting for an ambulance to take him to Polyclinic Hospital. Rothstein wouldn't talk. His attorney visited him the following day and wrote a new will for him. Rothstein died on Nov. 6.

The police did not get to the hotel suite until 2 a.m. A card game had been in progress. On the table were glasses of half-emptied drinks. No fingerprints were taken. There was no blood in the room. The police seemed to be unusually inept.

A warrant was issued for McManus. He surrendered on Nov. 27. Two other men who had been in the room were arrested. A fourth, Hyman Bilber, never was found.

The first stories were a wild spate of rumors. McManus was reported to have owed Rothstein $51,000. Later, it was reported that Rothstein had owed those in the room more than $400,000. Police Commissioner Joseph A. Warren was not talkative. District Attorney Joab Banton said the case would not be difficult to prepare. Meanwhile, Bridget Ferry, a chambermaid in the hotel, asked to be arrested for her own protection; and was held 34 days as a material witness.

The case collapsed in court. The chambermaid, who was expected to identify McManus, said he was not the man in the room.

Red Dolan wrote the first stories for The News. Frustrated, he started his stories with boxes headed "Helpful Hints for Wistful Warren"—such as "Where was Detective Joe Daly when Rothstein was shot, and who told him the shooting took place in Room 394 before this fact was known to the hotel management?" Dolan kept up the needling for days. Then Mayor Jimmy Walker took action.

Warren, a boyhood friend of his, was relieved as police commissioner. And to everybody's surprise, Grover Whalen was appointed. Whalen at the time was general manager of Wanamaker's Department Store and had been the city's official greeter, best known for his suave handling of distinguished visitors. He proved to be a hardboiled commissioner. One deputy inspector was fired, one demoted; the confidential squad was broken up. And there were many lesser demotions.

The Rothstein will, which left one-third of his estate to a woman he had been living with, was contested by his wife. The nurse on duty at Polyclinic testified that Rothstein had been unconscious when the will was signed, and his attorney had guided his hand to make an X. The will was thrown out.

Rothstein's holdings kept coming to light. He was linked with a fake subdivision near Middle Village, Long Island; later with a dope ring. Three years afterwards Rothstein was even blamed for the failure of the

Bank of the United States because of an unsecured loan of $42 million made by the bank.

John O'Donnell, Forrest Davis, William Rice, Lloyd Acuff, Robert Conway, Gilman Parker, Arthur O'Sullivan, Tom Cassidy, Sanford Jarrell were News reporters whose bylines appeared over stories of Rothstein's activities and affairs.

In its many ramifications, the Rothstein case was one of the longest running of newspaper soap operas. Despite Commissioner Whalen's zeal and efforts, the case was never solved. A dozen years later, Jack Lait, then editor of the Mirror, claimed to have found the solution; that Rothstein was shot by a drunken ex-pugilist who had been trying to get a loan from one of the characters in Room 394, who claimed that he couldn't make it until Rothstein paid him. The stalling had been going on for days. Lait said the frustrated fighter bumped into Rothstein in the service entrance, recognized him, and shot him in a rage.

* * *

Another newcomer was Mrs. Elsinor S. Belk who became the Sally Joy Brown of the "Friend In Need" column. The Depression years with the big increase in the indigent and needy magnified the activity of this department greatly, as well as its personnel. Later she became the assistant to Fritzinger until her retirement on Jan. 1, 1960.

* * *

1929

In retrospect 1929 was a wild, free-wheeling, uninhibited year. Speakeasies opened faster than Prohibition agents could close them. The supply of liquor for medicinal purposes, available on doctors' prescription, dropped so low that the Government authorized the distilling of 2,000,000 gallons. Capt. Molyneux, Paris designer, who had started the short skirt vogue, protested that women's skirts were now so short there was no place for them to go but down. Low waists, bobbed hair, and long necklaces went with that popular knock-kneed dance, the Charleston. The youth were flappers and cake eaters, portrayed by John Held and Carl Ed in his "Harold Teen" comic strip. Movie stars announced their betrothals as soon as they filed divorce actions. Breach of promise suits proliferated with prosperity. The whole country was buoyed by the phony euphoria of an ever-rising stock market. The first three quarters of the year was summertime, and the livin' was easy!

Palestine and the Arabs were at each other's throats much in the 1969 mode. Murders were many and violent. American tourists thronged Europe, to the envy and resentment of the natives. The international scene was troubled and turbulent. Fascism ruled Italy and Mussolini won approval because he made the trains run on time. Germany, throttled by the Versailles Treaty and continuing inflation, was ripe for revolution and the Brownshirts.

Planes made news, chiefly by crashing. While 1927 was the year for trans-Atlantic flights, and 1928 the season of Pacific crossings, 1929 was given to endurance flights, sustained by refueling and revictualing planes. The Germans astonished the world with a giant Doerner DO-X seaplane that carried 69 passengers in a flight of more than an hour above Lake Constance in Switzerland; but the 12-engined monster was probably too complex to maintain in commercial service.

* * *

During the first weeks of 1929, the Rothstein murder continued to be the nation's most publicized crime but on Feb. 14 it was crowded off the front pages by a far more shocking case—the St. Valentine's Day Massacre in Chicago. As News headlines told the world, seven men were lined up in a building in North Clark St. and machine-gunned to death by beer war rivals who posed as police officers. Later it was charged that police actually were in league with the killers but this was never proved.

* * *

Despite violent recessions in the stock market on Dec. 9, 1928, and on May 8 and 9, 1929, the speculative fever raged unchecked. Space in the Equitable Building on lower Broadway rented for $12 a square foot; and two years later brokers' subleases could be had for $2 a square foot. Call money rose to 20%. Brokers did business with one-day million dollar loans from one or several banks; paying off the loan with the first proceeds of the day, and having it renewed for the next day.

In early October, a sharp decline in steel production and automobiles went almost unnoticed. But on Tuesday, Oct. 29, the market dived suddenly. The selling increased during the rest of the week and more than 250,000 telegrams were sent by brokers to customers demanding more margin. Curiously enough, on Saturday the news was optimistic. A consortium of brokers would rescue the market, stop the slide. The country was economically sound, said President Hoover; bankers and economists echoed him. Brokers condemned the selling as short-sighted and pathetic; and many of them sold short their closed out accounts three and four times. The News "Trader" (Raleigh Curtis) urged readers not to sell because the values of stocks "are based on the greatest prosperity the world has ever known."

During the next week, diners in downtown New York restaurants would see men suddenly drop their heads into their plates, dead asleep, overworked brokerage employees.

The effect of the market crash was cataclysmic. Affluent families suddenly found their equities worthless, often their jobs or businesses gone. Many were cash poor, unable to meet their rents, pay their servants, or mortgage interest. There was a wave of suicides. And many who were unwilling to destroy themselves, found they were destroyed anyway, in loss of purpose, character, ambition and hope.

The market reached a bottom on Nov. 13, and an uptrend started. Investors who had pulled out of the market earlier, rushed in and bought; and were wiped out by further declines the following year. Beside the destitute who tried to sell apples, or stood in line in front of soup kitchens, there were the poor who were not obvious, saddled with families and responsibilities. And the elderly were hurt worst of all.

The year came to a gloomy and uncertain close. But so ingrained and habitual was the optimism of the '20s that a miracle was still expected.

* * *

The year brought more reinforcements to The News staff:

Theodore Prager came in January as night police reporter, was the friend and confidant of police and lawyers, worked on many important stories until his death in May 1961.

As Albany correspondent, Louis Ruppel caught the eye of Gov. Roosevelt, went on to a government post in the New Deal; was later managing editor of the Chicago Times, and an executive with Crowell-Collier until his early and untimely death.

Dominick Unsino was a night copy boy until he finished St. Francis College; then worked as police reporter, and makeup man on the Brooklyn section. He distinguished himself in 1936 by finding a photograph of an Italian pilot who had lived in the Bronx, served with the Loyalists in Spain; and at the time was in a Spanish jail. He was subsequently suburban editor until 1968, when he elected to transfer to The News Westchester office.

Stuart Rogers, who had worked on Boston and Connecticut papers, started as a reporter in December, moved later to rewrite, and became an assistant city editor. He left in early 1944 because of ill health, returned five years later and served as night city editor until his retirement in 1963. His son, Stuart Rogers, Jr., worked in the circulation department, joined the Royal Canadian Air Force in 1941, was cited twice for bravery as a Spitfire pilot, was killed over England on Feb. 7, 1943—the first News man to be killed in combat in World War II.

MOVING MOUNTAINS

With circulation spurting from the limerick contest, the circulation department was a happier place in 1920. Sullivan's work day ran from 2:30 p.m. to 2:30 a.m., and in the early years seven days a week.

Sullivan noticed certain discrepancies in dealer orders. One store or stand would order three or four times as many copies as another similar store or stand. Sullivan wondered why, and began to pry into the problem. He found that the American News Company made dealers pay in advance on Thursday for the following week's papers. If the proprietor was not around when the driver called for his money, he was dropped from the dealer list. ANC was gradually attenuating its outlets. But the cut off dealer merely had a nearby store or stand increase its order to supply him. Some deliveries were for three or four outlets.

One night early in 1920, Sullivan left his office, and took the subway out to the end of the Coney Island line and started to *walk* back along the subway route, listing stands and stores that sold newspapers. In his first night, Sullivan found outlets that were not on his ANC dealer lists. He made these checks two or three nights a week; and after he knew the city better, used his car. In two years he compiled a list of 7,000 dealers, about 2,000 more than ANC was serving. Sullivan's research was to wreck the combination delivery system, and start The News on its way to the largest circulation in the United States.

Independent distribution was the obvious next step. Tribune directors, apprehensive about the amount of money that had gone into equipping the Park Place plant, balked at spending more for trucks and horses and wagons.

Annenberg found a solution. He persuaded Sam Booth, later president of Interborough News Company, and Charles Levy, a Chicago distributor of magazines and newspapers, to form the News Distributing Company. Henry Friend, Chicago businessman and Levy's father-in-law, supplied the capital as a loan.

The News Distributing Company was installed in the first floor on the Murray St. side of the building. It started operation on Dec. 31, 1921, with 83 employees, 42 one-horse wagons and 18 trucks, under the management of Abe Newman, an experienced circulation man. Joseph Schiffman, then a routeman and later city circulator, recalled: "We used the trucks for delivery to Canada points (distribution centers) at night; and to push snowbound wagons out of the drifts in the daytime."

Daily circulation in 1921 reached around 400,000, with Sunday about 100,000 less. By the end of the year, even the Tribune directors were sold on direct delivery. The whole staff of the distributing company was absorbed by the circulation department, with the exceptions of Messrs. Booth, Levy and Newman.

* * *

In September, Sullivan brought William B. Denhart to New York. Denhart had grown up in Champaign, Ill., carried a newspaper route, and worked for a news company (distributor) while in high school. He relates that one Sunday morning in 1913, the Chicago Tribune order for two jointly owned hotels had been increased by 160 copies. Denhart thought somebody in the Tribune's circulation department made a mistake. He called the hotel owner, who said casually "That's all right. Sully says they'll sell." That was his first mention of Sullivan. The date was when the "Adventures of Kathlyn" serial started.

Denhart enrolled in the pharmacy course at the University of Illinois. His mother died during his freshman year; and he decided that he preferred newspapers to pharmaceuticals. So he began to work full time for the news company.

He came to the notice of Moe Annenberg, Max's brother and then Hearst's chief of circulation, who also owned a number of news agencies. One in Springfield, Ill., had never been profitable. Annenberg persuaded Denhart to go to Springfield and take charge, promising him an agency of his own in the future. Denhart's recipe for running the agency was simple: "Find out who's doing the stealing, and fire them!" The Springfield agency showed a profit in his first month.

Denhart waited for his own agency, thought Annenberg was tardy in keeping his promise. He wrote Sullivan in New York, and Sullivan told him to come on. His first chore for The News was to prepare figures for the audit bureau's annual audit. Later he traveled in New York state and New England. He was loaned to Liberty magazine for a few months in 1925; then returned to The News as assistant circulation manager. He retired in 1952, died in May, 1969.

After the move to Park Place, Sam Steiger was made delivery foreman. With little formal education, he could appraise news stories and pictures for their local interest and sales potentials.

First edition in hand, he read headlines and opening sentences, scanned pictures. Fire in Flatbush, new school for Astoria, celebrity feud, parents' protest dangerous crossing in Brownsville, murder on Morningside Heights, local boy or girl making good or bad at something. He sensed the interest and appeal of a story—ethnic, economic, religious, political, personal.

Fifteen minutes later he would be out on the delivery floor, ordering certain routemen to increase their draw, telling them why.

At one time certain fights in Madison Square Garden brought increases as high as 30,000 copies on the Lower East Side. Other fights drew nothing. Sullivan was puzzled, couldn't see the pattern. Steiger wasn't puzzled. The Lower East Side wasn't interested in the Dempseys and Tunneys, but in a kid named Ruby, a prelim fighter, and a local idol.

Steiger was always ingenious. When heavy snow in the early winter of 1925 was making deliveries difficult, he found a whole fleet of wagon sleds somewhere in New Jersey, and rented them temporarily.

In later years, Patterson and other News executives would bring dinner guests down to the delivery floor to watch Steiger in action; and introduce him. Steiger was modest, almost shy. He knew he was good, but wasn't vain. He had tremendous loyalty to Sullivan; and in turn had Sullivan's respect and admiration.

* * *

An important part of the operation was a crew of inspectors; their duties were to check newsstands and dealers, settle complaints, and book increases. By 1923, Sullivan had four traveling representatives: Julius Grieco, Jack Gordon, Sam Kaye, and Eddie Lewis (who later became the paper's first city circulator). This group worked within 200 miles of New York. They called on news agencies, told them about new features and promotions; decided how much of an increase the agency was good for. And then they called on the agency's dealers and booked individual increases to make up the agency's increase. This procedure was unique at the time, helped account for the paper's continued growth. By March '25, each had a company car, a new Ford, to increase his mobility and efficiency.

* * *

By 1925, the early edition with pink outside pages, issued about 7 o'clock the night before, had become a big part of the total circulation. The "Pink" led to a curious custom. In residential neighborhoods when the weather was good, men would go out to take a walk, or air the dog, or pick up a beer; and then assemble near a newsstand to await the arrival of the Pink. By the time the paper was delivered, groups as large as 50 would be waiting for it. These impatient readers became neighborhood clubs, in session from the '20s up to the late '40s, when television came in.

The "earlies" also brought problems, as the boys and men sold them for 5 cents weekday nights, and 10 cents for the Sunday edition. On Saturday nights, the mob waiting for the Sunday News jammed Murray St., stopping traffic. In May '25, the Saturday night sale was discontinued. The circulation department waged a long war with the itinerant salesmen to get the paper sold at its proper price. The front page of the daily for years carried a large display line "2¢—Pay No More!"

The demand for the Sunday paper became so great that a predate edition was printed on Tuesday morning for points beyond the normal delivery distance on Saturday night. This edition had little hard news, became the lowbrow New Yorker that out-of-town people bought to read about movies, the theaters, entertainment, columns and gossip. After the gravure section was added in 1926, the out-of-town sale of the Sunday issue climbed steadily.

The News was not very old before it was discovered that it had an all day sales appeal. Just as men bought the Pink early in the evening, women bought later editions when they did their shopping the next day. In the baby carriages parked outside the chain stores, a News was often tucked in with the baby.

In the late '20s, Brooklyn spawned subdivisions and miles of apartment buildings. Sullivan, or his inspectors, would find a candy or notions store just opened in a new neighborhood, and pay a small subsidy—$10 a month, $5 a week—for the proprietor to stock newspapers. The merchants soon realized that The News was a traffic builder, brought in people who bought something else.

In December, '25, the daily circulation was 1,000,740. January brought a drop, but in February, '26, the million mark was passed again. In August the daily passed 1,100,000.

* * *

A million copies of a 32-page News weighs 100 tons. As the circulation grew, and the size of the issues increased, the sheer tonnage moved each day by the circulation department reached impressive totals.

THE RELUCTANT ADVERTISER

Classified continued to grow in the early months of 1920, running over six pages some days. On March 13, the four-column page became five columns. The reason for the change was classified; the canny Field added one column more per page, without reduction in rate. No advertiser protested.

Some retailers showed interest. Gimbel's Downstairs store ran spreads on Fridays. A. S. Beck, Ovington's, McCreery's sampled the paper.

The circulation growth attracted some national advertisers—Borden's, Colgate's Toothpaste, Pond's Cream, Woodbury's Facial Soap, Chesterfield Cigarettes, Knickerbocker Beer, and far too many proprietary medicines.

One regular advertiser was Lifebuoy Soap, with weekly pages. Two years later The News was to learn that Lever Brothers advertising manager, the prestigious Grafton Perkins, had decided the paper was a comer; he was the first national advertiser to place heavy schedules.

The volume of Female Help Wanted was partially responsible for the "Stenographers' Gazette" label hung on the paper during its first few months, a label that took years to outlive.

By mid-1920, the business climate changed for the worse. Deflation had set in. When John Wanamaker slashed prices by one-third in October, the dumping of merchandise was widespread. National Outlet Stores, Western Trading Company and others ran clearance sales. A shoemaker offered 160,000 pairs of women's shoes, made to sell for from $9.50 to $12.50, for $5 a pair. Other groups of manufacturers ran sales in Grand Central Palace, other halls and auditoriums, to the benefit of The News.

News linage in 1920 was 1,723,000 lines.

Advertising rates were raised four times in 15 months: January, 1920, maximum 25 cents per line, minimum 16 cents; April, maximum 40 cents, minimum 32 cents; July, maximum 50 cents, minimum 42 cents; September, maximum 60 cents, minimum 52 cents.

The increases were justified by circulation growth, but they were a serious deterrent to News salesmen. Often when a prospect was interested, and trying to find a place in his budget for The News, another rate increase would kill the sale. Advertisers were confused and annoyed by the frequent increases. This penny-wise policy prevailed for years, and delayed the appearance in the paper of many advertisers whose business The News would have been glad to carry.

* * *

In September, 1920, the paper surprisingly made a small profit and, as previously noted, boasted about it in an October editorial. By this time, the debt to the Chicago Tribune was a few thousand dollars over a million—certainly little enough to establish a newspaper in New York. As Field (presumably) pointed out in an editorial, many of the early advertisers were getting four times as much circulation as they were guaranteed under prevailing rates.

There were much needed staff additions that year:

The wisecracking Elmer Flagler, who had been on the Tribune and served in the signal corps during the war, was sent to New York as classified began to grow on The News. He was irrepressible and indomitable. Flagler was later manager of the Chicago office; and retired in 1952, as classified display manager.

Lyle W. Finch was a stripling from Whitewater, Wis., who had studied law in Chicago. He had attended the navy officers school at Peham, was commissioned ensign, and assigned to navy communications in New York. After the war he could find nothing to do back home in Wisconsin, and returned to New York. In his first job as a bookkeeper, he found out he wasn't one. His next occupation was selling a tax service. He called on Holliss one day, and Holliss sold him on coming with The News. He started on retail accounts; later was switched to national, and spent the rest of his life on the paper.

Another acquisition from the Tribune was Lee J. Mohr, a slight blond who was a very aggressive salesman. He had gone through the classified routine, had some retail display experience, and was a welcome addition.

Two other Tribune men whose wives were unhappy in New York returned to Chicago within the year.

In 1920 life in the Tribune's eastern office at 215 Fifth Ave. which also served as The News advertising office showed little change. The going was hard. Cochrane, Sherwood, Finch, Tuttle, Mohr and Flagler came in at 9 a.m. with shining faces; came back after 5 dejected by a day of refusals, rebuffs, even insults. And by the nightly miracle that makes a salesman, came back the next day for more.

The News was too radical, too apart from the conventional newspaper, for many conservative stores and advertising agencies. Even the rapid increase of circulation seemed suspicious.

But business was better than the year before. A number of factors were working in The News' favor.

In the 1920s, every woman in New York wanted a fur coat, which for most was muskrat, under trade names such as Hudson Seal, priced from $75 to $250, and payable for as little as $1.50 a week. Small fur stores ran little ads, with illustrations filched from out of town papers, crude copy, newspaper set, and sold more and more coats.

Brooklyn and the Bronx were beginning to fill up with small houses and apartment building; the new tenants would need furniture, and buy most of it on credit.

Every family seemed to want a phonograph or player piano. Sears Silvertone, Victor and Columbia were big names. Gimbels, Bloomingdale's, Aeolian, Story & Clark were among the early advertisers of musical instruments in The News. By 1923 radio sets were in demand; and people sat up half the night "logging" distant stations; and told the next day how they got Miami at 2 a.m. In April, '23, RCA advertised its revolutionary Radiola—no storage batteries needed, just dry cells, and only $142.50. A little later Victor announced a victrola and radio in one small two-part cabinet!

* * *

As 1921 opened, Holliss' big headache was still the department stores. Then Hearn's came in on March 15; Macy's, on April 4; Bloomingdale's on Sunday, May 15; and Wanamaker's on Sept. 14. In May Franklin Simon ran a sale ad, and stopped. Even after his appointment as assistant general manager in April, Holliss spent his mornings in the uptown office.

The reason for the stores' appearance was simply price. By March, '21, the paper had 400,000 circulation; Macy's (and probably other department stores) had a minimum rate of 15 cents a line. The low cost proved to be a disadvantage; The News got the weak departments with low budgets. The store advertising departments placed little value on News space, used it for odds and ends. Macy's one day carried in its two columns three items: Czechoslovakian fruit bowls, long woolen underwear, and lessons in painting parchment lampshades—not prime attractions.

Holliss had been talking to a string of high-powered salesmen with department store experience, who wanted astronomical salaries. By the end of the year he found the answer in John H. Glass, who had arrived in April.

Glass had grown up in Louisville, attended high school a couple of years; then won a University of Chicago high school baseball scholarship, which lasted only one year. He started soliciting classified on the Tribune, came to New York and worked at various advertising jobs. In 1921 he was with the Garment News, a daily trade paper that was not doing well. He had an employment contract with six months still to go; and he gambled on a smaller salary with The News. The gamble paid off for both Glass and the paper. In 1956, after Cochrane's retirement, he was appointed advertising manager; at the time of his death in December, 1965, he was an adviser to the management.

Glass understood the psychology of the retailer, talked his language. His effectiveness was evident shortly with the furriers. He won their confidence, persuaded them to buy larger stocks, use larger space and sell more fur coats. By the end of the year, Holliss put Glass on department stores.

Lynden S. Dickie was hired in May. He had grown up in Montclair, N.J., worked in a print shop, been a reporter, and had just finished 20 years as manager of a travel and resort bureau for Hearst papers. His department had been abolished in an economy wave; and his News salary was a fraction of what he had earned formerly. But Dickie was always cheerful, quickly made friends of his accounts. He was a valuable member of the staff until his retirement in 1947.

* * *

Holliss, meanwhile, was not getting along with Myhrum. In September, '21, Ray T. Wilken resigned as advertising manager of System, and Holliss wanted him. Field and Patterson had no objection, but Gene Parsons in Chicago had, felt Myhrum had not been given a fair chance. On the second Sunday in September, Holliss caught the Century for Chicago for a showdown. He won his case. Wilken came in at the end of the month. Myhrum went back to Chicago, worked in the Tribune's national department until his death.

Wilken was tall, good-looking, with a pleasant personality, and a good all around athlete. He and Holliss had been classmates at Hyde Park High School in Chicago. Wilken attended the University of Chicago for two years, had sold classified briefly at the Chicago Record-Herald, then gone with A. W. Shaw Co. as a salesman on System Magazine. Later, he was made advertising manager and moved to New York. He and Holliss were neighbors in Bronxville.

Wilken settled down to learn his new trade. He was a better organizer than Myhrum, loved system, order, figures. After the first few months he began to make calls with the salesmen; and gradually made it his business to become acquainted with the department stores. He was always a good listener, and never pretended to have the right answer; but after study and consideration would advance a solution to the problem.

He was well liked by the men. If the salesman was in difficulty with an account, he tried to help; and in the event of personal troubles, he went out of his way often to tide a man over, with sympathy, and if needed, money. By and large, the department was well run and as happy as any struggling sales organization can be.

* * *

In March, '22, Macy's dropped out. The store had a new advertising manager, just promoted from stable boss. He didn't profess to know much about advertising, but he did know that a Macy buyer was supposed to get bottom price! The News minimum rate had doubled in a year. He offered to stay with the paper at the old rate, which, of course, was not acceptable.

Gimbels, which had used the Sunday paper for its downstairs store in the first year, had also stopped. Glass worked through '22 to bring them back. Newspaper salesmen are not welcomed by buyers and merchandise heads, but Glass managed to meet most of Gimbels buyers. One, Mark Max, headed the piano and musical instrument department, was a power in the store. He was impressed with Glass's story, and began to work for him. In late 1922, when the question of using The News again came up, the paper got a big majority vote of the buyers and merchandising managers.

Glass persuaded Bloomingdale's, which had been using the paper virtually for pianos alone, to try other merchandise.

* * *

One point given special attention when Macy's stopped, was the store's claim that ads in The News had not been resultful. To avoid a recurrence of the charge, Glass determined to find out what kinds of merchandise and at what prices the paper sold best. He set up what was called the patrol system.

An ad for a store department advertised was posted in a scrapbook, and the weather noted. The salesman on the account visited the department advertised on the afternoon of the day it appeared; and on the morning and afternoon of the day following. At first the men could report only on traffic in the department. But as they came to know the sales people, they could get guarded reports; business was good, or it wasn't. This report was added to the scrapbook page.

Eventually, another important source of information was discovered. No buyer will ever give a paper the results for his department; but he does brag to his business friends. Sometimes the friends told The News salesmen.

In time, a pattern began to appear; The News learned the kinds of merchandise, and the prices, for which the paper was productive. If a $15 dress sold well, then the salesman went after other items of interest to the $15 dress buyer; the millinery, coats, footwear, hosiery she would want. And started solicitation on the next higher and lower price classifications.

After the pattern was known, News salesmen did not hesitate to discourage a store's advertising department from using News space to advertise items which previously had a poor response. One time Glass turned down a full page ad for mattresses which are notoriously slow moving. "Give it to the Times," he said. "You don't expect sales from the Times. But if we flop on it, you'll be crying."

Women's apparel was a tough classification. The New York Sun was the darling of the apparel buyer. It kept its circulation stable, around 300,000, and had reasonably low rates. When a buyer bought $10,000 worth of dresses, he could spend 10% of that amount for advertising; and buy one large and one smaller ad in the Sun. If he (or she) had guessed right on fashion, color, material and price, the two Sun ads would be enough to move the dresses. As News circulation grew, its ability to move merchandise in volume discouraged smaller stores which could not handle volume sales.

* * *

On April 14, 1921, a small box on page 3 announced that three and one half columns of advertising had been omitted from the issue because of lack of space, and ushered in a problem peculiar to The News.

Increases or reduction in issue size must be made in units of four pages. The three and one half columns omitted were in excess of the advertising limit for a 24-page paper. To include them would have required a 28-page issue—including finding 16½ additional columns of editorial matter between 5 and 7 p.m, which was well beyond the capacity of the 1921 staff. The problem was (and still is) chronic during peak advertising periods in spring and fall; though today there is rarely any lack of staff or capacity.

The omission of advertising, painful to the advertiser and the salesman, was the province of Emmett Gordon, who was responsible for the advertising makeup of the issue—and earned him the pseudonym of "Omit"

Gordon. In the September '24 issue of NewsPix, Lynden Dickie voiced the salesmen's complaint:

SPOKEN FROM THE HEART

by Lynden S. Dickie

There was a man in our town
And he was wondrous wise.

He had some goods he couldn't sell
Said he "I'll advertise.

A column in the Daily News
Will move them without doubt."

He got his copy in, in time
But Gordon left it out.

By 1923, Gordon was chafing at the responsibility of the job, and demanded an opportunity to sell space. He was given a list of accounts and started to call on them. Before very long, Wilken, Cochrane, Sherwood and Moyer found themselves in hours-long meetings on makeup, involved with unhappy advertisers and altercations with editorial. After three months, Gordon was recalled to his old job, and was given some help. Richard Gill was his first assistant. Advertising makeup gradually grew into a staff of six, as borough and suburban editions were added. Gordon kept the job until his death in 1963.

The makeup problem resulted in the elimination of classified in May '25 because a classified page may include scores of small advertisers who in a space emergency cannot be phoned and told their ad is being omitted and asked for a later scheduling.

* * *

In '21, when The News had 400,000 circulation, many advertisers assumed that only women read the paper. To determine how much male readership it had, a number of News salesmen began to check sales of all morning papers at newsstands where traffic and paper sales were heavy. Two men worked as a team, noted the number of papers sold to men and women. Twenty such checks were made. The tabulated results showed that The News sale before 9 a.m. was 50.53% men, 49.47% women. The after 9 a.m. sales tipped the balance in favor of women.

When the figures were questioned by some retailers, they were invited the following year to accompany News men on newsstand checks. Sheldon R. Coons, then advertising manager of Gimbels, later president of the advertising agency Lord & Thomas, and for the last two decades business consultant to a group of important companies, was among the earliest to accept an invitation.

The following year, agency men also were invited to participate, with dinner and the theater the night before as an extra inducement. Then agency men began to ask to be included. In '24 when News circulation had passed 750,000 there were 56 guests on these reader checks. The George Batten agency sent five; three came from H. K. McCann Co. Of the two from Barton, Durstine & Osborn, one was Ben Duffy, then a space buyer, later president of BBDO. By that time the percentage of men among News readers had dropped to 30; but The News still had more men reading it than any other New York morning paper, *and* more women than the Times and World combined.

The newsstand checks had one other value; they destroyed the concept that any paper had a reader type. The slatternly woman might pick a Times; a man who looked like a bank president might buy the American. But every kind of person bought The News.

The agency people said it was the hard way to sell newspaper space, but very educational.

* * *

In the Sunday issue of Jan. 8, '22, The News had its first automobile show section; carried the advertising of the Overland, Gray, Auburn, Nash, Stutz, Hupmobile, Cadillac, Oldsmobile, Early, Columbia Six; and Dort offered a sedan for $210.

In June, W. C. Durant announced his new Star series of cars, his first venture since leaving General Motors. In August, the new Overland models were announced; and the following month, the new Gardner at $895, with a full year's guaranty!

Also of automotive interest, the Twentieth Century Cab Company offered books of coupons that saved 20% on rates; 16 cents for the first third mile, and 24 cents a mile thereafter. Yellow cab rebutted with "Every Cab a Clean Cab, Every Driver an Escort."

Franklin Simon tried to attract Saturday shoppers, and Altman's ran some well-mannered ads, with a minimum of copy. One Altman offering was "Canine Accouterments/Sixth Floor." It brought The News a phone call from an indignant male reader who wanted to know what in hell were accouterments; and a letter from a lady do-gooder who thought it sinful to spend money on dogs when so many people were in need.

S. Klein, whose specialty was to buy whole floors from overstocked apparel manufacturers, ran a small ad that read "Sale/Dresses $2" that filled Union Square with milling females and called out extra police. His sales were stage-managed superbly. From time to time, two burly men would open the doors and shout "Only fifty women, only fifty," and make Herculean efforts to close the doors. A hundred women would pour in, and start snatching garments off the racks. Another Union Square shop cancelled its ad because the overflow from Klein's was keeping its store full!

* * *

In '22, there were a number of new men.

Early in 1922, Wilken persuaded Benton L. Moyer, New England manager for System, to switch to The News. Ben Moyer had grown up in Chicago, gone to college for two years, and then, as many young men were trying to do at the time, had gone back to the land. For five years he homesteaded in Texas, fought flood, drought and insects, and gave up. After selling automobiles for a season, he joined the advertising sales staff of System. He was an asset because of his disposition; Moyer was born with built-in rose-colored glasses, was immune to the discouragement and setbacks so frequent at the time. He was made eastern manager shortly, and gave encouragement to his small staff of stalwarts.

John W. Bleakney had grown up on his father's ranch near Albuquerque, N.M., toured Europe with Buffalo Bill's Wild West Show; spent two years in the University of Pittsburgh Medical School and quit. He was a reporter on the Pittsburgh Press, and eventually was promoted to horse & mule editor. He served on the Mexican border with the Pennsylvania National Guard, went overseas with the army engineers, was gassed and spent 14 months in army hospitals. After a spell as an advertising salesman with the New York American, he came to The News on retail; and stayed on until his retirement in 1957.

Thomas F. Hickey, Jr., grew up in Brooklyn, served in France with a New York National Guard regiment; was gassed and had his back torn with shrapnel. Two years in Walter Reed Hospital in Washington followed. Lying on his back kept the back from healing; lying face down, his gassed lungs gave trouble. Hickey finally decided that if he were going to die, he'd die at home. Back in Brooklyn he joined the YMCA, started working out in the gym. In a year he was sufficiently recovered to look for a job, and started in News classified.

Earl Dixon, ex-sergeant of infantry in France, another young veteran who had some sellling experience, started in classified, later was assigned to the Brooklyn section, was the section's advertising manager until his death in 1966.

Arthur H. Mason grew up in Montclair, N.J., had aspired to be a musician, and was an amateur organist. He sold musical instruments in Minneapolis, then space with La Prensa, the Spanish newspaper in New York, before coming to The News to cover retail men's wear. He was manager of retail at the time of his death in 1959.

Arthur B. (Sam) Poole was a big, sandy-haired jovial Texan, an ex-infantry sergeant who sold trucks before coming to the national department. His territory was Philadelphia and the South, with N. W. Ayer & Co. his special charge. When the Metropolitan Sunday group was formed in 1930, he became its Chicago manager.

John E. Eckert attended Penn State for two years, worked as a bookkeeper with a railroad, sold shirts and collars, later paper drinking cups. He too started in classified, moved on to resorts and travel, then retail; and stayed with the paper until his retirement in 1968.

Frank B. Walsh came as secretary to Wilken, kept asking for a sales job; and later went into retail on the furniture classification. Among Walsh's prospects was a furniture store owned by two brothers in the Bronx. Walsh finally persuaded them to try a two column ad. It rained steadily the day the ad ran. Walsh dropped in to commiserate with his new advertisers. The store was empty, both brothers staring out the window.

"How much circulation did you say your paper has, Mr. Walsh?" asked one of his clients.

"Almost a million," said Walsh.

The questioner shrugged, and turned to his brother. "Almost a million—and not even a dog comes in." Weather is as much the ally or enemy of the retailer as the farmer!

By Washington's birthday the advertising department was installed in the Park Place first floor. Big fans at the top of two windows blew in a fine deposit of street dust, or made a partial vacuum when they blew out. Despite the difficulties and discouragements, it was a hard-working, dedicated group.

* * *

Something else was under way that spring of '22 that was to be very important to The News. The Newspaper Advertising Managers Association of New York had decided to make the first survey attempted of the New York City market. The two Hearst papers had the most information about the market; and they and the Worlds did not join the effort. But 12 city and suburban papers did; and each agreed to pay $83.33 per month for a year for the survey. New York University's Bureau of Business Research was picked to do the job. Porter Carruthers, advertising manager of the Tribune, was chairman of the research committee.

McGivena of The News attended the first meeting with Wilken, and subsequent ones without him, as his deputy. For weeks nothing happened, nobody would agree on a course of action. After several meetings, Carruthers announced that he was leaving the Tribune for the Post, and resigning as chairman of the committee. McGivena, to his own surprise, was made chairman. His program was to do for New York what the Tribune had done for Chicago a decade before.

By great good fortune, the NYU bureau had the superbly right man for the job, Horace Barney, a graduate of the University of Colorado and a fellow at the bureau. He spent months traveling around New York, and established 104 districts in the five boroughs. His next step was to key family income in six grades, from under $3,000 to over $12,000; rent was used as the base, estimated at 20% of income.

The income grades were to be shown in color on the district maps. The cost of the color plates required was estimated at $18,000. Augustine J. Powers, of the Powers Engraving Company, was persuaded to supply the plates on condition that the engraving business of the Mail and the Post was returned to his company. The company was also given a credit line on every map sheet.

When some specimen maps were printed, dinner was held for the advertising staffs of the subscribing papers. With something specific to show from the survey, their cooperation was secured.

Barney, meanwhile, had some help from another young NYU bureau fellow, Harry Corash, a recent graduate from Clark University. When Barney died suddenly the following year, Corash carried on.

* * *

Another highlight of 1922 was the start of The News' advertising promotion with the "Tell It to Sweeney" series. Sweeney, a brainchild of McGivena, was the statistical average New Yorker, as derived from the 1920 census.

Sweeney was born of a convention then prevalent in the advertising business, that every publication, even the lowliest trade paper, had an elite readership. The convention was based on the snobbish assumption that the general public was only a subsistence customer for necessities. The assumption may have had some validity in the past but it never had substance in this country, with its consistent record of creating wealth and raising living standards.

The first ad was titled "Tell It to Sweeney! The Stuyvesants will understand—" The idea was novel at the time. The copy was readable and convincing in a period when most media promotion was dull and consisted of unsupported claims and boasts. The text was set by a fine typographer, A. Colish, when most promotion was publication set. Holliss and Wilken were afraid of the idea, feared it might subject the paper to ridicule. But Field approved.

The series made its debut in Printers Ink, then the bible of the advertising business. It came out on Thursday, and by Friday afternoon virtually everybody in the business had at least thumbed through it. Today the field is so fractionated that no one publication reaches a majority of it; and the advertising business is, of course, so much larger.

The reaction to the Sweeney copy was almost immediate. News salesmen heard about it from the people they called on. Then requests for copies started to come in. Reprints were made in folders with flaps that carried more information. The first folder was reprinted five times.

Later it was realized that the folder was a medium itself. It was changed to a magazine format, with the Sweeney ad in the center spread; and News pictures and excerpts were reproduced.

The Sweeney series today means nothing. Ever since radio network began to peak in 1937, advertisers buy the mass audience; and the idea of class has disappeared.

Doing advertising promotion was exciting and fun. A lot of sacred cows were kicked.

One day somebody in the advertising department remarked that it was rare to find a copy of The News left on a subway train. Some News merchandising men checked a large number of trains, and confirmed the fact. From subway headquarters it was learned that discarded newspapers were gathered at terminals where the trains were cleaned, and sold to a waste paper dealer.

A News merchandising man arranged with the dealer to have the discarded papers counted for a week under his supervision. Sure enough, The News had the fewest discards, and the venerable gray Times topped the list. This information was published in an ad titled "So we asked the garbage man—" and Holliss got an indignant phone call from Louis Wiley, business manager of the Times.

The effect of the promotion could not be measured. But advertising department executives learned that if their salesmen believed in, and liked promotional advertising, it was a good investment. News promotion raised morale, offset the rebuffs and refusals, which declined with the passing years.

Staff additions in '23 included Paul C. Hinz and William B. Dixey, Jr. Hinz came from Moving Picture World, a trade paper, and began the long assault on Detroit for automobile linage. Hinz left in two years because of ill health.

Dixey was an older man. Graduated from the University of Pennsylvania, he had spent most of his business life with the Philadelphia Ledger and was its advertising manager before he came to New York in 1919 to be advertising manager of Garment News. He had been hired tentatively by Utassy to head an advertising staff for the Hearst tabloid scheduled to appear in January '23. The project was postponed, although the New York American began to carry a picture section of eight tabloid pages folded in the standard size paper. Glass got Dixey to come with The News. Another Utassy selection came with Dixey—Len Pinover, a very young man not long out of grade school, who started as a night clerk in the advertising publication section.

Dixey was an asset. His long experience with department stores in Philadelphia qualified him to work with New York stores. He was in charge of department store advertising until his retirement in 1939.

* * *

By 1923, national linage began to look up. Lever Brothers, with Lux, Rinso and Lifebuoy, was the largest account. The cosmetics, cigarette and food product advertisers were drawn to the paper by the rising circulation which kept the rates low.

The Sunday paper developed a surprising quantity of mail order advertising—"They laughed when I sat down at the piano" type of copy, for books and courses on etiquette, dieting, self-improvement and cosmetics. Ruthrauff & Ryan, then the leading agency in this classification, made the discovery that returns on Monday from a Sunday ad approximated about 10% of the total, so the pull of an ad could be determined within a day after it ran.

* * *

As soon as the survey district maps became available, a start was made toward allocating circulation to the districts—which The News alone among New York newspapers could do because it had independent distribution. This allocation showed where News readers lived, and supported the paper's claims that family coverage in good districts was fairly uniform with that in poor.

Martin Gurnea, in charge of the Chicago office, died on Dec. 4, 1923. Members of The News staff were shocked to learn that he had been fighting cancer for more than a year. Lee Mohr was sent out the week before Christmas to replace him.

* * *

With the department stores and strong growth in retail, The News in 1923 carried 4,392,034 lines of advertising, ranked 13th among 16 papers; and had its first first place—in jewelry advertising!

* * *

In 1924, the Mirror and Graphic promised some competition which never materialized. The big stores hoped that the Mirror might become a rival of The News. Neither Mirror nor Graphic ever reached 4,000,000 lines in the 1920s.

On Jan. 13, 1924, the Brooklyn Section of the Sunday News was started with Glass in charge, and Dixon helping out. The section was successful from the start. The rate was low, and Glass was able to persuade Brooklyn merchants to use sizeable space units, and feature several specials at a time—to give the woman reader more than one reason to make the effort to shop.

There were three papers published in Brooklyn at the time. The long-time leader was the Eagle, which up to 1928, was third among New York newspapers in linage, running from 16 to 17 million lines. The Standard Union was second, and in 1924 carried more than 7 million lines. The Brooklyn Times was third, with from 4 million to 6 million lines.

However, all three papers failed to grow with the borough which virtually doubled in population during the twenties. The newcomers felt themselves to be New Yorkers, with no special loyalty to the borough. As Maj. Benjamin H. Namm, president of the Namm Store, summarized the situation a couple of years later: We support the Eagle because it is the watchdog for the borough; but we use The News to sell goods." The Eagle at its peak had 56,000 circulation; and by 1924, the Brooklyn circulation of The News was over 200,000.

* * *

The advertising department had settled down to some semblance of organization. Sherwood was national manager, and Moyer, eastern manager, with New England and New York state as his province. Cochrane was retail manager.

Staff additions in 1924 were:

National—John J. (Jack) Reilly, an older man who had previously been with the Chicago Tribune; Lyman Worthington, Dartmouth alumnus, exagency space buyer; Frank Walty, who had lived abroad during his youth, served with the French Foreign Legion during the war, and was shortly transferred to the Chicago office; and David Sampson, who had been with Minneapolis newspapers. Worthington was later eastern manager for the metropolitan Sunday group; and Reilly was in charge of its Detroit office.

L. Marshall Greene, ex-Hearst salesman, was brought in to work on radio set linage; and did a magnificent job by learning the industry thoroughly.

Capt. Milford Simis, army pilot during the war and later a member of Lieut. Maynard's flying circus, began to develop real estate advertising in the Saturday paper. George Mulder, another La Prensa alumnus, concentrated on jewelry. Bill Dietz, ex-Bristol Myers, worked on retail drugs.

Publicity (advertising promotion) was growing slowly. In addition to Fannie Rosenberg, secretary; Sinclair Dakin was writing copy as well as getting out NewsPix; Robert P. (Bob) Lawless, ex-St. Peter's College, moved up from the publication desk in 1922, and took over mechanical production, and odd jobs; Bob was an excellent amateur photographer. The next year came Gurdon Simmons, who had been Field's office boy on the Chicago Tribune before the war, served with the British army and stayed on in London for a couple of years afterward.

Our 1924 arrival was Jean Russell, tall, slim, very good-looking. After two years at Colgate, he enlisted in the army during the war, ended up with the tank corps, was in London when the Armistice came. His ambition was to be an actor, and he was in and out of the theater, professional and amateur, in various capacities. His talents ran more to humor and whimsy than to prosaic promotion copy. At parties, he would swirl some girl's wrap around his shoulders and declaim Hamlet's soliloquy in full; and then improvise a one-man ballet. He made life in the advertising department more interesting.

* * *

In 1924, with the Globe and Evening Mail out of business, News linage for the year was 5,850,580—almost 1,500,000 lines over 1923. The News ranked 11th among New York newspapers and also gained first place in drug products advertising.

* * *

Meanwhile, the market survey made progress. The last phase was an ambitious census of about 15 types of retail outlets and service businesses, to be used as route lists by advertisers' salesmen. The census took about five months, and each paper furnished a man for the job. The News man was Hickey. Afterwards, he spent two months in Chicago, working with the Tribune's merchandising service; and came back to start one for The News.

His first staff was three men: George Knoche, graduated from the purchasing department; Charles D. Chapman, who had sold silverware; and Charles W. Donahue, fresh out of Notre Dame, who had worked summers in the Chicago Tribune's advertising department.

The merchandising service became The News training school for salesmen; taught them the geography of the five New York City boroughs, transportation, neighborhood trade centers, local buying habits; and the distribution and sale of a variety of products.

By 1925, the merchandising service had five men. Thereafter six to 10 men were hired every year. "These men, by the way, are not drifters," said a 1925 advertisement, "but college men with selling experience and some sales background . . . We train these men for our own selling staff and graduate them into our national sales department. In other words, we pick men good enough for our selling jobs to help with yours."

And to make sure that merchandising men could be graduated, they had to be accepted by all advertising department heads before they were hired for merchandising. After 12 to 18 months, they put in an additional six months in research, to gain some familiarity with figures and data, and to learn how to prepare presentations.

The result of the system was that News salesmen knew more about the New York market and the advertisers' businesses than those on the other papers.

In 1925, with its five-man staff, the merchandising service helped introduce into the market a mineral water, a mayonnaise, breakfast food, candy, face cream, toilet accessory, radio set and a food specialty. Thirteen surveys were made in the drug field, four in groceries, one in candy, one in apparel, two in radio sets; and a number of small spot surveys.

* * *

In 1925 the staff additions were:

Emerson Dye, quite young, had sold classified for Conde Nast magazines briefly, and car card space for Baron Collier, was given a list of retail accounts; William Delaney, ex-Fordham, from the media department of Barton, Durstine, Osborn, was assigned to national; and Lester Mercelis, formerly advertising manager of La Prensa, came in to handle department stores. Chapman and Donahue started in merchandising; so did Alfred J. Hailparn, fresh out of a training course at Filene's of Boston.

Capt. Horatio V. S. Negus (called Rache), was an older man, was brought in to cover resorts and travel. He had worked in this field since

1905, with the New York Evening Post, and had a wide acquaintance in the travel field. In 1910 he had gone to Bermuda, raised $500 from resort owners there, and ran two pages in the Post gravure section, the first Bermuda advertising to appear in this country. In time, his work was very resultful. He retired in 1946.

Floyd Noe, also an older man, had been a salesman for Class, an industrial magazine, and earlier spent a dozen years in the varnish business. He was brought in to cover the automotive classification which had been giving The News a lot of resistance. Noe spent about half his time in Detroit, and his doggedness and persistence eventually brought a lot of automotive linage to The News.

And Harry Corash, who had worked on the New York survey with the NYU Bureau of Business Research, became first manager of research. He was later transferred to Metropolitan Sunday Group and became its treasurer.

* * *

In the next few years, The News made a number of important contributions to metropolitan marketing.

New York had a reputation as a graveyard market, where none but the very big companies could succeed. Out-of-town business men thought it was the Manhattan they knew from their business trips; but were utterly ignorant of the populations of the lower East Side, the West Side, and northern portions of Manhattan; of the burgeoning boroughs of Brooklyn and the Bronx, and the to-be-filled communities of Queens; and the vast suburban belt that was the largest quality market in the country; and how 10,000,000 people were housed, fed, clothed, transported and amused. Their advertising agencies were no better informed.

Many felt that their objective was to get a single department store to stock their line; but no one store, not even mighty Macy's, sold more than a portion of the market. Some thought that acceptance by a single chain would establish their product, although no one chain, then or now, dominates the market. Others looked for a single jobber to cover the market.

There was no realization of the size of the market, and the number of outlets. The News preached constantly to sales managers that three items on the shelves of every third outlet was *distribution;* and two cases in every fiftieth store was not.

Inadequate distribution was accompanied by inadequate advertising. The product was not available in enough places for an interested prospect to find it. And in the early '20s no one newspaper had sufficient circulation to create widespread demand. After The News passed the million mark

Terrorism in Wall St. Scene at the corner of Broad and Wall immediately following the explosion Sept. 16, 1920, of a bomb carried in a horse-drawn cart. Blast killed 30, wounded 100. Edward Jackson, photographer.

Through the ropes. One of the greatest of all sports photographs shows Jack Dempsey whirling out of Polo Grounds ring in first round of heavyweight championship fight with Luis Angel Firpo, Sept. 14, 1923. Dempsey returned to ring, knocked Firpo out in second round. Hank Olen, photographer.

PICTURES TO REMEMBER

Here are some of the most notable photographs made by News cameramen during the fifty years of the paper's history.

The Vestris tragedy. Scene aboard the British ship Vestris just before the vessel foundered off the Virginia coast Nov. 12, 1928. Death toll was 110. Photo was taken by a crew member who sold the film to a News staff member. This is one of the few pictures in this book not made by a News cameraman.

It happened on Lafayette St. Widely published human interest photo appeared in The News July 29, 1925. Cat had carried several kittens across street before cameraman arrived. He persuaded animals to make one more trip, with this result. Photographer, Harry Warnecke.

Bricks fly in Washington, D.C. Discharged servicemen demanding federal bonus battle police in nation's capital during riots in summer of 1932. This was one of bloodier encounters, leaving two dead and 40 wounded, before regular army troops were called in. Photographer, Joseph Costa.

J. P. Morgan obliges. Giant of financial world puts circus midget Lya Graf into spotlight before testifying at Senate banking committee hearing June 1, 1933. Press agent arranged stunt, to consternation of senators. Photographer, William Hoff.

Death chair. Only picture of its kind ever made in Sing Sing prison shows Ruth Snyder at the moment of her execution for the slaying of her husband. Photo was made Jan. 12, 1928.

Uproar at the UN. Soviet Premier Khruschev pounds desk with his shoe at United Nations meeting Oct. 13, 1960. Photographer, Frank Hurley.

Holocaust. German dirigible Hindenburg explodes and burns at Lakehurst, N.J. mooring mast May 8, 1937. Death toll 36. Charles Hoff, photographer.

in February, 1926, it was the first medium to reach enough of the market to get action, to make sales; to persuade dealers to stock a new product because News advertising was potent enough to move it.

News market researchers analyzed conditions for various types of products; found different trade practices, margins and pricing; tried to find out if the newcomer would need warehousing, brokerage, jobbers, arranged introductions, and helped route his salesmen or specialty crews more expeditiously. News merchandising men accompanied the advertiser's salesmen; and while they sold their product, The News men sold advertising as a reason for stocking the product and assurance that it would move.

The district maps were invaluable in merchandising; they spotted the location of the store, showed the retailer the class of customer in his immediate area, and the volume of News circulation that helped him.

* * *

One of the major headaches of The News during its first decade was the readership survey. Whenever an advertiser or agency made one, The News showed up badly; while the reports of Times and Herald Tribune readership were proportionately larger than their actual circulation warranted. Many News readers were status conscious and unwilling to disclose that they read a tabloid. In '26, and again in '27, the readership survey became crucial.

The American Association of Advertising Agencies in 1926 proposed a major research of media. New York newspapers were to be its first study, conducted by the eminent Dr. Daniel Starch. News market researchers learned, via the grapevine, that preliminary results were not favorable to The News, and obtained an appointment with James O'Shaughnessy, then the 4A's executive secretary, and Dr. Starch.

Dr. Starch's principal business was finding out the advertising readership of national magazines. Over a period of years, he and his people had painstakingly formulated average salaries and wages for every conceivable occupation.

The News' objections to his research were 1) that his compensation scales were too low for New York; and 2) that obtaining the exact occupational status of the household head was virtually impossible. Miss Sinclair Dakin, using Dr. Starch's questionnaires, had spent two days on calls on housewives, and was unable to get a full set of answers. The stumbling block was occupation. If a woman said her husband was a broker, the interviewer had to press for details. Was he a partner in a Wall Street firm, customer's man, clerk or board boy? Or employed by a commodity trader? At this point the woman being questioned either ended the interview abruptly; or else said she didn't know. Dr. Starch admitted that this part of the interview required finesse on the part of the interviewer. The News researchers left the incomplete questionnaires with O'Shaughnessy—and heard no more about the 4A media study thereafter.

A year later The News learned that General Motors was conducting a readership survey in New York. A News delegation went to Detroit to see Henry Grady (Buck) Weaver, in charge of the project; and for good measure he threw in GM's advertising committee. He was told advance information about the survey was that it was unfavorable to The News. In view of GM's reputation for research, The News would have to fight it, with common arithmetic. The meeting was shown some district maps with allocated circulation figures.

Weaver was icily polite. When General Motors needed the help of the New York News, it would ask for it. And thank you very much. The confrontation with the committee seemed to be a complete flop.

Two months later Weaver came to The News advertising department. After a thorough check of his study, he had scrapped it—which took considerable courage for a man in his position. In one Park Ave. apartment building, the discarded News copies sent down in the dumbwaiter, and counted by the building superintendent, were more than three times the number reported by his interviewers. Weaver thanked The News for helping GM retain its reputation for good research, and was a good friend of the paper ever after. In the next few years, his customer research program kept GM from building cars with features the public didn't like, and he became important in the GM hierarchy.

FINDING THE FACTUAL SWEENEY

The Sweeney idea was now almost four years old, and had been getting some acceptance among advertisers. Almost every Sweeney advertisement was based on a specific instance; but The News wanted realistic evidence, in volume. So it turned to Manhattan's Lower East Side.

The Lower East Side was New York's ghetto, slumland, the depository of the newly arrived, poor, ignorant immigrant; and its status as a market was zero. Census estimates gave it a population in 1925 of 377,010; of whom almost 300,000 were Jews—Russian, Polish, Austrian; with some 70,000 Italians, the Chinatown enclave, colonies of Greeks and Spaniards, and a smattering of descendants of the original Irish settlers. In an area of less than two square miles, there was a population equivalent to that of Cincinnati or Indianapolis.

Miss Dakin, short, slight, guileless, set out to explore the district. She visited scores of tenement flats with a utility employee and a real estate agent; and during countless interviews gathered enough case histories to fill tomes.

There was plenty of poverty in the area, she found, but there was also buying power and affluence beyond any economist's imagining.

Rents were low. Families were large, often with more than one wage earner. A News delivery man, unmarried, lived with his parents in a six-room flat; working brothers and sisters brought the family income up to $600 a week. The area supplied most of the city's garment workers, who were well paid. The Jews were the most provident, put their money in banks that were open from 9 a.m. to 8 p.m.; bought real estate and mortgages. Many owners of small stores, long established in business, were affluent; but with the stores open from 6 a.m. to 9 p.m., could not afford to commute or live elsewhere.

The term "dowry" was unknown, but parents often bought the newlyweds a house, or furnished their apartment, or set their son-in-law up in business. They married young, moved out to Brooklyn, Queens, the Bronx or the suburbs; and introduced their parents to washing machines, vacuum cleaners and other appliances. Many came back to the old neighborhood to buy clothing and furniture because the values were better. Young doctors and dentists opened offices in the neighborhood; and as their fortunes improved, opened second offices uptown. Mornings they served the downtown patients who paid cash; afternoons were devoted to the uptown patients who took their time paying their bills.

Fruits and vegetables came to the Lower East Side first; were sold from pushcarts. Most of the first watermelons to reach New York were sold in the district, by the slice from pushcarts, and grossed $5 per melon. Food was the common extravagance. Immigrant women pointed to packages on the shelves before they could name the products. Pushcarts vending foodstuffs paid $1 a day license to the city; and averaged $136 a week, according to a U.S. Department of Agriculture study. Many had sales of $600 a week. Kitchens were small, ice boxes miniscule, storage space scarce; and like Europeans, the women bought food for quick consumption.

Miss Dakin's study was no dry treatise. She sprinkled it with colorful vignettes and anecdotes.

About Sadie, the manicurist, who earned $30 to $40 a week in a beauty shop. She had three girl friends, all about her size. One girl would buy a suit or dress from Millgrim's for $150. The quartet then took the garment apart, copied the parts in materials of their own choosing; and made several replicas. With their ingenuity and industry, they had *haute couture* at low cost.

About the old woman who had started selling crockery from a pushcart, then graduated to a small store; and had a savings account passbook with more than $100,000 entered in it!

About per capita sales of pianos, imported English baby carriages, and Russian caviar, highest in New York!

Car registrations in the district were relatively low—3,294 among 80,000 families. But the makes of cars owned were surprising; Rolls Royces 2; Packards 80; Cadillacs 119; Cunninghams 6; Franklins 7; Locomobiles 6; Pierce Arrows 46. Ford led, Buick was second.

Even today, more than 40 years later, this study stands as a milestone. Much to the surprise of The News advertising department, sociologists gave it a lot of publicity.

Later that year, Miss Dakin made a study of Greenwich Village—as a medium size Italian community, fringed by Bohemia.

The following year, a study was made of Battery Park, the downtown financial district, which had a resident population of 12,427, living among the 100,000 workers who thronged the district each weekday.

A fourth study covered Midtown East, Third Ave. to the East River, from 14th St. to 69th St., an area of old settled neighborhoods before the district became fashionable.

The four studies took time to make and were expensive but it was felt they proved a point: that the Sweeneys of New York were worthwhile customers for any advertiser.

In 1928, Miss Dakin made another study of the Upper East Side, the exact antithesis of her first. This time there was less talking with the *habitants*. She interviewed merchants, who told how long they had to wait for their bills to be paid; doormen, rental agents, employment agencies. She also discovered the "Park Avenue Poor," the families that might have lived middle class comfortably, but whether for business or social preferment, sacrificed much for a good address. Some lived without cars or servants, women made their own clothes, did no entertaining, to meet the high rent they paid, or to send children to private schools. Many of them had less spendable income than Lower East Side Families. And in many ways, the Very Best neighborhoods made relatively poor customers. This study was issued as a separate brochure, and raised some eyebrows in advertising agencies.

THE GREAT CAMPBELL'S SOUP SURVEY

This was another 1926 effort.

The idea was probably Hickey's. Campbell's were magazine advertisers, had never used New York newspapers. In his calls on grocers, Hickey was impressed by the volume of Campbell's that was sold in the market;

and became convinced that Campbell's advertising was reaching a very small share of its active customers.

Merchandising had learned by this time that the retailer's estimate of his sales of any product was usually optimistic, from 15% to 20% above actual. Hickey picked several hundred stores in middle and lower middle-class areas. News merchandising men had called on grocers enough to make them realize the selling power of the paper. So on the basis that Campbell's advertising in The News would sell more soup, the grocers were persuaded to bring out their jobbers' invoices; and let our men copy deliveries of eight kinds of Campbell's Soups during a six month period. The assumption was that six months purchase was equivalent to six months sales.

The job took six weeks. Mrs. Emmett Gordon, then Viola MacAvoy and Hickey's secretary, recalls how she and the other two girls in merchandising worked night after night, typing reports and making tabulations; and came to hate even the mention of Campbell's Soup.

When the study was finished, an appointment was made to present it to F. Wallis Armstrong, Campbell's agency in Philadelphia.

After the presentation was finished, a tall young woman in the agency's research department said disdainfully, "Your figures don't mean anything. You've left out lunchrooms and restaurants." She was answered, rather sharply, that restaurants and lunchrooms sold soup, not Campbell's Soup; and their customers ordered soup, not Campbell's Soup. She sniffed and left the room. So the end of the session was anticlimatic—no sale.

Nevertheless, our national salesmen made effective use of the study, impressed other advertisers with the enormous tonnage of soup sales that came out of ordinary neighborhoods; and were able to get considerable business.

The story, however, had a happier ending. We didn't know that the F. Wallis Armstrong people were enough impressed to pass along the study to Campbell in Camden. And somebody there was interested enough to come to New York, and check jobbers' records, and confirm our reports. The following spring, a contract came in the mail—for 10,000 lines for Campbell's Soup, the first newspaper advertising they had ever used in New York.

* * *

In 1926 the advertising department added:

Wilfred E. Everist, Baltimore City College graduate, former third baseman for the Philadelphia Athletics, had been selling motor trucks; and was assigned to retail. He succeeded Noe in automobiles; and retired in '55 because of ill health.

Putnam E. Stowell, ex-Boston College, had played professional football, and been in retail shoe business. So shoes became his classification. He was with the paper 22 years.

Karl M. Roberts, who was shortly put in charge of department stores, had a checkered career. Born in New Mexico, he had attended schools in eight states; been a reporter, press agent, salesman, and during the war was with the army food administration in the Southwest. Roberts never made a call without bringing a new idea. He made Macy's his particular target; and was rewarded in 1928 when Kenneth Collins, advertising director of Macy's, made that store one of The News' big advertisers. Roberts retired in 1957.

To publicity came a tall young Pittsburgher, Bernard M. (Steve) Broudy, a B.S. from Carnegie Tech, and an M.B.A. from New York University. Steve was probably the only advertising production man in New York who used a slide rule!

To merchandising came:

Joseph W. Linahan, from Binghamton, N.Y., who had sold space in Macfadden magazines; stocky, apple-cheeked, nature lover, hunter; who later spent many years in the Chicago office.

Omar Latimer and Warren Bush, University of Pennsylvania; Latimer left to become an osteopath. Bush retired Dec. 31, 1968, as the paper's national advertising manager.

Tom Beebe, 1926 graduate of the University of Illinois, who in 1969 was still active in the national department, has spent his whole business life with The News.

Robert Kelly, recent graduate of Ohio State; Philip E. Pelletier, who had attended Newark Institute of Technology, sold chemicals and tea; Harold Schehr, a refugee from the auditing department; Murray Martin, ex-Annapolis and Navy, one-time sports editor on a small Mississippi newspaper; Hugh Dolan, De La Salle graduate, Navy chief petty officer in the war, and recently with the foreign department of National City Bank.

* * *

Another step forward was the start of the Sunday gravure section on Oct. 26. Jack Reilly and Jack Bleakney were assigned to it, but the whole staff pitched in. The initial print order was to be 1,350,000—but before the start of the press run, Sullivan uped the print order 100,000, and had a net sale of more than 1,400,000 copies.

The rate was low for the time; $2.50 per line one time, $2.40 for 13 insertions or 5,000 lines. In the 10 weeks preceding the first appearance of the gravure section, 53 advertisers placed orders for 203 pages. The names of the advertisers give an indication of how far the paper had come—Listerine, Fleischmann Yeast, Cellucotton Products, Ivory Soap, Colgate, Pepsodent, Camel Cigarettes, Chesterfield Cigarettes, Hickok Belts, Rem, Sealpax, Cutex, Ovaltine, Converse Rubber, Ponds Cream—representing the acceptance by the leading national advertisers.

Len Pinover who had started as night clerk on the publication desk in '23 was put in charge of advertising makeup in the gravure section; and in another three years took over the production of the section, and proceeded to make himself an authority on gravure. He resigned from The News in 1936 and started his own very successful gravure production company.

* * *

There were more staff additions in '27:

Belton O. Sullivan hailed from Jackson, Tenn., left Vanderbilt College to enlist in field artillery, made sergeant and spent 15 months in France. He had been in the cotton business, owned a Ford dealership in Albany, and sold street car advertising, before his advent with The News. He was with the paper at the time of his death in 1956.

Joseph G. Babini, infantry captain in the war, ran a men's wear shop, sold space for a trade paper. Bab was immediately popular, told a story well; started with a group of Westchester accounts, and later covered New York State for national until his death in 1962.

George W. Ward, an older man, took over banks and financial. A University of Minnesota graduate, he had been an actor, a playwright, editor of trade papers and publisher of one. His previous job was as an editor on American Banker.

Seward Davis had been preparing for Annapolis when the war started, joined the merchant marine and earned a quartermaster's rating. Later he was a steamship purser for three years. He had been on the advertising staffs of the New York Herald and Sun. After merchandising, he was assigned to national, spent some years in the Chicago office. He was national manager when he retired in 1964.

A. D. Van Allen, an earnest young man just out of the University of New Hampshire, had intended to go to Filene's of Boston as a trainee; but changed his mind and came to merchandising.

Late that fall, publicity acquired Howard W. Roper, an M.B.A. out of Harvard Business School. Roper was slight, with a pompadour, small moustache and glasses, had a *Herr Professor* look about him, although his antecedents were Plymouth Rock English. He came from a needy family in Milwaukee, had worked from his earliest years at an extraordinary assortment of jobs; turning out lights in store windows at night, replacing records on phonographs in a Polish dancing academy on Saturdays, checking coats at a Greek dance hall.

His first ambition was to be a chemist, and he managed a B.S. from Wisconsin. He got a job in a dye plant, and was allowed to work two shifts a day, at $35 a week for each shift, which he considered sheer affluence. However, he picked up some sort of poisoning, and his skin discolored, He was put in a sanitarium to bleach out. The time was the mid-twenties, when advertising contests were popular, and Roper concentrated on winning them. He left the sanitarium six months later with $12,000 in the bank, got married, and entered Harvard Business School.

During vacations, he had worked with the American Appraisal Company at various jobs—one was on an employees' house organ, which caused him to become interested in writing. He had answered a News ad for a copywriter, and was hired.

As part of his indoctrination, Roper was assigned to merchandising at an unfortunate time.

The E. Fougera Co., pharmaceutical manufacturers, had brought out a product called Vapex, nose drops for the treatment of colds. Vapex was packed in small glass vials priced to sell at $1 retail and Fougera's advertising agency, because of the price, estimated that there were not more than 400 possible outlets in New York. Hickey scoffed at this estimate and brashly promised 1,000 outlets in two weeks, if the agency gave him six specialty salesmen. It permitted him to hire the men but the price proved an obstacle, and very few outlets were obtained.

Hickey, desperate, in the second week sent his own men out to sell Vapex, which was contrary to the department's own rules. So Roper spent Monday morning with one of the specialty salesmen in Brooklyn; and after lunch was on his own.

Hickey's men and the specialty salesmen began to come in after 5. They had one, two, three orders; one hero had six. Roper was the last to appear, hot, tired, bedraggled. Hickey's reception of him was brusque.

"Oh, you. Did you get anything?"

Roper started to explain diffidently that he had never tried to sell anything before.

"Never mind. Get anything?"

Roper laid down on Hickey's desk 17 signed orders. Hickey flicked through them, and in an awed voice, said, "Sit down. What did you say? What was your approach?"

The introductory offer was one free with a quarter dozen. In his morning calls with the specialty men, Roper noticed that the druggists were more interested in the margin than the product. In the afternoon, when he entered a drug store, he laid down the four small bottles on the counter, and said to the druggist: "Costs you a dollar-eighty. Sells for four dollars." And the invariable response was "I'll take it. What is it?"

Following the Roper formula of stressing the profit instead of the product, the rate of sales picked up promptly. Hickey was almost able to make good his promise, and Roper acquired an impressive reputation with News salesmen.

With his interest in writing, Roper took courses at night at Columbia. In 1932 his novel "Beauty Lies Beyond Hell" (largely autobiographical) was published by Ray Long and Richard Smith. It was a *success d'estime*. Satisfied that he could write a book, he never wrote another.

He was a remarkable student and researcher. Any News salesman, facing a session with, or a presentation to, a prospect about whose business he knew little, could bring his problem to Roper. He would start with the World Almanac and any other reference books in the office, disappear into the New York Public Library; and a few days later come up with a study that reeked of authority. Thirty years later he earned a Ph.D. at the New School for Social Research; his subject, economic forecasting. And in addition to everything else, he was a gifted mathematician; and worked well with Corash on market research. Both contributed greatly to News effectiveness of our promotion and sales.

THE GREAT CEREAL SURVEY

In January, 1927, one of the major advertising agencies asked The News to survey the cereal product of a client, and the product thought to be its principal competition. Preliminary digging exposed the fact that the client's products had several competitors. The formulation and testing of the questionnaire took several weeks. Six weeks of field work followed, with calls on 1,002 stores, both independent and chain. The tabulation of the data took five months. The finished study comprised 295 chart sheets, covering 30 products; distribution, price range, order of sale, frequency of order, average weekly sale, estimated quotas and consumption. Location of the products and use of display material were also included. Never before had such a comprehensive study been made of a food classification.

The soup and cereal studies made important news in merchandising circles and were important to The News. They got advertising salesmen past the junior media men to senior space buyers and account executives of major agencies; past the product managers to the advertising and sales manager of principal companies. They made a welcome for the men and their message. And they established The News as the top marketing authority in New York.

Such studies demanded excessive efforts by the people who made them—service men, secretaries, researchers; they eventually loathed the mention of cereal names as well as soup. But no other medium in any field was making such comprehensive and detailed surveys.

As the reputation of the merchandising service grew, many advertisers bought The News to get the benefit of the service.

* * *

For three years, 1925 through 1927, The News ranked ninth in linage among New York newspapers—a remarkable showing, in view of the paper's tabloid page. In 1926 there was a gain of 1,000,000 lines over 1925; and 1927, with a total of 9,311,191 lines, was almost 1,500,000 lines over 1926.

News rates, daily, were virtually twice those of the Times. The high rates had lost many of the small retailers who used the paper in its earlier years. But the huge and growing circulation (1,145,481 daily and 1,433,578 Sunday in March '27) brought in the big stores. The paper had 100,000 line contracts with Bloomingdale's, Gimbels, Hearn, Wanamaker; with the Namm Store, Loesers, Abraham & Straus in Brooklyn, while Altman had a 50,000 line contract, and Best 20,000 lines.

There were six furniture stores running more than 100,000 lines, and another on lesser contracts. The paper took the lead in furniture and household advertising, and never lost it.

Some other classifications were spectacular successes. Radio set linage was 6,818 in 1923, and 541,718 in 1927—largely the result of Marshall Greene's efforts. The following year, Glad Henderson, editor of the Talking Machine Journal, commented:

> "Quite a change is occurring in the newspaper situation in New York City. With the Daily News getting the bulk of the business, dealers tell us that half of their sales can be accounted for from their advertising in The News, which is a tremendous proportion for one paper to create. One department store ran a $500 advertisement in The News and sold nearly $20,000 worth of radio sets . . . The markup was 38% and with an advertising cost of about 2½%, the sale was considered a most profitable one."

Automotive linage—12,000 lines in '22 had grown to 198,000 lines in '27—came from Nash, Overland, Oldsmobile, Willys-Knight, Chrysler, Moon, Oakland, Hupmobile, Pontiac, Studebaker, Erskin, Whippet, Hudson-Essex, Cadillac, Peerless, Marmon, Chevrolet, Paige, Dodge, Ford, Elcar, Auburn, Buick, Durant, LaSalle, International Trucks, Indian

Motorcycles, General Motors institutional; and Socony, Watson Stabilators, Simoniz, Tydol, Whiz Products, Gabriel Snubbers and Steelcote Enamel.

Automotive advertising involved a dual sale, to the factory and the local dealers. The next year Floyd Noe got a helper, Seward Davis.

And The News probably had more food accounts—though not more food linage—than any other New York paper.

In 1928, The News added another 1,000,000 lines—10,432,709 total for the year; moved up to eighth in rank among New York papers; and sold more than $10 million worth of space.

Warren Rinenberg, formerly advertising manager of a garment trade paper, joined the national department.

To merchandising came: Alfred Hailparn, who had been editor of a house organ for Filene's of Boston; John F. Morrissey, with previous experience on St. Paul newspapers; Ken Lee, who had been with a firm of publishers' representatives.

Publicity had a fledgling writer, Harold A. Smith, eldest son of Gus Smith of the composing room. Smith got his first job in the auditing department five years earlier. He was slugging his way through Columbia at nights. He left the paper in 1937, later had his own public relations company; and is now with the public relations end of J. Walter Thompson Company.

Auditing lost another man to advertising that year. Vincent F. Sullivan had served with the army in France, later wrote a book on his war experiences. He joined auditing Feb. 28, 1922, was later responsible for advertising billing. In February, 1928, Wilken made him his assistant. Sullivan remained with The News until his retirement at the end of 1968.

After The News circulation passed a million, the enormous response to advertising became more and more apparent.

Hessel, Weinberg & Hertz were manufacturing furriers who were hard hit in the 1920 deflation. They opened a store on 37th St. near Sixth Ave., called it Wilson's to distinguish it from their manufacturing business. Morris Hessel was one of the merchants John Glass talked to in 1921. After a few cautious trials, Hessel placed an order for 100,000 lines. The business grew furiously. In 1927, the firm opened another store called Selberts', Ltd., also on 37th St., just a few feet off Fifth Ave., stocked it with higher priced furs. For four months the new store spent $10,000 a month in nine newspapers; and found that most of its customers, like those of its old store, were coming from The News. By 1929, the two stores were using more than 200,000 lines of News space annually.

Curiously enough, the big department stores lagged in the proper use of the paper. It was not until years later when they had branch stores in the suburbs that they began to get the full benefit of the paper's power.

Today, one big store will not list two of its branches when they have a big promotion—simply because the two branches cannot stock enough merchandise to meet demand.

Occasionally The News learned of outstanding results. On Thursday, May 4, of that bleak year 1933, Willys Overland ran an 800-line advertisement for its seasonal model. By Saturday night, May 13, it had delivered 291 cars to purchasers and had unfilled orders for 416 more. The sale of 707 cars represented $282,000 in gross business—from one four-column ad!

At one time, manufacturers would pay for a page advertisement of their product for Ludwig Baumann, one of the big credit furniture stores; and would get orders from credit furniture stores all over the country.

A few years ago, a three-quarter page advertisement in the Sunday News for an electrical applicance priced at $24.95 brought 12,000 sales—and two-thirds were telephone orders!

The response was not limited to retail. A salesman for a medicine manufacturer got a proprietary product of his own. He wrote his own copy for two small ads. Week after week on Friday afternoon, he came to Sherwood's office, wrote a personal check to pay for two insertions during the coming week. He was so successful selling his new product that he later added others and built in substantial business through The News alone.

* * *

The ways of getting business are devious, often unfathomable. In the summer of 1926, Frank Walty of the Chicago office visited New York. One of his accounts was Listerine, based in St. Louis. Walty called on the agency, Lambert & Feasley; the principal Lambert of the agency was also a principal in the Listerine Company.

Walty asked for a space buyer he knew, but the man was out. Brashly he said to the receptionist, "Is Gerry Lambert in?"

The girl assumed he must know the boss; and told him where Lambert's office was. Again brashly, he entered the office.

Lambert and another man sat behind a table of blueprints.

"Know anything about boats?" Lambert asked Walty. The other man was a marine architect.

It happened that Walty knew quite a bit about boats. He looked at the drawings, and (he said) made some suggestions that seemed to him to be obvious. They pleased Lambert. The architect began to sketch the changes on tracing paper and it was 5:30 by the time he finished and left.

"What did you want to see me about?" asked Lambert.

Walty told him about the new gravure section that was to start in October. Lambert was familiar with The News, had bought a lot of space in it.

"What's your rate?" he asked again.

Walty told him. Lambert reflected for a minute or so, and then said, "Would an order for 26 pages make you happy?" And that's how Walty *sold* 26 pages of gravure!

* * *

Another highly improbable sale came to Bob Kelly, who had gone through merchandising, and was on the national staff. He was also taking courses in business administration nights at New York University, and was invited to join a fraternity. Kelly was a joiner.

As part of his initiation, he had to talk a full hour on five Thursday nights. To the chagrin and amusement of his new fraternity brothers, Kelly talked five hours about The News.

When his fifth hour was finished, one of his listeners came up and said, "Can you get the X account assigned to you?"

"I don't know," answered Kelly. "Why?"

"If you can, I'll see that you get a 52-time order. You've sold me." He was an agency account executive.

So Kelly asked Moyer for the X account, and got the 52-time order!

* * *

The year 1929 started out as the best of all possible years. Business was very good and The News continued to gain in advertising every month until February, 1932; and after 14 months of decline, began to gain again in April 1933, a phenomenal performance at the very bottom of the Depression.

This volume was attained despite 10 increases daily and Sunday in retail rates in its first decade; and 14 increases daily and 15 Sunday in national rates.

There were the usual staff additions, but with a difference. Out of the dozen men hired for merchandising, only a few stayed with the paper for any time. The others wanted the experience, and then moved on to other endeavors.

One exception was Richard S. Tincher, just graduated from the University of Southern California. He started in merchandising in August, 1929. In 1946 he became western advertising manager; returned to New York in 1952 as classified display manager, and remained in that office until his death in September, 1959.

And publicity gained a young man who was also a stayer—Harold

Garrett. Ex-Fordham, he had sold silks, worked for a year and a half in the circulation department of Macfadden magazines. To Garrett fell the task of helping publicity prepare its annual circulation distribution study. Sullivan said, "I've spoiled a circulation man, but made a statistician. So publicity better keep him." Which was done, until his retirement as manager of research in January, 1967.

* * *

The stock market crash which started in October, '29, had a depressing effect on everybody, including those who were not in the market. Nobody could foretell the effect on general business or the general public.

One young salesman in the advertising department had inherited some money, and made a lot more in the market. The weekend before the first drop, he was dickering for a secondhand Rolls Royce at $6,000. A month later he said he couldn't afford even a tricycle.

MONUMENT ON 42d ST.

By the summer of 1927, the need for more space was so urgent that a search for a new building site started in earnest.

Harry Corash made a center of population study; and found it was in Queens, across the East River from midtown Manhattan. The difficulty of newsprint transport, and the delivery of printed papers made the site impractical at the time; but did suggest 42d St. as an axis.

East of Lexington Ave., the south side of 42d St. looked like the street across from the railroad station in any small city; a row of old, assorted, unpretentious structures. The real estate firm of Douglas Elliman Co. was commissioned to acquire a plot in the vicinity. Joseph P. Landauer, over a period of time, succeeded in assembling an L-shaped area. The conclusion of the deal was held up for months by the owner of a paint store with a long lease; after a lot of haggling, he was bought out for $25,000.

The plot had a frontage of 125 feet midblock on 42d, running through to 41st, and an additional 230 feet on 41st running east to Second Ave. The total cost was something over $2,500,000.

The original concept seems to have been a 20-story office building on the 42d St. side and a manufacturing plant on 41st. What eventually came off Raymond Hood's drafting board was far more impressive.

* * *

Raymond Hood, himself was a Horatio Alger character.

In 1921, the Chicago Tribune announced a $100,000 prize competition for the design of a new building. Twelve architects of repute were extended invitations accompanied by $2,500 fees.

Hood, at the time, was out of a job and had a sick wife. One day walking through Grand Central Terminal in New York, he met John Mead Howells who had been a classmate at the Beaux Arts in Paris. Howells, of an old Boston family, had the means and connections to open his own office and had done very well. Hood, without money or status, had worked for a number of architects. That day he congratulated Howells on his invitation to enter the Tribune competition. Howells said his shop was so busy that he couldn't accept the invitation. After they parted, Howells turned on his heel, called out to Hood and brought him back. He suggested that Hood, if he were interested, could use his office to work on the Tribune Tower plan, and keep the fee—which was a godsend to Hood at the time.

Out of 260 plans submitted, Hood's modified Gothic tower won first prize. A new firm was formed, Howells & Hood with Andre Fouilhoux later admitted as a third partner. The commissions on the Tribune Tower came to more than $300,000; and Hood was never in want again.

His second success was the black and gold American Radiator Building on West 40th St. across from Bryant Park in New York. The radiator company asked Hood to redesign its building in London, a section of a seven-story block. British architects immediately went into a flap, protesting the entry of an alien who had no respect for British tradition and would probably attempt something barbaric.

When his plans were ready, Hood went to London, called on the president of the architects society, and demanded a meeting. An evening was set and some 200 architects attended. Hood opened with a stinging rebuke: he had studied, respected and loved the best of the English traditions in architecture; and he recognized the architect's obligation to preserve and perpetuate the best of tradition. Then he uncovered his rendering. The black and gold faced building was seven stories tall; and its roof line was level with the other buildings in the block. The normally phlegmatic English architects gave him a standing ovation.

This London incident had an amusing sequence. The following year the other owners of property in the block sent a committee to see Hood, and asked him to reface the entire block in the same style!

* * *

Like every good architect, Hood was eminently practical. An early member of the "form follows function" school, he was a fascintating talker, and could sketch as fast as he talked. He was also a practicing psychologist, and a superb salesman.

He had seen enough of Patterson while the Tribune Tower was under way to know that he differed radically in taste and temperament from McCormick; wanted no cathedral motif, and would even prefer the unconventional.

He also sensed that Holliss and Barnhart were wary of him, expected to be overwhelmed with technicalities of architecture and art. So he showed up at their weekly meetings with nothing but floor plans, talked about rentable space. After a few meetings they recognized him as a fellow business man, concerned with the best revenue aspects of the building.

The meetings went on for about 10 weeks. Then Hood said that he would be unable to see them the following week; and suggested that two weeks hence they meet in his office. At that meeting, he unveiled a 39-inch high plaster model of the proposed 36-story News Building and 9-story plant with all the other structures in the block modeled to scale.

Hood said he had learned the model technique from Joseph Urban, Vienna born architect known in this country as the designer of Ziegfeld Follies sets. Most laymen found it difficult to visualize the proposed structure from drawings of front, side and back elevations whereas the plaster model showed them exactly what the finished building would look like.

Patterson, Holliss, Barnhart and other people concerned walked around the model for the next three weeks. It was approved with two immaterial changes. The third story setback on the 42d St. side was raised to the seventh story; and the setback on the 41st St. side was lowered to the seventh floor; both changes were within the mandatory building requirements.

There was one contingency. Hood believed provision should be made in any tall building for light and air. He had learned that plans were under way to raze the Commercial High School, adjacent to the News Building site on the west; and erect a new Board of Education office building. He proposed that The News give up a 25-foot strip on the west side of its lot; and that the Board of Education be asked to code 25 feet on the east side of its property; so the resulting throughway would assure both buildings of light and air.

Getting the Board of Education to do anything was a formidable job. Fortunately again, The News had the man for the project. Clarence Worden had started as a copy boy with the Brooklyn Standard Union 14 years before, advanced by stages to reporter. He was 17 when he enlisted in the army in 1917, served in France with the 470th Aero Squadron; returned to his old job after the war. In 1924 he came to The News as City Hall reporter. Worden was a favorite of Mayor Walker, and president of the Inner Circle, the association of City Hall reporters, and had considerable standing with the politicians. In June 1928, he had been appointed secretary of the Board of Education; but after four months decided he was not the man for the office, and came back to The News. Worden was tapped to prevail upon the board to relinquish the 25 feet desired.

He did his homework well with Hood, prepared a presentation showing that sacrificing the strip on the side of its lot was to the permanent advantage of the Board of Education Office building. The approval of 30-odd officials of the Board of Estimate, various commissioners, and officers of the Board of Education was required. Worden started with the officials he knew, got introductions and appointments with those he had not known before. And in two months secured the 30-odd letters of recommendation required. The measure to use the school property for the throughway was formally approved.

After watching Worden's operation, Holliss concluded that he was wasted as a reporter, made him his assistant. Worden's victory, however, proved to be pyrrhic: After the 1929 market crash, the plans for the new office building for the Board of Education went down the drain. Forty-one years later, the same old Commercial High School is still doing business at the same old stand. There is no 50-foot throughway but The News has its private 25-foot alley.

When the model got final approval, Hood took a pair of calipers, summoned his secretary, and called off the dimensions of the structural steel required, without waiting for blueprints.

Hood wanted the building to be faced with Bedford stone. Patterson opted for white bricks. F. M. Flynn, then Barnhart's assistant, and liaison man with the architects and contractors, relates that the decision to use white brick caused a crisis; there were not enough white bricks available, nor were they being made in quantity. Eventually, three brick-making companies were pressed into service to supply the quantity needed.

* * *

Barnhart had been planning the plant floors ever since the decision to build had been made. He was assisted by Lockwood, Greene, engineers. The general contractor was Hegeman Harris Co.

In the next two months, models of the production floors to be occupied by The News were prepared, scale one-half inch to the foot, at the Brooklyn plant. Scale model presses were supplied by Goss, linotypes by Mergenthaler. Wooden blocks, to scale, represented other machinery. Mechanical department heads, engineers, draftsmen, electricians, and technical representatives of suppliers spent hundreds of hours determining machine positions, materials flow and traffic, provisions for gas, current, water, ventilation. This thorough pre-planning is commonplace today, but was radical 40 years ago. It made installations and moving easier, reduced changes after moving to a minimum.

In January clearance of the site was started, finished in February. Foundations followed, then the steel erection, with masonry a few stories behind. The building proper was finished in November, and nearly three months were required to install the machinery. Barnhart had planned to start the presses on the night of Feb. 21, 1930. Some delay on the part of the electricians necessitated overtime around the clock for a week. Offices were moved on Feb. 22. The front of the building and the lobby proper were not to be completed until midsummer.

Above. Globe and meteorological instruments in lobby of News building are popular with New Yorkers and out-of-town visitors.

Left. Bust of Joseph Medill Patterson, founder of The News, is the work of C. D. Batchelor, who knew him well during the years when Patterson was editor of the paper and Batchelor editorial cartoonist. Funds for the sculpture were raised by voluntary contributions from News employees. Bust was placed in News building lobby June 26, 1948.

Marble facade over main entrance to News building was inspired by Abraham Lincoln's observation that God must love the common people since he made so many of them.

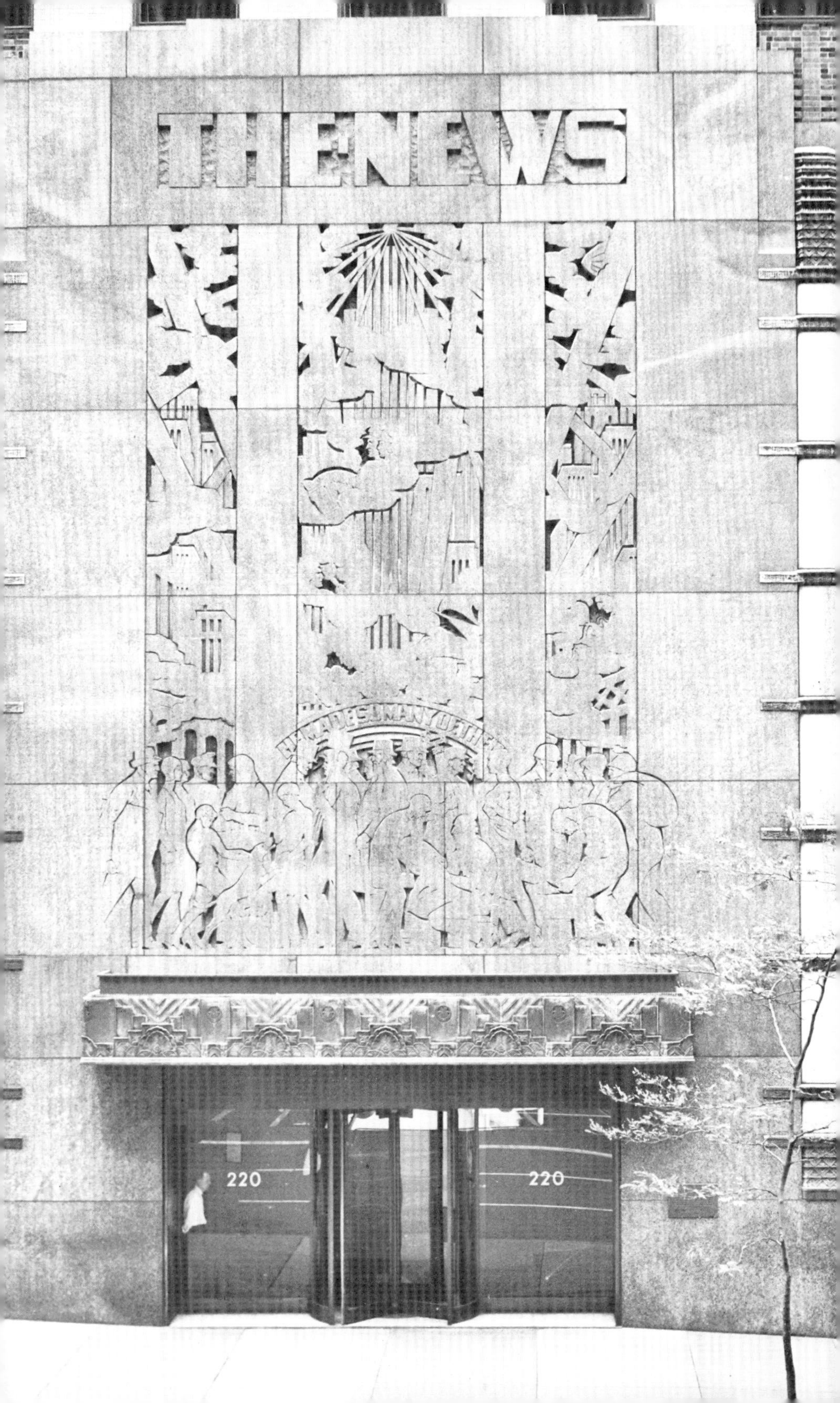
THE NEWS
220
220

The lobby was Patterson's idea. It was circular in shape, walled with panels of black glass, four stories high. In the center, a globe 17 feet in diameter turned slowly in a well of concentric steps, lighted from above and below. In the terrazzo floor, bronze compass points are inlaid, with mileage from New York to the principal cities of the world. Wall panels hold a barograph, wind direction and velocity indicator. A circle of clocks show the time in every time zone. The daily state of the weather is marked on a glass overlay above a map of the United States.

* * *

Another unusual feature, also inspired by Patterson, was the massive marble facade over the main entrance of the building on 42d St. It consisted of eight carved panels with THE NEWS at the top and at the bottom over a group of working men and women, the legend, HE MADE SO MANY OF THEM. These words are attributed to Abraham Lincoln who is said to have observed, "The Lord must have loved common-looking people—He made so many of them."

* * *

The executive suite was on the eighth floor, advertising occupied the sixth, seventh and eighth floor of the tower area, editorial the plant area of the seventh floor. The composing room, engraving and stereotype departments occupied the sixth. The pressroom occupied the equivalent of the second and third floors, a novelty at the time, as presses because of their weight were usually in basements. But this unusual placement of the pressroom followed the gravity flow of casts from the sixth floor to presses on the third, to printed papers in the first floor mailroom where they are bundled for delivery and loaded on trucks.

* * *

The second floor, incidentally, is where the rolls of newsprint are moved on tracked dollies, and fitted into the reels of the presses.

The fourth and fifth floors were left unfinished, and used for paper storage.

Despite all the careful advance planning, the growth of the paper rapidly made inadequate certain facilities of the new building. Within two years, an additional line of presses was being installed.

The building's principal tenants, aside from The News itself, were and still are today the United Press and International Paper Company. While

1930, after the market crash of the previous fall, was not a year for optimism, nevertheless by June, 1930, the building was 85% rented.

* * *

The News building, with its clean lines, the stark shaft of white brick, bare of any ornamentation, was striking and beautiful in contrast to many of the *moderne* structures that went up in the next decade. Almost 40 years old, it is still striking and beautiful. On weekends and in summer, it continues to draw a horde of camera fans who crouch on the curbstones in the block to get their own individual perspective. It is another monument to Raymond Hood; and Hood was to have few more, because he died in 1934 at the age of 53.

The building did a lot for the paper. It was substantial evidence of its success and prosperity, commanded the respect and admiration of the business community. The building also did a lot *to* the paper, as well. The single elevator at Park Place was the funnel where you met everybody; or if you didn't meet them, you knew who they were. On 42d St. the smallness, the sense of community have gone. People sought their floors by different banks of elevators. Sometimes a year would elapse before you ran into somebody you had seen every day at Park Place.

* * *

There is a story, probably apocryphal:

Time, Inc. had its offices in the Bartholomew Building, on the north side of 42d St. just east of Third Ave.

One day in 1929, Henry Luce observed with amusement a sign which had gone up across the street, announcing that on this site the Daily News would erect a $10,000,000 building.

Amused, Luce is supposed to have asked: "Where would that outfit get that kind of money?"

Some of his better informed associates told him.

Luce sent for copies of the paper and began to study it, and continued to study it the rest of his life. The epithet "gumchewers' sheetlet" disappeared from Time's columns. The News was recommended reading for the Time staff, for its terseness and brevity, for the bite and cleverness of its captions, and for its occasional significant and telling photographs. For years Luce thought of publishing a newspaper in New York. Within the last decade a Time study group surveyed the newspaper situation here, and is reported to have arrived at the conclusion that 10 years and X millions of dollars would be required, with no assured payoff point.

* * *

As the circulation of The News continued to grow, more and more trucks were bought to cover the delivery men's routes; and the use of horses and wagons declined. The paper at one time had three rented barns and a rented downtown garage. Shortly after the erection of the News Building, a garage was located at 23d St. and the East River. In 1946, however, the paper had to vacate the premises to permit the building of Peter Cooper Village, a huge apartment complex.

Land was bought on 41st St. and 40th St. between Second and Third Aves. Five dwellings were demolished to make room for a garage. A year later, more old buildings were torn down and The News garage extended from 41st St. to 40th St. The first structure was one story, with a ramp that permitted trucks to park on the roof.

* * *

Jim Brown had been having trouble with paper rolls delivered by ship; and finally gave up a Hudson River site for one on the East River. Over the years he fought steadily against labor racketeering. In one instance, a half-unloaded ship had to sail to Philadelphia to complete the unloading for delivery by rail. On Aug. 7, 1947, when newsprint was still rationed, a fire in the Kennedy trucking premises downtown cost The News 2,000 tons of paper which was badly needed.

Brown had planned a newsprint terminal over a long period. In 1951, a waterfront site was secured in the Red Hook section of Brooklyn, and the terminal erected. The building roughly covers a square, about 330 feet on each side. It had dock frontage, and a rail siding; and a storage capacity of about 32,000 tons.

When Brown retired in June 1961, he was succeeded by Robert C. Lundin. August Hempel, who had come to The News in 1929 as a secretary to F. M. Flynn, had been Brown's assistant; and remains today as an advisor.

In 1947, also, an additional floor was added to the plant wing to provide space for WPIX, the television station started by The News. A 300-foot antenna was erected above the tower; it was in use less than two years, as WPIX joined other stations using a common antenna system on the top of the Empire State Building.

By 1957, many departments of the paper and News Building tenants were in need of more floor space. An 18-story wing was built east of the original tower; and five stories were added to the plant wing. The garage had added stories, and was connected with the plant by a bridge across Forty-first St. at the third floor level. In the upper section of the garage air conditioning machinery was installed. Running the conduits through the old building was an enormous job; walls were pierced, ceilings removed. The days were filled with the noise of the workers, and plaster dust was tracked over the floors.

The architects for the new wing were Harrison & Abramovitz, successors to Hood's original firm. The addition provided another 270,000 square feet of floor space.

The new wing, the extra stories added to the plant section and garage, and the air conditioning plant cost $20,000,000—about two and one-half times the cost of the original News Building in 1929.

Part III

A great editor once wrote: "The '20s were a fool's paradise—the '30s were a fool's purgatory. In the '20s economics were unsteady, the social system was rotten and men lived carefree and gay and thoroughly enjoyed their lousy world. In the '30s we scuttled economics and reformed the social system. It was the decade of the great despair."

Great despair, unquestionably, to the nation and much of the world but not to The News. To The News it was a decade of physical, fiscal and editorial growth, of reaching for maturity, of coming-of-age. In 1930 the daily circulation was 1,299,000, the Sunday circulation 1,624,000; not bad for a paper that had started from scratch a little more than 10 years earlier. In 1939 the daily circulation had become 1,841,000 and the Sunday circulation 3,363,000; not the least bit bad for 10 years of struggle in a fool's purgatory.

The News started the despair decade by moving into its new building on Feb. 22, 1930. It celebrated its 15th anniversary in 1934 by paying off the $4,000,000 mortgage on the building and looking ahead questioningly:

"How about the paper's future? People grow up, grow mature, grow old, and die. So do newspapers. We don't know whether we have reached our peak, or whether we'll grow stronger yet. Nobody can tell."

The News grew stronger yet.

The '30s were dominated newswise by Franklin D. Roosevelt and the New Deal but the decade was studded with other great stories, at home and abroad. Because it was more mature, The News covered them well. It was writing history.

'THEY HAVE STOLEN OUR BABY'

Soul-searing as they were for millions, the Tragic Thirties—the second decade of The News—had high spots as well as low spots, particularly for those who worked for a newspaper which was thriving and gave a percentage of salary (depending on length of service) as an annual bonus instead of cutting wages every few months, as most of The News' competitors were doing.

The NRA (National Recovery Administration) with its symbol, the Blue Eagle, calling for a reduction in working hours and other benefits designed to put more men to work, came into being with massive ballyhoo in the middle of 1933, three months after the birth of the New Deal, and was expected to do some powerful pump-priming.

But The News had already adopted part of the NRA code before the eagle was hatched. Patterson believed, as Roosevelt did, even before he took office, that one logical way to fight the depression was to provide more jobs and one way to do that was to initiate a five-day week.

Early in 1932 Patterson suggested informally that employes working the six-day week (except union men, who were covered by contracts) take an extra day off with a one-sixth pay cut. That idea didn't seem to generate much enthusiasm so, after mulling it over for awhile, the publisher installed a five-day week without pay reductions. The paper said it would report on the results at the end of the year.

"By and large, the new system has worked well . . ." said an editorial the next New Year's Day. "There have been occasional hitches here and there—key men, for instance, being off two days a week and losing contact to some extent. But there has been a correspondingly valuable training of understudies; and maybe—who knows?—the sight of the understudies in the wings has spurred the energies of the overstudies. 'Twas ever thus, or almost ever . . .

"A few of the top salaries have been reduced somewhat, so that more people could be hired in places where the work could not be staggered. You can't, for instance, run six elevators with five elevator men or six trucks with five truck drivers.

"Less than one-half of 1 per cent of salaries—and those the higher ones—have been reduced."

When Roosevelt went on the air July 24 to urge all employers to sign and abide by the NRA code and to convince the public it should patronize only those businesses which flew the NRA emblem, The News said it was a great speech and urged compliance—having already warned that "either it works, or we all go to hell."

"But there are sure to be sticking points. One of them has cropped up in The News organization of about 2,000 employes. Except in the building department (where the situation is being corrected) and in the delivery department (union), The News employes are within the blanket code. Our 150 newspaper delivery drivers, however, work 80 hours a week at $80 a week (including overtime). This is newspaper custom in New York. The men themselves would rather handle all of every night's editions at $80 a week than go on the blanket code's 40-hour week for less money.

"Yet to halve their work time would necessitate practically doubling our delivery force. There would be trouble for us—inexperienced men, routine altered, new shifts of foremen, and so on—and there would be less pay for the men now earning $80 a week. But more men would be put to work, and purchasing power spread to 150 men who now have no purchasing power and are a drain on the community's resources."

The News was certainly more than cooperative with New Deal plans—the NRA gave it a pennant for good work—but Patterson was not one to be pushed around. The NRA had asked a number of newspapers, including The News, to run a full-page ad, free, explaining its principles. Also it asked for a two-year subscription—likewise for nothing.

Both requests were turned down. The News was in business to make money, Patterson explained curtly, and would therefore be foolish to give away valuable space or copies of the paper.

But a month later The News carried a coupon-pledge on page 3 in which the signer agreed to patronize shops that flew the NRA emblem. The pledge was to be sent to The News Information Bureau, NRA section. Thousands sent or brought them in and received a Blue Eagle for their own.

Some newspapers had asked exemption from NRA on the ground that reporters were professional people and Patterson editorially derided them. When the Newspaper Guild was formed, he said he couldn't blame reporters and rewrite men for organizing.

"Nor can we see how the papers can avoid taking their own medicine. They criticize Henry Ford for not signing the automobile code; they urge the President to use the Big Stick on the coal barons; they exhort the public to sign NRA consumer pledges. If, then, their own workers organize to press demands for compliance with the spirit of the NRA, how can the papers complain?"

When the NRA was killed by the United States Supreme Court on May

27, 1935—because a couple of Brooklyn brothers named Schecter had presumably killed and sold a sick chicken in their poultry market—Patterson called in the chairman of the Newspaper Guild unit of The News.

"I want to sign an agreement with the guild to keep the five-day week," he said. The guildsman was astounded. All publishers, including Patterson, had insisted that the guild deal collectively with the Publishers Association. "I'm not being eleemosynary," Patterson continued. "The fact is that The News can afford to do this but the other publishers will be hurt. I want to put them on the spot."

Milton Kaufman, the executive secretary of the New York Newspaper Guild, was summoned by phone and rushed over in a cab. The agreement was drawn up, typed, signed and hung up on a bulletin board in less than an hour. It didn't really mean much but it was the first break in the publishers' solid front.

The Depression itself, of which all this was a result, produced many interesting phenomena, not the least of which was the march on Washington by bonus-seeking veterans of World War I. It occurred in June, 1932, and was covered by Dick Lee, who was still at work for The News when he died at 80 in 1968. In his dispatches Lee referred to himself as correspondent with the B.E.F. (Bonus Expeditionary Force).

Vice-President Charles Curtis wanted to call out troops to patrol the capital but Brig. Gen. Pelham D. Glassford, superintendent of the Washington police, said he could handle the situation. How well he did so is recalled by Joe Costa, who was there with his trusty camera for The News:

> "The veterans set up camp on the banks of the Potomac and steady rains turned the area into a quagmire, somewhat similar to that which plagued a much more recent group of Washington visitors —the Poor People's March. Things were rather static for a while and during that period Capt. Patterson, as we always called him, visited the encampment several times. He trusted his reporters but he preferred to see for himself how things were going.
>
> "Washington was in the throes of what would be called an urban renewal project today. Several blocks of buildings had been condemned and demolition had already started. Many of the marchers established themselves there, building shacks of sheet tin, linoleum, pieces of wood, anything they could find that might form some kind of habitation. The area was dubbed 'Hooverville,' after the President, and the same designation was given to shantytowns around the country.
>
> "After a while Superintendent Glassford told the leaders of the bonus march that the men would have to vacate the area, as the

demolition work had to continue. The marchers, who had become decidedly embittered by this time, refused to leave and the police were ordered to carry them out bodily, as has been done so often of late during civil rights protests.

"This was the sort of thing I had been waiting for and I managed to get some good shots. At the first lull I hurried to the airport, unloaded the glass plates in a porter's closet—working on the floor after having first stuffed some towelling under the door to make it light-tight—and shipped them back to the office via plane. Then I reloaded my plate-holders and hurried back to Hooverville.

"The battle had been renewed, this time in earnest. Out of the debris that littered the place the marchers had picked up pieces of pipe, two-by-fours, jagged sticks and such and were fighting as viciously as they ever had on the wartime front. The police were outnumbered and, since they were under strict orders not to use their weapons, had to run for their lives. I had been concentrating on operating my camera and when I looked up I discovered that a barrage of bricks which I thought was meant for the police was being aimed at me. I rapidly joined the cops in undignified retreat."

Nevertheless it had been a very successful day for Joe. The picture pages of The News the next day were devoted exclusively to his photos, which were among the best ever taken of a clash of that nature.

On July 21 President Hoover gave the bonus army two weeks to get out of town and assigned Gen. Douglas MacArthur to see that the order was carried out. Another battle started on the day of ejection but it was an unequal struggle. Tanks and tear gas were used by the troops, who then set fire to the veteran's shanties. Only a deep scar in Hoover's career remained.

* * *

Since the early '30s were the heydey of the bootlegger and the gangster, violence of another sort was far from rare. One of the members of the underworld most frequently shot at—so often that a favorite sobriquet was The Clay Pigeon—was Jack (Legs) Diamond, a sort of favorite of The News who deserves mention. The center part of the name was earned as a boy because he could outrun any cop who caught him lifting a package off the back of a truck.

Diamond, starting as a bodyguard and gradually muscling in on other racketeers, had been a colorful local character for some time but attained international fame in 1930 when he arrived in Belgium while touring to avoid questioning in the murder of an upstate innkeeper. Belgium heaved him over the border, where he was picked up by 30 German cops and sent back to the U.S.

Several News folk had come in more or less intimate contact with Legs. John O'Donnell had done a series on his career. Bob Conway had covered one of his trials. Tom Cassidy had spent a cold and miserable week at Acra, N.Y., where Legs had been a target for the fifth time as he stepped out of his "castle" there.

And Grace Robinson had an interview with him. Ishbel Ross, in her book, "Ladies of the Press," tells how it came about:

> "Jack Diamond sent for Miss Robinson when he was on trial in federal court on a liquor charge. He had read some earlier stories she had written about him. Then, when he saw that she was covering the federal trial, he sent a message by an indirect route that he would like to be interviewed by her.
>
> " 'Don't let anyone know who I am, for I will be thrown out,' he warned her. 'Come to this hotel and ask for Mr. Jones.'
>
> "Miss Robinson went to a well-known commercial hotel in mid-town New York. She found him looking ill and nervous. He presented his bodyguards to her, mumbling the names of the strange assortment of thugs who filled the small hotel room. They were all deferential to her. Diamond ordered them out of the room. Then his wife, Alice, came in. She fussed about, rouging her cheeks and doing her hair.
>
> " 'Go on up to the roof where it's cool, honey,' he suggested. And she went.
>
> "Miss Robinson was now left alone with him. He locked the door and took careful observation out of one window. He seemed to be in constant fear. The waiter came. Supper was served. They ate and drank. He was anxious to propitiate Grace. He held up a copy of her paper. It carried a banner line about him.
>
> " 'See,' he said indignantly. 'These jurors walking through the lobby see just that. I want you to know I'm not a bad fellow.'
>
> " 'Mr. Diamond, you say you are not a gangster,' said Miss Robinson boldly. 'Just what do you do for a living?'
>
> " 'Well, that's a little difficult to explain,' said Diamond evasively. 'I can't describe how I make my living. I couldn't now, anyway, because I'm afraid the government is going to investigate income taxes.'
>
> "Miss Robinson could get nothing out of him. She fell back on the stock tintype questions—what size shoes he wore, what food he preferred, what he read, how he passed the time. Jack worked hard

to make a good impression on her. He fancied himself as a smart and scholarly fellow. He was far from being either. The interview made an entertaining Sunday story."

At 34, Legs was handsome and rather virile despite his many punctures. His wife was demonstrably fond of him despite his preference for the company of Marian (Kiki) Roberts, an auburn-haired curvaceous showgirl. When Kiki decided to turn herself in in October, 1931, her surrender (she was a supposed accomplice in one of Legs' crimes) was arranged through John O'Donnell, who had an exclusive on the story.

But closest of all to Diamond was night editor Gene McHugh, who really liked underworld people and was the confidant of many of them, including Legs. The acquittal of Diamond on a kidnaping charge in Albany was a page one headline on Dec. 18, 1931. After the first edition, one of McHugh's underworld friends phoned him and told him Legs was due to be killed, probably that very night. Gene passed the word around the office but nothing happened.

When the last edition went to press at 4 a.m., McHugh got into a card game in the studio with George Kenney of rewrite and Jack Kenny, the night picture editor. The bonus checks were to be given out the next day and they had decided to wait until the cashier's cage opened.

About 8 o'clock Bromley Gray, the lobster-trick city editor, rushed in waving a bulletin from the wire room. "You were right, Gene," he said. "They got Diamond this morning in an Albany rooming house!"

McHugh's first thought was to get out an extra, even at that unprecedentedly late hour. Fortunately he had just the right editorial help there in the room with him but how about mechanical? He raced down to the pressroom and found everybody gone but Charley Everitt, a machinist. "The boys will be waiting up for their Christmas bonus," he told Everitt. "Go to every neighborhood ginmill and say I need enough pressmen and stereotypers for an extra. Step on it!" Unbelievably—and probably for no one but their friend McHugh—they began to scraggle back.

Upstairs George Kenney had started to write the story from clippings and Albany dispatches. Jack Kenny found enough cuts (photo-engravings) in the library to make up new front and back pages. Since printing crews worked around the clock, there was no difficulty in getting the stories and captions set in type. By 8:35 the miracle was accomplished and the presses were rolling with a new page one banner: "DIAMOND MURDERED." Even the delivery department dug up enough help to race the extras to the middle of town before the first afternoon papers reached the newsstands.

McHugh was too excited to sleep but he hardly expected Patterson's reaction. When he arrived at the office and learned of the feat, Patterson gravely informed McHugh that he had violated a long-standing agreement between morning and afternoon papers about encroaching on each other's time and a somewhat similar contract with the news services. But how Patterson really felt was made clear a few days later in a bonus and a salary raise. The "Legs" extra is still a city room legend. Paul Gallico romanticized it in a memorable magazine story called "Scoop."

* * *

The decade had begun rather prosaically in the area of stimulating news. Very little of real significance occurred in 1930 but The News, which had developed the knack of making minor local stories sound important, rarely seemed dull. It was an era in which any airplane crash which resulted in a fatality was worth front page recognition. Human-interest stories predominated. A page one banner proclaimed "Murder On Roof For $50."

There were frequent references to love cults, a term which had been pretty well preempted by the Tantrik Love Cult of the Omnipotent Oom at Nyack, N.Y. Breach-of-promise suits, long since outlawed, were a steady diet. Headline writers had a favorite name for them—heart balm.

Reporters and rewrite men had developed a vocabulary which was becoming a part of the language—sex fiends, white slaves, love nests, torch murders, cry-baby bandits, bobbed-hair bandits, sugar daddies, on the spot, trigger men, gun molls, crooners, gang slayings, muscling in, death pacts, torso murders, dream girls, tiger women. Blondes were svelte, brunettes were vivacious. Each new crime launched its own phrase. Somebody was always popping up who had some connection with the Hall-Mills case, the Arnold Rothstein shooting, the Kip Rhinelander divorce, the Dot King murder and other instant-recognition happenings.

An almost daily byline on page 2 or 3 was Alfred Albelli, who covered the courts for The News then and still does today. Fresh out of Yale, he joined The News in 1925. While a member of the college boxing squad, he became acquainted with Tommy Manville, the marrying asbestos heir whose didoes made his name a household word in the '30s and '40s. Albelli was involved one way or another in Manville's acquisition of most of his 11 wives. He wrote a book-length series, "Tommy and I," in 1967 for the National Edition of The News.

The 1930 disarmament conference in London was covered rather consistently, both in the news columns and editorially, but as a rule it required little short of a national catastrophe or a revolution to justify publication of a story from abroad. An exception were the foibles of King Carol of Romania and his fiery girl friend, Magda Lupescu, which received frequent mention.

Feats of aviation also made headlines. On March 1 a plane carrying pictures of the Scott-Sharkey fight to The News set a new speed record (9 hours, 57 minutes) from Miami to New York. Alicia Patterson, one of the publisher's daughters, who had been a pilot for only two years, set a record from Philadelphia to New York on Oct. 28 and from Albany to New York three days later and both accomplishments were recorded on page 3.

Capt. Dieudonne Coste of France (with a co-pilot) rivaled Lindbergh with the first flight from Paris to New York. This was noted in the issue of Sept. 3, 1930, which also carried the first report of the disappearance (still unsolved) of Supreme Court Justice Joseph F. Crater, who came close to dominating the news for the rest of the year.

Unemployment became the subject of many stories and editorials. One editorial said "this writer" had walked down the Bowery and had been accosted only once, which seemed to indicate that "professional bums are laying off to give tragic newcomers a chance."

An editorial on Oct. 31 was headed "Buy Now and Bring Prosperity Back." It was the beginning of a campaign which was pushed vigorously for the remainder of the year. Prizes of $10 were offered for the best "Buy Now" slogans carried each day. These were displayed in boxes on every available page of the paper.

A girl reporter, Peggy Burrows (she didn't last long; maybe was scared away by this assignment), spent a night in a flophouse to "taste the horrors of the jobless" and wrote a series about her experience.

Locally the chief concern of editorials in 1930 was parks and playgrounds. Nationally it was Prohibition. The News was vehemently pro-wet. Its hopes for repeal of the dry law were bolstered in December when Federal Judge William T. Clark, in Newark, ruled that the 18th amendment never legally became a part of the U.S. Constitution. The paper warmly approved of his decision, although noting that it seemed to have no effect on enforcement.

On Christmas Day The News reported on the whereabouts and recent activities of some whose stockings had been well filled with publicity during the year—Texas ("Hello, sucker!") Guinan and Belle Livingstone, both proprietors of fashionable speakeasies; Edward (Daddy) Browning, who was still battling with Peaches, his Gander Girl; and oft-married Peggy Hopkins Joyce, the most famous of the girls around town.

The elaborate lobby of the brand new News Building was not completed until July 22, when the 12-foot globe (on which so many countries have since been added and subtracted) began to revolve for the first time and the many meteorological instruments became functional.

Guided tours through the building, starting every hour from the Information Bureau off the lobby, began late in the year. A new garage was bought; The News commercial portrait studio was started. It had to give way before long to new demands for space, but a lot of mothers were made happy with pictures of their offspring.

Certainly 1930 had not been a happy year for the country or the world and, if anything, 1931 was even worse. The News, still reluctant to give much space to events beyond the seas, linked a lot of the world's headaches together on May 27 and reported, in a single story, with a paragraph devoted to each country, that there had been violent political unrest the day before in Finland, Spain, Italy, Poland, Greece, Romania, Hungary, Burma, China, Honduras and Cuba.

* * *

But there was one story that year which, for a while, at least, seemed to justify the attention being paid to hometown happenings.

About mid-afternoon on June 8, 1931, city editor Harvey Deuell sang out to a rewriteman: "Take this call from Frogge. He has something about an unidentified girl found on a beach. Two or three paragraphs, maybe."

John Frogge was a staff correspondent based at Mineola, L.I. He reported that the body of a young woman had been washed up by the surf that morning at nearby Long Beach. She was wearing only a dress and stockings. Her body was badly bruised and her brown hair was matted with salt spume. An identification was hoped for soon but until then . . .

The identification was established about an hour later by her stepfather, a manufacturing chemist. Her name was Starr Faithfull and she lived with her parents and a sister in an apartment three doors from Mayor Walker's home. She was described as beautiful and cultured. She had been missing from home for three days. Her stepfather spoke mysteriously of a diary that had been destroyed.

By 6:30 p.m., when the first (Pink) edition of The News went to press, the "two or three paragraphs" had become a smash on page 3, a streamer on page 1 and the start of a deluge of words that swept other news aside in New York papers for the next month. How Patterson felt about it is clear from this editorial in the Sunday News of June 14:

A GREAT MYSTERY STORY

Leave it to life to outdo the writers of murder stories when life gets good and ready.

The case of Starr Faithfull, washed up dead on the sands of Long Beach last Monday morning, proves that reasonably ancient thought anew.

That name alone—Starr Faithfull—starts your imagination spinning plots, dreams, poetry, depending on what kind of imagination you possess. As a name for the central figure in a grisly drama of death, Starr Faithfull is so good that an acute friend of ours at first suspected the whole affair of being a press agent stunt. But it's real.

Since the body's discovery, the case has been unfolding by the minute: detective story material, romance, color, human interest, commentaries grim and footnotes gay on this age we live in, and almost every other kind of food for your brain and your emotions that you care to name.

The young woman lived a double life—a Jekyll-Hyde existence. About this, her mother and stepfather (who always saw that she should have chemically tested gin to drink) knew something, though not all.

She had an "alibi" in Boston, Francis Peabody Hamlin of one of the first families of Massachusetts, who was and is admired and trusted by the family. Starr used to say she was going out with this Dutch uncle almost every time she set out for a party.

Starr Faithfull knew men on great steamship lines, nobles in London (nobles chiefly of the pipsqueak variety, it would seem, but nobles none the less), Manhattan playboys, Boston politicians—a whole galleryful of these times' most colorful human products.

Somehow, for reasons which prosecutor Edwards of Nassau County swears he will clear up in time, the beautiful girl was done to death. How? When? Where?

Whether those questions are ever answered or not, the story remains a real-life mystery story of the first caliber. Some of the characters even look and talk like people out of a Conan Doyle, Edgar Wallace or J. S. Fletcher thriller—Stanley Faithfull, stepfather of the deceased girl, descendant of Oliver Cromwell; Sylvia Tucker Faithfull, Starr's sister, who likes to be called Tooka, and wonders wistfully whether her picture will make all the papers; Frank Wyman, Starr's father, from Boston.

Like Vivian Gordon, Starr Faithfull kept a diary. She wrote in the diary that she had "experienced every sensation life holds." Poor little girl, she overlooked the greatest experience a woman can have—motherhood.

The mystery may be solved. Or it may join the company of the Hall-Mills and other unsolved mysteries. Whatever happens, it is one of the most thrilling and sinister true stories life has seen fit to write in many a month.

Besides a Dutch uncle and a father in Boston, Starr had a frequent escort, Andrew J. Peters, that city's millionaire ex-mayor. Peters, who was married and the father of six boys, was Mrs. Faithfull's second cousin-by-marriage and had often entertained Starr and her sister Sylvia Tucker when they were young.

The diary that Stanley Faithfull had said was destroyed was found by a Nassau County detective behind books of philosophy and psychology (including Krafft-Ebing) in the Faithfull apartment. In it the 25-year-old Starr detailed 14 years of sexual escapades, beginning with her seduction at 11 by an "AJP," who was often mentioned but only by the initials.

AJP, of course, was Peters but the Faithfulls didn't find that out until 1926, when Starr returned from a two-day binge with Peters and told all. Faithfull obtained photostats of registrations in various hotels where Starr said she had been with Peters and turned them over to a Boston attorney. The following year Peters paid the Faithfulls $25,000 "for medical services and to restore Starr to a normal outlook." In return the Faithfulls signed a release to protect him from further claims.

There were many other sensational developments in the case, including Starr's infatuation with the ship's doctors on a couple of Cunard liners, but when, after a month of headlines, her death remained as much of a mystery as ever, most papers turned to other news.

The Starr Faithfull stories in The News had been written by Warren Hall, who was hired from California in 1928 to write captions but had been shifted to rewrite. Patterson, however, was reluctant to drop such a promising story and had what he considered an ace in the hole.

The ace was Sidney Sutherland, author of a book named "Ten Real Murder Mysteries," who had been under contract to Liberty and still had some time to serve after the magazine folded. Patterson assigned Sutherland to make a study of the Faithfull case and write a series of articles for The News. He was told that reporters would help him investigate any new angles that might turn up.

In the hope of finding something for the reporters to work on, The News offered a reward of $5,000 for information which would clear up the tragedy. Nothing very startling developed but the series by Sutherland, "Nationally known magazine writer and analyst of famous crimes," began late in July and continued well into August.

Father Faithfull was outraged. He filed a criminal libel charge and Patterson and Sutherland were brought before Magistrate Overton Harris. Hearings, tersely and objectively reported in The News, were held sporadically for months and it was not until April, 1932, that the magistrate dismissed the charge.

Meanwhile the Faithfulls had brought libel suits against all New York newspapers and the three major press services. Stanley asked for $350,000 damages from The News and his wife wanted $100,000. When the first of these 19 suits—Stanley vs. The News—finally came to trial in St. George, S.I., in February, 1935, The News found itself in an unexpected bind.

The legal aspects of founding The News had been supervised by Weymouth Kirkland, a former law partner of Col. McCormick. Patterson in the early 30's asked Kirkland, whose Chicago law firm represented the Tribune, to establish a New York branch to represent The News. Kirkland found this would be impossible but he put two young lawyers, Marion B. Stahl and Stuart N. Updike, into a suite in The News Building and gave them his blessing.

It had been understood that Harry Van Aken, who defended Patterson and Sutherland in the criminal libel action, would head the defense in Faithfull's civil suit but at almost the last minute he withdrew. Kirkland came on from Chicago, assimilated the massive intricacies of the case in a week, and became trial counsel with Updike as the attorney of record.

Kirkland advised against any news coverage of the trial, which may have been a wise legal move but deprived readers of a share in one of the most fascinating courtroom battles of the decade. Arthur Garfield Hays, a savage bulldog of jurisprudence whose name was a household word, represented Faithfull and was pitted against Kirkland, a dapper little fox terrier who always aimed for the throat.

Each session of the trial, which lasted more than three weeks, opened with a parade headed by Hays and his nephew, Allan Hays, followed by an entourage of porters with handtrucks piled high with filing cases of records and exhibits.

The judge, John McCooey, son of a Brooklyn political boss, often appeared to be dozing but whenever a question arose, he could cite the last ten questions and answers verbatim. He had a biting sense of humor which was a boon to the defense.

At one point Hays was holding a copy of The News up before the jury to exhibit a page 1 headline which he considered particularly damaging to his client. The back page headline, recording the victory of a famous horse in a famous race, faced the bench. Judge McCooey said: "Mr. Hays, when you finish would you be kind enough to look inside and let me know what Twenty Grand paid in the Futurity?" The outburst of laughter completely ruined whatever point Hays was trying to make.

When Mrs. Faithfull was on the stand, Kirkland asked casually if she had ever written her husband's Boston lawyer about the $25,000 Peters settlement. She said she hadn't. In the next half hour of cross-examination Kirkland rephrased his question half a dozen times, each time getting a denial. Her husband, she insisted, handled the affair without her knowledge.

The lawyer turned and made a motion toward his counsel table, where sat Updike; another young attorney named Tom Sunderland (who recently retired as board chairman of the United Fruit Co.) and the legendary legal investigator, Tom Cavanagh. They quickly produced photostated copies of a letter which were passed out to each member of the jury, the judge and finally the witness.

"Mrs. Faithfull, do you recognize that signature?" Kirkland asked.

The letter, which had been obtained from the Boston attorney, showed that she was deeply involved in the transaction and when she reluctantly acknowledged its authorship, her effectiveness as a witness was completely destroyed.

Updike, who presented the direct evidence, and Kirkland, who conducted the cross-examinations, managed to prove or disavow most of Faithfull's allegations: that The News had implied he murdered Starr, had said he concealed evidence in the case, hampering the authorities, had said he and his wife lived on Starr's earnings as a prostitute, had called him a blackmailer.

But one of Sutherland's statements was too hot to handle: that when Stanley and his wife had married each had believed the other was wealthy and that they had been woefully disillusioned. This, as Hays pointed out to the jury, was libel per se.

Nevertheless Kirkland, in his fiery summation, so thoroughly denounced Faithfull as utterly dishonorable that the jury brought in a verdict for the defendant. Mrs. Faithfull's suit was settled for $17,000, less than it would have cost The News to try it.

Next at bat was the Mirror. Stahl & Updike gave the Mirror's counsel every record it had on the case, including a complete transcript of the trial, and Hays lost again. The other suits were either settled for minor sums or dropped.

Stuart Updike is dean of The News law firm, now a huge concern known as Townley, Updike, Carter & Rodgers. Kirkland died in 1965 in his 87th year. As Patterson half anticipated in his editorial, the Starr Faithfull case has joined the company of unsolved mysteries. But he had done his best to make it otherwise.

* * *

There has to be a new edition of The News every day and every effort is bent to make it as lively and informative as possible, but newspapermen really live on the hope and expectation that the next hour, the next minute will provide the big one, the story they can recall for the rest of their days. Such a one did arrive, out of the blue, on the night of March 1, 1932.

In The News city room, that evening there was a threat of boredom. About 9 o'clock Warren Hall and Robert Conway, who were at adjoining desks, began to play "Battleships," a paper game conducted in low-voiced concentration. The contest ended at 10:30 when Hall left to catch a train to his Scarsdale home.

Then a world-shaking story broke. While the game was going on, the most famous baby in the world, Charles A. Lindbergh Jr., was being kidnaped from the Lindbergh estate near Hopewell, N.J. Conway wrote this story that night and then became a semi-permanent resident of Hopewell. Hall, called in early the next day to write the story for the duration, didn't get home again for three weeks.

The curly-haired blond Lindbergh boy, 20 months old, had been put to bed in his second floor nursery at 8 o'clock. His nurse, Betty Gow, looked in on him at 8:30 but when she returned at 10 o'clock the crib was empty. She told the young mother, Anne Morrow Lindbergh, who was preparing for bed, and then ran downstairs to inform the father. Lindbergh checked the nursery, saw clay smudges on the floor and on a window sill, saw an envelope in a radiator grating, and said: "Anne, they have stolen our baby."

He had the butler call the police station in Hopewell and then he put in a call to the New Jersey State Police.

A friend of Thomas "Jeff" Burke, The News night city editor, was covering Hoboken police headquarters for his own independent news service. Reading the tape on the recently-installed interstate police teletype system, he caught the first flash of the abduction and immediately phoned Jeff.

Conway had his overcoat on and was headed for the elevators. "Hey Bob," Burke shouted, "come back here!"

"He told me the Lindbergh baby had been kidnaped," Conway remembers. "I said, 'You're kidding.' He said, 'Like hell I am. See if you can check it.' "

Conway called the home of Mrs. Lindbergh's parents, the Dwight Morrows in Englewood, N.J., and got a busy signal. He was acquainted with Morrow's sister, Alice, who also lived in Englewood, so he tried her. She told him it was true; the baby was missing.

Moe Kivel was Burke's assistant that night. Harvey Deuell, the city editor, was sitting in a vacant slot on the city desk, working on a cabled report on the Chinese war sent in by Peggy Hull, whom he later married. Deuell immediately took over, keeping Burke and Kivel on the phones while Conway wrote a bulletin for a replate (an "Extra") and then started on the story. Gil Parker, the only other man left on the rewrite battery, was put to work writing background material from the envelopes of Lindbergh clippings.

When the two-star edition appeared at midnight, there were two columns of story about the kidnaping in large type on page 3, a front-page banner and a picture of the baby substituted for one of the four news photos on the first page. Every paper in town was scooped. But that wasn't all. The flash and the bulletins furnished by The News to the Chicago Tribune Press Service had gone to papers all over the country from 15 to 25 minutes ahead of all reports issued by other news agencies. Congratulatory telegrams poured in the next day.

Back at the big, rambling new house near Hopewell, Lindbergh had taken a rifle and gone outside to investigate. He was soon joined by the Hopewell police chief and his constable. They found two holes pressed into the reddish yellow clay directly beneath the southeast corner nursery window, and, some 60 feet away, a wooden ladder built in three sections. Where the middle and bottom sections joined, one of the rungs and a side rail were badly split.

The discovery of the ladder was announced in the final edition of The News. So was the disclosure by Mrs. Morrow that her daughter was expecting another child and might be seriously affected by the shock. A note had been found, believed to be a demand for ransom. A mysterious car, seen near the home, had been driven away at high speed. Troopers had thrown up road blocks at all important crossroads.

The story ran on and on, covering all of pages 3 and 4 and part of 6. A picture of the baby took up all of page 1 and there were pictures on the back page and a full page of pictures inside—all these, of course coming from The News library.

While all this was causing feverish activity in The News plant, Deuell was deploying his troops like a general. He called Stuart Rogers' home in Red Bank, N.J., learned Rogers was in a speakeasy in nearby Rumson and dispatched him to Hopewell from there.

Walter Kelleher called in to report he had taken some excellent pictures of a bus crash on Transverse Rd., in Central Park. "Forget them and come in at once," he was told. Half an hour later he was on his way to Hopewell in a car. Tony Marino wanted to unload a story about a shooting. "Hurry to police headquarters and cover for George," Moe Kivel told him. "Deuell has sent George (Moe's brother) to Hopewell."

"I had flown to Penns Grove, N.J., with an office boy to get shots of a fire that threatened to destroy the town," recalls Walter Ranzini, now picture assignment editor. "Dick Lee came down to write the story. After a tiring day, I sent my negatives in by a boy and Dick gave his piece to Western Union and we took the ferry to Wilmington. We checked into a hotel, phoned the office, had a late dinner and were ready to flop into bed when the phone rang.

"When Moe Kivel told me the Lindbergh baby had been kidnaped, I wouldn't believe him until Deuell got on the phone. 'Get cracking,' Deuell said. We got a train to Princeton, rented a car and arrived in Hopewell about 3 a.m."

Alfred Albelli wandered into the office from the Broadway beat and was immediately sent to Newark on a hunch by Deuell that New York gangsters, recently driven across the river, had made the snatch. He stayed there three months, buying drinks, frequenting gambling joints, looking for a tip. His final expense account was $7,500, promptly cut in half by editorial auditor Mike Feerick.

Called into the office from his nearby apartment, Jack Miley telephoned his bride, Norma Abrams, who was covering a murder trial in Poughkeepsie. He told her he was leaving for Hopewell and Deuell added: "Tell Norma to be here tomorrow morning." She spent the next few weeks camped in a car outside the Morrow home with photographer Eddie Dowling.

"Every paper had a car there," Norma recalls. "There was a feeling that the ransom might be paid there."

"The bartender at the speakeasy where Deuell located me was a former state trooper," says Rogers, who retired five years ago as night city editor. "He closed the place up and drove me to the Lindbergh home like we were flying. I was the first newspaperman there. I got what I could and phoned it in from Gebhart's in Hopewell. On the way back to Lindbergh's we almost ran into a car containing Marty McEvilly. He had come from the office and was the first photographer there."

It was fortunate that the kidnaping tip came in before Conway left the office. He had covered the birth of the baby and knew the Lindberghs. Furthermore, he had recently talked to a friend who had visited the Hopewell mansion and described it in detail. The next day he was sent to Hopewell, where he spent many busy weeks.

The Lindberghs, like Deuell, believed the abduction was the work of gangsters. They authorized the kidnapers to deal directly with two underworld characters, Salvatore Spitale and Irvin Bitz. The extensive real estate holdings of Spitale and Bitz included a speakeasy on the ground floor of a four-story building on 41st St., directly behind The News building.

Late one night Burke and Tom Cassidy, idly looking out of a window near the city desk, saw a light flash on in the speakeasy's top floor, which had a skylight. The ransom deal must be going on right under their eyes! They hurried downstairs, crossed the street and made their way to the roof of the adjoining building, which was the same height.

"You get the cops," Burke told Cassidy, "I'll keep an eye on them until you get back."

Crawling across the roof, Burke reached the skylight, tried to rub off some of the grime and suddenly crashed through. He grabbed a support in time to keep from falling directly on top of a startled couple making love in an unused room.

Burke pulled a few glass splinters out of his hide and went back to his desk. Poor paunchy Cassidy, who probably hadn't run 100 yards in 10 years, wasn't so lucky. On his dash to the nearest police station he collapsed and spent the next couple of days in a hospital.

There was rarely a dull moment in the Lindbergh case. An elderly intermediary, John F. Condon, known as Jafsie, paid $50,000, to "John" in a Bronx cemetery; Gaston B. Means bilked Mrs. Evalyn Walsh McLean of $100,000 which he assured her would bring the baby back; John Hughes Curtis, a shipbuilder of Norfolk, Va., vowed he was in touch with the kidnapers who were on a boat.

Rogers and Lee were sent to Norfolk on the Curtis story. Lee believed Curtis' tale might be authentic. Rogers phoned Deuell to say he was convinced it was a hoax (which it turned out to be). This difference of opinion resulted in a fist fight and Rogers was called back to the office.

On May 12 Col. H. Norman Schwarzkopf, head of the New Jersey State Police, summoned reporters to the Lindbergh garage, locked the doors and told them the Lindbergh baby, apparently killed when the kidnaper fell from the broken ladder, had been found in a shallow grave four miles from the house. Gov. A. Harry Moore, meanwhile, had given the news to a politically-connected Associated Press reporter, so the story of this denouement, to Deuell's great annoyance, carried an AP credit line.

Most of the $50,000 given to "John" had been in gold certificates, which went out of circulation a year later. The FBI issued a list of the serial numbers. One of the wanted bills was used on Sept. 15, 1943, to buy five gallons of gasoline at a Manhattan gas station. The two attendants jotted down the license number on the bill. When the driver was arrested and charged with the Lindbergh kidnaping, they were heroes.

Gene McHugh and Curley Harris did a little abducting on their own. They waltzed the two attendants off to a hotel and entertained them regally for two days while the other papers were looking for them.

The trial of the accused kidnaper, Bruno Richard Hauptmann, was covered by Marty Sommers. Bob Conway and Grace Robinson were in Flemington, N.J., to help him. Every paper and wire service wanted to be first with the verdict. Like some of the others, The News had arranged to receive a signal from an attendant as soon as the jury had reached a decision.

Conway was in the courtroom balcony and Joe Austin, a telegrapher, had set up a key in the hallway just outside the balcony door. A code had been arranged so no eavesdropper could function. If the verdict was guilty with the death penalty, the message to the office would be "Sommers will file new lead." If the jury recommended mercy, it would be "Robinson will file new lead." If not guilty, "Conway, etc."

The signal came and Conway wrote the "Sommers" message and slipped it under the door to Austin. Soon The News presses were rolling out the word that Hauptmann faced the chair.

Some minutes later, but still ahead of the official verdict, the Associated Press bulletined that Hauptmann had been convicted with a recommendation of mercy. Max Annenberg wanted to stop the presses but Deuell, wisely this time, insisted his staff must be right, and for good reason.

Joe Costa, possibly the greatest newspaper photographer developed during that era, tells the story of one precaution taken by Deuell, in addition to the code used in the Conway message, to insure against any mistake. Here is Joe's account:

> Equipped with a radio transmitter built into an ordinary briefcase, I located myself at a window of the courtroom, which was jammed to capacity. We had an office directly across the street, where the picture assignment editor, McEvilly, was stationed with a radio receiver. He had an open telephone line to The News office, with a rewrite man parked at the other end.
>
> It was winter time, and cold, fortunately, so that I was bundled up in an overcoat. I used the overcoat to cover the briefcase, and also to cover my body up to my chin. Thus, I was able to speak into the microphone with the coat serving as a sort of canopy.
>
> As the judge, jury and opposing counsel came in, going through all the usual courtroom formalities, I kept up a running description, which McEvilly was instantly relaying to the office. A second or two after the jury foreman spoke the word 'Guilty!' the verdict reached the city desk, which apparently already had it.
>
> I kept a running description going while the judge was discharging the jury and performing all the formalities that go with the rendering of a verdict. Unfortunately, I kept at it a little too long. By that time

the courtroom was pretty well cleared, and a suspicious deputy came over to inquire what I was doing. I said, 'Not a thing,' but he insisted I had some kind of radio on my person. He took my briefcase and put it to one side, and I was taken to another room to be searched. Of course, they found nothing on me personally. Meanwhile, the transmitter was still in operation, and McEvilly, aware of what was going on, closed up the shop across the street very quickly and departed.

The late Dorothy Kilgallen was covering the story for Hearst, and she had taken a perch also on a window sill, leaving the window slightly ajar. Her plan was to drop a note containing the verdict to a confederate on the outside. But a court attendant, spotting the open window, closed it and locked it securely, and poor Dorothy was unable to carry out her plan.

So The News was first on the street with the verdict, an accomplishment considered highly important in those days. Today it would probably be greeted with a yawn, since TV viewers would have been acquainted with it some time before the paper reached the newsstands.

Elaborate preparations were made to be first on the street with the Hauptmann execution. After several last-minute reprieves, the prisoner was due to meet his Maker the night of April 3, 1936. A guard signaled from the prison roof to a News reporter on the ground who waved to another who was waiting in a window a block away with an open phone to the office.

The headline and story had been set, cast and plated on the presses. The moment the man at the office end of the open wire shouted "He's gone!" Deuell phoned the pressroom: "Let 'em roll!" The papers spewed into the mailroom, were loaded on the waiting trucks and in a few minutes were being snatched from newsstands all over town.

It was a clean beat on the wire services . . . five minutes . . . ten minutes . . . fifteen minutes . . .

Lowell Limpus, who was on the desk that night, recalled later:

"I had taken a frantic call from Trenton. There had been a mistake. 'He's gone' merely meant that Hauptmann had left his cell for the electric chair. There was plenty of time for a reprieve before they turned on the juice.

"I hated to tell Deuell. When I did he just said 'Let's go to my office.' There he rubbed his chin meditatively, probably thinking of his own fate as well as Hauptmann's, and then he said: 'Lowell, let us fall to our knees and pray to a Divine Providence for the early extinction of one of our fellow men.' "

The presses were stopped but it was too late to retrieve the papers. After a wait that seemed like eternity, the official word came through that Hauptmann was dead. The day was saved but it was a day Deuell never forgot.

* * *

On March 4, 1933, when Roosevelt was sworn in for his first term as President the nation was in a dreadful state. Even Republicans admitted that.

The stock market crash of late 1929, which sent a number of erstwhile millionaires leaping to death from skyscrapers, was followed by a period of unparalleled economic distress.

As time wore on, the situation did not improve. It deteriorated. Savings were wiped out, jobless men sold apples on the streets, and public employment offices, opened by State and Federal governments, were thronged with men and women hoping against hope to obtain jobs even half as good as those they had lost.

There were runs on banks. Hundreds failed. Farmers were losing their farms through foreclosures. Manufacturing sank to unbelievable lows. Coal mines closed or went on part-time operations. Steel mills let their fires go out. The railroads were hard hit. Not a few conservative citizens even began doubting if their beloved capitalist system could survive.

In addition to the Lindbergh kidnaping, the Roosevelt landslide and the bonus riot in Washington, the top stories of the previous year had been voted by editors to be the collapse of Samuel Insull's financial empire, the Japanese invasion of Manchuria, the solo transatlantic flight of Amelia Earhart, the imprisonment of Al Capone, the Ghandi hunger strike in India and a couple of crimes—the Massie case in Honolulu (in which the mother of a supposedly ravaged girl took vengeance into her own hands) and the mysterious death of Smith Reynolds, the tobacco heir.

The outstanding news events of 1933, again according to editors, were Roosevelt's recovery program, the pre-inaugural assassination attempt made on him in Miami, the rise of Hitler in Germany, repeal of the 18th amendment, recognition of the USSR, the enforced bank holiday, the destruction of the dirigible Akron, a California earthquake, the war on kidnapers, and the U.S. departure from the gold standard.

The News had greeted the year with an editorial listing the top events of the previous year and adding:

> But the big question in the minds of practically all of us today is: "What will happen to *me* in 1933; to my wife, my children and myself?" Will the depression be lighter and jobs decidedly more plentiful 365 days from now? Or will times be worse still? And what

will either of those developments mean personally to "my wife, my child and myself."

That, nobody can foresee; and that's what makes New Year's Day so terrible if you're a pessimist, and so interesting and exciting if you're an optimist.

But there was little room for optimists as the decade wore on, except perhaps on The News itself. The depression did *not* get lighter and jobs did *not* become more plentiful. Ex-President Hoover attacked the New Deal, denounced the spending "joyride," saw "huge waste," warned against inflation and declared that taxes or "repudiation" were the only alternatives.

On the top of all the other troubles that plagued the land, vast portions of the Middlewest had been turned into dust bowls. Deforestation, intensive farming and a prolonged drought had lowered the water table and impoverished the soil. The condition was at its worst in 1934 and Fred Pasley, accompanied by photographer Walter Ranzini, was sent that fall on a tour of the stricken area.

Patterson, reading the Pasley reports as they appeared in the paper daily, wasn't exactly skeptical but he thought Fred's sympathetic nature might have influenced his reportorial judgment to some extent. As usual he decided to see for himself. Ranzini remembers:

Mr. Patterson flew to Omaha, where we met him in a rented car and started to drive toward Bismarck, N.D., where we had set up temporary headquarters.

Almost immediately we ran into a shower. Patterson smiled somewhat cynically, but we assured him it was far too little and too late. On reaching North Dakota he saw a green stand of corn, seven or eight feet high, beside the road. We pointed out that there were no tassels or ears on the stalks. The ground, we told him, was just dust. There would be no crop.

"Stop the car, please," he said. Getting out, he climbed a fence and started to dig with his hands. It was the easiest digging he ever did. He went through nine or ten inches of light dust before he hit anything resembling solid earth. There wasn't a trace of moisture.

Patterson rose slowly to his feet. "Let's get back into the car," he said. From then on he was sold on the dust bowl story.

After Patterson had returned to New York, Pasley and Ranzini were driving through the Bismarck area and stopped at a farm which seemed even more parched than most. They talked to the farmer, Henry Wetzel, while his wife and 10 children gathered around.

"We pray for rain every day but it don't do no good," Wetzel said. That gave Pasley an idea. "The folks back in New York don't realize how bad things are out here," he said. "You and the family just kneel down out there in that field and we'll take a picture."

The Wetzels trooped to the field and dropped to their knees but they were self conscious and didn't look very prayerful. Pasley wasn't very religious but he was resourceful. He knelt down, facing the family but out of camera range, and raised his clasped hands in supplication. "Now you do like I am and repeat the words after me," he said. Then he recited the Lord's Prayer, or a reasonable version thereof, and the Wetzel family, caught up in the spirit of the occasion, joined in as Ranzini clicked his camera. It was an inspiring picture that was reprinted many times.

Pasley may not have been the best reporter The News ever had but he was unquestionably one of the most prolific. He could write exhaustively yet entertainingly on almost any subject. Among the topics he tackled in the '30s:

Biographies of Legs Diamond; Herbert Lehman; Ella Boole (Prohibitionist); Billy Mitchell (famous flier); Fred A. Victor, state superintendent of the Anti-Saloon League; Mrs. Charles A. Sabin, a noted opponent of Prohibition; Bishop James Cannon Jr., head of the Anti-Saloon League; Ellis Parker, noted New Jersey detective; Samuel Insull; George (Machine Gun) Kelly; James Doolittle; Eugene O'Neill, et al.

Some of the other subjects Pasley covered, usually appearing in at least five installments, were: House of Barrymore; the NRA as it affected the automobile industry; financial condition of the principal cities of the United States by comparison with that of New York City; Japanese-American problems (from California, at the time the Japanese were invading China); the drought; the Depression as it affected the entire country; kidnapings; How it Feels to be a Down-and-Outer; the agricultural situation in the Middlewest shortly after New Deal reforms for farmers were being put into effect, American wines (after the death of Prohibition); firetraps in New York; Supreme Court decisions (the result of the Supreme Court's killing of the NRA); economic conditions in Great Britain and Ireland.

In addition, he did numerous local stories in between his various trips across the country and abroad. On the day that Dutch Schultz died of wounds as the result of a surprise visit by some of his enemies to a tavern in Newark, Pasley wrote a 3,000-word story of gang battles in the space of a couple of hours that could well serve as a capsule history of the underworld during that era.

The comings and goings of Fred were a subject of considerable amusement in The News city room. He believed in being fully equipped for the job, right down to the last suit of underwear, and the sight of Fred starting off on a trip, trailed by four or five copy boys bearing his suitcases, was a common one. One oldtimer insists that one entourage of Fred and his baggage boys, on their way to Grand Central Terminal, passed another group of boys toting Fred's luggage from Pennsylvania Station, where he had arrived that morning from an earlier expedition.

On some of his trips Fred had a companion—Patterson himself. Since JMP was always the epitome of the man in a hurry, these journeys were made by plane, and frequently, The News plane. On such trips all wore parachutes. During the course of one Patterson suddenly announced:

"I'd like to make a jump."

Not a word was spoken for almost a full minute. The next voice was that of the pilot, Duke Krantz.

"Mr. Patterson," he said, "you are my boss, but I am in charge of this airplane, and I forbid you to jump. You might get down all right but—" and at this point he surveyed Patterson from head to toe—"you're a big man, and the chances are that you'd break a leg."

A little startled, Patterson meekly nodded in agreement.

"However," continued Krantz, "there is no reason why Fred couldn't make it. How about it, Fred?"

Despite the fact that Fred always enjoyed his groceries to the limit, and was never known to refuse a drink except during a period when he was on the wagon, he, in addition to being short, was on the slight side. His weight probably never ran much above 120 pounds.

But jump? His shouted refusal wasn't even polite.

Pasley, who had been with the Chicago Tribune, came to The News in 1931. Patterson had promised not to hire him away but when he learned Pasley was in Hollywood, giving technical assistance in the filming of his book, "Scarface," the deal was off. At the end of the decade Pasley was assigned to the Washington bureau and his later career is told in another chapter. He died in 1951.

The 1930s hadn't been going so well for everybody. Hitler consolidated his power in Germany through Nazi blood purges and Chancellor Engelbert Dollfuss of Austria was obliterated. Samuel Insull, the dethroned utility czar, was chased halfway around the world, brought home, tried—and acquitted. John Dillinger, the country's No. 1 badman, was extinguished by the FBI. Lucky Luciano, the Mafia king of his day although he was merely called a vice lord, was convicted and exiled. A happier note was provided by the birth of the Dionne quintuplets in Canada.

A New York housewife named Nancy Evans Titterton was murdered in her apartment in 1936 by a rapist, a 24-year-old upholsterer's helper

Battered. C. D. Batchelor created this character in mid-1936. The near-naked former plutocrat appeared in many editorial page cartoons in that and following years.

who was trapped by a fragment of twine and a non-human hair. Readers of The News were not kept uninformed of the circumstances which eventually led the killer to the electric chair, and that may have prompted a letter which in turn prompted an editorial on March 31, 1937.

The letter, printed in the previous day's Voice of the People and reprinted at the top of the editorial column that morning, accused The News among other things, of "lurid sensationalism," and the editorial writer (undoubtedly Patterson talking through Maury) said managing editors were faced almost every day with the problem of what news a newspaper should emphasize. "An especially dramatic posing of the problem occurred Monday," he went on.

> Two big news stories broke. The United States Supreme Court reversed itself in the women's minimum wage law case, O.K.'d the Railway Labor Act counterpart of the Wagner Act, O.K.'d the Frazier-Lemke Farm Mortgage Moratorium Act, and again dodged a decision on the Wagner Act. And some person, at this writing unknown, murdered Veronica Gedeon, a model; her mother, Mary Gedeon; and their lodger, Frank Byrnes, under circumstances most atrocious but most interesting, in a Beekman Hill, Manhattan, apartment.
>
> Which story deserved the big headlines? Our managing editor decided to give both stories banner headlines on the front page—an unusual makeup for The News—but with top position and picture awarded to the murder story.
>
> We think he was right, even though most of our esteemed contemporaries played up the court story.

The esteemed contemporaries didn't remain aloof very long. Like the Starr Faithfull case, the murder of Ronnie Gedeon et al. was real big while it lasted and part of the reason was that she, like Starr, was young, beautiful and promiscuous—and had a name that rolled off the tongue.

The crime was discovered—on Easter Sunday—by Ronnie's father, an upholsterer who had become estranged from her mother after arguments about Mrs. Gedeon's permissive attitude toward her daughter. He had been invited to Easter dinner and found the nude body of Ronnie on her bed and the body of the roomer, who had been stabbed many times with a sharp instrument while he slept.

There was no sign of the mother but police, when they arrived, discovered her body under Ronnie's bed. Both women had been strangled.

The motive was not robbery. The only thing missing was an alarm clock belonging to another lodger, Mary Beacco, 19, who fortunately had been away for the weekend.

After an ex-lodger had been arrested and then cleared, the father became a prime suspect, not only because the household dog hadn't barked but also because the walls of the room in which he slept behind his shop were covered with magazine pictures of nude women and an elaborate mirror was poised above his bed.

Six days of intensive investigation produced no real clue and the police, in desperation, began to go through railroad station lockers on the theory that the killer, if he had left town, might have checked something there. It was a needle-in-the-haystack, one-chance-in-a-million search, but it paid off. In a Grand Central locker they found a valise which "ticked" and inside was the missing alarm clock.

Also in the bag was a numbered pair of blue denim trousers which were traced to a mental hospital and the number identified them as having been issued to Robert Irwin, 29, who had been a voluntary patient there three times.

Irwin, a divinity student who dabbled at sculpture, had been a previous boarder in the Gedeon apartment and immediately became the object of a nationwide hunt. Although his trail seemed constantly fresh, he eluded capture and finally, in June, surrendered to a surprised and delighted Chicago newspaper editor.

He said he had been "spiritually" in love with Ronnie's older sister, Ethel, and had dropped in at the apartment hoping to see her. Learning she had since married and left home, he became enraged and strangled Mrs. Gedeon. He waited several hours until Ronnie returned home and prepared for bed. Then he choked her to death and finally, fearing that Byrnes, the boarder, might somehow identify him, he did his third killing with the ice pick that he usually carried with him to carve on cakes of soap.

Irwin was sentenced to 139 years in prison but, a month later, was pronounced insane and transferred to Dannemora State Hospital at Clinton, N.Y., where, at this writing, he is still being held.

Often it is difficult to obtain pictures of a murder victim but Ronnie for a while had earned her living by posing for girlie magazines. On the day after her death a free-lance photographer brought in dozens of photos of her—all in the nude. The News bought them and an artist painted a discreet veil on those which were used. As they passed through the engraving and composing rooms they had a tendency to disappear. Even in the library they weren't safe. Today not one of them is left in her folder.

The News said goodby to 1937 with an editorial which noted that, for all our troubles, the rest of the world fared worse during the year than we did. "England and the Scandinavian countries were the only spots on the map whose brightness compared with ours." Anyhow, it had been a bright sports year. Don Budge had pushed the U.S. to victory in the Davis Cup tennis matches, War Admiral won the triple crown in racing, Sammy Baugh shone in "a new and great sport—professional football."

But then there was '38 with the Munich Pact, the McKesson & Robins scandal, and other unpleasantness, and 1939 with the most unkindest cut of all, the outbreak of World War II.

Until the hostilities started, at least, The News had managed to keep its sense of humor and its fondness for the ridiculous. Almost every day there was at least one story with a laugh in it and many of them were written by George Dixon, a transplanted Canadian who could treat anything flippantly, even a full-panoplied visit from the royalty he traditionally should have revered. When King George and Queen Elizabeth arrived in Canada in May, 1939, on their way to visit the New York World's Fair, Dixon was sent there to keep News readers in touch. Some of those readers must have been startled at the resulting page one headline:

NEWS REPORTER GABS WITH KING

The first page carried an AP wirephoto of the royal pair arriving in Ottawa and, with the caption "Hand That Shook King's," it also had a picture of Dixon's outstretched paw, which the library had been able to provide. And smashed on page three was the story, which began:

> "Your correspondent is about to have a cast made of his right hand for the Smithsonian Institute, to be preserved for posterity. This work-hardened paw, calloused by years of honest toil, has just shaken the hand of His Britannic Majesty George VI, King of Great Britain and Ireland and all the British Dominions beyond the seas, and the hand of Queen Elizabeth.
>
> "It was positively the first occasion that a pressman, as we are called in Dear Ol' Lunnon, ever had been presented to the present sovereign, and that goes double for Her Majesty. The setting was the reception room at Rideau Hall, residence of the Governor General of Canada, Lord Tweedsmuir.
>
> "Please reassure the boys from down under press No. 6 and in the composing room, however, that I will still continue to be the same democratic, lovable fellow they have always admired. Don't

> stand on ceremony with me. Just step up anytime and call me plain Sir George Dixon, K.C.M.G., K.C.B., K.C.V.O., O.M., C.V.O.
>
> "Note: This positively does not apply to copyreaders."

The story continued in the same vein but there was another on the same page with the unusual byline "Also By George Dixon" which treated the occasion with a modicum of decorum.

That was fun, but all in all it had been a rather grim decade—except on The News.

"Come on in. I'll treat you right. I used to know your daddy" Editorial page cartoon by C. D. Batchelor. It was published April 25, 1936. Awarded Pulitzer prize the following year.

THE HORIZON WIDENS

During the early '20's, one of the biggest headaches in the editorial department of The News was how to pretend that the telegraph copy (stories from out of town) was being handled properly without actually having to read it. The sheets of copy from the wire room were dumped on the city desk and whoever was stuck with the job ruffled through them and picked out anything that seemed important, leaving the final judgment to the news editor. At least 99% of it went into the wastebasket.

At that time The News was receiving out-of-town copy from two sources—the United Press and the Chicago Tribune Press Service. It had applied for membership in The Associated Press, but the consent of all other AP franchise holders in the area was necessary before this could be granted and there was at least one blackball.

In January, 1927, however, the picture changed. The News purchased the moribund Commercial Bulletin, a Wall Street newspaper which was an AP member. It paid $150,000 for the name, goodwill and equipment, none of which it wanted, and $350,000 for the AP franchise, which it seemed to want very much.

When the flood of new copy came in, it was too much for the city desk to handle. Besides, telegraph stories seemed of more importance because of the high price paid for the AP membership, not to mention the yearly cost of the service. H. Armand deMasi, a young but experienced copyreader, was put at a table in a corner. Provided with a couple of dozen spikes, an atlas and a few reference books, he became the first telegraph editor.

The gold-plated nature of telegraph copy didn't impress Ed Bean, who was the news editor. The right-hand column on page two was headed: "The NEWS in Tabloid." It contained summaries of the day's events—local, national, foreign and sports—each 15 or 20 words long. Half a dozen of these tidbits came from the telegraph desk, and that was often the total of the day's grist, which meant that the spikes on deMasi's table were loaded with assorted copy that might as well have stayed where it came from.

When telegraph stories got into the paper, they usually were from Chicago, which was the liveliest newspaper town in the country outside of New York, or from Hollywood, where movie stars were always making news. A week could easily go by without anything from abroad being published other than the tiny items on the second page.

After about a year, deMasi became an assistant city editor and was replaced at the telegraph table by Orville Welch, another copyreader. (DeMasi left the paper in 1929 and didn't return until 1961, after he had retired as head of the copy desk of the New York Journal-American. He still puts in a day or so now and then on The News.)

Welch was no more successful than his predecessor in selling his wares to the news editor but the job apparently had a little more significance because Hugh Schuck was taken from the copy desk to help one night a week in preparing advance copy for the Sunday paper and to replace Welch on Saturday, his day off.

The stirring of unrest throughout the world, signified by the Japanese invasion of Manchuria in 1931 and by the seizure of Argentina by rebels the year before, began to whet the interest of the Sweeneys as well as the Stuyvesants for foreign news. Tenold R. (Billy) Sunde, who had been head of the copy desk and was assistant news editor, advanced the idea of a separate telegraph desk with more help. So it happened that when Welch's health failed and he developed disorders from which he was to die, Sunde was given the job of telegraph editor with Schuck as his assistant.

When the Italians invaded Ethiopia in 1935, the concern of the reading public seemed sufficient to justify a Morning Glory edition, which went to press at 6 a.m. to take advantage of the time differential between New York and the battlefront. Schuck was brought in late each night to put it to bed. His orders were that even if no late news broke, the Morning Glory was to have a new page-one line on the war.

Civil war in Spain, which broke out in July, 1936, broadened the interest in European affairs, particularly when American volunteers began to get involved. The telegraph desk was active but still small. Sunde, Schuck and Harold Davis were the only regular members.

The first European correspondent of The News was Donald K. Mackenzie, a rather fabulous Australian-born globe-trotter who had been a major in the British Black Watch in World War I before becoming a combat pilot in the Royal Flying Corps. He was shot down in France but landed his plane safely despite six machine gun wounds in his abdomen. He had traveled widely in China and India before becoming a London newspaperman.

In the latter part of 1936, Mackenzie's dispatches from London kept The News and its readers on top of the rapidly-developing crisis over the determination of King Edward VIII to marry Mrs. Wallis Warfield Simpson, a twice-divorced American beauty. When the affair seemed to be nearing a head, Fred Pasley was sent to London from New York to provide additional coverage, and on Dec. 10 The News scooped all other papers in the city with the definite announcement that the king would abdicate that day.

The lead story, however, was written by David Darrah, a veteran correspondent from Chicago. The story was copyrighted by the Chicago Tribune-New York News Syndicate. Pasley had a scoop of his own, the revelation that one of Britain's foremost obstetricians had flown to Cannes, where Wallie was in seclusion, to "protect the romance from the blighting torch of scandal." There was a rumor in France that Mrs. Simpson was pregnant.

On the same page in the last edition was another story saying that the flight to France, as revealed by Pasley, had caused a flood of telephone inquiries to The News but local physicians had been consulted and readers could be assured that, as the head announced: "Stork Is Rare Caller At 40."

The telegraph desk was steadily gaining in importance and so was another News adjunct—the Washington bureau, to be considered later—but competition on fast-breaking stories was coming from an unexpected source. Radio, which first became a rival worth noticing during the Lindbergh kidnaping, was providing regular newscasts which often managed to score beats.

The News decided to fight fire with fire and employed Clifford Denton, an electronics expert. At first there was some indecision on how to use him but at the suggestion of the publisher and with the enthusiastic cooperation of the managing editor, Deuell, who was something of a radio buff, a radio reception center was set up which came to be known as the listening post.

Six 40-foot antenna towers arose on the roof of the 36-story News Building and the finest short-wave receiving sets obtainable were installed in five booths in a corner of the editorial department. Several capable linguists were hired, as well as a couple of men who understood the Morse code.

The first story on which the listening post worked effectively was the election of Eugenio Cardinal Pacelli as Pope Pius XII on March 2, 1939. By listening to a radio broadcast from the Vatican, the operator was able to report first that a new pope had been chosen, as indicated by the tell-tale smoke from the burning of the ballots, and then identify him.

But that didn't seem very impressive in 1944 when one of the listeners, Blaine McLean, reported in Newspix on the operation, which was still functioning well (it ceased after the end of the war):

"The first big story our listening post monitors got was Hitler's speech on Sept. 1, 1939, which started German troops moving on Poland. In

March, 1940, we got a scoop on the bombing of Scapa Flow. Another was the Germans invading Denmark, April 9, 1940, and then the invasion of Holland, May 10, 1940, and disclosure of the first new, or secret, weapon, May 12, 1940, during the capture of Liege Fort. A story no one else had until the next day was that of Paris being declared an open city."

He neglected to mention one of the biggest scoops, for which Peter J. Wallenberg, one of the interpreter-listeners, received a nice bonus. One of Pete's chores was to listen every night to the 11:15 Berlin broadcast. Promptly on time the evening of Sept. 21, 1941, he sent a note to the telegraph desk:

"Something has gone wrong in the Berlin short-wave radio station. Will keep you informed."

A little later there was another note:

"The news due at 11:15 hasn't gone on the air yet. At first, the same piece of music was repeated over and over to the accompaniment of considerable yelling. I can hear loud voices speaking in German, but cannot make out what they are saying."

His next note enabled The News to beat all other papers to the streets with a headline that covered all of page one and a story which started:

"Adolf Hitler declared war on Russia at dawn today and sent his troops marching into a campaign which smashes the 21-month-old Nazi-Soviet pact and threatens to revolutionize Europe's military and diplomatic alliances.

"The fuehrer's proclamation, as read by propaganda minister Paul Joseph Goebbels over the Berlin radio at 11:30 p.m. New York time and heard by The News, announced that German legions, flanked by the armies of Finland and Romania, had been sent against Russia in 'the greatest march the world has ever known.' "

When the war started, a war desk was set up as an adjunct of the telegraph desk but it was soon absorbed into the telegraph operation which, under Sunde's guidance, expanded until it seemed to dominate the city room. The News, which in 1930 frequently didn't carry a single telegraph story, now had room for very little other than dispatches from Washington and abroad.

Mackenzie, the man who had been covering the United Kingdom, resigned as news editor of London's "Daily Mirror" in 1940 and joined The News, eventually becoming assistant telegraph editor. After the U.S. entered the war, he was sent back as a war correspondent and his exploits in news gathering became legendary. During the invasion of Normandy he flew over the beaches in a B-26 and his eye-witness accounts of the landings were among the first and best to reach New York.

One of the many stories of Mackenzie's audacity was his "liberation" of a French town after Allied forces had broken out of the Normandy beachhead and were racing toward Germany. Mac and his sergeant-driver had outdistanced Gen. Patton's tanks and were first to reach the town. The Nazis, eyeing Mackenzie and his correspondent's uniform ablaze with campaign ribbons, were convinced he was a ranking officer and insisted on surrendering to him. Patton later commented with affectionate sarcasm, "I wish Mac would let me fight this war."

When Mackenzie left London to join The News, he was replaced, at his own recommendation, by Graham Miller, who became the first News correspondent with a guaranteed income. Later, as a staff member, Miller covered the fighting fronts and continued to serve in London for several years.

Another News war correspondent was John O'Donnell, who later became one of the most controversial members of the staff. His more or less accidental presence on the scene at the outbreak of hostilities will be discussed later.

Jack Turcott, who became Westchester County correspondent of The News in 1934 and then was transferred to rewrite, was dispatched early in 1942 to Australia and saw some of the toughest fighting of the Pacific war. Although he won no Purple Heart, he probably deserved one because he emerged with a permanent mastoid condition caused when his plane, under Japanese fire, dropped suddenly from 22,000 to 5,000 feet.

In 1944 Turcott made a brief return to carry out a confidential mission. A Presidential boom had been launched by admirers of Gen. Douglas MacArthur, the Pacific commander who was based in Melbourne. MacArthur wanted Patterson to advise him on whether to accept a "draft."

The answer that Turcott took back was quite specific: a soldier who left his post in wartime for a political campaign would not have the backing of American voters—or of The News. MacArthur stayed put.

After his return from the Pacific in 1945, Turcott served with distinction as labor editor of The News until his death in 1965.

The number two man on the telegraph desk, Schuck, was an old hand at wars. He had been a sergeant in World War I and attached to Allied forces in Russia during the early months of the Communist revolution. Later he was news editor of the Japan Advertiser in Tokyo.

He was packed off to the European theater in 1944 and covered the fighting fronts with outstanding zeal until he was bogged down with the Ninth Army 16 miles from Berlin. Disgusted, he returned to New York.

Sunde, who was becoming bored with directing a telegraph staff of 16 while others saw action, greeted him warmly. "Thank God you're back," he said. "Now I can go." Sunde covered the Quisling trial in Norway and later the war crime trials in Nurnberg.

Although the number of men on the telegraph desk dropped off after the war, it became even larger in a way because it was technically in control of the reporters covering the new United Nations. While the UN was at Lake Success, the bureau chief, Lowell Limpus, had a staff of 18, most of them editorial trainees. Now the UN bureau has only four men, headed by Wallenberg of listening-post fame, who returned to The News after serving as a staff sergeant in Guadalcanal and elsewhere.

Limpus too was technically a war correspondent—at least he wore the uniform—but his trip to Japan was in 1945 after the hostilities had ceased. He spent several months with the occupying forces.

While in the area he had lunch with a couple of visitors from home. Patterson had been invited to Japan by Gen. MacArthur, presumably to discuss revived White House ambitions. He accepted the invitation and took O'Donnell with him. Patterson did not disclose the topic of the conversations but The News never did support MacArthur for President.

When Limpus died in 1957, his self-written obituary, found in a sealed envelope, was printed in The News and reprinted by many other papers and news magazines.

"This is the last of the 8,700 or more stories I've written to appear in The News . . . It must be the final one because I died yesterday . . . Most of my adult life was spent working for The News, and I think I may claim that I helped a bit to build it. I wrote half a dozen pretty fair books ('Twentieth Century Warfare' among them) and one good one, espousing pacifism, for which I never found a publisher . . . I had a number of very fine friends, some of whom were very famous men . . . Mourning would be especially inappropriate because I'm off on the greatest adventure of my life . . . the biggest assignment any newspaperman could have."

Perhaps it should be mentioned here that Sunde, who died two years later, also was widely obituarized, although not by himself. He left the telegraph desk in 1954 to organize and become editor of the special features department, which, under his guidance, won many journalism awards for The News. He had been a president of the New York State Society of Newspaper Editors.

Like Topsy, The News' Washington bureau was never born, it just grew. In 1932 Patterson sent Dick Lee to Washington, perhaps with the thought of having a permanent correspondent there eventually, but after filing several stories and a few columns headed "Capitol Stuff," Lee returned to the office.

O'Donnell and Grace Robinson were assigned in March, 1933, to cover the Roosevelt inaugural. Grace was sidetracked on another Washington assignment but when O'Donnell tried to pay his hotel bill the following

Monday and return to New York, he ran into trouble. All the banks were closed, under FDR's bank holiday order, and the office couldn't send him any money.

"I became a Washington correspondent because I couldn't get out of town," O'Donnell was fond of saying.

While he was waiting, big news began to pop. Patterson decided that as long as O'Donnell was there he had better stay. Before long he was joined by his wife, Doris Fleeson, and their daughter, then a year old, whose arrival had almost interfered with Doris's coverage of the Jimmy Walker hearing.

"Capitol Stuff," the heading under which Lee had written, was picked up by O'Donnell at Patterson's orders, since it was his brainchild to begin with. The column began to be signed "By John O'Donnell and Doris Fleeson," and it was so popular with Patterson that a News stylebook, which specified the type size for double-bylines, specifically excluded that one, which was always larger.

Although there seemed to be no question about the permanency of the arrangement, O'Donnell was not officially listed as Washington correspondent on The News personnel records until Jan. 12, 1936, which undoubtedly meant that he received a substantial raise at that time. By the same token, he was not listed as bureau chief until March, 1942, although his authority had never been questioned. Another kitty-sweetening there too, probably.

O'Donnell and Fleeson, taking their daughter with them, sailed on July 26, 1939, for a working vacation in Europe. They put the little girl, then 8, in a school in Switzerland and began to tour the continent. They filed a story together out of Berlin on Aug. 24 and doubtlessly cabled Patterson a private prediction that war was imminent.

He ordered O'Donnell to London and instructed Fleeson to come home. She hurried to Switzerland, picked up little Doris, and caught the last boat out of France before the outbreak.

Over the years, the pair had operated the Washington bureau pretty much on their own with the assistance of "junior reporters"—Bill Murtha, Jack Purcell and others, none of whom stayed very long. While they were in Europe Fred Pasley, Bob Conway and Carl Warren took turns filling in but it soon became apparent that more permanent help would be needed.

Early in October, O'Donnell left London with a group of other uniformed war correspondents to cover the war from British general headquarters back of the Maginot line. It appeared he might be there for a long time.

Seven weeks later, on Thanksgiving Day, he made a radio address from Paris over a National Broadcasting Company hookup. This was the period known as the "phony war" and O'Donnell prophesied "that the hour of the inevitable armistice will arrive without the world witnessing a blood bath." The only good thing about the war, he said, was that we weren't in it. And he didn't forget where his own interest lay.

"News developments in Washington are more important than anything happening here," he told the country. "London and Paris editors put their own war dispatches on the spike to make room for news from our White House, particularly if it concerns the 1940 Presidential campaign."

He didn't remain at the front as long as had been anticipated. When Undersecretary of State Sumner Welles was sent abroad early in 1940 as Roosevelt's personal envoy, Miss Fleeson accompanied him and her husband joined her in Rome, from where they filed a joint story. They came home together, presumably on the same ship with Welles, although his arrival in Washington the same day was covered by Pasley and Warren.

At any rate, O'Donnell resumed control of the Washington bureau with a firm hand. Pasley remained and took over the White House beat. Guy Richards, Turcott and some others from New York helped out occasionally but the bureau remained substantially stable until the Japanese attack on Pearl Harbor.

Patterson arrived in Washington a couple of days after that momentous event (the reason for his visit is told in another part of the book) and decided expansion of the bureau was necessary. Pasley's bride of six months, the former Virginia Schmitz of the Chicago Tribune, was added to the staff. Bill Murphy was brought down from New York to be a sort of super-copyreader (that didn't last long—too many sacred cows), other help was acquired and for a while the place was a beehive.

The following February, Patterson and O'Donnell went to Hawaii to view the after-effects of Pearl Harbor. While O'Donnell was sending dispatches to The News describing the need for vast new armament and more troops "because Pearl Harbor and Honolulu can be raided again," and Rube Maury was quoting the dispatches in editorials, Patterson was cornered by rival newsmen on the scene.

He told them that Japan, not Germany, was the real enemy of the United States and that our battlefront was the Orient, not Europe.

The O'Donnells were encountering both ideological and domestic differences and in April, 1942, Doris obtained a Reno divorce. For a while, however, (she later, for many years, had a syndicated column in other newspapers) Doris remained with the bureau. When Frank Holeman arrived later in the year as a junior reporter, things had settled down quite a bit and the basic members of the bureau were O'Donnell, Fleeson,

Pasley and George Dixon (who also later had a syndicated column elsewhere).

Holeman was a vastly tall, vastly likeable stringbean who was called "Colonel" because his drawl was reminiscent of Kentucky. With eight other college graduates (a degree was a requirement then for a News editorial office boy), he had been interviewed by Harry Nichols, assistant city editor, in March, 1941, for a vacancy that needed immediate filling.

Each was questioned individually and one of the questions was why they would rather work for The News than for any other New York newspaper.

"Hell, I don't care what paper I work for," Holeman said. "I'm broke. I haven't eaten anything but peanuts since yesterday morning and I slept last night on a bench in Bryant Park. I just need a job."

His frankness so delighted Nichols that he was hired (pay, $19.20 a week) on the spot. It was a wise decision, because Holeman became not only one of the most memorable of all News copy boys (they were mostly girls during the war, and that gave rise to many complications that will never get into this book) but also one of the most popular Washington correspondents and served as president of the National Press Club in Washington.

Holeman had a jolting introduction to Presidential press conferences. With O'Donnell as a guide, he attended his first one in December, 1942, and saw FDR, as the conference was breaking up, hand an Iron Cross to Earl Godwin, a radio commentator, with the comment "When you see John O'Donnell, give him this."

Godwin was too embarrassed to do anything at the time but called O'Donnell later at the office and told him if he really wanted "that little decoration" as a keepsake, he could have it. FDR said later that he had made the award for what he considered "the unfairest story of the war."

Actually the column he referred to was completely innocuous. Meeting accidentally in Australia, Turcott and George Durno, a former INS White House correspondent who had become a captain in the Air Transport Command, had amused themselves by writing facetious notes to O'Donnell, some of which he had quoted. They said, among other trivia, that they had taken up flute and piccolo playing "just to keep our fingers nimble for the time when censorship lets us beat the keys of our portable typewriters."

Obviously that referred only to Turcott, since an army officer couldn't write news. Turcott also complained that Durno, a friend of the President, had drunk up all his Scotch.

"I'm completely bewildered by the President's action," O'Donnell said in a statement, but he really felt it had nothing to do with his jocular column about the boys in Australia.

Months earlier, in April, 1941, O'Donnell had written in The News that charges would be made in the Senate that the government was using U.S. ships and men to convoy lend-lease supplies to Britain. The morning it appeared FDR authorized his press secretary to denounce it as "a deliberate lie."

The next day there appeared in the Philadelphia Record, published by J. David Stern, an editorial commenting on the President's denial. It charged that O'Donnell was a Naziphile. "On numerous occasions," it said, "to all friends and barflies within hearing, he has broadcast his sympathy with most of Hitler's aims—such as destruction of the British Empire, suppression of labor unions, and liquidation of Jews."

The Record's editorial went on, exonerating Patterson from any responsibility for O'Donnell's views: "We do not criticize Mr. Patterson for opposing the President's policies. At a time like this sincere opposition to Administration policy is a healthy element in our body politic . . . But when opposition to the Administration resorts to what the President feels necessary to denounce as a 'deliberate lie' then it also becomes right and proper that the public know the kind of a man who is writing such news."

If the Record had waited another day before excoriating O'Donnell, the editorial might not have been printed because the convoying charges *were* made in the Senate, exactly as the story in The News had predicted. O'Donnell sued the Record for libel.

The suit became a long and involved action. About it O'Donnell wrote in 1947:

"The first trial ended in strange and peculiar circumstances. Just as this writer's side of the case was going strong, the defendant paper came out with a story about the trial which the trial judge held to be prejudicial to this writer's interests. Our side said we were willing to go along and take our chances. But the Record wanted a mistrial and the mistrial was granted—in other words, the defendant paper profited by its own admitted misbehavior.

"Then up came the second trial. By that time we were at war. Stern and others close to the Record were close to the White House. They wanted to win the libel suit, to get a jury verdict against the Washington newspaper writer who represented a paper critical of the Roosevelt road to war.

"The re-trial was scheduled to start the first Monday in January, 1943. At his last press conference before leaving the White House for a Hyde Park vacation, FDR pulled the Nazi Iron Cross deal.

"The writer was present in the White House at the scheduled press conference. At its conclusion, he and the others walked out, passing the Roosevelt desk and in full view. If FDR wanted to make the presentation of the Iron Cross in person he had his chance. But he didn't take it. He wanted publicity, not the possibility of facing natural resentment.

"He wanted to influence a jury and not take the chance of inflaming a temper. So he called back a reporter who had lingered after the conference had ended with the 'Thank you, Mr. President' and handed him the German decoration which he had received as a souvenir a few days earlier, with the off-hand sneer, 'Give this to John O'Donnell.' "

When the case finally reached a jury, O'Donnell was awarded $50,000 damages. In a post-trial poll, all jurors said they had read of the Iron Cross incident. The Record won a re-trial, resulting in a $25,000 verdict and another Pennsylvania court scaled that down to $8,000.

The paper, not wanting to pay even that much, incurred considerably more in legal expenses by carrying the case to the Pennsylvania Supreme court and then to the U.S. Supreme Court, which upheld the verdict in effect by refusing in 1947 to review the case. By then the Record had gone out of business.

O'Donnell was called a liar by President Truman, too, but he had to share the distinction with several other columnists. In an article written for a magazine in 1952, South Carolina Gov. James F. Byrnes had wanted to include a letter to him from Truman attacking columnists but the editors refused to use it because they were afraid the columnists might sue for libel.

So O'Donnell, in his column, printed the letter in part: "I never read or listen to Walter Winchell, Westbrook Pegler, George Sokolsky or John O'Donnell, or any of the liars for the simple reason that it just stirs you up to no good purpose." O'Donnell added: "After all, when you have won against such professional, high-grade, adroit and skillful liars as the late Franklin D. Roosevelt, for example, you shouldn't be lured into controversy by clumsy amateur insulters . . ."

Always rather frail (although he was a good enough high school baseball player to be taken to a Red Sox spring training camp, along with a guy named Babe Ruth), O'Donnell had a lot of trouble with his health in his later years. He retired officially as bureau chief on Sept. 1, 1961, after having been on extended sick leave since the first of the year. He died in December.

O'Donnell was succeeded as bureau chief by Ted Lewis, who had joined the group in 1944. When Fred Pasley and Virginia left in 1945—Fred going to The News UN bureau—Jerry Greene and Paul Healy were hired. Lewis, who carried on "Capitol Stuff" without rancor but with no stuffiness, was recently named chief Washington correspondent, a new post, so he could devote all his time to the column. Greene became bureau chief and now heads a staff of 15, of whom 10 are writers.

The copy turned out by those writers goes to the telegraph desk but it's only a drop in the bucket. The desk also handles the output of the Albany bureau and the UN bureau. Except for Long Island, it takes care of everything that comes in from any place more than 50 miles distant from Columbus Circle—and there are usually a couple of arguments a week with the city desk over whether some Podunk is 49 or 51 miles away.

When Sunde turned to special features, he was succeeded as telegraph editor by Schuck, who recently retired. Between them, they acquired an excellent array of foreign correspondents. Henry Maule sent The News an exclusive from London on the budding friendship of Princess Margaret and Capt. Peter Townsend and was hired to replace the retiring Miller.

Bernard Valery was the representative of a French newspaper at the United Nations when Sunde met him in 1950 and recognized his capabilities. Sunde sent him back to France for The News and he has since been the source of countless dispatches, many of them exclusive. He was recently made a chevalier of the French Legion of Honor and elected president of the Anglo-American Press Association in Paris.

Then there are Reynolds Packard and his wife, Eleanor. They had covered, mainly for the United Press, the Ethiopian War, the Spanish Civil War, the Italian Invasion of Albania. They ran the Rome bureau of the UP from August, 1939, until Italy's declaration of war on the U.S. closed it down. They stayed on in Siena, more or less as prisoners, until May, 1942—all of which inspired a well-received book, "Balcony Empire."

The Reynolds were in China in 1948, and involved in a complicated disagreement with the UP, when Sunde hired them to cover Rome for The News. They have been doing that ever since, and have scored innumerable beats inside and out of the Vatican.

An unknown named Joseph Fried called Schuck and asked if he could represent The News in Israel, where censorship was pretty tight. He cleverly slipped many items through. When the arrest of Adolf Eichmann was announced, no one was allowed to say where it had happened. Fried sent two seemingly innocuous messages to The News that afternoon. One mentioned the pampas. The other used the word gaucho. Schuck drew the obvious inference that the arrest took place in Argentina, and The News had another beat. (Wallenberg, an expert on Israeli affairs, was detached from the UN bureau to cover the Eichmann trial.)

Eventually Fried was in so much trouble with the censors in Israel that he asked to be moved. He and his wife were sent to India for a while and wrote from there that Vietnam was in turmoil and appeared about to explode. He was sent to Vietnam, arrived about the time the first monk set fire to himself and has been, it is generally agreed, the best correspondent on the scene ever since.

Russ Braley, in Germany, is another staff correspondent and there are special correspondents all over the globe, some of them with rather odd names. Prokash Jain, who had won an M.A. degree at the University of Missouri, sent an article from Delhi: "What America Means To Me." It wasn't suitable for newspaper use but Schuck suggested some changes, sent the revised manuscript to an agent, and a sale to the Saturday Evening Post made Jain happy, proud, a bit richer—and a News correspondent. A somewhat similar transaction converted Jaap Boekkooi into an excellent correspondent in Johannesburg.

Some members of the telegraph desk are sent out of town on assignments as are star performers of the city desk and all their copy is part of the 2,000,000 words handled daily under the direction of telegraph editor Sidney Feingold. The staff numbers about the same as at its wartime peak—16—and the operation is a far cry from deMasi and his spikes on a battered table in a dim corner.

THE PICTURE MAKERS

Down years once smoky with flash powder, now lit by an electronic light so swift and pure it can catch the most fleeting expression on a face and paste it down on page 1, men with cameras, wild men and quiet ones, sly as snakes and all a little daft, have been chasing around, cabbing and flying and climbing bridges, getting shot at and getting their rear ends frozen off, all with one obsessive notion, to advance the cause of The News. And this they have done, admirably.

There are now 51 photographers on the staff of The News, among them John Tresilian, 82 and ill at this writing but still on the staff, reluctant to leave it all to the young ones. In addition to the professionals, The News is also served by an unseen army of amateur photographers with a profound respect for "New York's Picture Newspaper," its ability to recognize a good picture and its willingness to fork over generously for one. One amateur on the British steamship Vestris made some of the most dramatic disaster pictures ever taken.

When Tresilian went to work at Park Place in 1921, as he recalls it, there were about half a dozen photographers on the staff. His memory is pretty good. There were seven "pioneers" on the job—Eddie Jackson, Frank Ryberg, Marlborough Sylvester (Lou) Walker, Henry Olen, who got the great picture of Firpo knocking Dempsey out of the ring; Otto Baumann, George Schmidt and Harry Warnecke.

There were four darkrooms, and the photographers did their own developing and printing. This is unheard of today in the building on 42d St. Now the photographer returning from assignment hands his roll of film to an apprentice who steps into a strange and circular black chamber and feeds the film into an automatic processing machine that develops and dries the roll in four minutes. Then the film goes to one of 11 men whose sole task it is to print. The News has two automatic machines and they provide large volume and, therefore, greater selectivity, but on occasion one will break down and if the other's busy, then an apprentice will go back to the old-fashioned method of processing film, first developer then hypo bath.

Tresilian & Company hit the street with equipment that would look downright antique compared to the fancy little fast-shooting 35-millimeter Nikons and Rollies and strobe lights that the boys carry now. The cameraman circa 1920 was particularly partial to the Ica, a German job. Compared to the Speed Graphic and Graflex, which were usually used for sports, the Ica was compact and slim and you could wear it from a shoulder strap. It took a 4 by 6-inch plate and was equipped with an f/4.5 lens and a leather bellows.

You got your light from flash powder, which sometimes had the impact of a mini-A-bomb. You carried it in a flask and fired it with a 4-inch-square flash pan and when you went out on an assignment with it, your equipage should have included bandages and salve. Powder was unpredictable and cameramen who went unburnt were rare. Twice in a single year, Al Willard suffered major burns of the face and arms. After his second mishap, he spent three weeks in a hospital before one of his eyes was declared out of danger.

Cameramen were allowed right in the courtroom during the sensational Hall-Mills murder trial in New Jersey, but flash powder was banned because it would interrupt the proceedings, and Tresilian and his colleagues had to use time exposures. "Usually," Tresilian recalls, "it was open—wide open—and then close."

A highlight of the trial came when Mrs. Jane Gibson, better known as "the pig woman," was borne into the courtroom on a stretcher to testify against the defendants. Tresilian stole a march on the other photographers by quietly going upstairs to the balcony and shooting from there. It gave him a much wider range, allowing his camera to catch both star prosecution witnesses and defendants, and it also gave him a beat.

The floors of the Park Place studio creaked and sometimes a rat would drop into one of the darkrooms to see how things were developing. If you think that's primitive, go back to July, 1919, when Eddie Jackson, the Illustrated News' first photographer, joined the paper. At that time the News picture studio was situated on the second floor of an abandoned Consolidated Edison powerhouse adjoining the Evening Mail in City Hall Place. There were no print driers. The studio's equipment consisted of tanks, trays and an enlarging camera and that was all. Finished enlargements were half-dried between blowers, then carried to the roof and through a window to The News art studio. Crude, yes, but the men who fed it with plates made up for its deficiencies.

Jackson walked into his first big one on Sept. 16, 1920, and what with having some precarious picture experience at the Battle of the Somme, he must have felt right at home. A horse-drawn butter-and-egg wagon came to a halt at Wall and Broad Sts., outside the U.S. Assay Office and across the street from the J. P. Morgan & Co. building. The wagon driver, middleaged and foreign-looking, jumped to the sidewalk and broke into a run. He saw a solitary street sweeper and yelled at him, "Beat it! Get the hell out of here!" Then he disappeared.

The sanitation man, who probably figured the guy was a nut, glanced at the clock in Trinity Church steeple and saw it was 11:59 a.m. He ambled off, not because the nut had yelled a warning at him, but because lunch time was calling. Presently Eddie Jackson headed for the area. He was on his way to make a portrait of some financial big shot at his desk. That's one he missed.

Because at 12:57 p.m. a dynamite bomb in the wagon blew up with a tremendous explosion. It killed 30 persons, injured more than 100 others. Jackson himself was knocked flat. Seconds later, he dazedly got to his feet and almost instinctively started shooting pictures. Subsequently a flock of other photographers descended on the scene, including several from The News. Police set up lines around the blast area, barring them from close-in shots. But Eddie Jackson was already loaded with them and a little later showed up at City Hall Place with the first on-the-scene pictures.

Less than a month later, News photographer Lou Walker came up with a major innovation in camera technology. We are indebted for this story to John Chapman, drama critic of the present-day News and once a good cameraman himself. "In early October that year," Chapman recalls in "Tell It to Sweeney," his informal history of The News published in 1961, "the Cleveland Indians and the Brooklyn Superbas were playing the World Series, which Brooklyn lost. Lou Walker had for some time been tinkering with a camera. He had fitted an extra-long base and an extra-long bellows to a 5 by 7-inch Graflex and had fitted it with a lens of 24-inch focal length. This made it practically a telescope, for the standard lens for the camera had a length of seven inches.

"Crouched in the stand of Ebbets Field, Walker made pictures of plays on all bases of the diamond which were large enough on the negative plate to permit astonishing enlargement. The News featured a double spread of these pictures daily and made a mystery of its Big Bertha, querying on page 1: HOW DOES THE NEWS DO IT? The mystery did not last long, of course, for other cameramen could see what Walker had made."

Actually the Big Bertha didn't stretch or contract like a real telescope although there are some that do this today. Be this as it may, Walter Ranzini, present picture assignment editor of The News, says the long lens provided improved quality, high speed and made the subject bigger.

Now, for sports, The News teams up a Nikon 35-millimeter or 120 Hasselblad with a telefoto lens. Some of these cameras are five feet long. The pictures they take are beautiful but one has a suspicion that John Chapman still favors Big Bertha over them, and no wonder. Big Bertha helped him mightily once.

When The News was only a few weeks old, a Chicago picture service proposed an alliance, but investigation showed it had little to offer. One idea that cropped up was to buy one of the established picture agencies but when owners learned the rich Chicago Tribune was involved, their price tripled. So, toward the close of 1921, a new photographic syndicate was launched under the joint ownership of The News and the Tribune. It was called Pacific & Atlantic Photos. Charles L. A. Mathieu, who was in charge of the picture services of International News Service, got it under way. Within a month eight branch offices were opened in the U.S. and later more were established in Europe. One of the men assigned to Europe for P&A was Chapman.

The Zeppelin ZR-3 had just been built for the U.S. by Germany under terms of the Versailles Treaty and it was to have its trial flight at the Zeppelin works in Friedrichshaven on the German side of Lake Constance. Chapman had hoped to cover the flight but was dismayed to learn that P&A was excluded because two other American picture services, International and Times Wide World, had bought exclusive rights. The exclusion was drastic. Chapman wasn't permitted to set foot on the vast Zeppelin grounds.

Then he thought of Big Bertha. He contacted New York and it was shipped to him. Here, from his book, is his account of what happened:

"With Bertha I stood outside the high wire fence of the Zeppelin works and made my pictures as the ZR-3 was manhandled out of its hangar and loosed for its first venture into the sky. It turned out that I got better pictures than the Times and Hearst men did, for they were too close to the monstrous dirigible to get good shots. And feeling comfortable about having the story sewed up, they made no particular effort to speed their pictures west to the Atlantic and on to New York. But I hired a small motor boat, crossed choppy Lake Constance on a stormy night, took an automobile to Basel and caught an express for Paris. Soon the pictures were processed in Paris and on their way to New York by steamer."

For the benefit of those who were very small when Chapman went boating there was no Wirephoto in that era. The fastest thing a man could find for transmitting pictures was the plane, which wasn't much. Photographers flew World War I surplus, beat-up Jennies, although the pilots were first-class. Clarence Chamberlain, one of the early trans-Atlantic fliers, frequently flew News photographers or their photographs. So did Lindbergh himself, prior to his sightseeing trip to Paris.

Before The News began operating its own planes, it rented them from Chamberlain and Casey Jones. The photographer rode in an open cockpit, the back one. Usually, if taking shots from the air, he faced backward with his knees on the seat, aiming his camera over the craft's tail. Once Chapman, on such a jaunt, converted his Ica into an aerial camera by attaching cardboard to it with rubber bands to keep the wind from blowing the bellows out of shape.

On another occasion, an eclipse of the sun was coming up and managing editor Frank Hause told Tresilian to shoot it from a plane; if he could get high enough, to eliminate haze. Tresilian proceeded to Teterboro, N.J., where Chamberlain did his flying. It was winter and there had been a heavy snow and the Jenny picked for Tresilian had to be dug out of it. Because winter would give that wide open cockpit an extra bite, one of the fliers at the field offered him his flying suit and the photographer accepted it with alacrity. It was warm enough; only trouble with it was that Tresilian was five-feet-six and slim and the flier whom the suit fitted was a six-footer and brawny.

"We got to 10,000 feet," says Tresilian, "but I didn't get the eclipse because something went wrong with the plane. Either the engine froze or we ran out of gas. Anyway we were over New York when it happened so we scooted for Jersey, where there was plenty of open land, and came down on a snow-covered meadow."

Fairly nearby ran a road but it led nowhere near Teterboro, where Tresilian's overcoat was hanging, so Tresilian gave up on the coat, thumbed a ride to the nearest railroad station, entrained to New York and then switched to the subway. His fellow riders must have gotten quite a treat; it was no doubt the first time they had ever seen a straphanger in a flying suit. Not that they saw much of him since he was almost buried in it.

One September day in 1925, photographer Martin McEvilly got a phone call at home from The News city desk. He was told to grab his camera and go to Governors Island in New York Harbor. A plane would be waiting for him. He was to go up in aforesaid plane and cover the sinking of U.S. Submarine S-51, 16 miles north of Block Island off the eastern end of Long Island. A big rugged man, Marty disdained overcoats in September, he had no idea of how handy one might be in a plane since he had never been up before. Arriving at Governors Island he got into the cockpit of the plane. He was given neither goggles nor helmet and the plane was scarcely aloft when McEvilly went into a quick freeze; he couldn't even get his eyelids open. The pilot landed him at Curtiss Field, Mineola, L.I., where he was furnished with a leather coat, goggles and helmet and also a bigger plane that could carry a lot more fuel. But even that fuel wasn't quite enough. The plane reached the site of the sinking, marked by a swarm of navy vessels, and McEvilly got several pictures and would have shot more but the pilot signaled that his gas was low. The plane just got back to solid ground. It made a forced landing among 20 cows grazing in a pasture near East Quogue, L.I.

While the pilot trudged off to rustle up gas, Marty had his hands full fighting off hungry cows who, it appeared, had a strange predilection for the dope on the plane's fabric wings.

Land photography had its rigors, too. Phil Levine, who ultimately became manager of The News studio, set up his camera one day less than 100 yards from the point where an army plane bombed an ice jamb in Port Jervis, N.J. Another time he and reporter George Lang were assigned to cover a Ku Klux Klan convention in Middlebush, N.J. The hooded ones chased Levine out of the hall, so he proceeded to shoot pictures of Kluxers roaming around outside. The outdoor Klansmen got sore, too, and went after him. Levine ran, caught up with Lang, and slipped him his plates, then they ran in opposite directions. The majority of the Klansmen chased Levine, so Lang got away with the plates. Levine managed to outrun his pursuers and rejoined the reporter at the office.

While The News was busy covering the New York metropolitan area, P&A was working the rest of the world and, because of all the geography it had to cover, it became exceedingly adept in the arts of fast travel. It studied every available form of transportation for ways to speed up the delivery of photographs.

Joe Wurzel, a relative youngster, displayed a genius for working out plans to deliver negatives and prints in the fastest possible time, using trains, ships and planes. He later became head of P&A's London bureau, and continued in that capacity after the P&A foreign operation was taken over by the Associated Press in 1931.

The New York Central's vaunted 20th Century Limited had long been considered the fastest train to Chicago. Then P&A discovered two other expresses that beat the Century by half an hour. P&A's favorite couriers were Pullman porters. If there was no Pullman on the train, P&A's man at the railroad station would ask a passenger to take a parcel of pictures and hand them to another P&A man at the end of the trip.

One day P&A fotog Ralph Morgan boarded a steamer about to put out of New York harbor and spotted a middle-aged passenger who Morgan thought looked "like a regular fellow." Morgan asked him if he'd be kind enough to take a little package to London. When he arrived, Morgan went on, would he please phone Marcel Wallenstein? Wallenstein, a former News reporter, was in charge of P&A's London office and he'd arrange to pick the package up.

FROM THE AIR

The News has long been a leader in the development of aerial photography. Here are some of the more striking examples of this highly specialized type of picture making, which appeared in a 35-year period.

Fire at sea. The cruise ship Morro Castle, en route from Havana to New York, burned off the Jersey coast Sept. 8, 1934. Death toll was 134 of the 500 crewmen and passengers aboard. Photographer, Herb McCory; pilot, Duke Krantz.

End of a sea queen. The Normandie, pride of the French Line, settled into mud at 50th St. and Hudson River Feb. 10, 1942. Ship had been gutted by fire before it capsized. Photographer, John Hemmer; pilot, Buster Warner.

Touch of smog. Top of Empire State building juts through blanket of smog which brought discomfort to many New Yorkers Dec. 6, 1966. Photographer, Gordon Rynders; pilot, Al DeBello.

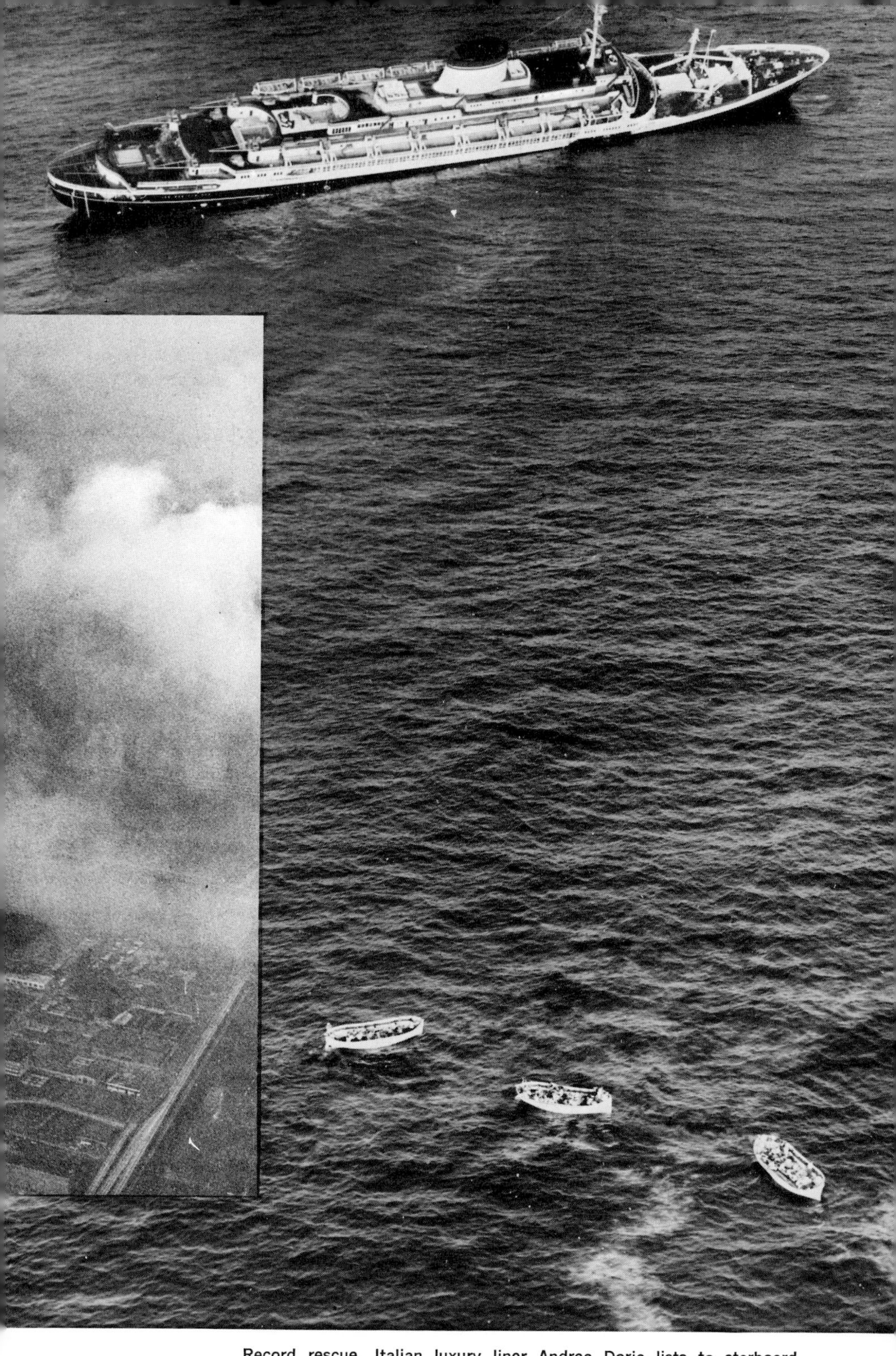

Record rescue. Italian luxury liner Andrea Doria lists to starboard before sinking off Nantucket light July 26, 1956. Vessel had collided with freighter Stockholm. Of 1,700 passengers and crew members aboard, five were killed, 83 injured. Photographer, Gordon Rynders; pilot, Al DeBello.

Death plunge. Air Force bomber crashes into street at East Meadow, L.I., Nov. 2, 1955. Nearby houses were set afire. Photographer, George Mattson; pilot, Al DeBello.

Inferno. Fireboats battle blaze following explosion which wrecked Pier 35, Bush Terminal, Brooklyn, Dec. 4, 1956. Photographer, George Mattson; pilot, Al DeBello.

The "regular fellow" said he'd be glad to oblige. Morgan asked his name and the man said Baldwin. Morgan gave him the package of pictures, thanked him and left.

Eight days later Wallenstein was astounded to receive a phone call from Britain's Prime Minister—Stanley Baldwin—asking him to please call at 10 Downing St., to pick up a package that "your Mr. Morgan gave me for you."

P&A ran up big expense accounts, which helped keep it in the red, by hiring launches and tugs to pick up packets of pictures from incoming steamers in the outer bay or even in Boston before they docked in New York. In that way P&A beat the opposition for a while but the syndicate's competitors eventually caught on and hired tugs too. These tactics, incidentally, could get you in trouble; frequently Coast Guard cutters mistook the picture running tugs for rum runners and chased them.

P&A officials had often dreamt of transmitting pictures by wire and they quickly latched onto Telepix, a process devised by Marvin Ferre, formerly of the Minneapolis News, and Joseph Wissmar, an ex-Western Union man. The process involved a graph with numbered and lettered squares. At the sending end an artist placed a transparent graph over a photo and then proceeded to trace outlines on the graph. The course of each outline was wired in sequence, such as B 6, A 7, C 5, etc. At the receiving end, working with a similar graph, another artist reproduced the coded outline. Directions were given for light and shadow. Retracing the coded directions was slow and difficult but occasionally results weren't bad.

Photographs of the New Year's Day, 1925, football game between Notre Dame and Leland Stanford were transmitted by Telepix over a 3,400-mile circuit from Los Angeles to New York and P&A began extending the system to other newspapers, but by this time the syndicate was already immersed in the development of a new form of wire transmission. It was the Bartlane process, invented by Harry Guy Bartholomew, a London newspaper art director, and Capt. Maynard D. McFarlane. The process involved the conversion of light values into telegraphic impulses at the transmitting end and reconverting them at the receiving end. A photo was wrapped around a circular drum and covered with a plastic sheet with fine lines on it. A light beam followed the lines around the drum, sending line by line. Another beam reconverted line by line.

The process had a weakness—its dependence on an integrated circuit, sometimes not possible on telegraph wires. If transmission were switched to another circuit, then the lines waved, causing a ripple in the picture. But experimentation continued and the process improved. When Lindbergh made his flight to Paris in 1927, the photographs of his landing were transmitted by Bartlane process and The News filled six pages with them. The pictures were widely used by other newspapers.

Eventually a new process—Wirephoto—would come into being and The News would be the first to use it. But another half dozen years would pass before that. Meanwhile things were happening fairly close to home and men, rather than machines, were the star performers.

Late one day in August, 1926, word came to The News of explosions at the Lake Denmark naval arsenal near Dover, N.J. Hause told photographer Al Willard to hop to it. Then realizing that Willard might risk worse injuries than the two flash powder explosions he had already experienced, Hause decided to share the danger and go along.

Willard, with an extra-sensory perception born of experience, foresaw the possibility that the authorities would bar newsmen from the scene. So he borrowed a uniform cap resembling those used by ambulance doctors. He and Hause then got into a car, with Hause at the wheel, and raced to New Jersey. The explosions at the arsenal were proliferating and as The News men drew closer to the scene, they heard roars suggestive of battlefields. Hause stopped the car and Willard put on the uniform cap and got out on the running board (they had running boards then). Sure enough, they encountered a police road block.

"Medical!" yelled Willard and he and Hause were promptly waved past the block.

The night sky was livid and thunderous and in its intermittent light the two men spotted a nice, cozy perch—a tower 300 feet high. They ascended it and for four hours, while 16-inch shells exploded and a powder depot uncomfortably close blew up, Willard took pictures. Curiously enough, he got out of this one without a single powder burn.

Early one Sunday on the edge of Spring in 1927, a big, blonde, sex-hungry suburban housewife named Ruth Brown Snyder teamed up with her lover to kill her husband. By this act, Mrs. Snyder achieved the dubious distinction of sitting for a photograph that became the most talked-about picture since the Mona Lisa.

Albert Snyder, art director of the magazine Motor Boating, was a middle-aged stay-at-home who had stopped making passes at Ruth years before. One day she met Henry Judd Gray, married, a father, and quite virtuous. He was a corset salesman by trade. Ruth got him to fit her for a new girdle in his office, and poor Gray never quite got over it. Slight, eye-glassed, seemingly the personification of a Casper Milquetoast, Gray turned out to be a real fireball in a hotel room. He and Ruth, their passions loosed by Prohibition whisky, pursued their extracurricular love affair in one hotel after another.

Ruth decided to get rid of her husband but first she maneuvered him into signing a blank application for a life insurance policy, purportedly for a small amount, and then she jacked up the amount to $50,000.

Snyder was killed, rather completely, one might say, with chloroform, manual strangulation and a sashweight in his home in Queens Village, Queens, which is part of New York City but was more like a village then than it is today. To make the crime look like that of a burglar, Mrs. Snyder was left on the floor with her hands and feet tied and her mouth gagged.

But Ruth and her sweetie had been a little too thorough. In addition to pulling out bureau drawers, which any burglar would have done, they had tossed around cushions, silverware and clothing, which seemed an awful lot of trouble to go to for a burglar. That put a glint of suspicion in police eyes, but what really got the cops going, when they thought about it, was why the hell would a burglar kill his victim three ways?

The burglar ploy, they reasoned, might well be a coverup for another motive, and the cops started looking into the background of the deceased and his good-looking wife. Their inquiries were quickly rewarded when they discovered the $50,000 policy on Snyder's life. That was motive enough for the wife and the cops decided maybe there was another guy in her life. Cops think like that automatically in such cases. The result was that more clues were uncovered and Ruth and Gray were arrested and charged with murder. Day by day, as details of their torrid love affair and its terrible culmination were unfolded, it became clear that this was the most dramatic and most sensational homicide of the decade. The lovers were put on trial, found guilty and sentenced to die in Sing Sing's electric chair.

A fortnight before the scheduled executions, two men began browsing, very discretely, in and around Sing Sing. One was shrewd police reporter George Kivel, who had the knack of talking like a cop and had endeared himself to bluecoats all along the Atlantic seaboard. The other man was good-looking, engaging Joe Costa, who carried no camera on this assignment. The two were employed by The News on a task formidable enough to make a CIA agent quail. It was to arrange to smuggle a photographer into territory where photographers were strictly forbidden—the Sing Sing death chamber.

While Messrs. Kivel and Costa pursued their secret mission in Ossining, N.Y., site of the big state prison, another photographer busily practised strange rites in a New York City hotel room. He was the man The News planned to smuggle into the death room. His name was Tom Howard and both his name and his face were unknown in the New York area. The News had imported him from P&A's Washington bureau.

Hour after hour, Howard sat in a chair in the hotel room and practised working a small camera strapped around one of his ankles. A long cable release ran up his trouser leg and, through a hole in his pants pocket, to a bulb in his hand. The bulb could open and close a shutter so gradually that there would be no betraying click. The whine of the death chair's electricity might drown out such a click, but then again Howard might not get a chance to shoot a picture until the whine had stopped. There would have to be a time exposure because in those days there were no lenses or emulsions fast enough to make snapshots in existing artificial light and that was another reason for the bulb.

Gently, very gently, Howard would push the release open and then ease it shut, over and over, with as little movement of the hand in his pocket as possible. In addition he had to be singularly careful to look straight ahead as though at the electric chair while practising aiming and operating the camera. This wasn't easy. The tendency was to drop one's gaze to one's foot while taking aim. It was a must, of course, that Howard be planted in the front bench occupied by reporters covering the execution. His pants cuffs must be down far enough to conceal the camera when he walked into the chamber. Then, when he was seated, he would have to gently tug the cuff up to let the lens have an unimpeded view of the subject—Ruth Snyder.

Presently Kivel and Costa scored a real find, a blueprint of the death chamber. This supplied Howard with the exact distance from the front bench to the hot seat, a vital statistic required for focusing the camera. The blueprint also provided the angle from which Howard would have to shoot. With this important data at his disposal, Howard revised his rehearsals somewhat. One gathers, considering the thoroughness of all concerned, that he did so under light closely approximating the illumination of the death chamber.

The indefatigable Kivel, meanwhile, pulled another coup. He arranged the secret installation of a signal system whereby The News could score a scoop on the execution story itself. Under prison rules, reporters assigned to the electrocution would be obliged to remain in their seats until the pronouncement of death had been made, and would be required to leave the death chamber in a body. Then they would have to make their way to phones. All this would eat up valuable time. Under the signal system arranged by Kivel, a good chunk of the wasted time could be saved. Two electric lights, one red and one white, were rigged somewhere outside the walls—but they were to be operated from somewhere *inside*. (Just where the lights were placed and by whom they were operated still remains a secret.) About a mile away, a phone was installed in a shack. A News reporter was stationed there on the night of the execution to watch for the lights with high-powered binoculars. A red flash would mean Ruth had just died; white, Judd. Once he knew the order of their dying and the time of death, the reporter would relay the information to The News by phone.

Patterson had hoped to have Grace Robinson cover and write the detailed story of the executions, but Warden Lewis E. Lawes refused to allow a woman in the death chamber, so Sidney Sutherland drew the writing assignment. Kivel was also among those present. And so was Tom Howard who was admitted to the death chamber as a "reporter." He made sure he got a front seat. Apparently he needed elbow room because he gave the newspaperman next to him a nudge and the man obligingly moved over.

Everything worked beautifully. The signal system arranged by Kivel got the bare details of the story to The News first. Then, as time went by, Sutherland's full story poured into the city room of The News and it was a fine piece of vivid reporting. The News, edition after edition, late Thursday night and into early Friday morning, carried a one-word headline on the front page:

DEAD!

Then The News sprang an extra. Under the same headline was a picture that almost filled Page 1. It was a photograph of Ruth Brown Snyder, taken as the deadly current coursed through her body.

As the caption pointed out, the picture made history. It was the first Sing Sing execution photograph ever made, the first photograph of a woman's electrocution anywhere. Since one of journalism's most sensational pictures was too hot to confine to an extra, The News ran it on the front page in all Saturday's editions and virtually every copy was sold.

The buyers included representatives of the crestfallen, badly-shaken opposition papers. Some of them, after recovering from the jolt, denounced The News for trickery. In certain quarters there were even cries of "fake" but this swiftly died down when investigation showed the picture was real, real as death.

Probably the finest tribute to The News' enterprise came, grudgingly, from a reporter on a rival newspaper. He was the man whom Howard had nudged on the front bench. In a memorandum on the execution which he filed later, he recalled how "a newspaperman nudged me to move a bit so he could get a view" and "I slid up maybe a few inches." It didn't mean anything to him at the time—not until Ruth Snyder in the electric chair leaped out at the reporter from the front page of The News.

"A beat, a real photo!" he declared in his memo. "There she was in that ghastly picture just as she had slumped at the touch of the current. And then I remembered that little squirt who had asked me to move up the bench. He had had a miniature camera strapped to his left ankle, concealed by his wide slacks. The little squirt! But it was a beat for all that!"

The picture evoked horror in some places, too, but it was the truth, and it ripped to shreds an element of hypocrisy which had long hampered newspaper photography. For years most papers had taken a squeamish approach to portrayals of death in any form. When a gangster was slain, the photographers would wait until the body was removed before taking a picture of the scene. Then it would be published with a caption that said "X marks the spot." The News picture of Ruth Snyder in the electric chair went far toward destroying that convention.

* * *

Death once provided The News with a photograph of haunting, even serene beauty. It came to the paper, not through a news tip, but through an appeal for help by a frantic woman reader. The News by this time had become something more than a newspaper. People called it when they were in trouble, as though The News possessed the magic to iron out every woe. Sometimes, if injustice had been done, no matter how petty, or if there was bureaucratic laxity, The News would do something. And not to get a story. Just to help.

That's the way it was late Christmas Eve when night city editor Bill Rice got a phone call from a distraught woman living in a flat in upper Manhattan. Her family, she went on to explain, had a boarder. The boarder, an elderly man, had gone into the living room and sat down beside the lighted Christmas tree. As he sat there, he was seized with a heart attack which was fatal. The woman had called, or tried to call, several city agencies to have the body removed, but she had gotten nowhere, probably because of the holiday. What upset her, aside from the fact that a pleasant old man had just died, was that her children's gifts were piled under the tree and she dreaded the moment next morning when the youngsters would troop into the living room and behold the body. She wanted to spare them that.

Rice told police reporter Julius Mahler to verify the phoned complaint and if it were bonafide to do something about it. Photographer Philip Greitzer went along with Mahler, partly because it was a dull night and partly because he could give Mahler fast transportation in his car. Certainly not for a picture. A man dead of natural causes was scarcely the stuff from which news photographs were fashioned.

The Newsmen reached the house, ascended five flights of stairs and were ushered in by the grateful woman and her husband. The boarder was seated in a comfortable wing chair, one hand resting on the chair's arm, his feet outstretched like someone completely relaxed. His eyes were closed and in the soft glow of the Christmas tree lights his face held a look of infinite peace. Mahler got on the phone. He had access to several officials, not only their office numbers but their home numbers as well, and finally he reached the right people. He hung up and assured the couple the body would soon be removed.

At this point Greitzer, now assistant studio manager, asked the couple for permission to make a picture of the scene and they said of course. He hadn't brought his tripod, but he made do with the backs of two chairs, on which he mounted his Speed Graphic. He had just finished making a few exposures when police and a medical examiner arrived. The official pronouncement of death was made and the body was quietly taken away.

In the morning the kids in the home where death had struck had a gay time of gift-discovery and The News had a poignantly beautiful picture. Had it not been for the caption, readers would never have known that the man seated in the glow of the tree was sleeping his last sleep.

* * *

The News has long encouraged amateurs to submit spot news photographs. If one brings in a picture not worth using, he is still paid a small sum to cover expenses he incurred in bringing it to The News. On the other hand, if his photograph has real news value, he may get $50 or even more, much more. And there's always a chance of his winning $500 in the contest for the best amateur news picture of the year. Naturally amateurs, when they've snapped something they're proud of, gravitate to The News picture assignment desk.

But there was one time when The News gravitated to an amateur. The British steamer Vestris foundered off Virginia Nov. 12, 1928, with a loss of 110 lives, but others were saved and rescue ships sped them toward New York. The News, in the faint hope that someone aboard might have had a camera and the presence of mind to use it, assigned several fotogs, including McEvilly, to talk to the survivors. McEvilly found a crew member, Fred Hanson, who said he had an undeveloped roll of film he had shot during the sinking. The News doesn't encourage buying pigs in pokes but McEvilly promptly shelled out $10 because of the roll's tremendous potential value. He assured Hanson he'd be paid much more if any of the pictures was a good one.

The pictures were great and The News paid Hanson $1,500. The best showed the sharply slanting deck of the Vestris as crewmen strove to launch a lifeboat. One of the sailors had turned his head so that his face could be seen quite clearly; in his eyes was pure fear. Another seaman stood leaning against a deckhouse, both his arms broken.

The picture made the front cover. That night, not long after the first edition was on the street, managing editor Hause got a phone call from Ted O. Thackrey, then the young and enterprising editor of the Telegram.

"I'd like to buy the Vestris picture," said Thackrey.

"It isn't for sale," said Hause.

"I'll pay $600—"

"No sale."

Thackrey proceeded, in stages, to raise his bid to $12,000. Hause politely said goodby and hung up.

Next day the Telegram, an afternoon sheet, printed the picture and didn't pay a dime for it, but the cost to its ego must have been immense. Its standard-size front page carried a full-sized reproduction of page 1 of The News with the caption, "This was the front page of The News this morning."

Free-lance fotog Ed Clarity, trudging the sands of Rockaway Beach, saw a woman chasing a very small and chubby boy and the sight was so appealing he swung his camera and shot it. What made it particularly amusing was that the woman was carrying the kid's bathing suit in her hand and the boy was completely bare. The camera caught the kid's back. Clarity sold the picture to The News and it went over big, especially with mothers.

After Clarity joined the staff of The News, whenever spot news was in the doldrums, he'd somehow always manage to find a barebacked baby. He had imagination and the theme was always touched with variety. For instance, one shot showed a big cop solemnly "arresting" a very young lady for nudity. Other newspapers, on discovering the special appeal that bare baby bottoms seem to hold for the public, enthusiastically joined the Clarity school of art, to a point where The News finally cracked down and put a stop to it.

In 1933, The News purchased its first plane, an Ireland Privateer that came to be known as "The Flying Camera." It gave the photographers coverage over a much wider area than before. The plane was christened with printer's ink by Patterson's daughter, Josephine. Later, a specially-built Stinson Reliant was acquired. All private planes, including those of The News, were grounded during the war.

In May, 1947, The News bought a bigger plane with much more zip, a Grumman Mallard amphibian, which was named Miss Daily News.

A few months later, while en route to the southern hurricane area, Miss Daily News performed a task beyond the call of duty; she rescued six persons marooned on an island in the Gulf of Mexico. Today, in addition to the Grumman, The News operates a modern Aerocommander, loaded with aerial and land cameras of the latest makes. Nobody freezes riding those planes. They're comfortable cabin jobs with just the right temperature inside.

There were other technological advances. A new machine was developed for the transmission of photographs via phone lines. It was Wirephoto and it was operated by the Associated Press. An ordinary print was wrapped around a cylinder that revolved under a small hoodlike housing containing a photoelectric cell. The cell was the "eye" that transmitted the photographs, and a sharp eye it was. Pictures sent out on the new machine possessed a fidelity and quality so fine it was difficult to distinguish between them and the original photographs on the transmitting cylinders.

It was a marvelous stride forward. But the service was inaugurated at the very start of 1935, in the depths of the economic depression, and few newspapers, comparatively speaking, could afford the fees charged. A certain sum was set for each major city and no matter how many or how few newspapers in that city subscribed, the set fee had to be paid. The charge for New York City was $150,000 a year. Had three or four newspapers in the metropolis agreed to become Wirephoto subscribers they would have shared the cost, but the only paper in New York to subscribe was The News. It had to pay the entire $150,000 but it had Wirephoto exclusively through 1935–1939, five history-making years. Hitler had come to power, the world was in turmoil and exciting events were taking place all over the U.S. FBI agents killed Fred and Ma Barker, long-hunted criminals, in a gun battle; the sensational Weyerhauser kidnapping broke in the Northwest. Pictures, great pictures, poured into The News and The News alone in New York.

The Associated Press came up with a portable Wirephoto machine and, by paying an extra charge, The News got one. It proved a boon. The machine was about the size of a suitcase and when a photographer went on an out-of-town assignment he could easily stow it in a car and hook into a convenient phone. Paul Bernius was a top technician and he was hired to handle the new portable.

The News transmitted its first portable Wirephoto pictures Oct. 20, 1937. Two photographs, taken at a trial in Elizabethtown, N.Y., in the Adirondack Mountains, were put on the portable sender at 2:30 p.m. They were received at the AP office in New York and the wirephotos were developed, printed and delivered to The News office at 3:50 p.m. The nearest transmitting station on the regular AP circuit was in Albany, 150 miles from Elizabethtown. Now the pictures can be sent directly to a receiver in The News office.

Although now assistant studio manager, Bernius still goes out with the portable. One big yarn his machine worked on was a damaging Texas hurricane. The machine comes in especially handy at political conventions when a second machine is rented to handle the heavy traffic.

Long before Wirephoto came into being, P&A, which had reached a peak with 1,600 correspondents and 250 contract subscribers, had been disbanded by The News and the Chicago Tribune. For one thing it was wallowing in red ink. The News retained its commercial studio and most of its camera staff, Associated Press picked up the foreign end of the syndicate and the rest went to Acme picture service.

The science, or perhaps art would be a better word, of taking action shots also progressed. A pioneer in prize fight photography at Madison Square Garden, Henry Olen boosted the sensitivity of plates by dipping them in a special solution. When enlarged, the picture was on the grainy side, but it caught the action. The coming of the flashbulb helped. But the introduction of the electronic strobe opened vistas. It hurled a brilliant flash in as little as a 30,000th of a second. The News, the first paper to use it, engaged the inventor to make some sets for night fights and football games. The strobes arrested swift action and held it frozen, with virtually no movement apparent. Attached to a camera, the strobe works on batteries, recycling in two seconds—that is, it takes no more than two seconds for this magic light to surge up for the next shot.

Joe Louis was known for his poker face but it contorted into an expression of naked fury when he delivered the goodby uppercut to Arturo Godoy. A stroboscopic flash nailed down this unprecedented moment. Costa made the picture, which was captioned, "Life in The Dead Pan." Instead of hooking a strobe to his camera, Costa had positioned four electronic units in the steel rigging over the ring. The fight was at night, out-of-doors. In the afternoon, it rained hard and Costa had some bad moments worrying whether the wetness would short circuit his rigging masterpiece, but it didn't.

In 1958 another News fotog, Charles Hoff, and Phil Levine, by then studio chief, spent hours experimenting with strobe, all to get a high-jump shot at a track meet. They also had to do some hard physical labor, lifting sections of the wooden running track to install a cable under it. A strobe was mounted on a mezzanine rail, hooked up to a light on Hoff's camera. A lot of theory went into it, and it all became reality

OFFBEAT

Half inch from death. Mrs. Pauline Weitz walks to ambulance with spent bullet in her breastbone. She was wounded by cop firing at escaping prisoner in Bronx. Picture appeared July 1, 1952. Photographer, Ossie Leviness.

Caught in the act (below). Burglary suspect Ruperto Rivera descends fire escape in Bronx, to be greeted by Patrolman Walter Carlson (holding revolver) and his partner, Edward Bracht. Date was Dec. 19, 1964. Photographer, Al Aaronson.

Misstep to tragedy. Arthur Bretton, father of three, falls from roof of five-story building after family quarrel. Photographer John Pedin made the picture July 29, 1954.

when Hoff snapped Bob Barksdale as he cleared the bar at 6 feet 9, then a world's record. The picture was flawless.

Hoff covered all kinds of spot news, including the explosion of the Zeppelin Hindenburg, which provided its own light, but his main forte was sports. When he was at a fight and sensed something big was coming, he would put his speed graphic on the ring apron, as did the other photographers, but, unlike them, he disdained looking through the viewfinder. He kept his gaze on the fighters. And he "fired" like the old gunslingers, from the hip, in a way of speaking. He had an uncanny flair for making the shot at precisely the right fraction of a second. He caught Ray Robinson's fist smashing against Kid Gavilan's tortured face, with the sweat spraying out, every drop of sweat, every line of pain. That picture took first prize in the sports division, best-of-show award at a New York State AP news-photo contest, and half a dozen other awards.

An album containing pictures taken by 26 News cameramen in 1955 was submitted to the Pulitzer committee and the following year all 26 were cited for a Pulitzer Prize for general excellence in photography. Special mention was made of a picture taken by George Mattson, who specializes in aerial shots. He'd been riding a News plane back to his base at Zahn's airport on Long Island from a routine assignment when he spotted a puff of smoke. A B-26 bomber had just crashed in East Meadow, L. I. Mattson signaled the pilot who positioned him for a shot and Mattson got a fine one of the burning plane.

The Pulitzer award totaled $1,000 and The News tossed $1,600 into the pot so that each fotog cited would get $100.

At Patterson's behest, The News had long briefed its reporters to go after not only stories but snapshots or studio pictures of people in the headlines. On some occasions, as when there had been a murder in the family, or a divorce scandal, a reporter really had to use his super-powers of persuasion to get a picture. Reporter Ben White, who had his own gentle way of wheedling things out of people, received a tip in 1952 that a former paratrooper from the Bronx named George Jorgensen had been converted into a girl through a series of operations performed in Denmark. Ben called on his (or her) parents. They'd learned of the conversion job, understandably were inclined to clam up on the subject, but under the spell of Ben's soft sell they corroborated the tip and gave him a story. He even succeeded in talking them into handing over letters from their son as well as a whole slew of pictures showing a good-looking and decidedly female-blonde. Her new name was Christine Jorgensen and Ben had cornered an exclusive, storywise and picturewise.

When The News was born, the cameramen it hired were experienced men, with solid training on other papers. But the bulk of today's staff started as office boys and learned photography at The News. They couldn't have found a better training ground.

The Speed Graphic, long the chief weapon in The News camera armory, has given way to Nikon, Hasselblad and Rollie. "The old Graphic," Ranzini recalls, "used plates, then film, could take rough handling, produced a big negative and could print wet. But it was hard to handle. You cocked the shutter, inserted the holder, removed the slide, put in your flash bulb, shot, then did it all over again. Now you just press a button, crank to the next frame and press the button again."

It's getting even simpler. Motorized cameras are coming into use so that you don't even have to crank, just hit the button. And yet all cameras have little complications and with the introduction of each new type, the men must train themselves in its use, train until it almost becomes a part of them. Among other things they must learn to turn the lens aperture, without looking at it, by the sound of its clicks.

The picture assignment desk, which immediately abuts the city desk, is equipped with a short wave radio which Ranzini and his helpers use to keep in instant touch with The News planes, with a fleet of 10 radio cars constantly patroling the city and its environs, and even with walkie-talkies sometimes used by the fotogs.

The radio cars move in prescribed districts and their radios are tuned not only for contact with the assignment desk, but for police and fire signals. Often, when a major crime or fire story breaks, The News fotog in the radio patrol gets there as fast as the cops or firemen. Sometimes even faster.

What's with the walkie-talkies? Let's say a disaster occurs in wooded country. A plane goes to the scene so the fotog aboard can get aerial shots. But the desk wants close-in shots, too, so other photographers go by car. They get to the area, but not the right spot, they can't see it. In such an emergency the plane sends them to the spot. They get the directions by walkie-talkie.

During the Columbia student hell-raising, walkie-talkies came in particularly handy. Half a dozen cameramen worked on widely separated fronts. If one man found the action getting hot in his area, too hot for one man to absorb, he radioed for help. If an obstruction impeded transmission to the nearest cameraman, then all he had to do was radio the desk, which in turn relayed the message to the second fotog. A motorcycle, also radio-equipped, was kept in readiness at an agreed-on spot. As soon as a photographer shot a roll, he passed it to the cyclist who dispatched it to the office.

Pretty soft, say The News pensioners, warming old bones in Florida or California. Now when we were lugging a camera . . .

Sure, it's easier for a fotog to get a good picture today, with all the gizmos at his disposal. But he can still get hit on the head with a brick, or slugged by persons hostile to photography, and in these riotous days there are plenty of persons like that around. And there are still, and always will be, moments when The News cameraman must use his wits, which no gimmick can match.

SPLASH OF COLOR

Some time early in the 1930s, Harry Warnecke, one of the top black and white photographers on the staff, and at that time assistant studio chief, suggested to managing editor Frank Hause that the subject of color photography might well be worth looking into. Hause, normally forward-looking, turned down the suggestion for the time being, but Warnecke decided to do a little research on his own.

Prior to that time the only New York paper that had done any experimenting in color was the World. Before its demise, its rotogravure section had been edited since 1922 by Richard W. Clarke, who had been lured from The News by the World. (The three big papers of that era, the World, the Tribune and the Times, were engaged in a struggle for Sunday circulation, and were building up their gravure sections to attract readers. The phenomenal success of The News had prompted that action.)

One of the features of the World's gravure section was the display on page 1 of a reproduction in full color of a work of art selected by Clarke from the great collection at New York City's Metropolitan Museum of Art.

The copying of those paintings was a laborious process, involving the exposing of three negatives through three different color filters. Much time and extreme care were required, since the slightest movement of the camera out of position following the first or second exposure caused the as yet unexposed negative or negatives to be slightly out of synchronization or register. This resulted in a blurred final image. Those three negatives, with another exposed without a filter, were the engravers' copy. He was also supplied with a small commercial print of the painting—the museum made them available to patrons at a small fee—to serve as his color guide.

Clarke, incidentally, returned to The News following the World's passing from the New York newspaper scene, and served subsequently as automobile editor, Sunday editor, managing editor, executive editor and finally editor until his retirement in 1968.

But Warnecke was thinking far beyond the copying of inanimate objects. His years of experience as a news photographer—he had been with The News, following an apprenticeship with a couple of commercial photographic studios, since 1922—had quickened his awareness of the public's interest in pictures of current events or of prominent personalities.

When, in the '30s, Warnecke finally did get the go-ahead signal from

Hause, he found himself facing a blank wall. The few men in New York familiar with the progress in color to that date were understandably uncooperative, and Harry soon came to the realization he would have to build up his own store of knowledge without outside assistance.

Meanwhile Patterson, having recovered somewhat from the failure of Liberty, which had not been too successful in attempting to print color, decided to have another go at it, and suggested to Harvey Deuell, when he succeeded Hause as managing editor, that a color studio be set up, with the eventual aim of reproducing one color picture each week on page 1 of the Sunday rotogravure section. Deuell, who had done a little dabbling in black and white photography himself, detached Warnecke from the black and white staff and assigned him the task of creating the color studio.

Warnecke went to work. Hours meant nothing. He was given space in the portrait studio on the seventh floor, and also took over a room in his own home where he worked at nights, frequently until midnight, testing, discarding and testing again.

There were then two or three color films on the market. Harry decided, after much experimentation, to work with Agfa, a German product. The colors were remarkably accurate, but the film so slow that time exposures of considerable duration had to be made even under brilliant light.

Harry decided to try out a radically different plate called the Finlay. A technical explanation would not only be greatly involved but also dull. Finlay's greater speed over the Agfa plate gave it a decided advantage, influencing Warnecke's decision to give it a try, which he did for a short period.

It had one serious drawback, a screen, similar to that used in ordinary black and white halftone engraving; and at times that screen produced an objectional moire pattern in the final reproduction. All things considered, the plate was an improvement, but Harry was not satisfied. An important consideration was the fact that an outside assignment was a painful procedure.

Two cameras were used, one requiring 8 by 10 plates, the other, a 5 by 7 size. Since they were never quite sure of the conditions they might face on the job, Warnecke and Rufus Cranston, whom he selected from the black and white staff as his assistant, carried both cameras, with several dozen heavy glass plates. The work was primarily portraiture, and had to be done under artificial light. Tall lamp standards with reflectors were needed for that purpose. There was other necessary equipment, and when the two men, with a couple of copy boys as assistants, left the building, observers might well have thought that the entire photographic studio of The News was in flight.

The News conducted a water circus at the pool of the President Hotel in Liberty, N.Y., in the summer of 1935, which Warnecke attended and photographed in color. It was a clear, bright day, and the pictures were of good enough quality for reproduction. They appeared in the roto section of July 28, to Patterson's great pleasure.

A sizeable space was then assigned to Warnecke for his working quarters. It was labelled the Three and One Studio—identifying the three primary colors and the monotone color, either black or brown that form the basis of color printing.

His selection of Cranston—known to all as Bob—was a most fortunate one. From the earliest days of radio he had been a "ham," and his knowledge of that intricate subject proved invaluable as the two men worked their way through the as-yet-uncharted field of color and light. One complemented the other—Warnecke with his unquenchable thirst for knowledge; Cranston with his uncanny ability at improvisation when they found themselves at a dead end mechanically, with nothing on the market that could solve their problem.

The ever-questioning Warnecke continued to regard the use of the single color plate as a stopgap measure. He was convinced that the three-plate system—one for each of the primary colors—was the ideal solution, but he also realized that the one-plate-at-a-time method was useless for the type of work he planned to attempt. Meanwhile he continued to work on a camera of his own design.

Hearing that a photographer named Cummings had constructed a camera employing a negative tri-pack with a single mirror, he investigated. He concluded he could get fairly good results with that until his machine was ready, and bought it from Cummings. Three negatives were exposed with the one shutter opening, a very desirable effect, but the camera had a defect. Two films were placed back to back, like a sandwich, and the resulting refraction of the light as it passed through the first film caused the second one to be slightly out of focus, or "soft," as the photographers term it. Fortunately, the engravers, made aware of that condition, were able to make adjustments that helped somewhat to overcome the error, but the results were still unsatisfactory by Warnecke's exacting standards.

His labors at home were finally productive. Although no engineer, he had laid out a set of plans for the construction of a camera that would have received at least a nod of approval from the most critical professional. He took the plans to a machine shop near his home in the Bronx, and after a lengthy period the camera was completed to his satisfaction.

It was a large aluminum box of peculiar shape with four openings: one in front for a lens, one on either side to accommodate a plate holder, and one in the rear for the same purpose. In the interior were two frames for the insertion of special, semi-transparent mirrors, made of a delicate substance called pellicles. These served to reflect the light passing through the lens to the negatives on either side, and through the mirror to the plate in the back. Each plate was placed immediately behind a filter.

It was a big day in the color studio when the camera received its baptism of fire. The receptionist, always the subject for such experiments, smiled her prettiest on this occasion, although apprehensive, as were the men, that this sitting, the most important, technically, to date, might be a failure.

Instead, it was a success, and great was the rejoicing. (Warnecke, who did not drink, was strongly tempted to go out and have at least one shot in celebration, but he restrained himself.) One giant step forward had been accomplished. Development revealed three crisp, sharp negatives, and when a carbro print—of which, more a little later—had been made, even the receptionist had to admit it was the loveliest picture of herself she had ever seen. From that time on the Cummings camera was put away to gather dust.

All of this would have been of little value to The News had not the administrative offices been cooperating. Provision had been made in The News plant on Pacific St., Brooklyn, for the accommodation not only of black and white presses to take care of the expanding Brooklyn and Queens circulation, but for some new color presses as well. When the Sunday News was started in 1921, the rotogravure section had been printed by Art Gravure Corporation. While satisfactory results had been obtained, the business office knew that eventually the paper would have to erect its own plant, especially since advertising color was becoming increasingly in demand.

Gustav A. Friess, who had learned his trade in Germany, and had learned it well, was selected as roto production chief. He took over in March, 1935, but his tenure was cut short by his death on Jan. 24, 1936. For more than four months John L. Zaugg filled in, being succeeded by Arthur Dultgen on June 15, 1936.

Dultgen not only knew his business thoroughly, he was also the inventor of a rotogravure printing method known as the Dultgen process, conceded to be a considerable improvement on the method universally used at that time. With the hiring of Dultgen The News also acquired the right to use his process, and to license it to other newspapers and printing plants throughout the country. Dultgen, of course, received royalties from the licensing. In return, The News had exclusive use of the process in the New York metropolitan area.

In the color studio experimentation continued. Warnecke and Cranston agree that far more time was spent on testing than in actual photography.

One of those experiments involved the hiring of an expert in carbro printing, Lee Elkins. This method had been developed in England. Each of the three color negatives is exposed on a sensitized gelatinous substance which, after careful washing to eliminate areas that do not contain the desired color, is then laid on a mounting board. The yellow is placed down first, then the red and finally the blue. Without question it is the most pleasing and accurate of any of the color printing methods.

But, like everything else in this or any other business, the carbro method had its faults, too. Until Elkins laid the final color down and surveyed the print, it could not be determined with accuracy whether the result was successful or not. Since it takes approximately a day and a half to make just one carbro print, it could be evident that it is not only time-consuming but expensive. The process was used, however, until the one-shot camera—as Harry's device was known—was finally abandoned in favor of color film. Another method, involving the use of dyes, called chromatone, had been tried out previously by Warnecke, but the colors were, in his opinion, inferior to those produced by carbro, which was settled upon as the better method.

To help with the carbro printing chores, Gus Schoenbaechler was drafted from the black and white studio. In addition, he assisted Warnecke in hundreds of color studio sittings.

Studio lighting was long a major headache. This was more in Cranston's line than in Warnecke's, and to the former should go a great deal of credit for its development.

In those early days even a hardened publicity seeker among the movie stars must have winced at the thought of posing for color. Studio lights of great intensity were universally employed, in Hollywood as well as here, and in a few moments the poor subject was cooked from rare to medium to well-done. Many of the female stars brought their maids with them, who between exposures dried them with towels and applied fresh makeup.

Fortunately, Warnecke had worked out an operations system that cut minutes down to seconds. Each man knew exactly what he was supposed to do during the sitting. Hardly a word was spoken as lights were turned on and off, new plates inserted in the camera, light readings taken to insure absolutely accurate exposure times, and the lens reset. The subject was then put on the alert for the next exposure. It was well known throughout the movie industry, which provided a high percentage of the subjects brought to the color studio, that their stars would be in and out in less than a half hour.

Nevertheless, the heat from the studio lights caused great concern, and when photoflash bulbs came into use in black and white photography,

Warnecke and Cranston worked out a method whereby they might be used for color. Again, because of the mule-train speed of the color plates or film, whereas only one flash bulb might be needed for a well-exposed black and white picture, six or possibly four times that number would be required for the same exposure in color.

In a short time they had the problem solved. At first they rigged up two boards, each with a dozen sockets mounted in series. Much experimentation revealed the number of bulbs required for a given light reading. The required number were placed in the sockets—they were of the bayonet type, to insure speedy insertion—and the exposure was made. This process was repeated for every pose.

A much better system was developed shortly thereafter. Light standards with double sockets surrounded the subject. Photofloods were placed in one set of sockets; photoflashes in the other. Readings were taken with the photofloods, which were then extinguished and the actual exposures made with the photoflashes. A couple of the photofloods were always left on during the sitting to eliminate the expanded-pupil stare that results in going from brilliant light to darkness just before the flash bulbs are fired. Again, all of this was accomplished in a few seconds, while the subject exchanged a few words with reporter Julia McCarthy, there to conduct an interview to appear in the next day's paper.

Many of these sittings Patterson himself attended, taking part in the conversation between Miss McCarthy, and the subject. He had made it very clear that any person visiting the color studio was to be regarded as a guest, and was to be treated as such. All interviews were to be of a friendly, chatty nature, with no embarrassing questions asked. Press agents were aware of those conditions, and were able to assure some doubting clients that their privacy would not be invaded.

All assignments for color studio sittings were arranged throughout the years by the picture editor. He kept himself thoroughly informed of the comings and goings of the stars between New York and Hollywood and he was also conversant with their professional standings. It was his painful duty on occasion to refuse the importunities of a friendly press agent trying to get a sitting for an over-the-hill star who might well be helped to obtain a role if her picture appeared on the front page of The News' Coloroto Magazine.

Patterson was very proud of his color studio. He knew of the great esteem in which it was held by the entertainment world, which strengthened his insistence that it never be used to assist in an unwarranted publicity buildup.

The 1930s were the heyday of the movies. Contrary to today's practice, virtually all the important stars were under contract to one studio or another, and there was little or no interchange. A 20th Century-Fox star appeared only in pictures made by that studio, and the same applied to those with Metro-Goldwyn-Mayer, RKO, Warner Brothers, etc. The star system was full-blown, and the success of a movie usually rested on the prominence of the stars appearing in it.

As soon as a color studio appointment is made by the picture editor—or, under the present setup, the magazine editor—he sends out a note to a number of his fellow editors in notification. (This is done primarily to avoid duplication of story or pictures on that subject in another section of the paper.) In the past, leakage of such information sometimes resulted in a traffic jam when the star got off the elevator on the fourth floor of The News building, where the color studio is located. He or she would have to elbow through a crush of young women—some men too, it must be acknowledged—many with pens and autograph books in outstretched hands.

Orders were issued that private secretaries maintain privacy, and today the stars are not bothered to any great extent on their arrival. But their departure still causes traffic jams, since they are invariably spotted passing through the main lobby on arrival. Information spreads throughout the building, and a half hour later the lobby often is crowded.

It might be noted that, long before civil rights became a burning subject, The News drew no color line when it came to selecting subjects for its Coloroto Magazine. Every black performer of consequence has been photographed and presented on page 1 from the very start of the use of editorial color. Ethel Waters, Bill (Bojangles) Robinson, Hazel Scott, Dorothy Dandridge, Duke Ellington are just a few of the many who were featured during the '30s and early '40s.

Following the development of stroboscopic lighting, The News bought a set of lights for use primarily at Friday night fights at Madison Square Garden. They proved their worth immediately; many sensational shots were obtained. The suggestion was made to Warnecke that a set be purchased for the color studio. Warnecke demurred, on the grounds of expense. He hesitated to ask for an appropriation of the thousands of dollars needed for the many lights that color would require. His present lighting equipment was working satisfactorily; he felt he could use that money for other and more necessary purposes.

During the summer of 1942 an assignment was made to photograph Paul Draper, the dancer. Both Warnecke and White, the picture editor, were on vacation, and the latter's place had been taken by John Chapman, just back from Hollywood after having done a tour there as the movieland columnist. He had been assigned temporarily to the picture department awaiting a permanent place in drama.

Having started his newspaper career as a photographer, Chapman was familiar with strobe lighting, since it had been put to use by the Hollywood studios for their publicity pictures. Not knowing that pressure had been brought on Warnecke to apply for a set of strobe lights, Chapman suggested to Patterson that the black and white set be borrowed to permit action shots of Draper going through his dances. The stop action photos were another step forward and, upon his return from vacation, Warnecke ordered the necessary equipment for color studio use.

Few persons of real prominence in the United States have failed to appear before The News color cameras. From 1936 to date every candidate for the Presidency has been photographed and presented in the Coloroto Magazine. Once a man has been nominated, he has virtually no time to call his own, and the problem of making color studio appointments is at times almost insurmountable. Since candidates seldom can spare the time for a special trip to New York and the color studio, photographers usually have had to follow them around the country in order to squeeze in a quick sitting. Many times they have set up a temporary studio in a hotel room adjoining the suite of a candidate, with the idea of promising to have the job finished in five minutes. And they always kept their word.

A sitting of John Nance Garner was made at his home in Uvalde, Tex., during the summer of 1936—he had been nominated to run for reelection as Vice President on the ticket headed by Franklin Delano Roosevelt. Garner was 68, and disinclined to do much campaigning. But he did agree to pose—at 6 o'clock in the morning! Warnecke and Cranston readily agreed to that, and had their camera set up well in advance of that time in a room adjoining Garner's bedroom. Mrs. Garner acted as his "maid," smoothing down his shirt and resetting his tie between exposures.

From Uvalde the photographers went to Topeka, Kan., to get some shots of Gov. Alfred M. Landon, the Republican candidate for the Presidency, and the man who was to suffer the worst defeat in U.S. history, winning the popular vote in only two states.

The matter of posing was put up to Landon in his office at the state capitol during a press conference and from his response it was apparent he had either not heard of The News, or considered it of very minor importance. He did not actually object to posing, but was far from enthusiastic. Finally a reporter from a Bismarck, N.D., paper spoke up:

"Governor," he said, "I'll have to stick my neck out by saying The News is quite important, not only in New York, but throughout the United States. Why, in our little city alone, Sunday News sells 650 copies."

The startled Landon immediately agreed to pose. What was good enough for Bismarck was good enough for him.

When Dwight D. Eisenhower ran for his first term in 1952, he was president of Columbia University in New York and agreed to pose in his home on the university campus provided only a few minutes was required for the job.

Cranston and his assistant, Daniel Jacino, set up their camera in a bedroom, with Ike momentarily expected to walk in. The drab-colored walls of the room offered little in the way of background. Finally Cranston snatched a blue spread from the bed and with the use of some heavy tape—he was never without aids of that sort—suspended it on the wall. The result was a most pleasing picture, and there were many approving comments on the "lovely background."

President Roosevelt was photographed in color many times, and he was always a gracious and patient subject. Not only were portraits made of him for use during his four campaigns—the first one in monotone, as color had not been introduced then—but also on many historic occasions, such as signing of bills, his inaugurations, the operating of telegraph keys to start dams in operation, etc.

The signing of the Social Security Act in 1935 provided a little unexpected excitement. Warnecke and Cranston were all set up, camera at the ready, as the President, seated at his desk with a convoy of Senators and Representatives in the rear, picked up a pen out of the dozen or so at hand for the official signing. Warnecke had deliberately refrained from snapping on the lights until the actual moment arrived, rather than cause confusion.

As the President poised the pen in air the lights were switched on—and everything went black, including the desk lights and the normal room lighting. The News photographers had blown a fuse.

Roosevelt took it all good naturedly, and in a few minutes a new fuse was inserted and the signing proceeded without mishap. This was before the reconstruction of the White House, which was done during Truman's administration, and the electrical system was in a shocking state. Short circuits and blown fuses were of common occurrence.

When Eisenhower posed for the official campaign picture during the 1956 campaign, arrangements were made for the sitting at the White House. The photographers were led into the room where the picture was to be made, and informed the President would be with them shortly. They set the equipment up and had everything in readiness when Ike came into the room from the outside, where he had apparently been practicing on the little putting course laid out on the back lawn. He hadn't been notified that the cameramen were there, and was as much surprised as they. He had apparently escaped the eyes of the Secret Service men, as none were in sight. The three, Ike, Cranston and Schoenbaechler went quietly about their business, and the sitting was almost over before anyone appeared to disturb them. It was one of the quietest sittings on record.

Cranston and Schoenbaechler were sent to San Francisco to photograph Richard Nixon during his unsuccessful 1960 campaign against John F. Kennedy. Although arrangements had been made for the posing, an unexpected development required Nixon's immediate departure for Los Angeles. He agreed, however, to pose there.

Since it was too late for Cranston to make flight reservations, he asked Nixon if he and Schoenbaechler might be accommodated on the official plane, an arrangement to which Nixon gave ready assent. As the plane reached Los Angeles airport and was about to land, the pilot suddenly pointed the nose of his ship straight up, gained altitude, and came down again. The performance was repeated. On the third try, they landed. A small plane had settled on the runway directly in the path of the big plane. It had apparently failed to notify the tower of its intentions. It was a very narrow escape for the candidate and his party.

Newspapermen frequently have more trouble with officious underlings than with the big men themselves. That was particularly true during the Kennedy administration, when the President's press secretary, Pierre Salinger, made many peremptory decisions about matters on which Kennedy had not been consulted.

It had long been the practice of Presidents never to give exclusive interviews or pose for exclusive pictures. In the event that only one reporter or one photographer was admitted for an interview or picture, anything obtained was shared with all accredited reporters or cameramen. That long-standing rule was broken by Salinger, who had, for some inexplicable reason, developed a dislike for The News, and seemed to take a grim pleasure in turning down its requests. He made it quite clear he was running his office his own way, even to the extent of turning over to one of his favorites an exclusive color assignment proposed originally by the picture editor of The News.

Roosevelt, too, had a few overly-protective men around him. Among the most attentive was Harry Hopkins, his intimate friend and adviser. On one of Winston Churchill's visits to Washington during World War II he displayed his "air-raid suit," a one-piece garment of his own design into which he could scramble in a hurry during London air raids. Warnecke and Cranston were assigned to get a shot of England's famous statesman, and he agreed to pose on the White House lawn. There was the usual admonition that only a couple of minutes were to be allowed for the job.

Churchill came out, planted himself in the chair, greeted the photographers graciously—he may even have recalled their faces, having posed for them on a previous occasion—and announced he was ready. Just one exposure had been made when Hopkins seized Churchill's arm and led him back into the White House. The picture, fortunately, was a good one, and appeared a little later in the Coloroto Magazine. Since, under White House press rules, the picture had to be shared with all photographers present, and copies therefore had to be made, the boys wanted to be certain of development time. Cranston substituted himself for Churchill and Warnecke made a second exposure, which was developed first as a precautionary measure.

In addition to making frequent trips coast to coast and border to border—each year a pair of color men were sent to Florida during spring training to get advance closeup pictures of baseball stars in action, an assignment not possible once the season starts, since camermen are not allowed on the playing fields—Warnecke and Cranston, or other members of their staff, also traveled out of the country on special jobs. Twice, for example, they visited Rome.

The first occasion was for the purpose of recording the elevation of the then Archbishop Francis Spellman to the College of Cardinals. Spellman knew both Warnecke and Cranston quite well, since they had photographed him at his residence on Madison Ave., and he greeted them as old friends when they boarded his plane.

In addition to the assignment concerning Spellman, the two cameramen had been instructed to get, if possible, a sitting with the Pope, Pius XII. He and Spellman were close friends. As papal legate in Washington, Pius, then Eugenio Pacelli, visited New York on many occasions as Spellman's guest.

Warnecke told Spellman of The News' desire to make a picture of the Pope and he promised to do everything he could to get the Pontiff to pose, although he knew that the latter was in rather poor health, and was being closely watched for signs of fatigue. The elevation ceremony was an especially tiring one.

Spellman had arranged a general audience for all members of his entourage, which numbered 150, but when The News photographers arrived at the appointed place, he motioned them aside, saying the prospect was excellent that the Pope would pose privately for them immediately after the general audience. Elated, they dashed back to their hotel to get their equipment and to get themselves in the formal attire required by protocol.

When they returned they learned to their dismay that the Pope, fatigued, had called off the portrait sitting. Warnecke and Cranston were all dressed up with no place to go. But they didn't figure on the persistence of their friend, the Cardinal.

A little later, he informed them that, not only was the posing to take place, but they were also to have a private audience, having missed the public one. For 15 minutes or more they chatted with the Pope about baseball, and particularly the Dodgers, who had been the favorite team of Pacelli when he was stationed in Washington. He presented each photographer with rosary beads, then settled himself for the posing.

The Rome assignment was a sort of combined effort of the Chicago Tribune and The News. A Tribune photographer, Edward Johnson, also attended the sitting, and at one point was confronted with a technical emergency as were Warnecke and Cranston.

Cranston discovered to his dismay that the collection of converters he had fortified himself with to be certain of using the Vatican's electrical system were of no use. However, he had a battery flash which he hooked up and the exposures were made with it. Johnson made his exposures at a given signal from Warnecke, otherwise he would have gone home empty-handed. His lights were useless, too, in the Vatican outlets.

Warnecke and Cranston made another trip to Rome, also with Cardinal Spellman, at the time of Pope Pius' death. After photographing the impressive funeral ceremony, they were instructed to await the election of the new Pope and his elevation to the Papal throne.

In covering this assignment, the elevation of Pope John XXIII, The News photographers found they had almost to be in two places at once. The first part of the ceremonies, the Mass, was to be held inside the Vatican, while the actual crowning, which followed immediately, was in St. Peter's Square.

After a visit to Vatican police headquarters, and a friendly exchange of English and Italian, with neither one understanding the other, but with another exchange that is universally understood, Cranston and the assistant chief of police reached an agreement. A most desirable spot in a balcony directly over the altar was designated as Cranston's very own, and he was instructed to erect his tripod there and lash it down, which he did. He was then directed to the colonnade looking down on the vast square. Another official, who also understood the medium of exchange, reserved a place for Cranston's use during the outdoor ceremony.

Another assignment had been given Warnecke and Cranston—that of photographing in Florence many famous works of art, particularly numerous paintings of the Virgin and Child. These were intended for use in future Christmas editions of the Coloroto Magazine.

To assist in making the selections, Richard Owen, the music and art expert of the Coloroto Magazine, accompanied the photographers on the trip. Owen was a distinguished-looking man, with a thick mane of silvery white hair and an impressive manner. He always carried a walking stick, which he used frequently and emphatically when making a conversational point.

Confronted on the day of Pope John's elevation with the problem of getting his early pictures out of the Vatican, since strict orders had been issued that no one was to leave the building during the ceremony, Cranston saw how Owen could be put to use.

"Here's the way to work it," he told him. "When I turn my film over to you, head right for the entrance. There'll be a guard there, who will insist you do not leave. Just as you approach him, double up with pain, and use your stick as support. Then you'll get through."

The trick worked. The spectacle of the dignified Owen simulating illness softened the heart of the guard, Owen got through, the films made the Acme Newspictures airmail pouch, and were printed the next day in black and white in The News, then used later in color in the Coloroto Magazine.

Most stage and screen stars are only too eager to respond to an invitation to the color studio, but there were exceptions. One of the most notable, of course, was Greta Garbo, who posed for no one and permitted no inteviews. Another was Bing Crosby.

There was nothing haughty about Bing's refusals; it was just impossible to catch up with him. When he paid a visit to New York it was strictly for his own entertainment. He wanted to cram in as many Broadway shows as possible, and he enjoyed a night on the town. For that reason the press department of his studio was never informed of his goings and comings.

On one of those visits to the big town Bing finally broke down and agreed to meet the press in a sort of general audience. The occasion happened also to be his birthday, and a cocktail party was arranged at the Rainbow Room in Rockefeller Center, to which all the movie reviewers were invited. An invitation was also sent to picture editor White of The News. Since he had been trying to get Crosby to pose for some time, he decided to violate a self-imposed rule against attending such affairs and see if he could break Bing down.

The invitation stipulated that the recipient bring along a birthday present for Bing, which in no case should cost more than a dollar. That gave White an idea.

He wrote a birthday greeting in verse addressed to Bing, had it set in type in the composing room, mounted, then had an artist draw appropriate illustrations around the border. In the final verse, Bing was asked to celebrate his birthday properly by agreeing to pose with his family some time in the near future.

This paid off. An answer came from Bing, inviting the color photographers to visit his ranch near Elko, Nev., where he planned to spend much of the summer, or at least all the free time his studio would allow him. His boys were all to be there. The first Mrs. Crosby (Dixie Lee) had requested that she not be included, so The News photographers had to be content with an all-male layout.

The ranch was definitely not for fun, Warnecke and Frank Livia, his assistant, learned on arrival. The boys were not "acting" as cowhands. They worked a full day in the hot sun, pitching hay, milking cows, performing all the other chores normal to a working ranch.

As a result, the picture layout showed the Crosby boys, and their father, engaged in a day's labor. The closing shot was of the group taking their ease at sundown on the front porch of the ranch house. It was used on page 1 of a subsequent issue of the Coloroto Magazine, while the other pictures made up the centerspread.

At times, so busy were the movie factories in Hollywood, that stars could not be spared to make annual trips to New York. There came a period when none showed up, and the stock of portraits in the color studio was almost exhausted. It was suggested to Patterson that color photographers visit the West Coast, to build up the supply and he gave his consent.

Ed Sullivan was The News Hollywood columnist at the time, and Patterson suggested he be informed of the cameramen's visit, so that sittings could be arranged in advance with a minimum loss of time. This was done, but somehow the letter to Sullivan went astray, and nothing had been done when the men arrived. Unable to reach Sullivan, who was out of town, Warnecke made his own appointments and the work proceeded at a rapid pace. He and Elkins made sufficient exposures to fill the barrel to overflowing on their return. A year or two later, a similar situation developed, and Warnecke and Cranston went to Hollywood again.

One of Patterson's favorite movie houses was Radio City Music Hall, and he saw virtually all pictures shown there. He also enjoyed the stage show, and the dancing of the Rockettes intrigued him. He suggested coverage of that famous dance line.

The closing act of the Rockettes performance, precision dancing involving the projection of their shapely legs toward the audience has always evoked a round of enthusiastic applause. That was the pose The News photographers went for, but intense illumination was required, since the exposure had to be instantaneous in order to avoid movement.

Warnecke and Cranston solved that by designing a dozen "coffins"—at least, these boxes bore that resemblance—each containing a row of five photoflood bulbs, which were turned on to get a light reading, then extinguished, and photoflash bulbs substituted. The girls were then instructed to go into their act, and at the precise moment the 60 bulbs were set off simultaneously. Harry brought along a crew of four for this assignment. and as soon as an exposure had been made all rushed to the coffins, removed the spent flashbulbs, and substituted fresh ones. In this way clear pictures of the Rockettes were obtained and another "impossible" feat achieved by The News color photographers.

Little by little the manufacturers of color film have increased the speed of their product. Today some of that film has a higher Weston rating than the film or plates used by the black and white photographers in the early days of The News. As a result, more and more outdoor events are being made in color, even high speed action, such as is seen in football games. With every improvement in film, the scope of the color photographers' work has been widened.

And every issue of the Coloroto Magazine is a testimonial to the amount of thought and plain hard work put into the development of color photography by those pioneers, Warnecke, Cranston, Elkins and Schoenbaecheler of The News.

FORMIDABLE FEMALES

As they are to most men, women were always a mystery to the founder of The News. But Patterson felt that even if he couldn't understand them, other women could—and women were avid readers of his newspaper. That was why he made Mabel McElliott, an ex-secretary, his first drama and movie critic. It was also why he wanted his women reporters to cover the most lurid murder trials, which was allowed although frowned upon, and to witness executions, which was never permitted.

The exploits of the gentler sex on The News could fill a book—and at one point almost did—but the legend most treasured concerns a fragile—on the surface, anyway—beauty who muffed her greatest opportunity just because she possessed those attributes that Patterson had felt should be her strength.

Her name was Imogene Stanley and she came to The News from Texas via Washington. She had experience, she had a flair and she had an ineffable charm that seemed sure to carry her a long way in her chosen profession. A commentator on the scene said she was generally regarded as the loveliest reporter who ever set foot in a New York newspaper office:

> Pale gold hair framed an arresting face. She was slim, tall, eager. She had grace and an ardent spirit. Lawyers slowed up in their summations and fumbled for words when she walked in and took her seat at the press table. Judges beamed on her and jurors were a little bedazzled. Only her skeptical colleagues looked at her with equanimity, wondering vaguely how so delicate a piece of humanity had got loose among them, and what she could possibly be doing that was useful.
>
> Soon she surprised them by proving that she was also a good reporter. She had brains as well as a perfect profile. There was little she couldn't get in the way of news. Doors opened automatically for her. Lawyers gave her secret tips on stories. Butlers thought twice before slamming the door in her face. Her paper was the Daily News and she was manna from heaven for a tabloid.

It was no wonder then that Phil Payne, the managing editor at the time, thought he was wise in sending her to Quebec when Edward, the

Prince of Wales and the secret passion of women on two continents, was passing through in the fall of 1923 on his way to his ranch in Alberta.

Imogene was thrilled at the assignment. She spent a large part of a week's salary on a new green evening dress to take along, even though she wasn't sure she would be able to use it. It might be helpful, she sensed, if she had the slightest chance to follow Payne's instructions to get an interview with the prince, a task that both he and she knew fell in the category of mission impossible.

In much less entrancing raiment she went to the Quebec Golf Club to watch—from a distance, with the rest of the scribes—his highness hack through a round in the September haze. She made her way to the telegraph office and filed a routine story on his game, how he had looked, the clothes he wore, the adoration in the eyes of any female who managed to get near him.

The prince was leaving the next day for the ranch, where no reporters would be allowed, so Imogene knew it had to be that evening or never. She returned to her hotel, the massive Chateau Frontenac, where she had a room and where the prince, who was traveling incognito as Baron Renfrew, had a suite with his retinue. There was a report that he might appear in the dining room that evening so Imogene donned her green gown, took extra pains with her toilette and, perennially hopeful, descended to do a night's work.

Fortune was with her. As she stepped from the elevator she encountered a New York society girl she knew who was on her way to the dining room with her mother. Imogene was invited to join them so she arrived on the scene in the obvious tow of a chaperon of quality.

The prince and his party were already seated and the stately dining hall, which itself might have graced a palace, was packed with Quebec's elite, already in a twitter of anticipation. Imogene's friends had reservations at a table which turned out to be directly opposite the royal group, although some distance away. Imogene went through the courses of the meal automatically, conversing politely but keeping her eyes—as were most of the others in the room—on the slim blond man who dined so elegantly but abstractedly, as if bored with it all.

Suddenly she noticed that the prince's glance had rested on her. Daringly she raised her glass with a brief smile in an unspoken toast and then looked down at her plate, hoping no one else had noticed.

When the band struck up one of the prince's favorite tunes he chose Phyllis Burstall, a Quebec debutante, as his first dancing partner and the floor was soon filled with swaying couples. Imogene watched carefully, taking mental notes for the story she would file as soon as the evening ended.

She was startled from her reveries by a tap on the shoulder. A man of military bearing introduced himself as Gen. Gerald F. Trotter, the prince's groom-in-waiting, and asked for a dance. Once on the floor, he told her he wanted to present her to Baron Renfrew and soon she found herself being introduced to the very person she had come to Quebec to see.

The prince wasted no time. He had obviously decided, as was his habit, on the one girl that was to be his partner for the evening and Imogene was she. Dance after dance they whirled around the floor together, a most attractive couple and increasingly the center of attention.

Speculation grew as to the identity of the mysterious girl in green. The photographer who had been sent along dispatched a wire to The News. "Imogene monopolizing prince. Everybody else nuts. Congrats." Payne could hardly restrain himself. "I knew she could do it," he shouted. "This will be the greatest story of the year."

But he started to worry when the night passed with no word from her. Imogene, oblivious to all mundane things, had gone to bed in her lonely room to stare at the darkened ceiling and relive that long succession of precious moments.

A wire from Payne awaited her the next morning. "File soonest first person story how it feels to dance all night with Prince of Wales. Full details, conversation, etc. Give it the works." Imogene wired back that she had no intention of betraying the prince's trust. He hadn't known she was a newspaperwoman and it would be unfair to reveal any of his confidences. No man, she said, could be expected to appreciate her feelings.

The telegraph office was busy all day handling an exchange of messages. Payne was furious but Imogene was unyielding. The first edition of the next day's News had a factual but dull story with a Quebec dateline which could have been written in the office from news service dispatches—and probably was.

Later editions, however, had more details. Under Payne's hammering, Imogene apparently had broken down a little but it was all written in the most detached third person, such as: "The prince, God bless him, has little of that excess baggage known as 'dance conversation.' His partner's mind is deliciously vacant. The prince doesn't spoil a purely esthetic delight by mental mushrooms."

There was one brief but innocuous quote from his highness: "Dance is work when the time is too fast," and a somewhat garbled explanation: "He likes a lingering foxtrot, if the orchestra would please him, beat the drum slowly and play the saxophone well, not too Ted Lewis." About his terpsichorean technique: "His grasp is light, tightened only at such vital moments as the pivot, in which he excels. One need not fear for her toes—or those of any other—the prince dances on his own feet."

The story went on and on, just as if somebody only remotely involved had interviewed a Cinderella who had been lucky enough to float in the arms of some prince charming before being forced to flee at midnight. There was no byline, no intimation of who might have written the story except for Imogene's picture—not a very flattering one—identified not by name but only as the "mysterious girl in green" about whom all the other papers were wondering.

Imogene returned from Canada and covered trials and other assignments but she never seemed quite the same. After a while she left and went to live with a sister on the edge of a desert in the Southwest. It seemed like a terrible waste of beauty and talent.

The first of the tough breed of women reporters who developed on The News—Imogene had been plenty tough before her heart was melted—was Julia Harpman, who later became the wife of columnist Westbrook Pegler. With a couple of years of experience in the courthouse pressrooms of Knoxville, Tenn., Julia arrived in New York eight months after The News was born. There had just been a newspaper merger and it was not a good time to be looking for a job but Payne gave her a difficult assignment as a test and when she came back with an exclusive, he decided to hire her. He never regretted the decision.

Payne did not believe in doing anything conventionally if a spectacular method could be found and Julia was just the girl to aid and abet him. In "Ladies of the Press," Ishbel Ross tells of a more or less typical episode. Although Miss Ross carefully avoids saying so, the case involved was the Hall-Mills murder and the suspect was Willie Stevens, the brother of Mrs. Hall:

> In one of the great murder cases of the period, still unsolved, Mr. Payne was convinced that the person least under suspicion had committed the crime. As an amateur ball player, Mr. Payne fancied the terminology of the diamond.
>
> "Let's pitch to this guy's weakness, if he has one," he told Miss Harpman.
>
> She happened to know that the man in question was interested in spiritualism. So Mr. Payne decided that he would frighten him into confession at a seance. He had the art department prepare a letter-head designed for a mythical Madame Astra. It had hoot-owls, cobras, black tomcats and toads surrounding a line-drawing of a veiled brunette with curtain-rings in her ears.

Bernadine Szold, an exotic-looking girl reporter then working on The News, was assigned to go the rounds of the New York mystics to pick up atmosphere. She was to be Madame Astra. Bernadine might have been born for the role. She went to Cain's warehouse, where the scenery of Broadway's forgotten shows is stored, and dug out a black velvet backdrop that had been used in the Follies, a plaster pedestal with a green snake coiled around the column, a large brass Buddha and a mock throne. She borrowed a crystal ball from an optician, and a scene-shifter set up the magic props in her apartment.

Madame Astra then wrote to the suspect, saying that her spirit control had news for him. The day after the letter arrived, Miss Harpman talked to him in his kitchen. He was used to hourly invasions by the press and it was quite natural for him to chat about the letters he received. He was an odd character—seemingly as simple as a child; actually very cunning. He asked Miss Harpman's advice about the letter from the seeress.

"Well," she said, "I don't believe in spirits but if you do I don't want to advise you against seeing this woman. But watch out for a trick."

"I was afraid of that," he said. "I won't go unless you go with me."

So they went together to Madame Astra's. They were welcomed at the door by a swarthy young man masquerading as a snake-charmer.

"You stay out," he told Miss Harpman. "The gentleman must come in alone to see Madame."

Behind the velvet curtain sat two stenographers, the prosecutor, two detectives and Mr. Payne. Every effort was made to crack the seemingly feeble mentality of the victim. All sorts of abracadabra was sprung on him. The legend on Park Row at the time was that his wife's ghost appeared with clanking chains but failed to make him turn a hair. Bernadine tried to break him down by subtle and obvious methods. She evoked strange images from the crystal. She recalled the looks and gestures of his wife. But the suspect rambled along in his characteristic vein and showed no signs of alarm.

By this time he was used to all sorts of inquisitions. For weeks some of the toughest tykes and brightest wits of the newspaper profession had been badgering him unmercifully in his kitchen and his inevitable reaction had been to lift the stove-lid with its holder and spit thoughtfully into the flames. They were just as unsuccessful as the police.

So the seance was a flop. The suspect didn't confess. He didn't even bat an eyelash. He was never charged with the crime.

But it was certainly a demonstration of the lengths to which Payne and his girl reporters would go on even the slightest chance of coming up with a good story.

For more than six years Julia handled murder after murder, trial after trial. She covered Ku Klux forays in Georgia and the last of Harry K. Thaw's sanity hearings in Philadelphia. She went to prize fights and World Series games. While flying to Atlantic City to do a feature on Luis Firpo training for his fight with Dempsey, the plane plunged into the ocean and she had a miraculous escape.

One of her jobs for The News, as is recorded elsewhere, was to accompany Gertrude Ederle in a boat, while she swam the English Channel.

Over the half century, The News has had more than its share of hustling, bustling Amazons and Valkyries but it has also had many less colorful yet perhaps more valuable contributors on its distaff side. Chief among them was Mary King, who later became the wife of the publisher. Although she never worked on a city staff or went out on a news assignment, she almost seemed to be born a newspaper woman.

Miss King was one of seven children of a Chicago physician. Convent schooled, she had taken a business course and obtained her first job in 1907 as second secretary to Medill McCormick, then publisher of the Chicago Tribune. When Patterson came back to the paper, she became his secretary, then assistant, then Sunday editor. Through Patterson's editorial apprenticeship, and the development of features and promotions that escalated Sunday circulation, she became so familiar with Patterson's thinking that she was almost his editorial alter ego and often contributed a point of view that escaped him.

She also made him conscious of the potentials of the woman reader, suggested features of service and consequence to women. These, and another of her ideas—that the Tribune carry reviews of motion pictures—were important ingredients of The News almost from the beginning, although Miss King did not come to the paper until 1921 and then stayed only about a year before returning to the Tribune. Except for that interlude, she was the Tribune's Sunday editor from 1914 to 1926, when she became woman's editor of Liberty Magazine.

Miss King's younger sister, Loretta, also joined Liberty as a manuscript reader. She had been with Essanay, a Chicago film producing company, and was later secretary to Henry Kitchell Webster, the author. Early in her career she sold a movie script, her first and last, to Selig Studios for $35. It was a short silent film called "Love vs. Pride." At Liberty she wrote a short story which had a movie-theater setting and which so impressed the editors that she was promptly promoted to movie critic.

When Liberty ceased publication in 1931, the King sisters both moved to The News, Mary as woman's editor and Loretta as assistant movie critic. In a way Mary King had been associated with the paper from its inception because she began buying novels for serialization in The News in 1919 while performing the same service for the Tribune. "Blue Ribbon Fiction" it was called and it included not only many of the best-known authors but was appearing in print for the first time. Miss King retired in January, 1969.

When Irene Thirer, who was head of the movie reviewing staff, left The News in 1934, Loretta King took her place, also assuming Miss Thirer's byline, Kate Cameron, a pseudonym concocted by Patterson (Cameron for Camera and Kate for its alliterative value.) She also kept the star-rating system, an innovation which had been suggested by Mary King.

Upon her retirement in 1967, Loretta was unable even to guess how many movies she'd seen but she was looking forward to watching some more without having to worry about what she'd write about them. Her favorites? It would have to be a toss-up between "Gone With The Wind" and "The Informer." She was succeeded as chief reviewer by her long-time associate, Wanda Hale, who came to The News in 1933.

Another Chicagoan who came to the paper in its diaper stage and left an indelible imprint was Antoinette Donnelly. She was born into a poor family of nine brothers and sisters in Mount Forest, Ontario, and was given her name because her mother was addicted to French novels. When her father, a station agent, died, her mother took the family to Buffalo, where Antoinette taught herself typing and shorthand and eventually found work on the Chicago Tribune.

Lillian Russell, a renowned beauty and sometimes actress, was writing (or at least lending her name to) a column on health and beauty. Laura Jean Libby, prolific author of sad and saccharine novels very popular with women, was officiating in a similar capacity devoted to love and romance. Miss Donnelly became their joint secretary. In time she took over the beauty column under her own name and the love-lorn column under the name of Doris Blake.

Both columns were syndicated. Those in The News drew as many as 10,000 letters a day. A staff of five helped with her correspondence, which either provided direct answers to problems or included helpful booklets, of which she wrote more than 125 covering an amazing variety of subjects.

When "Disappointed" wrote Miss Blake that she was 17 and had never been kissed or even had a boy friend, she was advised to send a stamped, addressed envelope for the pamphlet "Getting and Keeping Boys Interested." But there was a different answer for "Edna," who wrote:

"I am in love with a married man and he tells me that he loves his wife and kids too. He can't understand himself how he can love the both of us the way he does. Do you think he is kidding me?"

The reply: "If you continue to see and believe the polygamous gentleman, you are proving nothing if not that you put a fairly low price on yourself. See if it isn't the forbidden fruit that fires your somewhat wobbly imagination. That's what we think ails you, sister."

Her advice on health and beauty was always sane and sensible, based on counsel she received from physicians, psychologists, chemists, nutrition experts and cosmeticians. In addition to all her other work (she also wrote a small daily interview-and-personality column called "Chatter"), she was great at improvising newsworthy stunts.

In November, 1921, she initiated her first reducing contest in New York, with the blessing of Dr. Royal S. Copeland, the city's health commissioner. Fifty fat women were put on a diet and engaged in prescribed exercises in Madison Square Garden, with daily reports of their measurements and weight losses. The following year came "The Transformation of Ruth," in which a plain young woman was turned into a passable beauty with diet, exercise and attention to complexion, hair and clothes.

Miss Donnelly retired in June, 1963, and died the following year.

Two of Patterson's daughters by his first wife, Alicia and Josephine, had brief and unspectacular careers on The News but Alicia later evidenced the ink in her veins by founding, on Long Island, one of the country's most flourishing newspapers, Newsday.

Although The News in its early days made no pretense of catering to the upper crust, Patterson believed it should have a society column. The working girl and the average housewife, he felt, would be interested in reading about the doings of their wealthier sisters, particularly if they were misdoings. Several male members of the staff had been filling in as society reporters, at first using the byline Angela and then Debutante, but the first woman hired specifically for the job was Grace Robinson.

The society columns of most of the rival papers were stilted and formal and Grace's breezy approach to coverage of the haut monde was a welcome contrast. She went south for the winter social season, as The News society editor still does, and one afternoon while she was lingering on the sands at Palm Beach, she saw flames leaping from the roof of the Breakers Hotel, a mecca of the rich. She had never covered a fire before, but the way she handled that one convinced Patterson that she was too good a reporter to be confined to the social whirl.

Soon she was taking big assignments from the city desk and she probably wrote as many words on as great a variety of subjects as anyone, male or female, ever employed by The News. Her period of service lasted almost 43 years, ending with her retirement in 1964, because of ill health.

Grace was born in Beatrice, Neb., and was in her junior year at the University of Nebraska when her father died and she had to earn a living. She started on the Omaha Bee at $10 a week and held several newspaper jobs before she was hired to modernize the women's page of the New York Mail. She was spotted there by Patterson.

Her memory is sharp and vivid in detail, as witness her recent account of her first trip abroad when she was just an iron-willed wisp of attractive femininity with only a smattering of high-school German:

> In the summer of 1932 Greta Garbo announced she was taking a trip to Europe. She hadn't renewed her contract with M-G-M and Mr. Patterson thought this might mean that she planned to retire. He told me to get on the same boat with her, find out what I could of her plans, and send back a story every day by wireless.
>
> Harvey Deuell, then city editor, was delighted. He said he knew a code which would be just the thing because no one on the boat would know what I was sending. It was pretty complicated and involved the use of a big square of paper with letters both up and down and across. I finally learned how to use it and was all set to go except that Miss Garbo hadn't said what boat she was taking. I was living in Connecticut and had to stay in a New York hotel with my bags packed.
>
> Finally it was learned she was going on the Gripsholm so I booked passage and left with her. There wasn't much to report the first day out but I wrote a story and, with a lot of effort, put it into code and sent it.
>
> The next day Garbo didn't show up at all, but I wrote a story anyhow and coded it and took it to the radio operator. He grinned and said: "You're going to a lot of work for nothing. I'm an old Swedish navy man and I recognized your code the moment I saw it. It's one of the oldest there is."
>
> I realized then he had told the captain who had warned Garbo that a newspaperwoman was aboard. After that it became a sort of a game, with the entire crew trying to protect their famous passenger and the other 33 passengers trying to help me, because everybody now knew what was happening.
>
> My deck chair was removed from the top deck so Garbo could play games without being disturbed. Every time I managed to sneak up there she would run for her stateroom. She appeared in the

dining room only three times and would talk to none of the passengers except two or three who sat at the captain's table.

I sent a note to her stateroom every day but they were all returned unopened. Finally, on the last night out, I found Garbo's door unguarded and knocked.

"Who is it?" she asked in the voice I knew so well.

"My name is Robinson and I have to talk to you." I said.

"In the morning," she replied. "Not now. Go away."

A dozen Swedish reporters swarmed aboard the next morning and she was very nice to them. She just gave me a cold look and said "You're the one who spoiled my trip. I hope I do not see you again."

So there I was in Stockholm, with Garbo having vanished somewhere in the woodwork, and feeling that I had muffed an assignment through no fault of mine. Then I received a cable from Mr. Patterson. He said that since I was so near Russia, I might as well go there and bring back a story on how it felt to be a tourist in a country that nobody knew much about.

I knew it would be futile to try diplomatic channels so I just went to the travel agent in the lobby of the hotel and told him I wanted to go to Russia. He asked for my passport. In the space which asked whom to notify in case of difficulties, I had written "Paris edition Chicago Tribune."

Spotting that, he said: "Russia does not accept newspaperwomen."

I told him I was on a vacation and just wanted to go to Russia as a tourist, which was at least partially true.

"Oh, that's different," he said. "I'll see what I can do."

While I was waiting to see what would happen, I met a young Swedish reporter who worked for an afternoon Stockholm paper. He spoke English well and was very considerate, almost affectionate, in showing me around town. The Russian visa came through in a week, which was very fast. My friend escorted me to the boat which was to take me to Finland on the way to Leningrad, and as we parted he said:

"That visa came through too easily. Something may be wrong. Promise me you will write me and let me know you are all right." I promised.

I spent a week on a tour ($93 for seven days, second class) and another week on a trip which took me to Moscow, and I described it all in a long article in The News, accompanied by photographs which I took surreptitiously. Of course I didn't do any writing until I got back to New York. I found it was impossible to get any sort of message out of Russia. As a result, my friend's Stockholm paper carried a front page story with the headline "Lost In Russia," telling about the American girl who had left for Russia and hadn't been heard from since.

I left Russia through Poland and finally reached Berlin. It was just before Hitler and the streets were full of brownshirts. There were riots on the Unter Den Linden about every hour.

When I cabled the office of my arrival I received an answer from Mr. Patterson telling me to collect material for a series on the German economic situation, which was in bad shape. With the help of Sigrid Schultz, who was head of the Berlin bureau of the Chicago Tribune, I was able to get a comprehensive idea of conditions and I took some good photos.

Just as I was finishing up (incidentally, the series was never used), a message came from Colonel Hause, the managing editor. Jimmy Walker had resigned as Mayor of New York as a result of hearings before Gov. Roosevelt and was comforting himself in Europe. He was scheduled to sail for home on the Rex, a new Italian liner which was the pride and joy of the Fascists and was to make her maiden voyage from Genoa to New York.

"Pick up Jimmy," Hause had cabled. I took a train to Munich, from where I could get a plane to Venice. It was a misty, foggy day. There was trouble first about my luggage, which I refused to leave behind. Finally all eight pieces were laid in the aisle, which made the other 11 passengers nervous. They looked grimly out the windows as we began to thread our way through the Dolomites, which thrust up like stone needles through the fog on either side of the plane.

They fascinated me and I took out a small camera and aimed it. The steward quickly confiscated it, telling me in German that Mussolini had forbidden any pictures. When the perilous flight ended I discovered it hadn't been necessary because the Rex wouldn't leave for five days. I cabled for permission to take part of my vacation and spent the time in Florence and Rome. Fortunately I made my reservation ahead because I got the last cabin. Like everything else on the ship—except the machinery—it was magnificent.

The great new liner broke down at Gibraltar and we all went ashore. Walker planted himself in the Continental Cafe and assured us he would stay there until 5 p.m., so a couple of reporters from New York and I went on a motor trip. I discovered I was running out of money and notified Hause to cable me some at once.

Walker was getting restless. He had taken the Rex because it was scheduled to arrive in time for a Democratic convention. He hoped to start a stampede to nominate him for a new term. Finally, he announced he was taking a train to Paris to catch the Europa, a German ship. No money had arrived and I was frantic.

I sat in the cable office the next day and finally some money came—just enough to pay my fare to Paris. Walker was 24 hours ahead of me and I fretted through the two days and two nights on the train. I had wired the Chicago Tribune office in Paris to have someone meet me with money. It was a Sunday and a young man showed up with a few francs he had managed to collect from other reporters.

"Hurry!" he said, pulling me into a taxi. "You just have time to catch the boat train to Cherbourg." When we arrived at the platform, Walker was posing for pictures. "My dear child, where did you come from?" he asked as I got out of the cab. I kept close to him and got aboard the Europa as a member of his entourage.

As soon as the ship sailed I went to the purser and told him I had to have a first-class cabin which my office would pay for. He reluctantly consented. There were a few other newspaper people aboard, including a vice-president of the United Press. Walker, who had reconciled himself to arriving in New York too late for his anticipated blitz, summoned us to the smoking room and read a message he had radioed to the convention, which had convened at that hour. It announced his retirement from politics.

We all scrambled for the radio room. I tripped on my dress and fell, and the operator was so sorry for me that he sent my story first, line by line as I scribbled it on a note pad.

I know you'll think I made this up, but Doris Fleeson, sitting in the convention at almost the same moment, felt a piece of paper blow against her leg and picked it up. It was a copy of Walker's message to the convention, which hadn't yet been read. So The News had a scoop on the same story from two sources 1,000 miles apart.

Grace, who covered a thousand fascinating yarns for The News, has enough recollections to complete this volume. Some of them are strictly feminine, like the two mental images she has of Libby Holman.

Libby, a blues singer who made "Moanin' Low" famous, married Smith Reynolds, 20-year-old heir to $20,000,000 of the Reynolds tobacco fortune. When her bridegroom was shot through the temple on the bed they shared in Winston-Salem, N.C., in July, 1932, and she was later reportedly found in the arms of his best friend, things looked bad for her.

"I remember how beautiful Libby looked when she testified at a coroner's inquest in the living room of the Reynolds home," Grace says. "She was wearing a white peignoir and I thought she was either telling the truth or was a superb actress.

"The next time I saw her she was in black at the graveside. The seams of her stockings were crooked. I said to myself: 'Any woman that beautiful who didn't bother to see that her stockings were straight must really have loved her husband.' I was sure she was innocent and I'm glad the courts agreed."

There were so many lurid details in so many of the cases Grace encountered that she learned early to use polite euphemisms. Even so she was sometimes in trouble.

When a sportsman named Benjamin Collings was killed on his anchored yacht off New Rochelle in September, 1939, by a pair of husky pirates who climbed aboard from a canoe, his wife said one of the men was overly attentive to her. A reporter asked Mrs. Collings bluntly if his attentions had caused her to have a physical reaction and then told Grace, who was writing the story, that he didn't receive a satisfactory answer.

The police also questioned Mrs. Collings and Grace quite tactfully stated, far down in the story, that the widow had admitted "that the attentions of the older of the two pirates were not altogether disagreeable to her."

"The next day Mr. Patterson called me into his office," Grace says, "and told me that such a line should not appear in a family newspaper. At first I thought he was kidding but he was so serious that he took me off the story."

After Grace Robinson (the wife of Robert Conway, whose years on The News almost equalled her own) ceased to function as Debutante, a long procession of unidentified writers took over the task, ending with an elegant young man named Alec (Alexander N.D.) Rackowe, whose two-year stint ended in May, 1928.

City editor Deuell then called in Inez Callaway, who had been working for a year and a half in the Sunday department. "Starting tomorrow," he said, "you're handling the society column."

"You can't really mean it," Miss Callaway said. "What do I know about society? I don't like champagne and I buy my hats in bargain basements."

"Try it for a month, anyhow," Deuell told her. "There isn't anybody else and you may like it."

She tried it and she liked it, although she wasn't fooling when she said she knew nothing about the milieu into which she was flung. She was born on a cattle ranch in California and grew up in Caldwell, Idaho, which had a population of 4,000. She got her first newspaper job when she was 15 because she wanted silk stockings for school and her parents wouldn't buy them for her. She attended the University of Idaho, took a journalism course at the University of Missouri, worked a couple of years on the Tulsa (Okla.) Daily World and was hired by Patterson after she showed him her scrapbook.

One of her first assignments was to interview Hugh Walpole, the English novelist, who was staying with friends in Manhattan. She had read his books and she could hardly wait to meet him. When a tall, distinguished looking man with a British accent answered the door, Inez started her questions at once. "I am the butler," the man said. "I will take you to Mr. Walpole." As it worked out, Walpole spent most of the time interviewing *her* because the Hall-Mills case was on at the time and he wanted to know all about it. Later she became on speaking terms with some of the best butlers in the business.

Miss Callaway didn't want to use her own byline on the society column (which was just as well because she married the following year and was known thereafter as Inez Robb) and Patterson thought Debutante had become passe so they settled on Nancy Randolph, a debutantish-sounding name which has graced The News society column ever since.

During Inez' tenure of the job, the column attained a sparkle so compelling that it began to be read by the Four Hundred as well as the two million. When her assistant, Mildred Lovell, attempted to interview John Jacob Astor and he replied "Aw, nuts!" Inez gave the expression a degree of fame that it didn't achieve again until the Battle of the Bulge.

In 1938 Inez left the paper to become a roving reporter and a nationally-syndicated columnist. She was succeeded on The News by Frances Kilkenny, who had been her assistant, and then by Barbara Boston, a member of the Hudnut toiletries family, who turned out to be too close to the society forest to see the trees.

Julia McCarthy, who took over in 1946 and has been Nancy Randolph ever since, was as unlikely a candidate as might be imagined but has done remarkably well. Although Julia started out as an artist, she had become a hard-boiled reporter of the old school long before she joined The News in 1933. She had worked on the Journal and the World, where, among other things, she was famous for having written the story of gangster Frankie Yale's funeral in the argot of the underworld.

In her first 13 years on The News, Julia had tackled almost every kind of difficult assignment except anything to do with society but in the succeeding 23 years she has become the confidante of an amazing number of reigning dowagers as well as the bane of aspiring sprigs of the noveau riche.

Not all women reporters could write their own copy. Several, like Edna Ferguson, always needed someone to put their stories into the king's English. Rewrite men called her Faux-Pas Fergy. Anyone who did anything outstanding was, in her lingo, a toot sweet guy. If she had been out on a late assignment, she called it an all-night virgil.

But Fergy, who spent the major part of her lifetime on The News, was invaluable nonetheless. Possessing an airplane pilot's license and having worked as a wing walker and parachustist, nothing could faze her. When something seemingly impossible needed doing, she was the girl to call on.

A nefarious character named Larry Fay was in trouble with the law during a milk-delivery scandal and Edna was told to see what she could get on him. She altered her appearance only slightly—she was no Imogene Stanley—and resembled a gun moll sufficiently to walk brazenly into one of his haunts and pick up the phone when he called. Before Fay quite realized what was happening, he had given her some very damaging quotes which News readers got with their coffee the next morning.

The issue of Aug. 18, 1930, carried a story with an Edna Ferguson byline (but put together by a rewrite man) which began:

> In the bedroom of America's richest spinster, the 78-year-old mistress of $100,000,000 or more, two ancient high-backed twin beds stand side by side.
>
> One is for the fabulously wealthy heiress, Miss Ella B. Wendel, last of her line, and the other is for the creature now dearest to her—her faithful dog.
>
> The entire routine of the Wendel mansion revolves around the needs and comforts of this pampered animal, a small white poodle, The News learned yesterday. For yesterday the shuttered, sequestered Wendel mansion, at Fifth Ave. and 39th St., decaying symbol of a bygone age in a district now otherwise given over entirely to business, and long an object of curiosity, opened its doors to a reporter for the first time since its erection in 1856.

The reporter was, of course, Fergy. She had been told by the city editor to see if she could get inside, a chore clearly the equivalent of breaking out of the Tombs. She began questioning people who worked in the area and learned from the doorman of a nearby Fifth Ave. shop that Ella, the last of six Wendel sisters, was at her estate in Irvington, N.Y., and that all repairs to the mansion were handled by a carpenter who lived down the street.

Fergy telephoned the caretaker of the Wendel mansion and told him the carpenter was sending her to make an estimate on some restorative work. He told her the front door had been nailed and bolted for a decade but to come to the back. He let her in but watched every move suspiciously. She had to talk fast to convince him of her authenticity, chatting carelessly about a new patented process for restoring old ceilings, but she managed to see almost every room in the house and found out about the poodle. It was a swell story.

In 1933 Patterson decided that if the Morgan Library, a stately marble edifice in the center of Manhattan, was to occupy, tax free, a valuable piece of property it should stop catering to graduate students and such and should be open to anybody. Marty Sommers, whose thick glasses and slicked-down hair made him look studious, tried it first and got nowhere. His story the next morning, counting on the reader's remembering a recent picture of a midget sitting on J. P. Morgan's lap, began:

"So far as I was able to discover, a midget gets into the Morgan Library without any trouble at all, but other people stand no chance."

The next day one of the girl reporters, Rosaleen Doherty, made the attempt. She was polite and was turned away just as politely, so the assignment was given to Fergy.

Fergy was too much for the doorman to handle so he left her standing outside and came back with a Miss Green, the library director, who had handled such situations before but found herself helpless with a woman who just wouldn't take no for an answer. Finally, with a sigh, she capitulated. Fergy was let in and shown around. Patterson commented editorially on the experience of his reporters and after that the Morgan Library was a much easier place to enter.

Another tax-free piece of property was Gramercy Park, closed to all but the surrounding residents who were supplied with keys. Carl Warren tried to get in with no success. Fergy waited until two mild-looking ladies opened the gate to leave and then she nipped in, smiling gaily and waving a bunch of keys as though she could have entered at any time. A News photographer got a picture of her ingress and her ejection a few minutes later—and it was another good story.

Rosaleen Doherty, who didn't make it at the library, and Marjorie Colahan were a couple of attractive young women who may not have had the writing zing of some of their editorial sisters but were always around to help on Patterson's campaigns. They wore shorts and pajamas when he was fighting for cooler summer clothing, or slipped down one strap of a bathing suit on a public beach to see if they would be arrested, or learned to swim or ski or ride a bicycle, or smuggled cigarets into New York from tax-free New Jersey.

Rosaleen did get arrested for wearing shorts in Yonkers in violation of a much-criticized city ordinance and her mock-heroic "Now-I-am-about-to-die" story from a Yonkers cell helped to do away with the shorts ban, which was quashed by the court of appeals the following year when The News fought the case.

She started as a stenographer and held a variety of jobs until she was hired by Liberty as a script reader. She was transferred to The News in 1931 and remained with the paper until her death in 1950. Marjorie came to The News as a reporter in 1925 and stayed 12 years.

Some of those on the distaff side preferred to remain ladylike unless it was to their advantage to sound otherwise but felt they were as good as men on any level, including the use of rough language. When Florabel Muir and Irene Corbally Kuhn sat at adjoining desks in the Park Place office, the male reporters made a practice of trying to goad them into a fight with each other because such a verbal spat was always productive of so many new cuss words and colorful phrases of opprobrium.

Both were enterprising reporters, trained in the dare-devil, out-of-my-way school. Florabel started her career in Salt Lake City, moved to San Francisco, where she was the only woman copyreader in town, and worked on The News until she moved to Hollywood. She was a Hollywood correspondent of The News for years and has been the paper's Hollywood columnist since Hedda Hopper died in 1966.

Irene, a native New Yorker, was on The News twice. During one of her absences she attended a farewell party in Paris for Peggy Hull, a News war correspondent who was preparing to leave for Shanghai. Somebody suggested that Irene ought to accompany Peggy so, on the spur of the moment, she did. In Shanghai she met and married Bert L. Kuhn, a transplanted Chicago newspaperman.

Among other extremely capable women who helped to make The News go was Ama Barker. She came to New York from Knoxville, Ky., with a delightful Southern drawl, and even at the time of her retirement in 1965 no one would have accused her of being a down-Easterner.

But Ama's route to New York was not direct. After serving as a reporter on the Knoxville Sentinel, she tried her wings in Chicago on an illustrated tabloid section of the Herald Examiner before tackling what was then the Mecca of all newspaper people—New York City.

The big town didn't exactly open its arms to her. A canvass of all the editorial offices in the city was fruitless, but the young lady was not discouraged. She managed to sell an occasional feature story, while at the same time doing publicity for Consolidated Edison. One particularly good piece which she sold to The News attracted attention, and when an opening appeared in the Sunday department she was hired. That was in 1925.

From that time on Ama was a sort of "maid of all work" there. She wrote many feature stories, some of them under her own name, others under pseudonyms that the paper employed to avoid byline duplication.

She read copy, wrote heads, checked proofs, did composing room makeup. It is not surprising, therefore, that eventually she became Sunday Editor.

Mention was made earlier of Patterson's daily habit of making a round of the various sub-departments in editorial. Generally on Thursday, he made a somewhat lengthy call in the Sunday Department. A special chair was reserved for him on those visits, and it is still a treasured part of the furniture of the Sunday Department.

Patterson was an exceedingly restless man. As the conversation proceeded he would cross and uncross his legs; tilt his chair way back, causing considerable concern among those present that he would tip over backward but that never happened; get up and stretch, then drop his considerable bulk back into the chair again. He was a big man, not stout, but heavily muscled, and he kept himself in condition by almost daily sessions of handball.

Patterson's part of the conversations consisted mainly of questions. Although they were directed primarily at the Sunday editor, there was no official protocol. Anyone who thought he, or she, had the answer was expected to speak up, and it was on those occasions that Ama revealed her real worth. Many of the suggestions that later turned into stories came from her.

Another gifted girl who participated in those huddles was Ruth Reynolds. Readers of The News, particularly of the Sunday edition, should be quite familiar with that byline, since it has appeared over the weekly Justice story for more than three decades.

Ruth came to The News almost fresh out of Marquette University in Milwaukee—she had had a short period of newspaper work on the Wisconsin News before coming to New York—and her credentials were good enough to gain her an offer by managing editor Hause of a temporary job. She became a permanent member of the Sunday Department staff soon after her arrival. While she did, on occasion, work for the city editor, most of her assignments came from the Sunday editor.

"I've been with The News for 41 years now," Ruth said recently, "and I still haven't been told that my job wasn't temporary."

When Irene Schroeder and Glenn Dagu were sentenced to death for the killing of a cop in New Castle, Pa., in 1929, Ruth was there. It marked the first time she ever heard anyone sentenced to death.

Dutifully, she rushed to the nearest Western Union office, filed her story and then fled to her hotel room where she proceeded to bury her head in a pillow and "cry and cry."

Half an hour later, her tears dried and having returned herself to a reasonably composed state, she started negotiating for the right to cover the executions. That was what Patterson had ordered and she was going to obey, no matter how it hurt. She was much relieved when she was told flatly—as Grace Robinson was on another occasion—that women were not allowed in death chambers.

Two of the most active reporters on The News in the '30s were Doris Fleeson and Norma Abrams. Doris is referred to elsewhere. The story still persists today that the Seabury investigation, which she was covering, was delayed so she might give birth to a daughter.

Norma was teaching in Bellingham, a small town in Washington, and hated it. An uncle who had a pull with the local editor got her a newspaper job. She came to The News in 1929 and is still on the staff, being the paper's principal liaison with the FBI and the federal courts.

She has covered so many trials that her dreams are sometimes haunted by courtrooms but if there is one place that is fixed indelibly in her mind, every brick and stone and board, it is the Englewood home of Dwight W. Morrow. She spent six weary weeks in front of it waiting for an announcement of the wedding of Anne Morrow and Charles Lindbergh—only to have them release the story elsewhere. Then, as is told in another chapter, she spent a similar period on the same spot hoping for word of the kidnaped Lindbergh baby.

It took a certain type of woman to work on The News in the old days, as witness the case of Eleanore Kellogg, who was considered one of the genuinely first-rate news writers in the country. She spent three years on the paper and then was told, so she complained: "You're too calm and critical to work on a tabloid." It may even have been true.

Two bylines very familiar to current readers of the paper are Theo Wilson and Kitty Hanson. On their shoulders have fallen mantles difficult to fill.

Theo, once described as "a remarkable pixie," is a regular ringsider at murder trials. The more passionate the crime, the more purple her prose. In 1952, Theo filed more than 50,000 words from Cleveland as Dr. Sam Sheppard was brought to trial for the murder of his wife.

Dr. Sam was found guilty. Subsequently, he was released and when his new bride, Ariane, arrived form Germany in October, 1967, Theo was at planeside in Cleveland. Dr. Sam and Ariane embraced, but it was a very special kind of embrace or, as Theo's lead put it, "a kiss that must have wilted the purple orchid he was carrying for her."

Gary, Ind., is a steel mill town. Kitty Hanson, one of its natives, came away from there with a steely glint in her eye in 1954 when she joined The News as its education editor.

Aside from being the Kitty that got the mouse (she engineered a massive rat chase when The News decided to promote a clean-city campaign), she has won a wall full of awards for series on nursing homes and reformatories.

Her feature on the gangs of Spanish Harlem in 1955 led to more awards and a book, "I Lived With a Teen Gang." Reminiscing on that series and that summer, Kitty says, "I became quite adept at four-letter Anglo-Saxon words with a Spanish accent."

No wonder Patterson couldn't understand women.

JMP AND FDR

It is considered rather proper, when discoursing on an epic situation, to dig up an epic bit of doggerel to give it an overall sheen. Most suited, perhaps, to consideration of the strange relationship of Joseph Medill Patterson and Franklin Delano Roosevelt is Rudyard Kipling's observation that "there is neither East nor West, Border, nor Breed, nor Birth, when two strong men stand face to face, though they come from the ends of the earth."

These were certainly two strong men. In breed and birth and behavior they were quite alike, aristocrats who strayed from the common course of their ilk by caring for the common man, although one evinced that tendency much earlier than the other. They were close friends during most of the 1930s but when that friendship ended and they came face to face the sparks lit up the sky.

That Roosevelt was a potential President was clear to Patterson by 1930 and the thought didn't bother him although he had some reservations. On March 4 of that year, exactly three years before the Roosevelt inaugural, he observed editorially that FDR would be less than human if his dreams did not include something higher than the governorship of New York but expressed worry about the firmness of his stand against Prohibition. When United States District Attorney Charles H. Tuttle was nominated to oppose Roosevelt for governor that year, the editorial comment was merely that it looked like "an interesting battle," particularly since both were wet.

But on Oct. 25, after The News had taken a straw poll which showed Roosevelt in the lead, the editorial was headed: "It Looks Like Roosevelt But We Prefer Tuttle." Roosevelt won handily and went on, as Patterson had foreseen, to become the leading candidate for the Democratic Presidential nomination in 1932.

"Maybe he is the man of destiny in 1932," an editorial said that May. "We don't see as many objections to Roosevelt as President as some people see. He has been called a weakling, often. But he was the real Secretary of the Navy under Wilson, and an extremely able one."

There was still that nagging suspicion that FDR might not be as strong a wet as Patterson would like him to be. The editorial continued: "We're worried mainly about what he may do with regard to Prohibition. Leading drys call him 'the most satisfactory wet.' We wish Frank Roosevelt would let the country know exactly what he proposes to do about Prohibition."

When Roosevelt was nominated by the Democrats after a bitter battle with his old friend, Al Smith, Patterson, always looking for the human quality in any situation, wondered editorially what made these two men fall out. "If the true story of the Roosevelt-Smith feud could be known, we believe it would be one of the most interesting stories in American political history."

The News yet didn't say it wanted FDR to win, or even say that it thought he would win, but it gave him a good chance.

"The Democratic nominee's gallant fight against infantile paralysis, which struck him when his political future seemed assured, will certainly help him. He has turned that disability into an asset of great value. Since he first entered politics he was a dashing, dramatic figure; this illness, which he has fought to a standstill, has made him also an appealing figure."

There were three consecutive editorials on the situation and they ended: "It ought to be a lively campaign. Here's hoping it will be, to take our minds off our other worries."

By September the paper thought FDR was as good as in—"The News state-wide Presidential poll indicates at this time that Gov. Roosevelt will carry his state; and the man who carries New York this year will probably be the next President of the United States." In October The News announced its support of him, mainly because of his stand for repeal of Prohibition. On the morning after the election:

> As we said several times during the campaign, it seems to us that it's all for the best, this change of administration. Under President Roosevelt . . . we can hope for a quick disposal of Federal Prohibition and all the corruption and misery it breeds. We couldn't have hoped for that under President Hoover.
>
> There is another reform which we hope to see accomplished under President Roosevelt. Candidate Roosevelt, a few days before the campaign ended, remarked in one of his speeches that this immensely wealthy country up to now has yielded too rich rewards to the few and not enough rewards to the many. He demanded more equality in that matter.
>
> We think that demand was and is just.

Two days after the inaugural, Patterson took a step which was, for him, quite remarkable. He promised the new chief executive immunity from criticism, at least for a while.

> This newspaper now pledges itself to support the policies of President Franklin D. Roosevelt for a period of at least one year from today; longer, if circumstances warrant. . . .
>
> One of an editor's chief prerogatives in a free-press nation is his right to tell every one, from the President down, how to act, and, on occasion, where to head in. If the Earth should establish communication with the planet Mars, it is a safe bet that American newspapers—including, no doubt, this one—within a week would be telling the Martians how to handle the affairs of their little planet. This right to volunteer counsel to everybody is a right which most newspaper editors hold sacred. We feel the same way about it, in times anywhere near normal, and certainly expect to snatch up this right again when times worry around to normality again . . .
>
> We take the liberty, too, of respectfully asking other newspapers, even if they do not feel they can conscientiously make the same pledge, to at least give Mr. Roosevelt better than an even break—for the good of an embattled nation.

The very next day The News called Roosevelt a dictator. "Invoking the war-time powers of the Presidency, Mr. Roosevelt in his first 48 hours in office has ordered a nation-wide bank holiday, embargoed gold, made gold and silver hoarders outlaws, and thrown 125,000,000 people temporarily on a scrip basis. Could Stalin or Mussolini or Mustapha Kemal have done more, or done it faster?" But it was no criticism. "Fortunately, we seem to have turned over the power and the authority to the right man."

Patterson had another thought about the man he had begun to respect and admire. He wanted to preserve FDR's health and he envisioned one way to do it. The project became a real headache for Grace Robinson, now in retirement in Connecticut. She remembers it this way:

> There may seem to be no connection between an assassin in Miami and a swimming pool in the White House, but I can assure you there was. On Feb. 14, 1933, a wild pistol-wielder named Joe Zangara (later executed) fired five shots from a street crowd at the car of President-elect Roosevelt. He missed Roosevelt but wounded five others, including Mayor Anton Cermak of Chicago, who died 19 days later.
>
> The reason Roosevelt was unscathed may have been the brave action of Mrs. W. F. Cross, a Miami housewife who was standing near Zangara and grabbed his arm after he had started to shoot.
>
> Mrs. Cross became a national heroine. She visited New York

shortly before the inaugural and I was assigned to take her to Washington to view the ceremony as a guest of The News. From seats directly in front of the honor stand we watched the new President take his oath and make his memorable inaugural speech: "nothing to fear but fear itself."

That afternoon I introduced my guest to Eleanor Roosevelt at a White House reception. The First Lady extended her hand and said: "It was so sweet of you—what you did, Mrs. Cross, and I do thank you."

Mrs. Cross returned to Florida and I decided to spend the rest of the weekend (Inaugural Day was a Saturday) in Washington, little realizing what was ahead. Back in New York, Mr. Patterson—himself a strong and athletic man—was worrying about the possible effect of hard work and knotty problems on Roosevelt's health. He felt that the new President must have exercise to keep in physical trim.

But what exercise? Roosevelt, powerfully built and an ardent outdoorsman, had been deprived of most athletic pleasures by his tragic attack of infantile paralysis a dozen years earlier. However, he was still a swimmer—his shoulders and arms were as good as ever.

Patterson decided that a swimming pool must be built in the White House. There it would be easily accessible to the President at any time of day or night. He could wash off the fatigue and tensions of his difficult job whenever he chose. The News would spearhead the project by an appeal to readers for contributions. Conscious of the political considerations that might hamper a project sponsored by one newspaper, Patterson decided that other newspapers in New York state should be invited to help.

Thus it came about that on Monday morning, March 6, in my room at the Mayflower Hotel, I received a telephone call from Frank Carson in New York. He was our assistant city editor.

Carson informed me that Mr. Patterson wanted to build the President a swimming pool and that I must get the President to consent.

I was appalled at the assignment.

I had little experience in Washington. I had no special entrée to the White House, as some of the old-time press corps might have had. The News didn't even have a Washington bureau but had depended mostly on its "cousin," the Chicago Tribune, for such capital news as appeared in its columns.

I felt that it was useless to approach a Presidential secretary or other subordinate with such an unorthodox proposal. Every reporter knows only too well how expertly receptionists, secretaries and the like can entomb an idea so that it never again sees the light of day. I felt that I must get right *into* the White House with the pool proposal, and that immediately, because Patterson was an impatient chief who never understood delays.

Unluckily for me, it also seemed essential not to let other newspaper reporters hear of The News' plan. It might fail—be laughed down—goodness knew what ignominy lay ahead, not only for me, but far worse, for my employer-publisher.

Besides, the new Democratic administration was just feeling its way. One might expect wariness in all decisions, particularly those involving political feasibility. A personal luxury for the President, such as a swimming pool, seemed to me to have little chance in the welter of poverty problems facing him.

Mrs. Roosevelt's first hen press conference was soon called. (These interviews with the female reporters later became a famous fixture.) I went to the White House, hoping vaguely that I might corner Mrs. Roosevelt. This proved impossible. The result was that, in the midst of the usual girly-girly inquiries about her clothes and her social engagements, I blasted out my newspaper's wish to build a swimming pool for the President. The effect was like a bombshell. The other 20 or so newspaperwomen all looked disapprovingly at me.

The kindest and most gracious of ladies, Mrs. Roosevelt froze momentarily, frowned and after a slight pause said: "I can't discuss anything like that. You'll have to see Steve Early. Steve Early, not me."

Stephen Early, a former Associated Press reporter, was Roosevelt's press secretary.

At the conclusion of hen press, I hot-footed it over to the Presidential office wing of the White House, and managed to see Early alone. I anticipated a rebuff, but at least I could say: "Mrs. Roosevelt told me to see you," an introduction that could hardly be brushed off.

As it turned out, Early was not shocked at the idea of a swimming pool. I believe that his shrewd journalist's mind immediately saw the possibilities of favorable public reaction to a Presidential pool, financed by popular subscription.

Then ensued the most agonizing 10 days of my long reportorial life. Steve Early "took up the matter" with the various advisers, political and personal, who surround the man on whom the great white light beats.

Marvin McIntyre, the President's beetle-browed secretary on appointments, vigorously opposed the pool. Then there was Louis

McHenry Howe, the dyspeptic, nervous man who had been Roosevelt's adviser for years and was now a White House staffer. Howe thought the pool "politically inexpedient." There were others who objected. All was handled through Steve Early who from time to time gave me brief bulletins, none of which was optimistic.

For days it seemed that the pool hadn't a friend in Washington but me. I wasn't sure even of Steve. I wasn't certain whether he was advocating the pool behind the scenes, or, if he really did favor it, would yield at last, outnumbered by the opposition. At any rate, he felt sorry for me, or perhaps was simply the gallant gentleman. When he held formal briefings with the White House press corps and I started to leave with the rest, he detained me and said: "Stick around, if you wish. Come into this office any time. Feel free to loaf here."

He took me to lunch a couple of times at the Allies' Inn, that famous, good self-service restaurant near the White House, which dates from World War I. I felt that this friendliness was not advancing the pool, but at least it warmed my spirits.

Meanwhile, I wired daily or twice-daily memos to editor Carson in New York, to report my "progress." Not content with this, Carson, who could throw the most levelheaded reporter off stride, tortured me with telephone calls. Repeatedly he pressed me for my "opinion" on the status of negotiations—"how does it look?"—"is there any indication?"—"how is the wind blowing?"—until I could hardly sleep at night from worry. Finally, when he pressed me again by telephone, like a prosecuting attorney badgering a witness on the stand, I stammered that it looked "favorable" but that there had been no decision—*no decision whatsoever*—that all was really still undetermined.

I surmised, of course, that Carson in his turn was being pressured by Mr. Patterson, who wanted his idea speeded into fruition.

My "favorable" report, hedged and qualified as it was, had startling repercussions. When I picked up my New York Daily News next morning from the Mayflower newsstand I was horrified to see a page one picture of Roosevelt splashing in a pool—probably the one he had had at Albany.

I opened the paper with trembling hands. Inside, on page 3, the chief news-play position in a tabloid, was a story by Fred Pasley. Under his byline was an announcement that The News wanted President Roosevelt to have a swimming pool to ease the tensions of office and that The News invited its readers to send in money contributions for that purpose.

If I had been worried before, I was now on the rack. I could hardly bear to face Steve. But I kept my customary little on-and-off vigil in his office (the President's office was just beyond the wall). Steve treated me as usual—made no reference to what appeared to me as a débâcle. But the competing press, which by now had learned or surmised the reason for my hanging about, started a small campaign of ridicule. There were snickers of satisfaction and gloating when I encountered the regular White House reporters, who sometimes lounged and smoked in the large reception room in the Office Wing.

An Associated Press reporter, whose name I have forgotten, buttonholed me in Early's office.

"You've got yourself into one hell of a mess," he said. "Your paper is running stories and getting people to send in money for a pool, when there's been no consent from the President at all. In fact, they've turned thumbs down on the pool idea. I wouldn't be in *your* shoes."

I felt faint, but didn't quite collapse.

On that same day I read an Associated Press dispatch in a Washington newspaper which stated flatly that The New York Daily News had launched a campaign for swimming pool contributions but that the White House had given no approval of the project.

Meanwhile, newspapers all over New York State had joined in the fund-raising campaign and even a couple of papers in the Midwest had joined the drive.

Every day The News ran lists of principal donors. Some donations were in the form of services. Hood and Fouilhoux, architects of the News Building, were ready to plan the architectural lay-out of the pool, and the designers who had planned Patterson's private pool at his home at Ossining, N.Y., wanted to contribute services.

Meanwhile, I was called back to New York for a face-to-face report to my editor. Mr. Patterson wanted me to get Raymond Hood, his friend and architect, in to see the President. Pasley was to go with us.

At 7 a.m. on a dismal March morning, we three made rendezvous at the airline bus office in the West 40's for our flight to Washington. None of us had had breakfast. We were chilled and miserable. Both Hood and Pasley had sized up the situation. They understood as well as I that this errand was doomed—that as matters stood there wasn't the slightest possibility that I could get either of them in to see the President, despite my friendship with Early and Hood's great reputation as an architect.

Hood, kind and sympathetic, kept smiling. Pasley, with the gay irony which was his habit, bantered about our dilemma. However, we were all under orders and went through the motions required of us.

Arrived in Washington, I engaged a hotel room so that we could sit, and make and receive telephone calls. There was nothing that *I* could do, except make a silly, perfunctory call or two to Steve Early. There was nothing that *Early* could do, either. Hood marveled at the number of calls that Pasley and I made to our office in New York. Calls that meant *nothing,* but the nervous Carson wanted to hear from us anyway.

In the late afternoon, we three flew back to New York. Before departing I phoned and asked Steve whether I should leave Washington. He said I might as well do so, but to let him know where I could be reached by telephone.

I left my companions and went to the New Yorker Hotel.

In my room I fidgeted and wondered—fidgeted and wondered—then had my dinner sent up, not wishing to be away from a telephone. I was in an agony of doubt and worry. Finally I went down on my knees beside the bed and—yes, I prayed. It was the first time in my career that I had ever appealed to the Deity for help in a newspaper dilemma. It was about 10:30 p.m.

Suddenly the phone rang. It was Steve, calling from Washington. He sounded excited and jubilant.

"Grace," he said, "it's all arranged. I've just had dinner with the family. They want the pool. They're keen about it—"

"You mean it's all in the bag?" I interrupted.

"All settled. Can you get down here? The President will see you at 11 tomorrow."

"I'll be there," I promised joyously and Steve hung up.

Tons of weight slid off my back, but I still had a misgiving. Suppose the decision had been made at the Roosevelt dinner table in a mood of jollity that might pale by morning. Suppose—oh, well, I had Steve's assurance—I relied on that.

I telephoned my good news to the night city editor—Carson was a day editor only—and arranged passage on an early morning plane. As I turned in for a few hours' sleep, an old remark, that has been spoken by many since David first wrote it in his Psalms, came to my lips. It was: "Put not your trust in Princes . . ."

Next morning, a few minutes after the appointed hour, Steve, with smiles softening his somewhat saturnine face, escorted me into Roosevelt's office and then departed. The President, who was alone, murmured an apology for not rising—his paralyzed legs made this amenity difficult—and I murmured back understandingly.

The famous Roosevelt charm was all over the place as he shook hands across his desk, then went immediately to the subject of the pool.

Obviously, he had already given the matter careful thought.

He didn't want an outdoor glassed-in pool and he didn't want it to cost $40,000, the suggested figure. He wanted a $25,000 pool and thought it could be built underneath the corridor between the Executive Office Wing and the White House proper.

"I don't want to spoil the historic plan of the White House," he said. "An outdoor pool—and by that I mean a glass-roofed structure attached to the building, would mar the symmetry. Besides, there is the Fine Arts and Public Buildings Commission. It has control of all parks and public buildings in Washington."

"You shouldn't have any difficulty there," I countered, grinning. "Your uncle, Fred Delano, is the chairman of the commission."

He gave me a sharp look and smiled slightly. "Let me show you what I mean." He took up a scratch pad and pen and drew an outline sketch of the White House. Then with me leaning over, he pointed out how the two wings of the building matched each other and how badly an excrescence from one wing would look. Obviously, he felt keenly about our capital's architecture and the American history linked with it. After 20 minutes of such discussion, Steve Early poked his head in the door and I understood that the visit was over.

In my newspaper life I have never been a souvenir collector, but President Roosevelt's sketch was a souvenir that I craved. I had promised beforehand that no statement or quote from the President would be used in The New's pool promotion stories and such quotation would have been in bad taste anyway. I would not have dreamed of giving the sketch for such a purpose.

The negotiations had been prolonged, the pool had hung by a gossamer thread, and the President had trusted me. I decided not to give him any cause for worry nor to make the slightest move that might jeopardize the pool. After all, the digging hadn't yet begun.

So I left his sketch lying on his desk.

After the pool was assured and freely discussed around the White House, Mrs. Roosevelt made no secret of her pleasure.

"It will not only be for us but other Presidents will use it, too," she told a hen press conference. Then her voice broke into her occasional falsetto.

"After all, we can't take it *with* us!"

As Roosevelt had planned in the sketch that Grace didn't get for a souvenir, the green-tiled pool—52 by 18 feet—was built in the colonnade between the White House and the executive offices, thus preserving the original symmetry.

Gene McHugh, who had a wide acquaintance on Broadway, enlisted the help of George M. Cohan and Dan Healy in staging a huge benefit for the pool fund. Many other distinguished entertainers participated in the benefit. The President listened to the program on a special radio hookup for five hours and sent a wire of appreciation to all the performers. The benefit raised more than $10,000, which was added to the more than $17,000 contributed by readers of The News and 43 co-operating newspapers.

On March 30 Roosevelt sent Patterson a letter which said in part:

> I have just signed the Joint Resolution passed by Congress providing "for the acceptance of sums donated for the construction of a swimming exercise tank for the use of the President." The signing of this Resolution makes it possible for me to thank you, now that the legal formalities have been disposed of, for all that you have done. I am grateful to you, to the members of The News staff, and to the publishers and workers on each of the newspapers that co-operated in the campaign you launched.
>
> It is not alone the material contributions you and the others have made but the kindliness and generosity of all contributors that I appreciate. The thought that this campaign was initiated voluntarily, without my knowledge or sanction, and subscribed to so generously means as much, if not more, than the pool itself.

The News sent $24,000, which was the estimated cost, to Col. U.S. Grant 3d, director of Public Buildings and Parks at Washington. He supervised the construction and tried to arrange for use of some of the services and materials which had been volunteered. The balance in the fund, $3,392, was distributed among actors' relief groups.

There was some effort made to persuade Patterson to go to Washington and present the check to the President, which is standard procedure in such situations, but, predictably, he declined.

Roosevelt tried to get in a plunge in the "exercise tank" every night before dinner. President Truman used the pool infrequently but President Eisenhower enjoyed it often, particularly after his first heart attack. When John Kennedy took over the White House, his father engaged Bernard Lamotte, a noted muralist, to decorate the walls. The Johnsons were not swim devotees and it remains to be seen how often the Nixon family will make use of the facility. Son-in-law David Eisenhower ought to enjoy it—he swam there as a boy.

Surgeon general of the Navy Ross T. McIntire, in "White House Physician," a book he wrote in 1946, called the pool "the only health builder that any President will find in the White House. All else that I know anything about is decidedly destructive."

Roosevelt could not have had a more staunch supporter than The News during his early years in office. The paper endorsed all the Administration's policies and, where possible, even helped to put them into effect. It was one of the first major publications to sign up under the NRA labor-wage code and the famous Blue Eagle, with the legend "We Do Our Part," appeared daily on the editorial page.

Other active cooperation with much of what the New Deal stood for is described elsewhere in this book. It wasn't that Patterson was in any way a yes man. He and Roosevelt seemed to see eye to eye the problems the nation faced in large measure and agreed on how they should be handled.

An editorial on March 6, 1934, remarked on the pledge of support made exactly a year earlier. "We are glad to report today that we have never regretted that pledge; that we have been in sympathy with almost everything the President has done or tried to do or proposed to do; that we have never felt as if we muzzled ourselves to the injury of ourselves or of the public the newspapers are supposed to serve with accurate news and fair comment . . .

"Shall we renew our pledge, to support the President without hostile criticism for another year or for the rest of his term in the White House?

"No; we don't renew that pledge.

"We don't know what the balance of the Roosevelt recovery program will be, and we do believe the crisis has been definitely passed through the efforts of the Roosevelt Administration. Constructive criticism, as the President said yesterday, is now patriotic—because he has made elbow room for constructive critics."

The News vigorously supported FDR for reelection in 1936 and congratulated "both the American people and the President" when he won. "We believe President Roosevelt's first term has been one of the most fortunate things that ever happened to the American people. The New Deal up to now has spread mass buying power, lifted farm incomes to a sound parity with city incomes, kept millions of people from the kind of ragged-edge poverty that leads to revolution, and laid the foundations for a Social Security system which should provide a cushion when the next depression comes."

Roosevelt's thank-you letter for the pool had been addressed to "Mr. Patterson" but the one received a few days after reelection was to "Dear Joe:"

"I think I do not need to tell you how very splendid you have been throughout. I have a very strong feeling that The News was worth more to us in the city in the way of votes than all the political meetings and speeches put together. And, incidentally, you must be proud of The News poll—and I only wish you had been able to get the Literary Digest to back up their crazy poll with a million dollars."

This referred to a prominently-displayed box in the paper the previous Oct. 12 which was headed: "An Offer to The Literary Digest" and said:

"There is a wide discrepancy in the results of the election polls conducted in New York State by this paper and The Literary Digest. The News knows a man who will bet $10,000 to $5,000 that the poll of The News, as published in Saturday's paper, proves to be more accurate than The Literary Digest poll of the same date.

"He offers this bet to The Literary Digest, or anyone connected with it, or anybody else. If the whole bet is not wanted, he will split it. If agreed to in principle, details can be settled. The only stipulation is that the cash must be put up."

The anonymous bettor "known to The News" was probably Patterson although it might have been Max Annenberg, who cleaned up $125,000 (a year's salary) by betting 1 to 4 that Roosevelt would carry New York by a million votes. Max advised others to make wagers at the same tempting odds and was a hero to them when they collected.

Anyhow, the Digest (which conducted its poll by telephone and had Alf Landon well in the lead) did not accept the offer. Its failure to realize that most Roosevelt voters could not afford telephones led to the straw-poll debacle which resulted in its demise.

By this time, and for the next four years, Roosevelt and Patterson were not only patriotic colleagues but warm personal friends. Patterson's widow, the former Mary King, recalls that they lunched on the White House yacht, the Potomac; that Mrs. Roosevelt asked her to stay overnight at the White House ("I slept on the Lincoln bed"); that Patterson spent a number of nights there on different occasions and that they were both frequently entertained at the Roosevelt home at Hyde Park, which was only a short drive from the Patterson home in Ossining.

Roosevelt called Patterson "Joe," which only a handful of old associates on The News would think of doing, and he wanted Patterson to call him "Frank" when they were not in public. That Patterson refused to do, pointing out that the office of President transcended the man.

It was about this time that the editorial department of The News was abuzz with a report that Patterson was to be named Ambassador to the Court of St. James's. Nobody would have been surprised, except perhaps Patterson. He told Col. William Knox, publisher of the Chicago Daily

News, who called him about it, that he knew nothing of it and that was the end of that.

Somewhat later, in May, 1940, when Charles Edison was about to retire as Secretary of the Navy, Roosevelt's handyman, Harry Hopkins, asked a member of The News Washington bureau if he thought Patterson would be interested in becoming Edison's successor. The word got to Patterson, as it was expected to, and Patterson leaked back the information that he didn't care for that job but would very much like to fill a new cabinet post—Secretary for Air.

There wasn't any such post then (although it was created in 1947) but Patterson felt it was necessary to put the air forces on equal footing with the army and navy. Since he had flown with the Wright Brothers at Kitty Hawk in 1915, had flown as a war correspondent for the Chicago Tribune early in World War I and piloted his own plane, such a stand is hardly surprising.

When Gov. George H. Earle of Pennsylvania declared in June, 1937, that Roosevelt should consider running again three years later, The News ran a ballot on its editorial page asking readers if they wanted a third term. Perhaps that was too early to ask because only 6,844 ballots were marked and sent in. Any kind of a query usually brought far more than that, but the voters were 2 to 1 in favor.

"We don't think that the President wants a third term in person," said an editorial, "but if he is a consistent man he must want a continuation of his policies through an acceptable successor."

Patterson had already given a hint about how he felt on Presidents overstaying their time. When Calvin Coolidge died in 1933, an editorial said: "Mr. Coolidge takes his place in our history among the few Presidents who have refused to serve too long, as they saw it. Washington declined a third term; Jackson and Theodore Roosevelt arranged for their successors and stepped out. Mr. Coolidge could have been renominated and elected in 1928, but chose not to be. Whatever his motive, he put away the crown he might have had."

But this was different and by the fall of 1938 The News not only brought up again the possibility of Roosevelt running for a third term but rather approved the idea. This was repeated from time to time during 1939, although some misgivings were expressed about FDR's foreign policy. It was essential, Patterson felt, to stay out of any foreign war. On the day after Hitler's attack on Poland, an editorial headed "No Use to Get Hysterical" said: "Why any American should want to plunge into the European blood bath is beyond our comprehension."

Stephen Decatur's line "Our country right or wrong" was resurrected at the top of the editorial column (but was replaced in June of the following year by George Washington's "To be prepared for war is one of the most effectual means of preserving peace.")

The News urged a buildup of U.S. armed forces with an army of a million "sergeants," i.e., highly trained men capable of handling machinery. Also, 50,000 planes and 100,000 pilots.

For years The News had run an editorial each Monday on the importance of keeping armed. Most of them were headed "Two Ships For One" with an occasional "Two Planes for One." Roosevelt was so convinced that the paper's insistence on strength at sea had helped secure passage of the "Big Navy" bill in 1940 that he sent Patterson this note:

Hyde Park, July 24

Dear Joe:

On Friday last, July 19, I approved the Bill HR 10100, An Act to establish the composition of the U.S. Navy, to authorize the construction of certain naval vessels, and for other purposes.

Knowing of your great and helpful interest in this legislation, it occurred to me that you might care to have the pen with which I signed the Enrolled Bill. I am sending it herewith and with it an expression of my sincere appreciation.

I do hope I shall be seeing you soon.

Faithfully yours,
Franklin D. Roosevelt

When the Republicans nominated Wendell Willkie at the end of June, 1940, The News found several things the matter with him but added: "There's this much to be thankful for, though, if Roosevelt is nominated: That both candidates will be men who see the necessity of arming the United States to the teeth in a world full of danger for us."

On the three days preceding the Democratic convention the editorials were labeled: "Should Draft Roosevelt," and when he was picked on July 17, the paper breathed an editorial sigh of relief.

If Willkie, who had been called "the barefoot boy of Wall Street," by Secretary of the Interior Harold L. Ickes, had any grass roots support, Patterson believed it would show up in the corn belt. He assigned Fred Pasley to question small town newspaper editors in Indiana and Nebraska and Warren Hall to do the same in Illinois and Iowa, the result to be a series on how things looked.

Too interested to stay out of it entirely, Patterson accompanied Hall on the Illinois canvass. His questions to the editors were probing but his concern with the past was equally insatiable. It was necessary to inspect the reconstructed village of New Salem, where Lincoln spent his early manhood; to visit the Lincoln home at Springfield; to look at the grave in Petersburg of Ann Rutledge, Lincoln's first sweetheart; even to hunt out and gaze foundly at the boyhood home of Max Annenberg, "my best friend."

Gen. John J. Pershing on Aug. 4 sent up what was easily recognizable as a Roosevelt trial balloon: a nationally-broadcast exhortation to Congress to sell Britain or Canada at least 50 "overage" U.S. destroyers, relics of World War I.

Mr. and Mrs. Patterson had been invited to a luncheon on Aug. 6 at Hyde Park, which the President was using as a summer White House. On the 5th Patterson phoned Doris Fleeson, who was there with other Washington correspondents, and asked her to inform Roosevelt that they would not be able to attend. "It might be embarrassing," he said. "We are running an editorial tomorrow opposing the destroyer deal." Doris reported back that the Pattersons were asked to come anyway.

Actually, the editorial was comparatively mild. It said Pershing obviously voiced the wishes of Roosevelt, and that if we gave Britain 50 destroyers they would soon be bombed to destruction and we would be asked for more and more.

> Now, we should be sorry to see the British Empire fall. This country will be in greater danger if it does so. But it will be in greater danger still if it sends any considerable portion of its armed forces to Europe within reach of Hitler's bombers.

At the Hyde Park luncheon, which was in honor of some South American politicos, Roosevelt took Patterson to one side. "Joe, if you reveal what I'm going to tell you, I'll kill you," he said. Then he confided that the destroyer deal was reciprocal, that the U.S. was to receive in return some bases that it badly needed for defense.

Patterson was somewhat mollified and after the news broke three weeks later that Britain had agreed to our leasing air and naval bases in Newfoundland and the West Indies, The News editorially gave its approval.

The News continued to endorse FDR for another four years in office—"the argument about a third term leading to a Roosevelt dictatorship seems complete bosh to us"—and once again congratulated him when he won. But by the following January it had somewhat changed its mind.

The "lease-lend bill," later to become the more euphonious lend-lease bill, "is a bill to make the President dictator of the United States and hence its right name is the 'dictatorship bill.' " That charge was repeated in March, although somewhat softened:

> We think his (FDR's) motives are unimpeachable; that he sincerely believes he is wise and far-seeing enough to run our whole aid-British effort without a lot of time-killing talk from a lot of Senators and Congressmen. That is what many a dictator has felt—earnestly and sincerely and perhaps, in some cases, truly. But that is not the way a democracy operates. When it does operate that way, it stops being a democracy.

There were other highly critical editorials and then, in September, after the President had ordered the navy and air forces to shoot first at submarines in waters "we deem necessary for defense:"

> President Roosevelt by this latest act becomes out-and-out dictator . . . He has eliminated Congress . . . To make this dictatorship stick, it looks to us as if the President next will have to eliminate freedom of the press. If the war lasts until November, 1942, he may feel he has to eliminate the Congressional elections scheduled for that time, because in all likelihood the people will repudiate the war party if allowed to vote at that time.

On Dec. 6, 1941, Mr. and Mrs. Patterson went to Cain Hoy Plantation, a retreat on the Ashley River near Charleston, S.C., belonging to Patterson's son-in-law, Harry F. Guggenheim. Patterson took along Hal Burton, who had succeeded Fred Fletcher as The News outdoor editor (largely because he was a great skier, but that's another story which doesn't rightly belong here). Patterson didn't ski but he did like to shoot and fish and Burton became his companion on many expeditions. This time there was to be some wild turkey shooting.

The Guggenheim plantation was strictly for relaxation. There wasn't a phone or a radio on the place because those contraptions were always interfering with rest and mental lassitude.

Patterson and Burton went into Charleston on Dec. 7 for an early lunch with the captain of the Charleston Navy Yard and Maj. Gen. Charles P. Summerall, ex-chief of staff of the U.S. Army, who had been one of Patterson's wartime commanders and was now head of The Citadel, a southern military college.

The talk at lunch turned, as might have been expected, to the Japanese menace in the Pacific and the presumed invulnerability of modern battleships to bombing. When the lunch was over, Patterson and Burton returned to Cain Hoy, where they spent a quiet evening and retired early in preparation for the next morning's shooting.

They were up at dawn and out into the field, Burton, Patterson and his daughter, Alicia Guggenheim (who with her husband had founded Long Island's Newsday). About mid-morning, a chauffeur happened to turn on the radio in one of the Guggenheim cars and came running upstairs.

"I think you'd better come and listen," he told his boss. "I think we're at war." A few minutes later Guggenheim and Mrs. Patterson were in a land-rover, headed into the woods.

"We had just rendezvoused when they found us," Burton recalls. "I had my bird; I don't remember about the others. When we heard the news we forgot everything and hopped into the car." Patterson hurried to Charleston, phoned his office to give instructions and said he was going to stop off in Washington on the way home.

In Washington, Fred Pasley greeted him with some information that he didn't particularly like. Fred and Steve Early had been chatting and had come to the conclusion that now would be a good time to get their respective bosses together and heal the rift that had been growing between them. Consequently Early had made an appointment with FDR for noon on Dec. 11, but Pasley tactfully made it appear that the overture had come from Roosevelt.

It had been stated reliably that Roosevelt had promised Patterson that, in case of war, he would be a brigadier general in the Field Artillery on active duty. Even if this were true, Patterson apparently did not expect that his meeting with Roosevelt would be fruitful because on Dec. 10 he wrote this letter to the War Department:

> Gentlemen:
>
> I hereby apply for re-admission to the United States Army for service in any capacity in which I may be useful.
>
> I prefer service with troops because my military experience has been entirely with troops.
>
> This experience is as follows: In the spring of 1915 I enlisted in Battery C, first Illinois Artillery (N.G.). This was composed entirely of college men and was later expanded to officers, in large part, the 149th F.A. During the summer of 1916, I served on the Texas border as corporal and sergeant.
>
> At the outbreak of war in April, 1917, I served as recruiting officer and instructor to new troops. I sailed with the 149th F.A. to France in October, reaching there Nov. 1, 1917. I proceeded to Artillery School, Coetquidan, France. I was commanding officer of Battery B, 149th F.A., from Jan. 1 until Nov. 14, 1918. During this

time this unit under my command took part in five official major engagements. I was discharged in Jan., 1919.

I was a member for a period, as I recall, of five years as major in the organized reserves.

Most of my civilian life has been spent in the newspaper business. Am president of the company which publishes the New York News. I am 62 years old, accustomed to driving a car and am in good health.

Respectfully,
Joseph M. Patterson

The oval room in the White House, where Roosevelt had his study, presented an ordeal to even the most casual caller. The entrance was at one end and the distance to the Presidential desk, at the far end, was a rough equivalent of the condemned man's last mile. It was, perhaps by design, interminable.

Patterson, who had arrived a half hour early, was let into the White House by a side door to avoid reporters—"This, of course," he wrote later in a memorandum, "at the request of the White House." He had cooled his heels in an anteroom and, at the appointed hour, was admitted to the oval room.

As he marched toward the desk, Roosevelt had his head bent down, signing papers, and continued that activity for several minutes while Patterson stood at attention like a schoolboy called before the headmaster. Finally Roosevelt looked up. The two men shook hands.

"Well, Joe, what can I do for you?" Roosevelt asked, remaining, of course, seated.

"I am here, Mr. President, to see of what aid I can be in the war effort."

Certainly Patterson at that moment was not thinking about a military commission. There is little doubt that he was thinking of the assistance his grandfather and namesake, Joseph Medill, had given to Lincoln in another war. But Roosevelt's reply was a jolt, if not an insult.

"There is one thing you can do, Joe, and that is to go back and read some of the editorials you have written during the past year."

A lesser man might have turned and walked out. Patterson stood there, perhaps restrained by his feeling that it was the President speaking, not just a man with a grudge. In a memorandum that he jotted down while the incident was still fresh in his mind, Patterson stated:

I remained standing for 15 minutes while he gave me a pretty severe criticism for the way The News had conducted itself during the year 1941. He said he would give me a task, which was to read over the editorials for 1941. This I have since done.

He likewise said that as a result of our conduct we had delayed "the effort" by from 60 to 90 days. That Congress had read the editorials, which are also published in the Times-Herald in Washington, and had been encouraged to resist and slow up "the effort." He did not specify what he meant by "the effort," whether it was the war or preparation for the war. He said that on two occasions I had suggested revolution, which was, of course, very bad. He said that anyone who suggested that a united air force would have avoided the Pearl Harbor disaster was possessed of a childish mentality.

In all, I should judge I was there 15 minutes. At the end he seemed a bit mollified and told me to pass on the word to Cissy (Mrs. Eleanor Patterson, publisher of the Washington Times-Herald) to behave herself also.

I had thought that perhaps he was testing me to see if I could accept military discipline, on account of the application of the day before. Accordingly, I stood at attention and my only answers were at intervals "yes, sir" with the following exception:

When he told me to read over my editorials and realize their wrong-headedness (these are not his words, but the meaning of them) I did say, "Mr. President, those editorials were written in peacetime, not in wartime."

Another thing I recollect that he said was, "And you further suggested that there might not be any Congressional elections in 1942. Why, Joe, don't you understand that that would be unconstitutional?"

When he left the Roosevelt study, Patterson was met by Pasley. He must have been boiling, but all he said was, "Fred, don't ever make another White House appointment for me without consulting me."

It would be hard to overestimate the bitterness engendered by that confrontation or the lasting effects it may have had upon the country. As Roosevelt himself pointed out, The News editorials were also carried in Cissy Patterson's paper in Washington, were read by many members of Congress and doubtlessly influenced them in some decisions. What criticism there had been of Roosevelt's behavior before Dec. 11 was a mere slap on the wrist compared with the way most of his actions were viewed thereafter.

A couple of days after Patterson had returned to his office, an editorial listed many of the promises of peace that Roosevelt had made during the 1940 campaign. It also noted the warlike steps he had taken since then. The title of the editorial was "Why Should We Believe Him?"

But Patterson, in spite of the rancor in his soul, was eminently fair when he thought FDR had done something right. A News editorial the following Jan. 13 suggested that Gen. MacArthur, whose forces had been trapped by the Japanese in the Philippines, should be sneaked out of Luzon before surrender so he could eventually lead the struggle in the Pacific. (Since Dec. 18, the line above every editorial had been John Paul Jones' "We've just begun to fight.")

When, a couple of weeks later, it was disclosed that "our ablest fighting man," as The News called him, had indeed been sneaked out—"I shall return!"—and was in Australia in supreme command of the war with Japan, the paper said: "President Roosevelt did it. The entire credit goes to the President and there can be no room for anything but the highest and most unstinted praise."

The day after Roosevelt's ninth anniversary in the White House, The News observed that "those who don't want Mr. Roosevelt to have a fourth term had better begin thinking right now how to head him off." There would be the usual business about not changing horses in the middle of the stream, the editorial said, but "the democratic theory is otherwise. It is that a nation's democracy is bound to be weakened, if not lost, unless leaders are changed fairly often . . . The country may eventually be blessed with 16 years of Roosevelt instead of only 12."

As for the upcoming Congressional elections, it was observed that Roosevelt had said the next House should be composed of Representatives "who would support the Government in its conduct of the war."

"Our guess is that the Administration will campaign along this line; that the implication will be that you are some kind of traitor, Quisling, Cliveden Setter or Benedict Arnold if you think and say that the Administration can make mistakes in its conduct of the war."

A little later an editorial said:

> This writer [meaning Patterson, regardless of who put the words on paper] does not like President Roosevelt because this writer feels that he was tricked by the President's campaign promise into voting for him for a third term. If the President ever gives thought to such a minor matter, it is to be surmised that he doesn't like this writer either, because since Pearl Harbor we have editorially objected to some items in the U.S. war efforts instead of yes-yes-ing every move the Administration has made.

It can also be surmised that when FDR awarded an Iron Cross to O'Donnell (described elsewhere) he most fervently wished that he were able to give it to O'Donnell's boss instead.

But when the President died in 1945, The News praised him for some of his domestic and social reforms, adding that "it is too soon to try to make a complete evaluation of Roosevelt's place in U.S. and world history." And "we do say now that we'll be editorially respectful, friendly, and helpful according to our lights, toward President Truman for at least the next three months, and probably for the next six months."

Requiescat in pace, and let bygones be bygones.

Part IV

JOSEPH MEDILL PATTERSON

Joseph Medill Patterson, publisher of this newspaper and the man who directed this page from the day THE NEWS began June 26, 1919, is no longer with us. The story of his death will be found in the news columns.

Those who are left behind will do their best to keep this page and the paper what we believe he would want them to be.

Reproduction of editorial column, May 27, 1946

TAPS AND REVEILLE

If The News had been been a citizen in 1940, it could have voted. It was 21 years old. Looking back from the age of 50, that seems very young indeed.

There was plenty of importance from abroad to report that year, but not very much at home, except for Roosevelt's third-term election. Some of the local news was amusing. Frank Hoyt, arrested for trapping in Pelham Bay Park, told the magistrate he'd been catching mink, weasel, muskrat, opossum, raccoon, skunk and fox within the city limits for years. He said he made as much as $500 a year on Bronx fur and that Bronx mink was superior to Northern mink.

And there was trouble with the football score-guessing contest when a former clerk in the Rockville Centre post office seemed to have all the right answers with amazing regularity. Brought up on charges, he explained that on Saturdays, after the results were known, he'd fill out his slip and mail it in an envelope postmarked Thursday. "I just wanted to know if the contest was on the level," he protested. It was. He wasn't.

On the more sober side, there was the Battle of Britain and the fall of France as well as the German occupancy of Norway, Denmark and the Low Countries and Italy's war with Greece. Voted among the top 10 stories of the year was one still unwritten, the enigma of iron-curtained Russia.

When the war really was brought close to home toward the end of 1941, The News was in it neck-deep. Before it was over, 680 members of the regular staff were in the armed forces—almost 20% of the paper's employes at that time. Twenty-one were killed in action. The home staff kept in touch with service men through NewsPix, the monthly house organ. Copies were mailed to all those in uniform, as were copies of News From The News, a monthly publication issued by composing and editorial men especially for the purpose. There were also frequent gifts from the management and from those who were still minding the store.

The delivery fleet had been completely mechanized in 1935 with the retirement of the last 29 horses and delivery wagons but now, with the rationing of gasoline and tires, it was necessary to turn back the clock. Hastily the circulation department rounded up 70 horses and wagons for nearby city deliveries. It wasn't easy, either to acquire the equipment or to operate it. Drivers who had learned to turn a truck on a dime found themselves in a peck of trouble and several accidents before readjusting to Old Dobbin. Their woes were lightened somewhat when the Office of Defense Transportation ordered that after June 1, 1942, newspapers would have to limit dealer deliveries to one a day. (Max Annenberg, who died in 1941, had been succeeded by his son, Ivan Annenberg, as circulation chief, who was succeeded in turn by William Welkowitz. Welkowitz was followed in the post by Dudley Feldman and, in 1964, Jack E. Underwood became head of the department.)

Wartime newsprint shortages became a serious matter early in 1943. On Jan. 21 a News editorial headed "Don't Buy a News—Borrow One" cited an agreement entered into by newspapers and the government to limit paper usage. For a while the curtailment fell chiefly on circulation and advertising but eventually the editorial department had to use a little less space. That was a real hardship when the first page had been devoted the previous year to such headlines as "Corregidor Surrenders To Japs," "U.S. Army Invades N. Africa" and "Tokio Bombed." (A picture of a grinning Chinese holding a copy of The News with that last headline occupied the entire front page the next day, without caption, and for taking the photo Al Willard became the first photographer ever to receive the coveted National Headliners Club Award for journalistic achievement.)

The space devoted to news was also cramped because Patterson, whose addiction to maps had begun in his army days, insisted on full-page maps to illustrate any important war maneuver. Enough maps, both in black and white and in coloroto, were printed during this period to fill a shelf of atlases.

Some paper was saved when the price of the Sunday News was increased to 10 cents in Canada and states west of the Mississippi. Later, the Canadian circulation was eliminated entirely. News dealers' orders were carefully pruned in both city and suburbs.

Advertisers were put on quota, asked to cut space requirements by 10, then 15%. Advertising was eliminated from the country editions. Classified advertising, an early standby of The News, was reinstated for a six-month period in 1943, at the urging of Anna M. Rosenberg, Regional Director of the War Manpower Commission, and then dropped. It did not reappear, in a full-fledged classified section, until 1968.

At the end of 1943, when The News traditionally reprinted its important headlines of the year, the biggest and blackest were "F. D. R. Meets Churchill in N. Africa," "Rome Bombed," "Allies Invade Italy," "Italy Gives Up" (Sept. 9, a week later), and "Big 3 Meet In Iran, Plan To Crush Reich."

The entire center fold was filled with almost 100 of them, and they included such less important items as "Charlie Chaplin, 54, Weds Oona O'Neill, 18," "Attu Is Ours; Japs' Last Big Unit Smashed," "Army Halts Detroit Riot; 23 Die," "Shoes Put On Ration; Limit 3 Pairs a Year," "Patton Did Slap Sick Soldier, Army Admits," and "79,000-Ton Normandie Rises From Her Hudson River Grave."

That year The News saved more newsprint than any other of the country's 1,940 daily newspapers. The saving in 1944 was 50,000 tons and in 1945 just under that despite a lessening of paper control during the latter half of the year. Few U.S. papers used as much newsprint in a year as The News saved—and that despite the fact that it was a tabloid, already so compact, so condensed that every pound hurt.

The big, black, page-one screamers in the centerfold compilation at the end of 1944 included "Invasion Begins," "Generals Rebel, Try to Kill Hitler," "Allied Sky Army Lands in Holland," "Yanks Land in Philippines," "Beaten Jap Navy Runs From Fight" and "F. D. R. Wins 4th Term." Most of those from inside the paper were about the war, also, but there were a few from home, such as "Irvin S. Cobb Exits Laughing," "Quake Shakes N.Y., East Coast, Wisconsin," "Wendell Willkie Dies Suddenly of Heart Complication," "AEF Sarge With U.S. Wife Has Quads by British Girl" (a companion head said: "Bride Flabbergasted, Won't Divorce Sarge") and "Strangles Mother for $2 After Lifetime of Hate." Also: "Army 23, Navy 7" and "Cards Win Series."

A city-wide deliverymen's strike the first two weeks of July, 1945, gave dramatic evidence of News readers' loyalty. More than 10,000,000 copies were purchased over the counters of the information bureau adjacent to The News lobby. One Saturday night readers stood in a 17-block lineup for three hours to buy copies of the Sunday News. The promotion department made a color-sound movie of the scramble for papers and it was exhibited all over the country, in spite of the fact that The News was still trying to keep circulation down.

The centerfold collection of heads in 1945 was dominated by three reproductions of page 1 of The News. On May 8 the page was filled with a view of Times Square rejoicers over which was imposed, in big white letters: "It's Over in Europe!" On Aug. 15, black letters were imposed over a picture of women kneeling on the steps of St. Patrick's Cathedral: "It's Official: Japs Give Up." The third page 1 was a picture of a haggard-looking President with the line: "Roosevelt Dead." Other heads told of the capture of Bataan by MacArthur, the surrender of Berlin, the atom bomb destruction of Hiroshima, and the death of 14 when a bomber hit the Empire State Building.

As recorded in another chapter, Patterson went to Japan in the fall of 1945 at Gen. MacArthur's invitation. He apparently did not contract a strange oriental disease, as some of his friends believed at the time, but the trip may have been too much for his diminishing strength. It seemed to his associates that his health declined rather steadily after his return.

Patterson spent several weeks in bed at home in the spring of 1946 but was reluctant to relinquish the reins of The News. He discussed the affairs of the paper with his executives when they visited him but his span of interest was short. He was moved to Doctor's Hospital in New York and died there on May 26. This certainly did not bring an end to The News, which has flourished almost as long and as well without Patterson as it did under his control, but his death marked the end of an era. He could never be replaced.

* * *

Besides The News itself, there are various monuments to his memory. His large office was converted into a library called the Joseph Medill Patterson Room, which is open to members of the staff. It contains books, pictures and other memorabilia, including his helmet and gas mask from World War I, his aviator's helmet, the topee that protected him from the sun on safaris. Also in the library is the extensive collection of theatrical books of Patterson's old friend, drama critic Burns Mantle.

A few months after Patterson's death a bronze bas-relief plaque was dedicated by the composing room chapel with a moving ceremony. Later 2,685 members of the staff subscribed almost $6,000 which was used for a bust of Patterson sculptured by C. D. Batchelor, the editorial cartoonist, who had doodled a thousand faces of him from life as he sat in editorial conferences. It was dedicated on The News' 29th anniversary and stands in The News building lobby. The fund also provided a memorial plaque in the Brooklyn plant and the balance was given to Sally Joy Brown for welfare and charitable work.

Fordham University established the Joseph Medill Patterson Chair of Journalism and The News board of directors established two Fordham University annual scholarships in his name.

Holliss, the general manager of The News, had been named acting president on Patterson's death. He had been in office only three months when he was killed in an automobile accident.

The following evening, Aug. 30, McCormick flew to New York from Chicago through a torrential storm. In the next few days he had several conversations with F. M. Flynn, the business manager, and one with Flynn and Clarke, the managing editor. He said he was sure that his cousin must have had confidence in both of them, since he had named them as his trustees in his will. (The original three trustees were Holliss, Mary King Patterson and Clarke, with Flynn and James J. Patterson, the publisher's son, as successors.)

During his conversations, McCormick said several times that he had no desire to run The News, since he had little knowledge of the New York newspaper situation. He said he would not tell Flynn or Clarke what to do but that they should feel free to call on him in case of emergency. He lived up to this agreement scrupulously.

On Sept. 2, at a special meeting of the board of directors of News Syndicate Co. Inc., the following officers were elected: chairman of the board, Mrs. Eleanor (Cissy) Patterson (the founder's sister); secretary, Clarke; treasurer, Flynn. Clarke was appointed executive editor. Flynn was to continue as business manager. At the next regular meeting of the board, Flynn was appointed general manager.

McCormick had a feeling that important steps should only be taken at the annual meeting. If Holliss had lived, he would have been made president of The News at the annual meeting on May 19, 1947. It was then, after The News had been without a president for almost a year, that Flynn was given the title. Mrs. Eleanor Patterson, who had her own paper in Washington to worry about, did not interfere with the operations of The News but remained board chairman until she retired for reasons of health prior to her death on July 24, 1948.

Clarke was succeeded as managing editor by Robert G. Shand. The son of an engineer, Shand was graduated in 1917 from Massachusetts Institute of Technology where he studied naval architecture. He then attended the U.S. Naval Academy at Annapolis and served in World War I as a navy lieutenant, but for a postwar career he chose newspapering.

After working as a sports writer, reporter and rewriteman for the Washington Herald, he came to The News in 1923 as a copyreader and rose to chief of copy desk, makeup editor, Sunday editor and city editor. At school he had excelled at mathematics and math served him, and The News, well when he became managing editor. For instance, on election nights before computers came into use, he more than once projected the final count very accurately from early returns.

On Feb. 6, 1951, a Pennsylvania Railroad commuter train plunged off a 30-foot-high trestle in Woodbridge, N.J. As is often true in such cases, confusion dominated the reports of casualties. Miles from the wreck, Shand made an early estimate of the dead that was remarkably close to the actual figure, 84, announced next day.

As city editor, he was something of a perfectionist and frequently had rewritemen do their stories over and over again until they met his stan-

F. M. Flynn

President of News Syndicate Co. Inc. since 1947. Publisher of The News since 1955.

dards. But there was a soft side to him. A young reporter living in the suburbs was called in on his day off and arrived in the city room in beat-up shoes he used for gardening. One sole came loose suddenly, making a loud noise with every step, and there were catcalls from several directions. Not so from Shand. He called over the reporter and quietly said. "I like the work you've been doing lately. You're getting a $10 raise."

Shand never really got over being a sports writer. He went to all the big fights and pro football games and kept a sharp eye on the sports staff. Gene Ward wrote in a column that Shand "rode herd on the sports content of this paper like a good trail boss keeps recalcitrant cattle in line and on the move. If The News sports pages have been lively and controversial over the years, much of the credit belongs to Bob Shand."

He had a flair for photographs and for years chose the picture for the front page. He also judged numerous newspaper photography contests throughout the country.

Two years after Clarke became editor in 1961, Shand took over the executive editorship that Clarke had vacated. In 1966, Shand retired. Later the same year, he died after a long illness at the age of 70.

In the winter of 1941, Patterson's son, James J. Patterson, not quite 18 and just out of prep school, was getting ready to enter the U.S. Military Academy at West Point. Like sons of other wealthy men he might have spent those months gadding around in a fast car or sunning himself on some Caribbean beach. But young Jim Patterson had the newspaper bug in his blood and he hired on with The News. He started in the very lowest echelon, as a copy boy.

He ran copy and fetched coffee and sandwiches for rewrite men like any other copy boy and when one of them tipped him he took the tip with a polite word of thanks. "Not all of them tipped me," he recalled with a grin years later. "Only the good guys."

His salary in those days was $16 a week.

After his experience as a copy boy, he put in four years at West Point and his training there did more than make him a 2d lieutenant. It gave him self-discipline and the ability to keep cool on just about any occasion.

After his graduation in June, 1944, Patterson was on active duty with the army for five years. He served with an armored unit in Patton's 3d Army in Europe and was an army liaison pilot in Japan. He still flies weekends using a rented Cherokee 180, and also holds a glider pilot's rating.

He resigned his commission in 1949 and returned to The News. As a police reporter, he covered crimes of all kinds and fires. Later he was assigned to the United Nations. In 1950 he was recalled to active military duty during the Korean conflict. When he finished with the army, he was a captain.

A civilian again, he went to The News Washington Bureau and worked on some big stories there. He covered a number of sensational sessions of Sen. Joseph P. McCarthy's investigating committee, as well as several Presidential press conferences. At one conference held by President Eisenhower, he asked a question that made headlines across the country.

The French were pulling out of Indo-China as Vietnam was then called and Patterson asked the President if it were true the U.S. was going to get involved in that country. Ike said no (and he didn't get us involved at the time) and the press corps had a major story.

Patterson rounded out his journalistic training as a copyreader, telegraph deskman, makeup editor and news editor. In January, 1959, he was transferred to the Sunday department and the following May was named assistant managing editor with general supervision over the Sunday paper. He has charge of the regular Sunday paper, Sunday features, and the Coloroto Magazine. In addition, he works two days a week in the managing editor's slot.

Patterson also is a vice president and a director of News Syndicate Co., Inc., and a director of WPIX, Inc. and the Chicago Tribune-New York News Syndicate, Inc.

* * *

In 1968, Clarke retired as editor, but his connection with The News was not cut off. He was named a special editorial consultant and advisor to editorial conferences.

"Mr. Clarke has served The News ably and well for more than 41 years," declared publisher Flynn. "On behalf of the entire organization I extend our thanks to Dick for his long years of devotion to the newspaper. I look forward to our new relationship."

In addition to his consulting and advisory posts, Clarke recently was elected to the board of directors of the Tribune Company and reelected to the board of News Syndicate Co., Inc.

His retirement as editor brought with it three important staff changes. Clarke's top editorial post was filled by executive editor William A. Casselman. Floyd Barger was appointed to the newly created post of associate editor, making him the second ranking executive of the editorial department. And assistant managing editor Michael J. O'Neill, who had been a Washington correspondent, succeeded Barger as managing editor.

Casselman's career on The News went back to 1925. He signed on as a copyreader after various newspaper jobs in Milwaukee and Madison, Wis., in Baltimore and New York.

Casselman soon found himself sitting in the slot of the copy desk in emergencies and served several hitches on the telegraph desk.

When he was drafted by news editor Edgar Bean to work on makeup, Casselman entered the field that was his for most of his years on The News. That was the news desk, or—as he liked to put it—headlines and deadlines. After Bean died and Gene McHugh became night managing editor, Casselman headed the desk, beginning in 1946.

But first he worked a year on Liberty magazine, through parts of 1930 and 1931. He edited articles in that final year under Patterson-McCormick ownership, returned to The News when Liberty went to other owners.

Casselman switched from reporting to desk work, as he freely admitted, for a simple selfish reason: It was a road to promotion and pay. But he found a special satisfaction in handling the tools of production without which a newspaper doesn't publish. The composing room was familiar ground to him and he could talk the printers' language. He could also talk camera language. He was a keen amateur photographer and for years maintained his own darkroom. He made page 1 once.

After finishing a late shift, in July, 1933, Casselman accompanied a reporter to Floyd Bennett Field to watch an Italian aviator, Gen. Francesco De Pinedo, take off on a solo transatlantic flight. De Pinedo didn't get off the ground. His plane swerved off the runway, crashed and burned. Casselman got the only pictures of the tragedy. The pros had all clustered at the other end of the runway.

On the news desk, Casselman dealt with many of the major news stories of 30 years, laid out thousands of pages and wrote a goodly number of the front page lines that told the news and sold The News.

He was news editor until 1961, when he became night managing editor. He was made managing editor in 1963 and executive editor in 1966. He retired as executive editor Dec. 31, 1968, and Barger was named to succeed him.

Flynn announced Barger would be responsible for all divisions of the editorial department including editorial promotion and would also have supervision of the content of the editorial page. Under Barger's direction, O'Neill was made responsible for all news and feature content of the paper.

Barger is a graduate of Wittenberg University in Springfield, O., from which he received a B.A. degree. (Recently his alma mater awarded him an honorary Doctor of Laws degree as well.) After serving as a reporter with the Flushing Journal and as feature editor with the Brooklyn Eagle, he joined The News in 1942, working on the telegraph desk. In 1949, shortly after Israel became an independent state, he went there and did a 30-part series about the new nation.

He was later sent to New Hampshire to cover the sensational "mercy killing" trial of a country doctor charged with committing first degree murder by administering a fatal injection of air into the vein of a woman helplessly ill with cancer. Time and again throughout the trial, until the doctor's acquittal, Barger managed by speedy writing to get a full edition's jump on his Mirror rival.

Barger worked as a legislative correspondent in Albany, later in the Washington Bureau. He covered the "Big Four" conference in Berlin in 1954 and a year later traveled with Richard Nixon, then Vice President, on a tour of Central America. Then, in 1956, Barger made a dramatic trip by freighter to Baie Comeau, Quebec.

Baie Comeau, on the North Shore of the St. Lawrence, is the site of the Quebec North Shore Paper Mills which supply newsprint to The News and Chicago Tribune and two factors made Barger's trip memorable. There was a severe shortage of newsprint and the 5,670 tons the freighter had been assigned to pick up were sorely needed by The News; and the weather was frightful. The ship ran into howling storms and numerous ice floes and for a while the skipper thought "we were going to wind up on the rocks." But the ship got its newsprint and Barger got a fascinating series of stories.

On one of his last assignments as a reporter, Barger flew with President Eisenhower in 1959 on a tour of 22 countries. He became telegraph editor in 1961, night managing editor in 1964. He served as managing editor from 1966 until his promotion to associate editor.

Managing editor O'Neill has a B.A. degree from the University of Detroit and did graduate work at Fordham University. In World War II he served as an army combat correspondent in Italy and was awarded the Bronze Star. At war's end he became a police and court reporter for the old Standard News Association. He joined the United Press in 1947 in Detroit and was named Michigan sports editor. Later he served as Wisconsin state manager. In 1950 he was sent to Washington.

He covered the State Department, later became overnight editor, then day desk editor. In 1955, he covered the national events that resulted from the development of polio vaccine. As a result he won the National Headliner Club award for outstanding coverage of a major domestic news story.

He joined the Washington staff of The News in 1956. Before the year ended, war broke out between Israel and Egypt. Britain and France got into the thing with the announced purpose of guarding the Suez Canal. Meanwhile Israel had taken control of a chunk of Egypt.

The U.S. called on Israel to withdraw and early in 1957 O'Neill heard a report that Israel had decided to comply. Working against a deadline, he finally found an Israeli official who confirmed the report. O'Neill phoned The News and dictated the story, later corroborated by official American sources. It gave him a beat of nearly two hours on the opposition.

O'Neill has free-lanced stories for several magazines, including McCalls, and contributed a biography of Dean Rusk to the Book "Kennedy Circle," published in 1961.

HEADS WE WIN

When New York City had trouble shrugging off a thick snow blanket early in 1969 and one of the boroughs felt particularly neglected by the municipal trucks and shovels, readers of The News found the situation summarized in this head:

QUEENS CALLS THE MAYOR A SCHMOBALL

Some readers may have chuckled but most probably passed it by as merely another sample of the kind of headline-writing that helped to make the paper famous. If their memories were good they could recall such heads as:

SAYS WIFE MADE TIME
WITH A NEWSWEEK MAN

or

ROONEY, A PINT, BARES
MARRIAGE TO A FIFTH

or

TWO GALS IN ONE ANTIQUE BED;
GUY, 70, MADE IT A CROWD

Heads are written by copyreaders, a rare breed of men who first edit a story and then try to sum up its meaning in a few well-chosen words which have to fit a prescribed number of lines with a certain number of letters in each line. To spur these men to greater effort, The News has always given cash prizes for the best heads each week. It is recorded that Jack Kirkland, who later became a playwright and a collector of beautiful wives, wrote the prize heads for the last two weeks of July, 1922.

Just before, in cramped, temporary quarters, copyreaders sat wherever they could squeeze in, but when they moved into the Park Place office they were provided with the conventional horseshoe-shaped desk, which is built that way for convenience and not symbolic significance. The head copyreader, or slot man, sits in the center and passes out stories to those sitting around the rim. The stories come from the news desk, which in turn receives them from the city desk, the telegraph desk, the society editor, and others.

Each copyreader is responsible for any story he handles, both as to facts and style. He pencils in any changes he wants to make. To bolster his judgment, he is provided with a style book containing such notations as: "The News reads faster and livelier through selection, rather than mere compression; through the use of the simple, correct word and the simple sentence."

The basic News style book was compiled by Bill Murphy, slot man for more than two decades and a legend in his own time. It includes guidance on almost every problem a copyreader might meet, such as spelling, capitalization, punctuation, abbreviations, etc., and also has capsule advice:

"Do not call a woman *pretty* unless you know she is or have seen a picture which justifies the word. *Comely, attractive* will often serve the purpose. The writer who carelessly helps his story with *pretty* may be made a liar by the camera."

"Collective nouns may be considered singular or plural, according to the sense. *The couple were married* is more logical than *was married.* The latter would lead to this absurdity: *The couple was married in 1945 and it has two children.*"

Because some writers think a story is improved by cuteness, Murphy's book advised avoidance of such words as albeit, anent, foul play, galore, gut, nee, sans, vouchsafe, yclept. Abrasions and contusions are to be merely bruises and lacerations are just cuts.

But cuteness, as distinguished from triteness, was encouraged in headlines and Murphy's men turned them out whenever the story called for one—and sometimes even when it didn't, such as this one over a serious discussion on meat prices and inflation:

PRICES SOAR, BUYERS SORE
COW JUMPS OVER THE MOON

When a decision was due the first of the next week in the Gloria Vanderbilt custody case:

SIC TRANSIT GLORIA MONDAY

When child pianist Jacqueline Horner ran away and was found seven weeks later in a hotel:

LITTLE JAQ HORNER FOUND WITH
GOB, SAYS 'A GOOD GIRL WAS I'

When a strip teaser went on trial, the pun was irresistible:

3 JUDGES WEIGH
HER FAN DANCE:
FIND IT WANTON

In 1958 there was a promotional campaign on "the men who make The News great reading" and Murphy was one of them. The copy was written by Robert Sylvester, whose column, "Dream Street," qualifies him for the same category. The headline of the ad, quite appropriately, summed up its subject colorfully:

PERSNICKETY PERFECTIONIST . . .
HEAD HUNTERS' FRIEND . . .
BOSS OF THE SLOT . . .
BANE OF "BUG" MEN

Of Murph Bob wrote:

Ask anybody who has been steadily employed by Bill Murphy for any length of time and he'll tell you firmly that Murph is irascible, argumentative, persnickety, stubborn, finicky and often downright unbearable. Downstairs at the saloon, a few drinks later, the same guy will tell you (perhaps less steadily, but just as firmly) that Murph is one of the best newspapermen in the country.

Neither opinion bothers nor flatters Bill Murphy. He is the boss of the copy desk of the New York News. As such, he cannot expect love or adoration from either the staff or his own copyreaders.

It is Murph who has to decide how many of some rewrite man's superfluous literary pearls must be sacrificed. It is Murph who must argue with a veteran beat reporter on whether or not the facts check out. It is Murph who must keep throwing a headline back at one of his own men until the "head" says exactly what the story says.

William B. (for Bernard) Murphy lives in Port Chester with his wife and their eight-year-old daughter. For years, his main hobbies were golf, baseball and fishing. Recently he has slowed down the tempo of his hobbies and now sees all his baseball on TV, does a little gardening and a little bird watching.

For years, he was devoted to villainous-looking cigars, but he quit smoking three years ago when his cigars began to taste strangely. He had his first drink of rye whisky when he was 19 and has approved of it ever since. Unlike cigars, it still tastes as good as ever.

Murph is perfectly definite and sometimes violent in his likes and dislikes. He likes the N.Y. Giants, cats, Beethoven and, as writers, Hemingway, Maugham and Marquand, in that order. He dislikes the Brooklyn Dodgers, jazz, dogs, people who whistle and, as writers, Joyce and Proust, in that order.

Bill Murphy sits in the slot of the big, horseshoe-shaped copy desk of The News, and ranges a wary eye on 14 copyreaders. All are experienced, all are efficient, but Murph must handle them as individually as a stage director chooses and casts his actors.

Like all newspapermen, copyreaders are inclined to be over-opinionated on at least one subject, and often several. Thus, when the city desk sends over a hot divorce story, Murph must quickly take stock of whatever combination he has working for him at the moment. One of them may be sitting idly. But this is the fellow who just lost a tough divorce case to his second wife. He has his own violent ideas on wives, divorce courts and juries. Murph sighs and tosses the story to another reader who is already busy. This makes both copyreaders mad.

The next story comes from the telegraph desk. It is something about the Vanishing Redskin. The only copyreader doing nothing at the moment is, of course, the only one of the staff who thinks he knows all about the Vanishing Redskin and is mad at everybody who might have anything to do with making the Redskin vanish. Murph sighs and looks for somebody else.

No matter how hard Murph or any other desk boss tries to escape it, a few "bug" men will always find their way to the rim of the desk. A "bug" man is a fellow who devotes himself to the tiniest mistakes. He can argue himself almost into a fist fight over a misplaced comma. He will lug over the big dictionary to prove an alternate spelling. And when he's finished he'll let the story go through with a big, whopping boner right in the middle of it.

Now and then, fate being what it is, a copy fighter will also arrive on the rim. A copy fighter is a guy who changes "that" to "which" and the next "which" to "that." He takes "yesterday" and puts it somewhere else. He changes "said" to "stated" and "quiz" to "probe." Then he writes a headline a contest winner couldn't solve.

This is the job that Bill Murphy asked for many years ago after a long career in the writing and editing end of this racket. Born in Waterbury, Conn., Murph got his first job, as a youngster, on the Waterbury Republican. "It was a fine schooling," he recalls. "As soon as they found you could do a little of something, they gave you all of it to do."

He had finished Yale when World War I called. He went to France, rose gradually from private to corporal and saw some action in the Meuse-Argonne battle.

"I was assigned to the University of Bordeaux, for three months," he says, "and sharpened up my French, which I have never used since." He came back, did a year on Wall Street and then joined The News as a sports writer. That was in 1922.

As the paper grew, Murph moved to the editorial desks. In 1937, he "took over the copy desk on a temporary basis" and rapidly made it permanent. He's been there ever since, with the exception of World War II, when we had to call him major.

To the late Bob Sullivan, one of Murph's brighest rim men, a copy desk was always a "Gehenna of one- and two-syllable words." It has never been that to Murph. The News' headlines have drawn the attention of trade papers and serious analytical magazines as the brightest and most imaginative in the country.

Despite his wariness in casting his subjects, copyreaders to Murph have always been the most delightful men on a newspaper. "Just give me," he says blissfully, "a rim of copyreaders all of whom are not crazy on more than one subject. That's the place for the best conversation, the best exchange of theories and ideas—and the best and most stimulating headlines."

Even before Murphy, The News copy desk was producing better headlines than most similar hives of activity, in New York or throughout the country. On conservative, old-style papers the heads tended to be wordy and dull, consisting of several banks of type with each bank telling part of the story. Patterson said he wanted the heads in his paper to be short, understandable, applicable and bright. And they were.

In the '40s and '50s when The News copy desk gained national prestige, copyreaders everywhere began to hope they might some day be able to join it so they could write heads like the one over the story of the marrying street car conductor:

SHE FELL FOR HIS TROLLEY LINE;
DING DONG'S NO. 17 ASKS FOR A TRANSFER
or
PROF. TRUMAN, ELECTORAL COLLEGE '48, A COLUMBIA HIT

In the Park Place office the horseshoe desk was only large enough to accommodate six men at a time. The one waiting for the copyreaders when they moved to the 42d St. building was twice that size. Now 16 men are needed to keep the desk in operation from 1 p.m. to 4 a.m.

The first News slot man was William E. Plummer and others who preceded Murphy from about the mid-'20s were Ed Bean, Robert Shand, Grant Brightman, Tenold Sunde, Henry Surguy, William Casselman, Ralph Sharp.

Murphy was succeeded by Heizer Wright, the current slot man, who had nothing if not experience. He had worked in Des Moines, Denver, Chicago and Miami before sitting in on the rim in November, 1927. At various times since he has been lobster city editor, night telegraph editor and has been on special assignments but mostly he worked with Murphy until he became chief on Murphy's retirement in 1963.

He has written hundreds of prize heads but can't remember any of them. Murphy, who lives now in Piedmont, Calif., recalls one of Wright's heads which he considered the best of the year. It concerned two repulsive characters, the Lonely Hearts killers, Martha Beck and Ray Fernandez, who sat with clasped hands during a pre-trial conference with their lawyer:

LET'S HOLD HANDS, MY
LOVE, AND TALK OF MURDER

Heizer is also given credit for a terse but telling head over a story of a man who, while walking home in Greenwich Village, ran into an old acquaintance and got into a fatal argument:

A WORD, A BLOW,
A MAN IS DEAD

Even if he didn't write that one, there is a record that he wrote one of the ten hit heads of 1951. It was about a movie actor who told a House committee about his Communist past. It said:

ACTOR HAYDEN
WINS 4 STARS
IN 'I WAS RED'

One reason a vacancy on The News copy desk is hard to fill is that copy pours in gushingly as the deadline approaches and the man on the rim has to be fast as well as clever. He has only a few minutes to produce a gem like:

REDS SHOW FOTOS OF MOON'S BACKSIDE—AND IT'S BARE

or, when France's Premier Pflimlin was losing his support:

PFLIMLIN'S CHANCES
GROWING PFLIMSIER

But the desk is still turning them out at the same old rate and with the same brilliant wattage. On a story about awkward holdovers during the Johnson-Nixon switchover:

LAME DUCKS SLOW NATION DOWN TO A WADDLE

On details of what the state of New York was going to allow the city of New York in the 1969 budget:

HERE'S SLICE-BY-SLICE LOOK AT MAYOR'S HALF
A LOAF OF STATE AID

And when a couple of Miami-bound jets were hijacked to Cuba:

SKYJACKPOT: TWO IN A DAY

There is considerable similarity between caption writing and headline writing, but one important difference. The caption writer not only tries to get a clever head for the picture under discussion, he must also tell the story it concerns in a confined space that permits of no expansion.

In the early days of The News, under orders from Patterson, captions were kept much shorter than is the custom today. His theory was that the reader tires somewhat during the course of following a lengthy caption, and in time gives up before he comes to the end. His theory was later confirmed by reader surveys.

While reporters, rewritemen, special feature writers, map artists and photographers all receive bylines in The News today, the caption writer, like the copyreader, remains anonymous. But, so distinctive has been the style of several of the outstanding caption writers over the years, that their work can be readily identified by a knowledgeable editor.

When Eddie Fisher and Debbie Reynolds had a child, the caption on that memorable event read:

> BODY BY FISHER. If you listen real closely, you can probably hear Carrie Frances Fisher humming "Oh, My Papa," as she's held by her singer-daddy in Hollywood. Debbie Reynolds, Eddie's wife, completes the first family portrait.

A caption described a front page picture of a little girl, injured in an accident, arriving home from the hospital where her life had been saved:

> SHE'S WALKING—ON CLOUDS. Cookie Egan's face breaks out in a rash of pure delight as she's carried home in Hoboken, N.J., by her dad, George. Happy playmates form an impromptu honor guard for their homecoming pal who has just ended 43 days of hospitalization after losing her right leg when she was struck by a train while walking along railroad tracks. Cookie was home for a short visit before returning to hospital for additional treatment.

It should be noted that this picture appeared on page 1 for its sentimental value, rather than for its news value. As a result, the caption writer had to tell the entire story in the caption, since no further information would be carried inside the paper. All told in 76 words.

On a picture that doesn't have to be seen to be appreciated:

> ONE SLIP AND SHE'S AN EGGHEAD. It isn't that Mrs. George Winder of Crowborough, England, is a featherhead. It's just that she likes some kind of life in her hats. She has trained a hen to perch on her hair and a top piece is something to crow about.

Another one from Hollywood:

> GET'S BIG PART IN PICTURE. While his father, actor Charlton Heston, holds him, Frazer, 1, reaches out and grabs nose of veteran producer-director Cecil B. DeMille on movie set in Hollywood. Charlton had told his son to shake hands with the famous moviemaker. Later DeMille said: "This may prove that I've always had a good nose for actors."

A picture of little importance made attractive by a caption writer with wit as an asset:

> THE GOVERNOR'S STATE IS A HAPPY ONE. Gov. Robert Meyner of New Jersey plants a kiss on the lips of his fiancee, Helen Stevenson, on his arrival at Cleveland Airport. Meyner, 48, and Helen, 28, will wed today in Oberlin, Ohio. They courted during Presidential campaign of cousin, Adlai Stevenson.

Caption writers have to have catholic tastes. They must be completely familiar with whatever war happens to be going on at the moment, and also be able to write intelligible captions on trips to the moon, the pill, and any form of sport, from baseball to curling. Take note of this one:

> HE COULDN'T DANCE ALL NIGHT. Heavyweight Bob Satterfield exhibits a definite swayback condition as he sags against the ropes after arising from his third knockdown by hard-punching Harold Carter in the fifth round of their bout in Syracuse last night. Ref. Teddy Martin steps in to award Carter a TKO in 2:59 of round.

Every year papers throughout the country—Florida excepted, of course—print pictures of children with sleds right after Christmas. A caption writer in time is tempted to write "Here are more kids with more sleds. What are you going to do about it?" A not-so-jaded writer came up with this one:

THIS KIND OF WEATHER SLAYS 'EM. They wear boots and galoshes, are warmly dressed and have their sleds in tow, but somebody forgot to supply the snow. Four disconsolate youngsters trek through Central Park where yesterday's snow had already vanished.

Try this one on your laughmeter:

MAJORED IN HUSBANDRY. Blonde Mrs. Cynthie Dolores Corraditti, 23, contemplates her predicament in Dayton, Ohio, police station. She was arrested on suspicion of bigamy. Now pregnant, she has wed seven times. It was a fight between her last two hubbies which led to her arrest. She complained: "It was hard to find a guy I could trust."

Even a run-of-the-mill picture, showing women working for their favorite charity, gets top treatment by a good caption writer.

COUNTER ATTACK ON BLINDNESS. Customers and salesladies join in a common cause as 35th annual Christmas sale for the blind opened yesterday at 84 E. 42d St. Sale of articles, all made by blind persons, will continue until Dec. 15.

A photographer covering the arrival of the S.S. United States picked up a little feature picture of the ship's master and his dog. Here's what the caption writer made of it:

PART COCKER, MOSTLY CHOW. Chuta Peg, cocker spaniel owned by J. W. Anderson, skipper of the liner United States, views platter full of goodies he was treated to for upcoming 14th birthday.

When a baby arrives at the palace in Monaco it's big news:

NOW SHOWING AT THE PALACE. Princess Grace of Monaco leans over for a closer look at her daughter, Princess Caroline Louise Marguerite, in the royal palace in the first photo of the three-day-old baby.

Another picture that takes you back a couple of marriage ceremonies:

CARATS GOOD FOR EYES; HANDS, TOO. Holding her arm and gazing at her solicitously, Mike Todd squires his love, Elizabeth Taylor, to plane at International Airport. Liz and Mike flew to Mexico, where she'll recuperate from spinal operation. She is wearing 29-carat rock, a friendship ring, from Mike, whom she'll marry.

No mention of movie stars could possibly be complete without a word about the late Marilyn Monroe. Here it comes:

> SOME FIGURES LIE—NICELY. Marilyn Monroe makes like it's spring training as she throws her curves around at International Airport. She checked out with hubby Arthur Miller for vacation in Jamaica, B.W.I.

A caption, which some might consider as slightly off-color but is nevertheless regarded highly was written at a time when the American Tobacco Co. was conducting an intensive campaign with the slogan: "So round, so firm, so fully packed, so free and easy on the draw."

The picture was of Kim Novak, who could never be confused with Twiggy and who always believed that if a girl has attributes, she should make every effort to reveal them—discreetly, naturally. It follows that when one bends over to close a valise, particularly when one is wearing a loose-fitting blouse . . .

> SO FULLY PACKED. Kim Novak, her luggage bulging with European purchases, uses her knees to close her valise after customs check at Pier 86. Kim arrived aboard liner United States yesterday. The actress admitted interest in Italian financier, Count Mario Bandini.

All one needs to know to appreciate the next caption is that a pickpocket is known professionally as a "dip."

> 'SAILORS' TAKE A DIP. Disguised as sailors, Detectives Alan Gore (left) and John Dignon book William Capestro, 29-year-old ferry deck hand, on larceny rap at South Street police station. Working on complaints, cops feigned sleep on ferry and then nabbed Capestro as he allegedly took $5 from Dignon's pocket.

Another having a connection with policemen:

> NOW SHE'S A BLUE BLOOD. Patricia Kulpowsky registers appreciation for type O RH blood donated by Patrolmen Robert Kerner and Charles Corun as Nurse Dorothy Piazzi looks on at Kings County Hospital. The men in blue responded when auto accident necessitated amputation of Patricia's left leg.

One more:

> CHURCH MAKES LIGHT OF MORTGAGE. As others look on, the Rt. Rev. Horace W. B. Donegan, Bishop of New York, puts

flame to mortgage at St. John's-in-the-Village Episcopal Church. Burning took place on church's 100th anniversary.

All in all, there could be some justification for the slogan in a 1958 promotional campaign: "Nobody says it like The News."

* * *

Cradled in a contest at birth, nursed on a formula of community service and teethed on a schedule of special events, The News grew up in an atmosphere of promotional efforts. One characteristic in the first issue which has remained prominent through the years is promotion mindedness.

On June 26, 1919, the entire back page of that first copy was devoted to promotion—a Most Beautiful Girl contest.

As noted earlier, the infant paper stretched promotional arms into many fields and a near miracle was wrought for circulation by the first limerick contest. The sports department in the first of many competitions it was to feature offered ringside tickets and free transportation to the reader predicting most accurately the date and place the Dempsey-Firpo fight would be held, the division of the purse and the referee. It was the forerunner of the World Series and football contests which for many years have provided challenging and rewarding fare for sports readers.

Within the first year of publication, the paper sponsored the first annual women's swimming meet. This set the pattern for a growing and continuing series of special events that today include the Golden Gloves, Harvest Moon Ball and New York Relays.

Within the first year, Sally Joy Brown was busy at her desk dispensing through her Friend in Need features service to the community, assistance to the needy and rewarding groups of children who forwarded the "brightest" letters. The rewards were theater matinees in the winter; trips to Coney Island for a day at the beach in the summer.

Threaded throughout the paper from day to day, week to week, month to month were offers of $1 awards for material submitted and printed on such topics as Best Joke, Unusual Burglary Experience, Strangest Wedding, Stingiest Man, Nearest Approach to Death, Queerest Boss, Mental Telepathy, Best Vacation and many others.

Two of these promotional beads, Embarrassing Moments and Bright Sayings, appeared in the first issue of The News and are still daily features. The $1 award was upped to $2 in 1932 and is now $5.

In '21, the youngster was scrappy enough to match muscles with the Hearst organization in a promotional war that lasted two weeks and was ended through the intervention of the federal government.

In one of the biggest newspaper giveaways ever planned, The News distributed millions of numbered Gold Certificates and conducted drawings to award cash prizes.

On Nov. 25, the front page bellowed "You May Win a Fortune." On Dec. 1, a full page ad roared:

600,000 BUCK
WHAM!!
SHOOT THE WORKS!!

"Mr. Hearst started this thing," the ad read, "but we're ready to finish it. He started it because he couldn't sell his paper at three cents in competition with ours at two . . . . . we have appropriated a million dollars for this fight and when it's spent, we'll have another million ready. At the present moment we're offering 600,000 plunks in prizes."

Nine daily drawings were held and $31,400 was awarded. Then on Dec. 5, The News announced, "In accordance with a request made by Postmaster General Will H. Hays, upon the various papers conducting Christmas prize drawings and contests, The News announces that its gift certificate contest will end after today's drawing."

The war was over but the young paper continued poking a promotional finger into nests of potential readers. In 1922, Doris Blake's horoscope feature was awarding $175 a day to readers whose names were luckiest. Paul Gallico, not yet keeping his eye on the ball as a sports writer, was conducting a "Most Popular Movie Contest," and on another front the paper resumed its search for beauty with a "Queen of the Beach" contest.

Santa Claus and the Christmas spirit were invoked promotionally as early as 1921, an attention that so pleased Santa he continues to make his seasonal abode in The News lobby. The sports department in 1921, already sponsoring the Silver Skates, conducted a marathon at Yankee Stadium in May and came back in November with a cross country race in Van Cortlandt Park.

In 1923 The News ventured into political polling, asking members of the New York Bar Association to cast straw ballots for judicial candidates. In 1926 public opinion sampling was begun. Readers were asked to vote for or against the return of light wines and beer. In 1928, the paper took the full plunge into the Smith vs. Hoover presidential race by canvassing voters throughout New York State and parts of New Jersey. Election polls have been regular promotion features ever since.

The first punches in the Golden Gloves were thrown in 1927. The tournament, named by Gallico, who had become sports editor, was the outgrowth of a one year amateur boxing tournament sponsored by the Chicago Tribune in 1925 to test a state law. To comply with AAU regulations the Daily News AA was organized as the official sponsor. The tournament in New York was so successful the Tribune picked it up again in 1928 and within a few years Golden Gloves became a nationwide, coast to coast event.

As circulation climbed, promotion effort began turning toward still skeptical dispensers of the advertising dollar. Emphasis was placed on convincing advertisers that newspaper readers responded to The News.

In 1932, in connection with the opening of Jones Beach, the Women's Swimming Meet became The News Water Derby and was presented on a grand scale at New York's newest summer playground. Two days of activities drew more than 90,000. The derby was repeated in 1933 and 1934, drawing even more impressive reader response.

In 1936, The News staged its first Harvest Moon Ball. Suggested by Mrs. Mary King Patterson on the pattern of dance competitions she had observed in England, it was scheduled for the Central Park mall and was presented as an evening of music and dancing, admission free, everyone invited. A crowd of some 15,000 was expected, but at the 8 p.m. starting time more than 125,000 people had swarmed to the mall. So great was the crush, the event could not be held.

It was rescheduled for Madison Square Garden two weeks later. Tickets were printed and admission charged with the thought of controlling the crowds. Tickets were sold out well in advance. Nevertheless, on the night of the event, so great was the clamor for admission, extra police were summoned to handle the crowds which had tied up traffic on Eighth Ave. and side streets.

The financial success of the Harvest Moon, the Golden Gloves and the Silver Skates, became awkward, almost embarrassing. Promotion was primary, profits incidental. In previous years incidental profits were donated to children's agencies to send needy youngsters on summer camp vacations.

In 1937, The News Welfare Association—renamed the New York News Charities in 1968—was organized as a non-profit, charitable corporation. It became the sponsor of the paper's special events and is the agency through which annual donations are made to charity. Through the war years, the USO was the principal benefactor. Since then, donations have been to Protestant, Jewish and Catholic charities, the Red Cross and the United Hospital Fund. Total donations have amounted to $1,535,248.

Until the start of withholding tax in 1942, The News operated a special income tax office, to assist readers in completing tax forms. Staffed by Internal Revenue Service personnel, the office soothed the headaches of as many as 80,000 readers in one tax period.

As this office closed, the Service Men's Service Bureau opened. During World War II, it provided thousands of servicemen and families with guidance and information about federal programs and benefits for the military.

During the war years, because of the newsprint shortage, promotional effort was curtailed. As the shortage eased, springs uncoiled. In 1948, the All-Star Baseball Game poll gave readers a chance to vote for their diamond idols. The Football Contest, one of the first victims of the war shortage, was revived.

On one hectic football weekend, readers responded with more than 450,000 contest coupons. By actual count, 25,899 picked all 15 winners on the card, delaying the announcement of the prize winners for three days.

Community service activities were resumed in 1950 with a Blue Ribbon Block contest with cash awards going to groups who accomplished the slickest cleanup of their neighborhood. Promotional steam picked up. In 1950, the paper presented a huge Roller Skating Carnival, a Hopalong Cassidy Coloring Contest, and a Deer Hunting Contest. It also pitched in behind the U.S. Census Bureau with a "Missed Persons" feature. It accounted for 22,582 people.

Limericks—again—High School Beauties, Jazz Concerts, Drum and Bugle Corps Pageants, the Goren Individual Bridge Tournament, community service features ("How to Save Water") Baby Quips, "Sez I" Bonanza Bills (the Lucky Bucks of '27) all stepped onto the promotional stage and took a bow.

Some are still taking bows. The World Series Contest went to bat in 1952 and the Ike Golf Championship, directed then and still by Dana Mozley, teed off in 1953.

In 1956 came the most popular of all contests, the Little Fooler crossword puzzle. Offering $5,000 weekly in prizes, the Little Fooler drew more than 1,600,000 entries in one week and averaged more than 1,000,000 responses per week for ten weeks.

Through the constantly changing scene, the Golden Gloves continued to knock 'em dead and the Harvest Moon Ball to enchant capacity crowds with its artistry and entertainment. They remained the outstanding events of the promotional lineup.

The changing scene opened new avenues, however, and in 1964 The News began ploughing promotional furrows down the middle of two of them—Education and Youth. The biggest paper in the country joined hands with the biggest educational system in the country, the New York City Board of Education, and erected the biggest showcase of achievement for youngsters in metropolitan area schools.

With a pat on the back, The News sent grade and high school students dashing off into such activities as the Citywide Orchestral and Choral

Concert (1964), Art in The News ('64); Science Fair ('65); the New York Relays ('66); The News Physical Fitness Program ('67) and the Spelling Bee ('68).

The '68 Spelling Bee involved more than 600,000 students attending 1,212 schools in the city as well as in Nassau and Suffolk Counties. The citywide finals were held at the Felt Forum; the Long Island Finals at N.Y. State University at Farmingdale. The winners (two from the city and one from Long Island) participated in the National Spelling Bee at Washington, D.C., as guests of The News.

Fritzinger completed his 46-year tenure as promotion manager in January, 1968. T. Harold Forbes, Jr., who had served as mail clerk, copy boy, sports tabulator, sports writer, outdoors columnist and assistant promotion manager, picked up the reins. Promotion galloped off on still another highway.

Increased emphasis on public service cast The News in an even bigger role as a helpful, active, interested participant in community affairs, a big brother responsive to the needs of the public.

Through bright mail order ads and over-the-counter merchandising, the paper offered information booklets on a wide variety of current topics (Social Security and Medicare, U.S. Education Benefits, College Guides, Stock Guides); books of historical and educational interest (Eisenhower, The World in '68, The Swift Sword, Lightning out of Israel, World Almanac, Weather Almanac); compendiums of sports information (College and Pro Football Guide; Major League Baseball schedules).

Patriotic-minded citizens responded in vast numbers in '68 when U.S. flag decals (stickers), window flags and outdoor flag kits were offered. More than 400,000 decals were snapped up. Readers rushed to obtain 31,377 outdoor kits and 7,558 window flags.

Long years had passed since the promotion-minded baby had climbed out of the contest cradle in which it had first been presented to the public. It was no longer a baby but as it approached its 50th birthday, it was as promotion-minded as ever.

THE WHEEL TURNERS

A succession of men led The News through the circulation battles of the '20s and '30s, through the heady successes of the post-war '40s and the merger-ridden storms of the '50s into the button-down world of the '60s. Less vigorous competitors didn't make it, in many cases because of the failures of other circulation departments to make the wrenching adjustments necessary to keep up with the times. The Horse-and-Buggy Age became the Auto Age, which became the Air Age, then the Jet Age, the Atomic Age and the Space Age.

In the beginning, airplanes were curiosities, the subjects of quaint feature stories; but as the paper neared its 50th birthday, copies of the early editions were sped routinely to airports, to be loaded on planes and carried to readers in such places as Miami, Chicago, Boston and San Francisco.

In the early days, circulation departments battled for the biggest share of a seemingly limitless market; but as the competition shrank to the Post and the Times, the enemy changed its character. The enemy became traffic jams, fogged-in airports, radio and television, huge, powerful labor unions, disappearing newsstands and a lemming-like rush of middleclass people from the city to the suburbs.

In fact, according to an official in the circulation department in 1969, the most serious problems faced by all circulation departments in New York today are those attributable to labor union difficulties and shrinking newspaper outlets.

As the paper reached the half-century mark, the scene in the circulation department of the main plant on any given evening wasn't much different from the scene at the business end of a newspaper press in 1920.

The time is 6:30 p.m., 10 minutes from press time. Knots of husky mailers are gathered around the conveyor belts, trucks are backing up to loading platforms, long steel tables are being wheeled into position, huge wrapping machines are being tested and made ready.

As the minutes pass a tenseness fills the air. Voices become softer, held in check, as trained ears listen for the faint rumble from above that signals the start of the press run for the Night Owl edition, the first papers of the evening, which are rushed to newsstands for sale to the before-midnight customers.

Then, right on time, the endless springs of the conveyor begin to inch along, moving imperceptibly. Talk stops, and all eyes move to the belts, where they disappear up into the ceiling of the loading area.

Suddenly it's time, and the place springs to life. The building vibrates as the presses pick up speed and the ribbons of collated papers come snaking down from the press room to the strong, practiced hands of the mailers. The long room is filled with the yells of the men. Bundles of papers thump onto metal tables, which are trundled off to the loading docks. The paper bundles are heaved into the trucks, which speed off as soon as they are loaded. The scene is repeated, a few minutes later, in the Brooklyn plant, where mats (matrices of pages) have been rushed by car to the Brooklyn stereotype operation.

To the untrained eye the scene is one of utter confusion, as trucks, men and newspapers fly in all directions. How, the stranger might wonder, can these men put more than 2,000,000 newspapers into the hands of readers by tomorrow morning? Next week, perhaps, but not tomorrow morning!

"Actually, it's quite a sophisticated system," said Bill Carey, an assistant circulation manager who joined the paper as a laboratory assistant, testing newsprint, in 1946, when he was still a student in Columbia University.

"It used to be a business where you could get things done simply by being bigger and louder than anyone else. But more and more, management techniques are becoming as important as news instinct to the people in our department."

It is the news instinct which keeps Carey and other circulation executives glued to radio or television sets in their eighth-floor offices every night as the press run begins. Any big news break can change circulation and distribution patterns. A big story can mean including extra papers for all dealers; another kind of story may have a localized impact, and call for increases only in one area.

The minute that the circulation department hears of a big news break—most of the time from the editorial department—the man in charge goes into a quick conference with the news editors on duty for a full appraisal of the situation.

On the night of the shooting of Sen. Robert F. Kennedy in California, circulation executives huddled time and time again with editorial people, as reports of the seriousness of Kennedy's wounds filtered out of the hospital room. When it became obvious that the senator was gravely, even mortally wounded, the decision was made to print more than 300,000 extra copies of the late editions.

Similar decisions were made for the assassination of President John F. Kennedy and other big news breaks, including many sports stories. The biggest break of recent years came on Aug. 5, 1962, a Sunday, when Marilyn Monroe, America's sex and glamor queen, was found dead in bed in her Hollywood home, a telephone receiver in her hand, an empty sleeping pill bottle on a nightstand.

The story had everything. Glamor, in the person of the blonde with the husky voice, who rose from a calendar pin-up to the throne of Hollywood and was that city's reigning queen at the time of her death at age 36. Mystery—whom had Marilyn called in her last moments of conciousness? Sex—the body beautiful, nude, found on her queen-sized bed, a champagne-colored coverlet at her feet.

The paper sold out not only on Monday, but on Tuesday as well. In fact, the carry-over lasted more than a week, as the story of Marilyn's untimely death and her regal funeral was unwound by News writers. As usual, the circulation department came through and got the extra papers to where the readers were.

Getting the papers to the readers once was a comparatively simple matter, but in the second half of the 20th century the job became complicated.

In the paper's infancy, the newsstands of the city offered many different newspapers. There were so many sales that being a newsdealer was a reasonably rewarding enterprise. Stands were located in heavily trafficked pedestrian areas in business districts, in the theater district, at subway stations and trolley terminals. In the morning, commuters could buy papers from newsboys on trains, shouting headlines. In the afternoon, the messages of p.m. papers were cried from every corner.

In the late 1960s, however, the number of newsstands had shrunk, partly because of bureaucratic delays within the city's license bureau, partly because of the diminishing number of papers to be found on the stands. Dealers' profits fell. Longtime operators grew old and went out of business; their sons, whose college educations had been paid for out of the profits of newsstands, entered professions or went into other lines of work and did not take over pop's old place.

Circulation departments of all the city's papers, joining together in their common effort to open up new outlets, fought long and hard to make life easier and more rewarding for newsdealers in this city. The number of items which could be sold at newsstands was increased. Stands in poor locations were shut down; stands were opened in newer and better places.

Sensing the need for increased sales of early papers, circulation executives called for earlier and earlier press times, to permit the early editions to be taken to the suburbs and put into the hands of news-hungry readers before bedtime.

Another major effort was put into boosting home delivery sales, and much of the hope for the future was placed on those efforts, according to circulation management.

But even if the problems of shrinking news outlets can be solved once and for all, and promotions continue to create a huge demand for The News, the other major trouble—labor unions—will still have to be dealt with.

Not only does the cost of labor comprise the greater part of the cost of circulation—it totaled 76% of the $17 million circulation department budget for 1967—but trouble on the labor front can stop the trucks, and delay or arrest the entire publishing operation.

"That's where management techniques come into play," said Carey. "More and more of our people have training in the fine art of dealing with labor unions, and we think that's how it should be. In the past, many of the top level people in circulation were former mailers and delivery men themselves. And that's not always the best kind of background to have from the management point of view."

Could the circulation of the paper keep pace with the changing character of the times? That question was one which both circulation and production executives answered in the affirmative. In fact, the problem might not be one of demand, but of production.

During its first 30 years The News grew steadily, not only in circulation, but in size as well. In the 1920s, a 44-page daily paper was considered huge, and a 64-pager on Sunday was a monster. In 1940, the paper ran an average of 88 pages. But by the late 1960s, advertising volume had mushroomed to such an extent that The News was a far fatter item. The current record daily paper was a 288-page edition, including the main section and several suburban sections, for Thursday, Feb. 20, 1969. And the record Sunday paper was the one rolled out on the previous Dec. 1—868 pages, including main section, all suburban sections plus magazine and comics.

It was one thing to print 2,000,000 40-page papers; but it is something completely different to print 2,000,000 papers of 80 pages, or 180. And when 192-page dailies are published as they frequently are at certain periods of the year, production limits are really tested. With every press running at full speed, the maximum number of 192-page papers that can be processed in an hour is 289,000. Francis R. Walsh, who took over as production manager following the retirement of George Farley in 1969, put it this way:

> We're busting at the seams. There are days when we're printing at full capacity—when there's no more room for extra ad pages or extra

copies for newstands. They want more papers, they'll have to give me some more presses from somewhere.

Whenever out-of-town newspaper production men visit The News, it is always the Sunday suburban operation that leaves them shaking their heads in wonderment. The task is a monumental one, requiring exacting coordination between production and circulation departments. There are nine separate sections, some exceeding 80 pages, all of which have to be printed in advance. The sections have to be delivered to the proper dealers according to a complex system of routing. Everything must mesh in the right way, or a reader in Hackensack, N.J., could find himself with a Sunday paper filled with features and pictures meant for readers of the Bronx or Queens.

Another part of the operation that often amazes out-of-towners is the automated paper-handling system that permits the quick and easy transfer from warehouse to press room every week of an average of 8,426 rolls of newsprint, each weighing about 1,700 pounds. The system has become the envy, moreover, of many production people who had grown large muscles pulling and pushing paper rolls around the hard way.

Visitors frequently observe, moreover, that The News building is just about the perfect place to produce a big-city newspaper. This is because the building was designed for newspaper production, and upon its completion it was generally agreed upon by publishers that it was the most modern newspaper plant in the world.

People always seem to be curious about something and it is perhaps flattering that they seem to think that newspapers can provide all the answers. When questions about extraneous matters began to take up the time of the small, already over-worked staff of the fledgling News, most of those who answered the phones were annoyed but Leo McGivena sensed that a number of such queries might help to convince advertisers that readers had trust in the paper and therefore also in the merchandise it was hawking.

The Chicago Tribune had had such a service for years called the Readers Service Bureau and so he loosely set up a similar arrangement on The News. It struggled along until the fall of 1924, when a counter was installed in the newly completed lobby of the Park Place building and officially labeled Readers Service Bureau. It was under the direction of promotion manager Fritzinger.

Said News Pix proudly: "The new bureau gives information on auto routes, sells auto maps and radio atlases; carries back numbers of the Daily and Sunday News; takes pattern orders and subscriptions, and sells copies of Frederick J. Haskin's 'The American Government.' But most of all, the new bureau answers questions on all sorts of subjects. Probably one of the most unusual queries was one of those received the first week: 'What boat of the Hamburg line arrived five days before the Presidential election in 1912?' And the correct answer was forthcoming."

By 1929 the department had a staff of four and a new title: The News Information Bureau. It seemed that people's desire for facts was boundless, as each year's number of requests surpassed the last. In 1935, the department logged 574,186 calls; by 1968 the annual total had risen to 1,288,398, handled by a staff of 31 full-time and 16 part-time employes.

In addition to answering telephoned questions, the information staff provided a wide variety of other services. At any one time, News readers in 1969 could order from an assortment of publications—everything from a 10-cent booklet of favorite fish recipes to a complete collection of Phil Santora's interviews with statues and animals. There were also laminated color photographs of the late U.S. Sen. Robert F. Kennedy and the beloved Francis Cardinal Spellman, all available through the mail or at the bureau's store on E. 42d St.

"There have been some amazing responses over the years," said Edward B. Brother, head of the information bureau since 1936. "In 1942, when Gen. Douglas MacArthur and his forces were in trouble in the Philippines, we sold about 500,000 MacArthur buttons, at two cents each to callers or five cents by mail. And after the assassination of President John F. Kennedy, we sold about 35,000 laminated color portraits of him and 225,000 copies of two memorial books published by the wire services."

The week following the Kennedy assassination, Brother said, was the busiest single period in the department's history, with several thousands of calls received every day.

Over the years, millions of people have received direct assistance from the information bureau. During and after World War II there were special counselling services for servicemen and their families. This was one of the most successful programs in the bureau's history, with well over a million individuals receiving help they needed. In the days before the withholding of income tax from wages became mandatory, as many as 80,000 people a year were aided in preparing their income tax returns in a special Income Tax Office.

But the primary concern of the bureau continued to be the answering of questions from readers who assumed that The News knew everything there was to be known.

"We probably get more questions about Easter than any other single subject," says Brother, a quiet, bespectacled man who always takes a long pause before answering a question. "It seems that people use Easter

The News newsprint terminal in the Red Hook section of Brooklyn. It went into operation in October, 1951.

Brooklyn plant, occupied 1927.

Garage and newsprint storage plant on East 41st St., New York. Occupied 1958. Glass-enclosed conveyor moves newsprint to reel room in main plant. Air conditioning apparatus for both buildings is on roof.

as a benchmark in their lives, and since the date varies with the years, they're always asking when Easter fell in a particular year."

Another favorite question, one that comes in at least once every day, is for the names of Snow White's seven dwarfs. (They're Sleepy, Sneezy, Dopey, Happy, Grumpy, Doc and, the one everybody always forgets, Bashful.)

"We get a lot of superlative questions—the biggest this, the fastest that, the tallest something else," said Brother, "and as the world becomes more and more complex, we get more questions about people's dealings with government, the taxes they must pay, the military obligations they owe, the benefits to which they are entitled."

"The calls logged by the bureau are an accurate barometer of the public's interest in various topics," Brother said. "When space shots were new, we'd receive 5,000 to 6,000 calls every time a capsule was sent into orbit. But the most recent Apollo shot, with three men orbiting the earth, didn't bring one single call—people just take the space program for granted nowadays."

Another vital service of the Information Bureau bears a woman's name: Sally Joy Brown. It started on June 8, 1920, with an announcement that a new column would appear the following day, to help News readers help one another. Sally Joy began her work on June 9 as promised, publishing the names of people who needed clothing and those with clothing to donate.

Through the 1920s and the early depression years, Sally Joy's following grew to tremendous proportions, so much so that in 1937 it was decided to begin a direct distribution of clothing to those in need. From 1937 through 1968, a total of 465,763 individuals had been on the receiving end of the column's services.

Sally Joy always makes a special appeal at Christmas time for toys and other gifts for needy children. From 1949 through 1954, the Christmas program was carried on only in an expanded "Friend in Need" column, but in 1955, Santa Clause arrived on the scene in person, setting up shop in the Information Bureau and thanking youngsters who brought gifts for the needy. In 1957, Santa and his helpers moved out to the lobby of The News building where he set up a permanent pre-Christmas headquarters. During the 1968 season, 15,362 children warmed Santa's lap, while 15,048 anxious parents watched nervously from the adult side of the velvet rope.

* * *

Everybody talks about the weather; The News did something about it. Dr. James H. Scarr, the U.S. Weather Bureau's top man during the

1920s, helped design the meteorological displays which have fascinated visitors to The News lobby since it was formally opened in 1930. Instruments located in the tall Weather Tower atop the 37th floor are connected electrically to large dials in the lobby, which show temperature, humidity, rainfall and wind velocity and direction. Daily weather charts are kept up to the minute with the latest Weather Bureau data.

The man in charge of The News Weather Bureau right from the beginning is J. Henry Weber, who was working for the U.S. Weather Bureau in the Panama Canal Zone when he received a call from Patterson in 1929. Weber boasts a 40-year record of being right more than 85% of the time in his forecasts.

"In the beginning, before television and radio began to carry good weather information, we used to be swamped with calls every really hot or cold day," Weber said. "There was no air conditioning then, so that when it got up around 100 degrees, people would be sent home from work—that's why they called, really, to see if they were going to get home early."

The busiest day in the department's history was July 9, 1936, when the mercury rose to a sizzling 106 degrees, while the busiest cold weather day came on Feb. 9, 1934, with the lowest reading Weber ever recorded—15 degrees below zero.

Weber said the modern-day callers—of whom there were 40,000 in 1969—seemed more concerned with the weather in other parts of the country or the world. "They all want to know 'What's the weather in Miami?' " he said.

"People travel more, so they want to know about not only climates, but also times in foreign countries. The News has become a recognized authority on world time zones," Weber said, "and even the Telephone Company calls us to find out what time it is in places on the other side of the world."

Others who depend on the paper for accurate weather information include several major department stores, which utilize News records in charting the ups and downs of their sales departments. "They check with us to determine why such and such a week or month wasn't as good as it should have been," Weber said. "We tell them whether to blame it on rainy or snowy or cold or hot weather."

One popular service of the Weather Bureau is the annual Weather Almanac, printed since 1954. Each year, Weber said, nearly 20,000 almanacs are distributed to the science departments of city high schools, and a similar number are sold at 25 cents per copy by the Information Bureau.

Ironically, the story that Weber considered to be his best fell victim to a man named Adolf Hitler. "It was on Sept. 20, 1938, when I predicted that a hurricane was going to shoot up an unusual low-pressure trough along the Atlantic coast, and strike somewhere near New York." The story, written by rewrite man Warren Hall, was played prominently on page two in the early editions of Sept. 20. But it was the time of the Munich crisis, a world war appeared to be brewing, and the hurricane warning had to be dumped in the late editions for a story that carried the page one line: "German Army Masses for Invasion."

The following day, Weber's prediction came true, and the banner line in the next day's editions was "Many Dead in Hurricane." In all, Weber recalled, 600 persons died in the storm as it swept across Long Island and New England. Some of them might have been saved if they had been warned of the storm through The News, the only paper to carry the hurricane prediction. So Hitler may have been indirectly responsible for some American deaths long before the war began.

* * *

In the beginning when The News was published in the Evening Mail building, it had no library of its own. News writers and reporters used the host paper's reference facilities, or they consulted Frank Hause. His pockets bulged with clippings, and his command of facts helped win him appointment to the city desk. Besides Hause's walking file, The News had a haphazard collection of photographs. By the time the paper moved to Park Place, the stock of photos totaled 40,000. Early in 1922, Maurice Symonds was given the job of sorting them out, adding to the collection and setting up a systematic reference library.

Symonds had a staff of assistants that varied in number from two to three, a total of six filing cabinets and an open corner of the city room to operate in. He immediately increased the size of the photo collection when The News bought 100,000 pictures which Charles L. Ritzmann had collected during the previous 30 years.

Ritzmann, who wanted to retire, was asking $7,000 for his gallery of celebrities. But, as Symonds later recalled, he sold for $4,000 "when he was told that The News meant business." The paper further economized by selling half the collection to the Chicago Tribune for $2,000.

The Ritzmann archives were remarkable for the time and were put to use quickly. Rare photos of Lillian Russell in her heyday appeared in The News when the celebrated stage star died in 1922. Layouts on actress Maude Adams and the former crown prince of Germany also came from the Ritzmann collection.

Symonds was sent to Chicago early in 1922 to go through the Tribune's files and pick out photos which he thought The News might use. He selected some 12,000 and had them copied. Many of these photos were portraits of prominent persons, for the Tribune had been soliciting pictures from those whose names appeared in "Who's Who in America." A large number of the 25,000 in the "Who's Who" roster responded to the Tribune's circular letter, and, as thrift-conscious Symonds noted with satisfaction, their contributions were free.

By mid-1922, the librarian could report that The News' photo collection had soared to 200,000. He also stressed, in an article in NewsPix, that he was in charge of "a library, not a morgue."

"Our managing editor's edict about neatness is carried out to the letter," Symonds wrote, "and the library can always be found to look like the spotless town. This gives the place due respect by those having occasion to use it."

In addition to this concern for tidiness, a characteristic of the library to this day, Symonds dealt in that early report with another consideration. This was the need to select only items worth saving, because he already was engaged in an endless battle for space.

"The librarian," as he put it, "must have a 'nose for news' and a thorough knowledge of what to keep. A portrait taken six months ago may be demanded, while a dozen taken later are passed up. Therefore, ample space must be provided for increasing portraits and pictures so that a weeding-out process that may severely impair their value need not take place."

Weeding-out, of course, could not be avoided. But The News library grew vigorously, through the years at Park Place and at two successive locations on the seventh floor of the 42d St. building.

The space squeeze was becoming critical when Joseph F. McCarthy became head of the library in 1965, succeeding the late B. Michael Reddington who had been given that post following Symond's death in 1956.

McCarthy, whose service at The News dates back to 1933, studied newspaper libraries across the country for three years before launching a $100,000 project to ease the storage problem. Described as a "10-year leap into the future," the new filing system increased the library's capacity by 34%, although there was no addition to the department's 6,130 square feet of floor space.

Before streamlining, the library staff had to discard an equivalent amount of material from the files for all new items that were stored. After the modernization, McCarthy and his staff of 20 assistants could look forward to a decade during which this weeding-out process would not be necessary, except for removal of duplicate items.

The 1969 library inventory included an impressive 10 million clippings filed (at the rate of 6,000 weekly). The clips were stored in 800,000 envelopes and covered 8,000 subjects.

Pictures on file totaled 3.5 million, and 100,000 zinc photo cuts were ready for re-use. In addition, the library stocked 800,000 negatives and had 10,000 reference books and 6,000 pamphlets on the shelves.

The library is manned 24 hours a day seven days a week.

* * *

Not long after The News moved to 42d St., so the story goes, Patterson once was barred from the building.

The day was warm, and Patterson was in his habitually rumpled clothing. Worse, he had just been inspecting a new tunnel, and his suit was spattered with mud.

On duty in the lobby was a new man. He did not recognize the bedraggled individual and refused to let him enter. Words were exchanged. Finally Patterson prevailed on the man to call the then managing editor, Harvey Deuell, and it was only after Deuell had arrived and identified him that Patterson was allowed to enter his own newspaper plant.

Characteristically, Patterson laughed off the incident. He thought it a good joke on himself.

If this encounter occurred—and there is no reason to believe it is apocryphal—the man who refused admittance to Patterson was a watchman, one of the few plainclothesmen who policed The News offices downtown and for the first three years after the move to 42d St.

In December, 1933, these informal watchmen were replaced by uniformed men called the guards. The guards were organized by the circulation manager, Annenberg, a veteran of the fierce newspaper circulation wars in Chicago. Annenberg believed in being prepared. He went to considerable lengths to make sure that The News would not be victimized by gangsters who were operating brazenly in those mid-depression days.

At one time, the guards numbered more than 80 men. Among them were a few in civilian clothing who conducted hourly tours of visitors through the News Building.

The tours are no longer given, and the guard force in recent years has been cut to about 55 men, all uniformed. These bluecoats are the equivalent of a police force responsible for the peace and protection of a city of 10,000 population—the News Building—as well as the Brooklyn plant, the newsprint terminal and other property.

When Annenberg first stationed the guards, he wanted them to be seen by the public—and by any would-be holdup men who might have their eyes on News circulation receipts. One veteran recalls that when he joined the force, "there were always at least three of us in the lobby to make sure nobody put their feet on the globe or something."

They were an impressive outfit. All could meet or exceed the New York Police Department's entrance requirements. A number were commissioned officers in the guards. Commanding was a captain, Henry McKinley.

The guards came to be known as the "Annenberg Rifles," a name that was by no means facetious. For in the old days they carried high-powered rifles capable of piercing armor on a hijacker's getaway car. The rifles were held at the ready during the touchy minutes when circulation drivers delivered their cash collections, totaling thousands of dollars a day, and the money was taken upstairs to the cashier's office.

The old guards' arsenal also bristled with riot-control shotguns and tear-gas billies. For years one guard protected the circulation receipts with a Tommy gun.

Preparedness evidently paid off. No gunman ever tried to hold up The News during Annenberg's day. The only armed robbery to take place on News property, in fact, occurred April 6, 1961, when three bandits took almost $63,000 at gunpoint from the Brooklyn cashier's office.

Next day's memorable page 1 headline, written by managing editor Shand, trumpeted: "We Wuz Robbed!"

Five suspects were arrested within 19 hours and two men eventually were convicted and sentenced for the holdup, but the guards had no role in this case. Their job is crime prevention, not apprehension.

In this, they have been highly effective. Says Sgt. William Nicholson, in charge of the guard detachment at the News Building: "We're told that the crime rate on company property is only about 10% of that for the city generally. And most of the crimes here are minor, thefts from offices and the like."

Handling troublemakers is another assignment of the guards. Sometimes the bothersome visitors are merely eccentrics, wild-eyed advocates of bizarre panaceas for the world's ills who crave to see an editor and get their ideas printed.

It sometimes happens, however, that troublemakers come in gangs bent on serious mischief. Like the group of unkempt hippies who once took the elevators to the seventh floor all set to storm into the city room for a violent protest. Several guards rushed to the scene and headed off the intruders firmly and discreetly. It was a narrow squeak.

Still another problem is caused by derelicts or other undesirables who try to use News facilities. A number of drug addicts have been caught in lavatories, for instance, in the process of giving themselves "fixes."

The guards no longer carry rifles or shotguns but are armed with pistols and nightsticks. They rely mostly on persuasion and experience, however, in dealing with troublemakers. At one time, all guards had served in the U.S. Marine Corps. Today most of those who are not ex-leathernecks are veterans of other branches of the armed forces.

THE COMIC TOUCH

In 1894, the late Morrill Goddard, then one of Joseph Pulitzer's whiz kids on the New York World, took advantage of a primitive form of color printing recently made available to newspaper publishers. In the Sunday supplement he presented a crudely-drawn comic feature, "The Yellow Kid," in one color (yellow) and black.

There followed several years of bitter battle between Pulitzer and his arch-rival, William Randolph Hearst the elder, with both printing "The Yellow Kid" at times. As a result, Pulitzer and Hearst were labeled masters of the "yellow press." More importantly, newspaper comics were born. They appeared on Sunday, and were commonly known as the "funnies."

Most of the early funnies were poorly drawn. The characters bore little resemblance to anything, human or animal, in real life. The plots were as crude as the art work. But they won a substantial following among readers of all ages and both sexes. Reading the funnies was considered by many at least as much of a vice as is the use of marijuana today.

During the years when the circulation of the Chicago Sunday Tribune was soaring under Patterson's direction, he seems to have been indifferent to the appeal of what was described by some observers as a new art form. Not for long.

In 1917, Sidney Smith, who had been drawing a strip labeled "Old Doc Yak," came up with an idea for a family life comic which Patterson christened "The Gumps." He is supposed to have got the name from his mother, who referred to anyone of sub-normal intelligence as "a gump."

"The Gumps" was a trail-blazer in continuity strips—it told a running story, in addition to presenting a daily laugh. Some years later it set another precedent by killing off, without violence, one of its major characters, a most appealing young female named Mary Gold. Reader reaction to this episode was violent and highly unfavorable, but there was no attempt to restore Mary to life.

"The Gumps" was so successful that on one occasion when Smith's contract was renewed he signed up for $1,000,000—and got a Rolls-Royce as a bonus. Smith died in 1935 and was succeeded by Gus Edson, then a sports cartoonist on The News. "The Gumps" lost popularity. It was dropped by The News in 1955.

During the years of Patterson's war service, there were no additions to the Tribune's list of comics. In 1919, "Gasoline Alley" made its bow.

The artist was Frank King, who had been in the paper's art department since 1909. "Gas Alley" was originally a one-drawing panel depicting the tribulations of automobile owners who gathered in their alley on Sundays to tinker with their cars. The panel soon became a strip, with a story line.

Then came an innovation. On St. Valentine's day, 1921, bachelor Walt Wallet, leading character in the "Gas Alley" cast, found a new-born boy on his doorstep. The child was christened Skeezix, was legally adopted in due course. He has grown with the years, has children and grandchildren, the largest family in comic strip history. King, his creator, still has an interest in the strip, although most of the work is done by Dick Moores, long-time associate of King's. The Sunday "Gasoline Alley" since 1951 has been drawn by Bill Perry, another King helper.

Although the success of "The Gumps" and "Gas Alley" must have convinced Patterson of the pulling power of the comic strip, he never made any attempt to buy similar features on the open market, although several syndicates could have supplied them. He preferred to create and control his own. The impression developed that The News was closed territory to outside salesmen. In recent years The News has taken on several good comic features from sources not under its control.

"Harold Teen" was the third strip to appear in The News. The date was Sept. 25, 1919. Carl Ed (pronounced Ead) was the artist. He coined a number of expressions which caught the fancy of the younger set, and created clothing styles which became popular. Ed had the advantage of living with several teen-age children. This he lost when they grew up. The News dropped the strip in 1950. Ed died in 1959.

By the time The News was a year old, it had been labeled "the Stenographer's Gazette" by so many of its critics that Patterson felt some attention should be paid to this segment of its readers. He launched a comic strip which he christened "Winnie Winkle, the Breadwinner." The artist was Martin (Mike) Branner, former vaudeville actor.

Again there was an innovation. Winnie, the working girl, never appeared twice in the same costume. She made her own clothes, querying readers were informed. What she did wear was up to the minute in style. Credit for the designs should be given to Mrs. Branner who had been Miss Fabrini of the Branner and Fabrini dance team. "Winnie" was another family strip, and another in which a major character was removed, by disappearance if not by death. His departure left Winnie with two children and a mother and father to support.

Branner suffered the last of several paralytic strokes in March, 1961. This ended his drawing career.

Since then "Winnie" has been carried on by several artists and writers.

Currently Max Van Bibber does the drawing. The story is written by James Sparber.

During 1923 two strips were added. The first was "Smitty," drawn by Walter Berndt. It dealt with the activities of a sharp-witted office boy, his mother and father and small brother and his boss.

Next came a "Biff-Bam-Pow" comic. It was originated by Frank Willard, something of a roughneck. The central character, Moon Mullins, was even rougher than its creator. The title was by Patterson, Moon being an abbreviation of Moonshine, an appropriate label during prohibition days. From the time of Willard's death in January, 1958, his former assistant, Ferd Johnson, has carried on the strip.

The year 1924 witnessed the birth of a comic character, the like of which had never been seen: "Little Orphan Annie." This was the creation of Harold Gray. His ageless red-headed child, her companions and her multibillionaire guardian angel, "Daddy Warbucks," provided the most controversial plots in comic strip history.

"Annie" and "Daddy" are rugged individualists opposed to most of the restraints which control the majority of humans. Gray's creation disturbed or enraged many of the editors who bought the strip and caused them to discontinue it frequently. Except in a few rare cases, complaints from readers caused "Annie" to be reinstated, sometimes with apologies from the editor.

Gray died in May, 1968. Philip Blaisdell has taken over the art work. The story is written by Eliot Caplin.

From 1924 until 1931, there were no important additions to the list of News comics. Then came one which soon developed into one of the leading American newspaper features. This was "Dick Tracy," the brainchild of Chester Gould who had worked on various Chicago newspapers. It was offered under the title of "Plainclothes Tracy." Patterson thought a better label would be "Dick Tracy," "Dick" being a common term for detective.

Gould has a vivid imagination and the ability to coin names for his characters which catch the public fancy. Some samples are Tess Truehart, Flat Top, Vitamin Flintheart, Gravel Gertie and B. O. Plenty.

Gould devotes much time to criminological research. He has dreamed up a number of gadgets to assist Tracy in his pursuit of lawbreakers.

An aviation strip was introduced in 1933. Zack Mosley, a licensed pilot, offered his drawings to Patterson under the title "On The Wing." In a few months this was changed to "Smilin' Jack." Mosley flew his own plane and during World War II served as a captain in a coastal air patrol of the army's anti-submarine command. He found time to keep his strip going during that period.

The next important comic feature to be offered readers of The News was "Terry and the Pirates," which made its bow in October, 1934. Milton Caniff was the originator. His feature was a love and adventure conception with an Oriental setting. Caniff's ability as an artist and particularly his portrayal of seductive females won "Terry" immediate popularity. Caniff left The News in 1946. Since that time the strip has been drawn by George Wunder, an excellent artist and a former army cartographer.

A rarity among comic artists—a woman—broke into The News in 1948. Her professional name is Dale Messick. In private life she is Mrs. Oscar Strom. Her feature had long appeared in the Chicago Tribune, first as a Sunday page, then as a daily and Sunday offering. "Brenda Starr, Reporter" is the title. In many reader-preference polls taken by The News and other Brenda newspaper customers she is the No. 1 favorite among women.

Following the decline and eventual abandonment of "The Gumps," Gus Edson, who had taken over from Sidney Smith in 1935, came up with a totally different kind of comic feature, "Dondi." He worked out his plot with the assistance of the late Maurice Reilly, then sales manager of the Chicago Tribune-New York News Syndicate.

Dondi is a World War II waif, adopted by a former U.S. army man. He is a somewhat simple-minded youngster, now thoroughly Americanized. Irwin Hasen, who drew "Dondi" from its start in 1955, took over the story responsibility following Edson's death in 1966.

"On Stage," a beautifully drawn feature, started in The News in September, 1957. Its creator, Leonard Starr, is a veteran in the comic art field. The story recounts the adventures of a beautiful girl who wins fame on stage and screen. Most of the episodes have a strong psychological flavor.

A daily two-column panel "The Neighbors," by George Clark, came to The News in April, 1939. It had established a considerable following nationally prior to its appearance on 42d St.

Two Sunday half-page comics, "Smokey Stover," by Bill Holman, and "Pottsy," by Jay Irving, are old-timers which appear with fair regularity. A later arrival is "Flubs & Fluffs," by Jerry Robinson. The most recent addition in the Sunday-only category is "Super-Duper," by Rolf Ahlsen and Bill Kresse.

(Ed. note—Since the foregoing was written, The News has lost the dean of its comic artists. Frank King, creator of "Gasoline Alley," died June 24, 1969. He was 86.)

AT BAT FOR THE FANS

Several decades before George Plimpton took his life into his hands by playing quarterback for the Detroit Lions to write a best seller, Paul Gallico tried a more hazardous stunt just for one story in The News. Gallico was the possessor of a burning curiosity and he wondered what it would be like to get clipped on the chin by Jack Dempsey.

Gallico proved he had both courage and newspaper sense—if not common sense—by climbing into a ring with the immortal mauler to satisfy his curiosity. It was satisfied.

Gallico's experience was typical of the kind of "in-the-trenches" reporting that has marked the 50 years of The News' sports department, which has come up with more exclusives than any other paper in town.

Athletic ability and experience were never mandatory, but they helped and through the years The News sports department has been sprinkled with athletes and former athletes. Gallico captained the Columbia crew; Gene Ward helped set a bobsled record in St. Moritz; Bob Anderson ran in the prestigious Penn Relays; Neil O'Keefe went to Tokyo in 1964 as a member of the United States' canoeing team; Mark Dempsey was a varsity football player at West Point; and Mike Meltzer played varsity baseball for Michigan. A member of the department made the Baseball Hall of Fame in Cooperstown and one News writer set a World Series record for strikeouts.

The Illustrated Daily News was not yet two weeks old, in fact, when sports news crashed page 1.

It was the Dempsey-Willard fight in Toledo, O., and page 1 of the July 5, 1919, paper blared the news, "Dempsey Wins In Third" in bold, black headlines. Two days later, there were sequence photos of the knockout, a startling precedent and a portent of things to come.

Sports took up one page in those early days with only one byline. "Sportographs by Alcock" was the only regular feature, a collection of sports notes of the day, which made John Alcock the first sports editor because he made up the entire department.

Alcock stayed only a few months and Marshall Hunt, formerly of the American, became the one-man sports department and interim sports editor. In 1921, they gave him some help, a 14-year-old copy boy just out of grade school, Charlie Hoerter, who stayed 46 years and retired in 1967 as sports editor.

James Crusinberry came from Chicago in 1921 to become the first full-time sports editor.

"The first thing he did when he got to town," recalls Dan Daniel, long-time dean of America's baseball writers, "was call me up and offer me a job. I said. 'That damn sheet hasn't got a chance.' I couldn't see any place in New York for that kind of paper. That was my first mistake."

Daniel described Crusinberry as "an able guy" and it was under him that the first News sports staff was assembled—Marshall Hunt, Al Copland, Harry Newman, Jackie Farrell and Grant Powers, the paper's first sports cartoonist.

While Crusinberry was sports editor, the half million or so readers of The News began to accept it as the town's baseball paper. Baseball standings and box scores were musts and the start of the 1923 World Series was greeted with pictures on page 1 and the back page line: "P-L-A-Y B-A-L-L."

Crusinberry was one of the founders of the Baseball Writers Association of America and as one of two surviving charter members, he was asked to throw out the first ball in the 1958 World Series between the Milwaukee Braves and New York Yankees, in commemoration of the 50th anniversary of the BBWAA.

When Crusinberry returned to Chicago in 1924, Gallico took over as sports editor and the first regular sports columnist. His smooth, picturesque writing and his imaginative approach to fun and games soon made The News sports pages the liveliest in town. It was the Golden Age of Sport and Gallico's pages reflected the exciting and bizarre events of the day.

Gallico was in White Sulphur Springs in upstate New York on Sept. 9, 1923, covering Dempsey's preparation for his fight with Luis Firpo, when he got the idea of climbing into the ring with the champ.

Dempsey, at first, was reluctant. He finally agreed.

"Do you want to be killed?" Dempsey asked.

"Not exactly," Gallico replied.

"I see," said the champ, "just half killed, so that when you recover you can write about it."

That was it exactly, Gallico said, and the fight was on. Here is how Gallico described what happened:

> We feinted with our right. Suddenly there was a flash of a tawny forearm and something jarred us from stem to stern.
>
> The champion had whipped over a left hook that landed handsomely beneath our left eye. We covered and dodged and sought another part of the ring. The champion was on top of us. We would

just have time to see the flash of his arm, and then something would hit us. Dempsey was keeping his promise.

Sparring a moment, we poked our left in the champion's face. Nothing happened. We did it again. This was an error. We should have rested on our luck. He shifted suddenly and let us have it with both hands. We were consicous of two tremendous thuds that seemed to come from nowhere.

Then our head was swimming. We couldn't find Dempsey. We couldn't even find the floor. Dempsey caught us as we were headed there and held us up until our head cleared. Breaking, we poked at him again, and then suddenly we saw his right arm too late. He hit us squarely on the side of the jaw. There was a bump, and the next thing we knew we were on the floor.

We had experienced a knockdown. It's a good deal like having a building fall on you. We scrambled up before any mention of numbers was made and rushed into a clinch. We wanted to get as close to the champion as possible. That also developed into an error. While we clung to him he pounded the back of our neck. We left him and got clipped on the jaw as we did so. We felt trapped and helpless.

And then suddenly the timekeeper remembered the word he seemed to have forgotten and called time. It was over. Jack shook hands with us and we left the ring with a headache, a cut lip and satisfied curiosity.

If it was any consolation to Gallico for his headache—which it probably wasn't—five days later Firpo lasted only a few minutes longer against Dempsey than he had.

Jackie Farrell, a pixieish individual of small stature but large ideas, fit right in with the Gallico approach and the times. In 1927, he covered an NYU-Nebraska football game and Gallico told him to pick up the Notre Dame-Southern California game in Soldiers Field, Chicago, on the way home. A companion on the trip was W. O. McGeehan, celebrated columnist of the Herald Tribune, who suggested to Jackie they pass up the game and go to a Chicago gym instead, where McGeehan had arranged for the proprietor to have telegraph lines set up. Reports came into the gym from Soldiers Field and Farrell wrote his story and filed it to The News without leaving the premises.

"I got a $50 bonus for the story," Jackie remembers. "I almost wanted to give it back."

A promising career came to a screeching halt after Farrell wrote a series of articles exposing local college basketball players as pros for play-

Right to the jaw. Tony Anthony's face is twisted like a rubber mask by impact of Sonny Ray's smashing overhand right in bout at Madison Square Garden Nov. 15, 1958. Anthony was winner. Stroboscopic photo by Charles Hoff.

IN THE WORLD OF SPORTS

Sports of all kinds are a subject of major popular interest in America. The News cameramen have established an enviable record for depicting various forms of athletic activity in photographs which have won hundreds of prizes. They have led in the use of two comparatively recent developments in their field: the stroboscopic light, better known as speedlight, and the sequence camera. On this and following pages are some striking examples.

Handshake? No. Michael Herman of N.Y.U. and Gaylord Kaatz of St. John's seem to be holding hands as they clear high hurdles in 60-yard event at Madison Square Garden Feb. 16, 1957. Photographer Charles Hoff made the stroboscopic shot.

TUMBLING ACT AT YANKEE STADIUM

Sequence camera records highlight of day, June 11, 1961. Yanks' right fielder at that time, Roger Maris, backs against barrier in effort to snag long drive by Ken Hunt, of California Angels. Maris went end over end, but came up with ball which otherwise would have been a homer. Photographer, Frank Hurley.

Up and away. Rolando Cruz of Villanova clears bar at 15-feet-6 to win pole vault event at Millrose games in Madison Square Garden Jan. 30, 1964. Stroboscopic photo by Charles Hoff.

Three's a crowd. Trio of St. Louis Cardinals players tangle in effort to snare easy pop fly in game with New York Mets at Shea Stadium May 22, 1967. Cards are (left to right) Cepeda, Javier and Maris. Photographer, Frank Hurley.

Father takes a cut. The Rev. Capistran Ferrito (O. F. M.) gives his all in effort to get hit in game played at youth center he operated at 226 E. 113th St. during summer of 1965. Picture was made July 24. Photographer, John Duprey.

DAILY NEWS

NEW YORK'S PICTURE NEWSPAPER ®

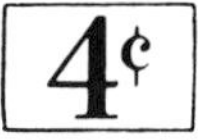

Vol. 37. No. 87 Copr. 1955 News Syndicate Co. Inc. New York 17, N.Y., Wednesday, October 5, 1955* 4¢ IN CITY LIMITS 5¢

WHO'S A BUM!

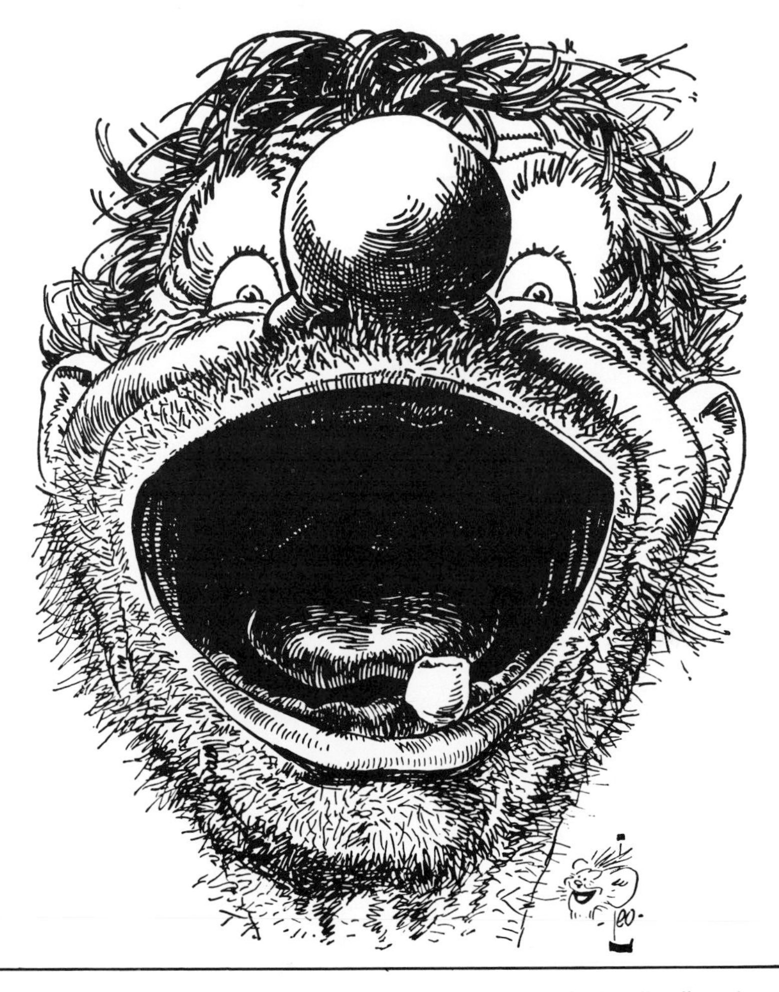

Triumph. Not a photograph, but it tells a baseball story. This is the front page of The News the day following final game of the World Series of 1955, when the then Brooklyn Dodgers became champions.

Stretch that failed. Robert Lutz, Los Angeles, makes valiant futile attempt to return ball in match with South African Ray Moore during U.S. national tennis championships, Forest Hills, L.I., on Aug. 31, 1968. He not only missed ball, but lost racquet. Photographer, Bill Meurer.

Going over big. High jumper John Thomas, Boston University, opens mouth wide and clenches fist as he clears bar at seven feet in track meet at Madison Square Garden Feb. 15, 1959. Stroboscopic photo by Charles Hoff.

ing outside ball for money. City College coach Nat Holman sued Jackie for $1 million.

"I didn't have it on me at the time," Farrell said. "So he settled for $1,500 and my job."

It consoled Jackie to know he was worth $998,500.

Another Gallico staffer accepted an expense advance to go to the Laurentians to cover skiing. Day after day, his articles appeared with date lines from exotic, faraway places. The writer never left his New York apartment. The one time he did, he made the mistake of taking a subway, forgetting that Patterson liked to use the subways to keep in touch with average readers of his newspaper. On this day, they came face-to-face on the subway and the skiing writer was an ex-skiing writer a few hours later.

They also tell of the rod and gun man who went to Florida on a fishing trip, bought a car and put it on his expense account. When the auditor brought the item to the attention of Patterson, the publisher said, "Give him anything he wants. The man is crazy."

Times certainly change.

And they changed in the sports department of The News. In 1934, there was a shakeup in the department because one staffer missed a big story. Several city room men were brought in to cover sports, among them George Kenney, Stuart Rogers and George Dixon. When Gallico left to devote his time to writing fiction, Jack Miley took over as columnist and Harry Schumacher served as interim sports editor. Later, Jimmy Powers became sports editor.

Under Powers, the department went through another major overhaul. Jimmy turned over most of the inside duties to his assistant, Charlie Hoerter, and devoted his time to his column, The Powerhouse.

Powers was a crusading columnist, one of the most widely read in the country. He was the first to campaign for Negroes in the major leagues; the first to suggest the wearing of plastic batting helmets; the first to advise the extension of baseball's foul lines; the first to recommend installation of "hit" and "error" signs in ball parks.

Powers and Hoerter put together a staff that included some of the best-known sports writers in America, most of whom came after World War II and are still being read today.

When baseball writers Jack Smith and Harry Forbes did not return to their jobs after the war, spots were open for men to cover the baseball beat and Powers and Hoerter filled them with capable reporters. Most of them were promoted from within The News organization, a policy the paper has long maintained.

Hy Turkin walked into the sports department one day with "nine or 10 inches of newspapers under his arm," according to Powers. "He had clipped them and circled all the mistakes we had in our box scores. I recognized him as a mathematical genius, a little Einstein, and hired him immediately."

Turkin started as a tabulator, advanced to baseball reporter and co-authored the Official Encyclopedia of Baseball before his untimely death at the age of 40.

Joe Trimble joined The News as a copy boy in 1937 and became the paper's man on the Yankees.

Dick Young graduated from the publication department to covering the Dodgers, then to his regular column, "Young Ideas."

Gene Ward went from copy boy in 1934 to boxing, horse racing and his column, "Ward To The Wise."

Jim McCulley was hired from the Cleveland News to cover boxing, baseball and horse racing, and did a hitch as columnist while Powers was serving as a commander in the navy during World War II.

Dana Mozley, the perennial best-dressed golf writer in the country, joined the staff in 1937 and was instrumental in originating the Ike Golf Tournament, one of the paper's successful promotions.

The sports cartoonist at the time was Leo O'Mealia, who originated the famous bum as the symbol of the Dodgers. Leo reached a milestone when his caricature of the bum made page one the day the Dodgers won the 1955 World Series. It was headlined, "Who's A Bum!"

Leo selected Venetian Way to win the 1960 Kentucky Derby, but died that morning and never saw his horse flash across the finish line in an upset victory.

His replacement as a cartoonist was Bill Gallo, whose creations, Basement Bertha, Yuchie and Two Kids Talking Sports, quickly captured the fancy of the reading public. Bill, three times nominated "Sports cartoonist of the year," and twice winner of a Page One award, is The News representative in Baseball's Hall of Fame, where 10 of his cartoons are on display.

Others who joined the staff in the Powers-Hoerter era are hockey writer Red Foley, pro basketball writer Joe O'Day, hunting and fishing editor Jerry Kenney, boating editor Don Price and racing writer Wes Gaffer.

Senior members of the staff are makeup man John Ebinger, who joined the staff in 1923; nightside sports editor, Lester Rose, who has been on the scene since 1929, and Carrie Quigley, Gal Friday to every sports editor since Gallico.

Hoerter got the title to go with the work he had been doing for years when Powers retired in 1957. Among his additions to the staff were pro football writers Norm Miller and Larry Fox and racing handicapper, Joe Gelardi.

Upon Hoerter's retirement in 1967, Bob Anderson became sports editor and under him St. Louis Cardinal pitcher Bob Gibson was hired to cover the 1968 World Series.

"By Bob Gibson" made page 1 the day the pitcher-writer set a series record by striking out 17 Tigers in the opening game. Anderson tried to hire Gibson as a full-time baseball writer, but couldn't match the Cardinals' offer of $125,000. He settled for Gibson's ghost writer, Phil Pepe, who was obtained for a somewhat smaller salary.

Outstanding characteristics of The News sports department have been its exclusive stories, its tenacious espousal of causes in behalf of the reader and its ability to cover sports in language the average fan can understand.

Dick Young has been called "the conscience of baseball" and, indeed, the entire department has been the conscience of all sports. Long ago, in the 1920s, The News became the first paper to pay its own way on baseball trips when Patterson said, "Our writers work for The News, not the ball clubs."

With front office support, it doggedly fought to keep the Dodgers in Brooklyn and when the battle was lost, The News stayed in the war and campaigned for the Continental League and was instrumental in the founding of the Mets and the building of Shea Stadium.

When the National and American football leagues merged, The News campaigned for a game between the town's two teams, the Jets and Giants. They have finally agreed to meet in New Haven in the fall of 1969 with The News Charities benefitting from part of the proceeds.

When it comes to exclusives, The News has been second to none.

Jim McCulley remembers getting the beat on the Yankee's signing of Casey Stengel to replace Bucky Harris.

Joe Trimble was first with the news that Johnny Keane would replace Yogi Berra as Yankee manager, that Gil Hodges would take the Mets' job and that Vince Lombardi would sign with the Redskins.

Dick Young had the scoop on the retirement of Whitey Ford and Mickey Mantle, on the Dodgers moving to Los Angeles and was first to spell out the details of Joe Namath's $400,000 contract with the Jets.

Young, who coined such phrases as "The Lords of Baseball" and "The New Breed" for the Mets' fans and who authored such memorable leads as "The tree that grows in Brooklyn is an apple tree," and "Long Gene made the world's most honored botch," summed up his sportswriting philosophy in this manner:

"The day to day quality is more important than exclusives because that's what the reader is interested in."

That also may be described as the philosophy of The News' sports department, which is bigger and better than ever after 50 exciting and glorious years.

Every decade or so, usually by dint of special effort, a story emerges that a newspaper can particularly call its own. That happened to The News in the '40s and again in the '50s. The next two chapters are examples of such stories. No one was closer to "The GI and the Orphan" than Joseph Martin and he reluctantly agreed to write it. The same task was imposed on Phil Santora, who, with Martin, won a Pulitzer prize with "Cuba Libre?" Fortunately, both men can handle words as well as predicaments.

THE GI AND THE ORPHAN

So, you want to be a reporter. You'll have to be able to prove fantasy is fact and fact is sometimes fantasy. You'll never be able to believe anyone until you have checked out the story. Not even your mother. She may be trying to get her name in print.

Always have a private concern for the defenseless and the poor. There are more great stories buried in Bowery bums than in the biographies of Wall St. brokers. Then learn to accept days of frustration when this business will drive you to the bottle. Either love this business or leave it. (Jeff Burke, newspaperman, to a copy boy in 1935.)

May 2, 1949, was typical of spring in New York. Cloudy skies, temperatures in the low 60s. The four-faced clock in the center of the city room of The News registered 5:30 p.m. demanding writers, copyreaders and editors meet the first-edition deadline.

The day's news was typical of the postwar years of the '40s.

Ingrid Bergman, leaving her husband at home, had hustled off to Rome to share light housekeeping with Roberto Rossellini. Leo Durocher faced a suspension ordered by Baseball Commissioner A. B. (Happy) Chandler for allegedly busting a fan in the face. The Giants had dropped an opener to the Braves in Boston and the Red Sox crushed the Yanks, 11–2, at Yankee Stadium.

Broadway had a fresh excitement and Times Square marquees glowed with box-office hits. Shirley Temple and Clifton Webb starred in "Mr. Belvedere Goes To College." Tennessee Williams combined Freudian overtones with a sweat shirt and offered "A Street Car Named Desire" to theater goers. Ralph Bellamy laid down an early foundation for a civilian review board with his role in "Detective Story." "Kiss Me Kate" and "High Button Shoes" gave cab drivers new tunes to whistle. White collar workers watching Lee Cobb in "Death of a Salesman" feared that one day their obituary would be written on the threadbare cuff of a tattle-gray shirt.

Red China's army was rolling through the Far East. With one exception, reports of victories in Shanghai and Nanking were of little personal concern to millions of New Yorkers. The Korean War was a year away.

To a 24-year-old ex-GI hesitating at the entrance of The News Building the Communist advance was a nightmare. He entered the building.

At a reception desk outside the news rooms he identified himself as Frank Chisari and said he wanted help in adopting a Chinese child. He asked to see the city editor. His request was relayed to assistant city editor Ted Dibble.

Dibble glanced about the city room and spotted reporter Joe Martin, heels hooked on the edge of the desk of a busy rewriteman, reading a newspaper.

"Joe," Dibble called, "there's a guy outside who wants to tell somebody something about adopting a Chinese kid. See what he has on his mind."

Martin, a former police reporter and ex-GI, glanced at the clock and grimaced. A 33-year-old bachelor, he was about to leave the office to keep a date in a distant bar in Queens.

He sauntered out to the reception room and introduced himself to Chisari. The GI's personality was warm and sincere. He had a quick intelligence. His vise-like grip went with his shoulders. He had been a Golden Glover. Here's a guy, Martin thought, you can depend on.

Slowly, chronologically, he began his story that had its start on the other side of the globe in Kunming—capital of Yunnan province in south China, terminus of the famous Burma Road and headquarters of the Far East Command of the OSS (Office of Strategic Services)—where Chisari, then 21, was a corporal in charge of radar maintenance of B-24s used to drop U.S. agents behind Japanese lines.

Four hours later Martin was still listening. Sandwiches had served as dinner. Thousands of words of notes had been taken on a typewriter. Chisari's story challenged the best of Hollywood scenarios.

"I was driving from the air base to the mess hall in a jeep early in June, 1945," he related, "when I had to stop at a railroad crossing for a train. It was like most Chinese trains, loaded with Chinese refugees.

"I heard a splash and saw a ripple in a nearby rice paddy. I thought something or somebody had fallen off the train. I got out and walked over and saw a woman's legs near the surface. I waded in and pulled her up on the railroad bank. She was a young woman, apparently a peasant, and pretty. And she was dead.

"There was nothing to do but notify the authorities. As I turned to go, I saw a bundle lying between the rails about 200 feet away. I went over, thinking it had belonged to the woman and might contain something to identify her.

"I picked up the bundle and saw the face of a baby girl. She seemed in a stupor. She wasn't crying, just lying there.

"Then I noticed the blood. Her quilted jacket and a dirty blanket around her were soaked with it. I opened the kid's jacket at the throat. She was so thin she looked only a year old, though her vocabulary later showed she was two or more.

"Cinders were ground into her face. Blood was pouring from a long gash running from the middle of her right cheek down to her throat. It looked like a knife wound, though she might have got it falling from the train."

Chisari carried the child to the jeep and laid her across his lap. Driving with one hand, he raced back to the air medical center where an officer firmly explained regulations prohibited the treatment of natives.

He drove to a nearby mission school. The priest in charge could do nothing. There was no doctor available. Chisari tried a small infirmary about a mile away. It was closed.

"I drove on totally confused. I kept my right hand pressed against the kid's throat. It wasn't septic but it checked the bleeding. The baby had regained consciousness and was repeating the Chinese word for 'water.' I passed a water vendor and got her a drink."

Chisari encountered a buddy named Howard Fener from Brooklyn. Fener knew of a French mission across town and went along to show the way. There they persuaded the authorities—with a cash offering and a promise of supplies the following day—to take the child.

Chisari returned late the following day with the promised supplies. The mission courtyard was deserted except for an old Chinese caretaker.

"She took me back to where the kid was. It was a dismal, damp hole. I saw the kid lying there. They hadn't even washed her face or changed her clothes. There was dried blood on her face. But she was still alive though they had placed her in a quarantine room where they put babies to die.

"In wartime China, lots of suffering was inevitable but I didn't want it to happen to this kid. I realized if she was going to pull through I was going to have to handle it myself."

Chisari had learned of a Chinese hospital in Kunming. He put the youngster in his jeep and headed for it but when he arrived at the hospital he found a line of patients a block long. Hitching the .45 in his belt, he bluffed his way past an attendant to a room where two Chinese doctors were treating patients. At first, he and the wounded child were ignored; then one of the doctors gestured, ordering him out of the room and back to the waiting line.

"I got sore," Chisari said. "Two days of runaround were too much. I slapped the .45 a couple of times. Then I grabbed the front of the doctor's jacket and slammed him against a wall and held him there. I was scared. One cry from him and the Chinese would have been all over me. I won. He called a nurse and instructed her to treat the kid. She washed the baby and cleansed its wounds. She gave it some shots, cut away the dead flesh and stitched up the wounds including one in the thigh that I had not noticed.

"I looked at the youngster's face, the part not hidden by bandages. She reminded me of my daughter, Adeline, just about the same age, back in New York. I knew I could never leave her to die—anymore than I could have left Adeline. I had to care for her myself. It was the only chance."

Because of round-the-clock flights of B-24s from the OSS base, Chisari had been permitted to convert the fuselage of a junked C-47 into a combination workshop and bedroom, making him readily available for emergency repairs on the planes.

He moved the child into his quarters. With the help of a friend working in the mess hall she was guaranteed a plentiful diet of rice, eggs and goat's milk. When he had to leave the youngster alone, a buddy in charge of K-9 dogs stationed one of the ferocious animals in front of the C-47 to keep intruders away.

The GI and his orphan charge became one of the best kept secrets of the OSS. If the brass knew anything they kept their silence.

Discarded parachutes were cut up and sewn into diapers. Chisari fashioned a harness to prevent the child from rolling off her cot and tearing open the stitches in her throat and face. Eventually, buffalo meat replaced rice. Slowly, he nursed her back to health and named her Ann, short for Antoinette, his wife's name.

"It was wonderful," Chisari remembered, "how she got stronger every day. She seemed to have forgotten her fright and loneliness. She smiled at me often. I was very happy and I was also very worried. I knew it couldn't last."

His loving care of the child ended abruptly. Chisari was summoned to the office of Lt. Noah Cohen, the OSS' communications officer. Gen. William J. (Wild Bill) Donovan was enroute from the States to inspect the base and it was expected he would be wilder than his name if he found an orphan baby living in a C-47.

Cohen suggested placing the child in the Kun Wei Orphanage, of the China Inland Mission. Chisari, after some difficulty, persuaded the German Lutheran Sisters who ran the overcrowded facility to accept the youngster.

"The next big job was to sell the kid on leaving me," Chisari told Martin. "She didn't like the idea. She seemed cold and frightened and looked at me appealingly. The deaconess-in-charge spoke excellent Chinese and talked to the child for nearly an hour; explaining that I wasn't going to leave and that I would be able to visit Ann every day and take her out, too. Later that day I had her baptized with my wife's name, Antoinette Chisari."

The GI and the child became a familiar sight at the base and around town. They ate together in the mess hall and he built a special seat in his jeep to ensure her safety while she watched him work on the planes. They strolled through the streets and markets where he would buy her food delicacies, toys and clothing.

About two months after he found her near death, atomic bombs fell on Hiroshima and Nagasaki, writing the final chapter of World War II and signaling the closing of the OSS base.

"I knew," Chisari said, "that we were going to leave in a few weeks. I decided the sooner the separation came, the better it would be for her, as the hurt would heal more quickly. Though it hurt to stay away, I only saw her once or twice a week.

"I'll never forget the last time I saw her. It was the day before I left for the States. We went out to a little farm owned by the orphanage. Gray little goats were grazing on the hillside. It was a nice day, sunny.

"I didn't know whether to bawl or not. I wanted to tell her I was leaving, but of course, I couldn't. I had brought along a list of questions written phonetically for me by a Chinese friend. Things I wanted to know. Did she like me? She nodded her head. Would she do what the sisters told her to? More nods.

"The last thing I asked her when I left her at the orphanage gate was, 'Who am I?' She said, 'My father.' I cried. I felt exactly the way I did when I left my family for Camp Upton.

"A sister came out and saw me crying and took Ann away. I watched her cross the courtyard and disappear into the building. She was wearing a little white apron, blue dress, blue stockings and black shoes."

Next day Chisari went over the Hump with a planeload of homeward-bound GIs.

Martin declares that when he encounters a great newspaper story a bell rings in his head. "As I listened to Chisari," he says, "I heard a carillon; Chinese temple bells and the bells of St. Pat's. It was beautiful. Having done the orphanage thing in my life, I understood this guy, how he felt, what he was talking about and what the kid meant to him."

The hour was growing late. The city streets, almost free of traffic, were growing silent. Chisari, showing the strain of an unexpectedly long day, stretched in his chair, then continued his story.

"When I got home I told my wife all about Ann, filling in the details I didn't know how to express in letters. I showed her pictures I made of the youngster at Kunming. She understands. Though we have two children now, John, 2, and Adeline, 6, she wants the child as much as I do.

"I make $70 a week at the Brooklyn Navy Yard and another $30 teaching electronics at the Delehanty Institute at night. I took the second job to pay Ann's passage here. I can't deprive my family of anything. I have $600 put aside.

"I have to get her here. I promised. I'm worried that I might have run out of time because of the war in China. The war reports frighten me. She may become trapped in the country.

"I never realized how difficult it would be to make the arrangements to bring her here. Everywhere I go I'm told it's impossible because of the limited quota covering Chinese people. The waiting list is years long. It will be too late if I depend on the quota.

"I had an appointment with an important Catholic Bishop today. When I got to his office his secretary apologized because it was cancelled. I felt it was my last chance for help. I was walking home and saw The News building. I never took this route before, maybe it's fate. I hope you can help. If you can't, I want to thank you for listening."

Chisari put on his jacket and headed home. Home was a flat in a tenement at 203 First Ave. that this family shared with his wife's mother and other in-laws.

Later that night Martin sent a cable to Kunming. Did the orphanage still exist? Was the child there or were her whereabouts unknown?

He left a memorandum for Harry Nichols, city editor: "I'll be a little late this morning and I didn't want you beating the bushes looking for me. I want to do some checking on a story that wandered into the office this afternoon. It's a helluva' story—if true. A fairy tale written from the Bible."

Martin remembered Jeff Burke's words, the editor he had served while a copy boy on the lobster shift. Fantasy or fact? Fact or fantasy?

The following day he reported to Nichols, filling him in on the details. "I hope it's true. It's a great story. Stay with it," Nichols told him. That afternoon Martin received a reply to his cable: "New York Daily News, Newspix, New York. Antoinette is well. Still here." He had the keystone to build on.

Though he had been deeply moved by Chisari's story, Martin approached his assignment like a cynical cop trying to break an alibi. Chisari was asked to return to the office and repeat his story word by word. The accounts were compared for discrepancies, even for the faintest alteration or embroidery of fact. There were none.

With the assistance of the Defense Department, Chisari's military service record was put under a microscope. It was clean—no court martials or even company punishment. The names of other OSS members in Kunming in 1945 were obtained. Questioned, they corroborated the authenticity of Chisari's story. School records were checked, friends and neighbors questioned.

Chisari survived an intensive investigation and on its completion, Neal Patterson, a craftsman of The News rewrite staff, was assigned to polish hundreds of pages of Martin's notes into more than 8,000 words recounting the touching story of the GI who found his heart divided between the Far East and Manhattan.

The News faced a major problem in trying to get the child out of Kunming with the mutual approval of the U.S. and Chinese governments. On May 23, Neal Patterson and Martin, armed with the unpublished story of the GI and Ann, left for Washington to meet with Watson B. Miller, then Immigration Commissioner.

Miller read the story. "If it means moving heaven, earth and the Capitol," he said, "we're going to get the youngster here." He arranged a further meeting with representatives of the State Department and the U.S. Attorney-General's office. They promised their aid.

The News consulted Madame Chiang Kai-shek, then in New York. On May 26 she advised Patterson that the Nationalist Government would issue a passport pending the approval of U.S. authorities.

For a week, Patterson and Martin lived the tense existence of expectant fathers. The future of the Chinese waif hung on a thread—a U.S. immigration quota number.

At the end of the week, the Chisari story was wrapped in a rainbow. Commissioner Miller phoned. He had learned that a quota number had gone into default as the result of the death of a Chinese emigree and was available to Ann. But, she must reach the U.S. by June 30.

The first of four, full-page stories by Neal Patterson appeared on June 8. It read in part:

"The News today begins the publication of one of the most moving human interest stories to come to its attention in years. It's the fascinating, true-life tale of a New York GI who saved a wounded little Chinese orphan under fiction-like circumstances, nursed her to health in the fuselage of an old C-47 when no other shelter could be found for the tiny victim—and who now seeks to bring her here to join his own family."

A final decision was made. Martin, accompanied by Bill Wallace, then a staff photographer, were to fly to the Far East to return Ann to Frank.

The legend of the Chinese waif touched the heart and captured the imagination of New York. Millions of people became concerned with the possibility of a race against time, the development of unexpected red tape and the problems of a bachelor escorting a tot across the Pacific. Mail poured in and switchboards at The News were flooded with calls from well-wishers and readers offering to help the Chisari family.

On June 11, Wallace and Martin were winging westward to Formosa. While they were enroute, Ann was to be brought from Kunming and would be waiting for them at Taipei, capital city of the steamy, craggy island 110 miles off the China mainland coast. After accomplishing routine international health and immigration requirements, they would depart for the return trip to New York.

Gen. J. L. Huang, a personal aide to Generalissimo Chiang Kai-shek, had been assigned to act as liaison between the Nationalist government and The News team.

Huang jolted Martin and Wallace into reality when they reached Taipei. The child was not there. She was still 1,200 miles away at the Kun Wei Orphanage. Huang explained that arrangements had been garbled in transmission through U.S. channels.

Though lacking a passport to China, Martin pleaded for official approval to leave for the mainland. Sympathetically, Huang refused. He stressed the dangers of travel through war-strained China with the child and the uncertainty of air travel. He promised immediate preparations would be made to send a Nationalist representative to Kunming for Ann.

Formosa in the summer is a roofless steam bath periodically washed by warm, torrential rains that turn roads into rivers of mud. At night, thumb-sized insects fly through open windows and create crazy symphonies that turn a bedroom into an Oriental version of the Savoy ballroom. Mosquito netting over beds denies the sleeper the benefit of an occasional breeze. Restaurants feature delicacies including fried roaches, raw lobsters and monkey brains. The stomachs of Martin and Wallace went on strike.

U.S. Marines, attached to the Naval Attache's office in Taipei, came to their rescue. They supplied the News team with American soups and bottles of nutritious Scotch until they developed a taste for water-buffalo meat.

Gen. Huang's agent reached Kunming and reported a major setback. Madame S. C. Liu, director of the orphanage, refused to release Ann. She was firm in her decision. She feared the commercial exploitation of the child upon her arrival in the U.S. Meanwhile, Huang had departed for Washington, D.C. on official business.

Considering making a down-payment on a rice-paddy or hari-kari, Martin cabled an SOS. Cable service from Formosa to the China mainland was as unreliable as smoke signals in a windstorm. During the following week, more than 5,000 words of cabelese were exchanged between New York, Kunming, Washington and Taipei in an effort to break the deadlock. Neal Patterson spent days on the phone with representatives of the State and Immigration departments.

On June 20, Madame Liu received the official assurance of the U.S.-Nationalist China governments that the future welfare of the child would be fully protected. She surrendered Ann. Martin thanked Buddha.

Buddha smiled, Martin and Wallace counted hours like prayer beads, unaware that new problems were developing. The new bad news traveled fast. Martin learned Ann was delayed leaving Kunming. Air transportation was unavailable. A scrap of cable, 24 hours later, reported she had reached Canton.

The ordeal at Taipei eased at 1 p.m., June 24, when a small Cessna, ordered into Operation Reunion by Gen. Clare L. (Flying Tigers) Chennault, broke through the mists over the Ping Mountain Airport, circled the field and landed.

Ann, a golden-tanned beauty of some 5-years-plus with black, braided hair, climbed from the plane. A slight wind ruffled the bright blue apron covering her blue, flowered dress. She smiled uncertainly. Martin hid the tears in his eyes from Chinese onlookers with a doll he had brought for her from the Chisari family. Expert photographer though he was, Wallace seemed to have unusual difficulty in putting the view-finder of his camera to use.

Chennault's plane had contributed invaluably in gaining time for The News team in meeting their June 30 immigration deadline in far away San Francisco. The ship had picked up Ann and Col. Shing Chung-Mei, who had been sent to Kunming for her, at Canton and had flown them to Amoy where fuel trucks were standing by. Refueled in minutes, the plane then departed on the final leg of its flight to Formosa.

Ann was taken to the home of Gen. Huang, bathed, fed and put to bed for a nap. Martin and Wallace should have celebrated. Ann was safe and with them. Celebrations were postponed. They knew the name of the game too well—trouble. And trouble came anew. Ping Mountain Airport was no LaGuardia field. And, there were no outbound flights for two days. Martin, temporarily, pushed the problem out of his mind.

When Ann awoke she was taken to a photographer's shop for photos needed for her Chinese passport and other exit papers. Martin waited for the pictures. He was taking no unnecessary chances. An appointment was made for 9 a.m. the following day with a local Chinese doctor. A thorough medical examination, including x-rays and blood tests, was mandatory before she could leave the island. Martin had a morbid thought. Suppose she broke out with measles requiring her confinement. He shuddered.

He found his Marine buddies and put the transportation problem to them. Try the MATS (Military Air Transport Service), they offered. Martin dashed off a cable to Neal Patterson, emphasizing the seriousness of the problem, suggesting possible rescue by the MATS. Patterson, working with Jerry Greene, military expert of The News in Washington, performed a miracle.

Patterson's reply hit Martin with the delightful impact of a homerun in Ebbets field. A MATS plane would be flown to Taipei to transport them to Hong Kong, terminal point of U.S. commercial airlines. The promise of the plane was gilt-edged. It had been underwritten by Louis A. Johnson, then Secretary of Defense.

The plane arrived in mid-afternoon, days before it was expected. Martin and Wallace hurried to the airport. It was a weathered C-54, a bucket-seat model. It brought Martin a new problem. The following day was Sunday and preparations to leave with the child were far from completed. If the plane left, it might be delayed in returning. Martin explained his worries to the pilot—Capt. Fay Adams. Adams said he and his crew had expected to pick up their passengers on arrival in Formosa, make a fast turn-around and be home for a late dinner. He radioed Tokyo for instructions. He was ordered to stay put overnight. His orders to hold the plane at Taipei touched off action usually reserved for Hollywood movie lots.

Within hours, Ann's Chinese passport was guaranteed to be available the next morning. Accompanied by a Marine friend, Martin jeeped to the x-ray technician's office. It was closed. Some 400 pounds of combined Marine-newspaperman opened the heavy door. Ann's x-ray negatives, identified with her name, were found in a filing cabinet. They grabbed them.

The next stop was the doctor's office. He checked the x-rays. Ann was okay. He filled out his reports of the results of the blood-tests and his examination. The child was in sound health.

The final need was Ann's U.S. visa. Martin and his marine pal sped to the home of Vice-Consul Scott George to appeal for help. George explained the visa would have to be prepared by his colleague, Wellington Z. Myers. George left a living room full of guests to go to Myers' home. Myers was not there. George left an urgent message that insured the visa would be ready in the morning.

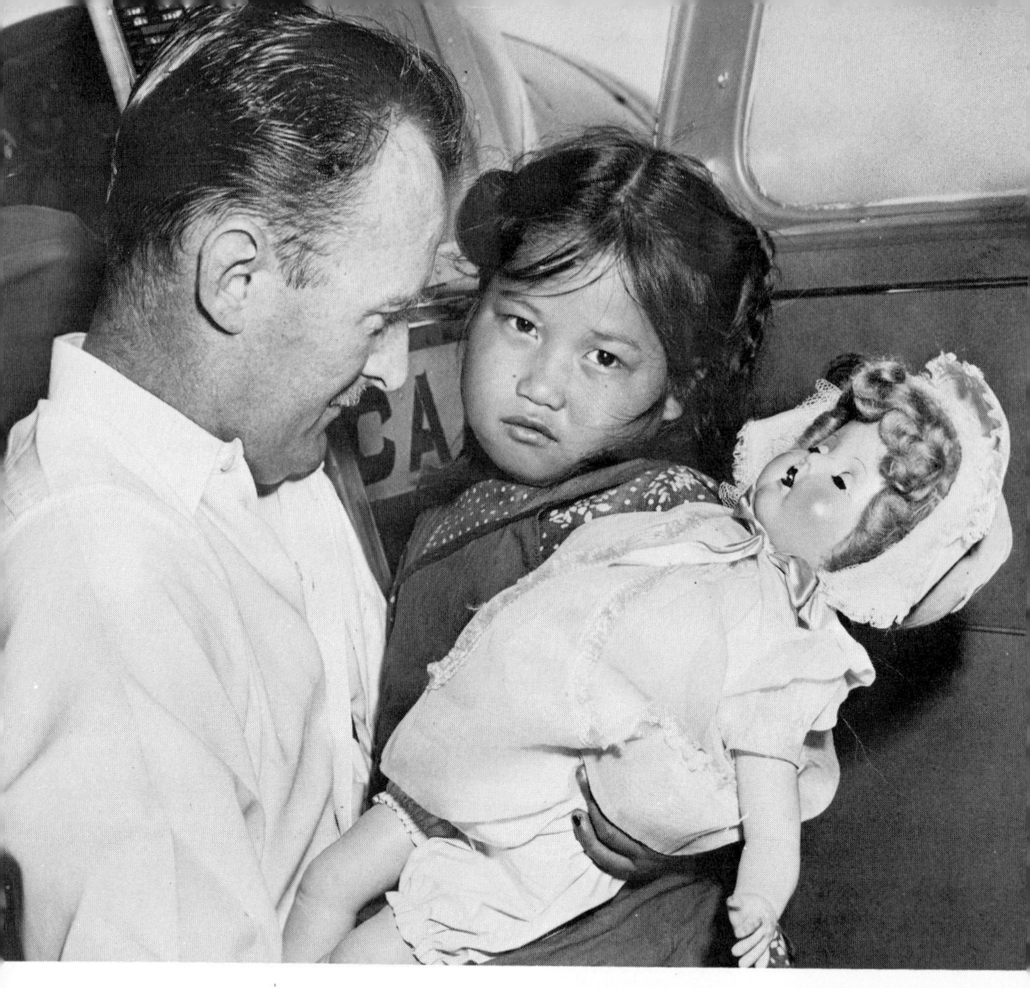

Mission accomplished. News reporter Joe Martin holds Chinese orphan, Ann, at Taipei (Formosa) airport, June 24, 1949, after her arrival from mainland China. Two days later couple started island-hopping trip to U.S. Doll was gift from Chisari family. Martin had lugged it from New York. Photographer, William Wallace.

Bride and bridegroom. Ann and Harry Dong toast each other following wedding Aug. 16, 1964. Photographer, Fred Morgan.

Day of smiles. Ann with her foster parents, Frank and Antoinette Chisari, at wedding reception. Photographer, Fred Morgan.

History repeats. Adopted Ann adopts a son, Kevin Frank, a bit more than a year old. Picture was made Feb. 28, 1969, at Dongs' home in Canaveral, Fla. Photographer, Bruce Gerard, Orlando Sentinel-Star.

Martin stopped off at a bar to purchase a brace of bottles of Scotch and rejoined the plane's crew who were preparing to bed down for the night on bare mattresses on the floor of his room. Hours later he went to bed. He slept soundly.

Sunday dawned bright and clear. Except for picking up Ann and necessary farewells, they were ready to depart. Martin got a wild idea. As a GI with the Air Force in World War II he had held a variety of jobs from crew-chief to man in charge of the preparation of travel orders for mass shipments of personnel homeward. The military, he knew, traveled on written orders as well as on its stomach.

Before departing, he had an earnest conference with the crew. He safely assumed they longed for the sight of home.

With a straight face, he asked Capt. Adams, the pilot, if the flight was covered with written orders. Negative. What were his verbal orders? To proceed from Taipei, he replied, to Hong Kong.

"I'm sure that's not the understanding of the Secretary of Defense," Martin said coolly. "I'm certain your Tokyo headquarters should be advised that we have an immigration deadline to meet and Secretary Johnson is aware of the urgency to reach the States as soon as possible. Why not query Tokyo?"

An hour later a dead-pan Adams reported, "It's okay. We proceed to the States. But they want you to know you may be transferred to another plane enroute and we'll be recalled to Tokyo." Martin wondered what the crew was grinning about.

At 1:15 p.m., Sunday, June 26, U.S. MATS plane—No. 5535, departed from Ping Mountain Airport and headed southeast on a Pacific Island-hopping flight to San Francisco.

Ann enjoyed her trip across the Pacific like a veteran air traveler. Stops were made at Guam, Kwajalein, Johnson Island and Honolulu where she had a chance to stretch her legs and enjoy the island scenery. WAC personnel took care of her personal needs. There was no relaxing the need to hasten. A mechanical breakdown could always ground the plane, short of its June 30 goal. Fuel trucks were standing by at every station to save precious hours. The plane was given priority landing and take-off clearances. Weather information was continuously fed to the crew via radio. And Ann was the hit of happy, furloughing GIs picked up along the way.

Faithful No. 5535 cleared the U.S. continental coastline on June 28 at 4:35 a.m. (Pacific time), descended through a Technicolor dawn and landed at Fairfield-Suisun Air Force Base, near San Francisco, beating the expiration date of Ann's quota number by two days.

Ann and her News escorts boarded a second MATS plane—leaving 5535 behind for maintenance work—for the final hop to New York.

The plane landed at 7:31 p.m., June 29, at LaGuardia Field. Ann's welcome equalled that of an Oriental princess. A crowd of several thousand jammed the plane's parking mat. Many had waited hours after an announcement of a delay in the ship's arrival time. Martin carried Ann from the plane and placed her in Frank's arms. He wept. After the Chisaris posed for newsreels and pictures, Vincent R. Impellitteri, then City Council President, congratulated The News on its successful mission. Said Chisari: "This is the happiest moment of my life—and I hope—of this child's life."

A motorcycle escort preceded the limousine that took the Chisaris and their new "daughter" to their home at 203 First Ave.

The scene outside their tenement home was bedlam. More than 5,000 people jammed the block between 12th and 13th Sts. requiring its closing to vehicle traffic. Well-wishers climbed the fire-escapes of the building, hoping to get a glimpse of Ann through the windows of the Chisari flat. The structures were ordered cleared by police to prevent their collapse.

Ann and the Chisaris waved from a window to the crowds below and then enjoyed a dinner of Chinese dishes including rice, noodles and shrimp. Frank smiled the smile of a man who had just received a guaranteed heart transplant. His family was reunited. He had kept his four-year-old promise.

Ann slipped quietly into her life as a New Yorker. She was rebaptized, acquiring an Irish godfather named Joe Martin. Inexplicably, she resisted her Chinese background and insisted on being enrolled in a local pubic school. Her orphanage training prevailed, she insisted on washing her own clothes. Lasagne, ravioli and veal cutlet parmigiana became her favorite substitutes for bamboo shoots and egg drop soup. She considered riding in subway trains a special treat.

Requiring larger living quarters, the Chisaris moved into Knickerbocker Village, a housing project near the lower, east-Manhattan waterfront. Chisari prospered through well-earned promotions as an electronics expert at the Brooklyn Navy Yard.

The family moved to Long Island in the mid-50s, eventually settling in a luxurious home in Searingtown, Nassau county. Frank's family had increased by two children, Frank and Camille, for a total of five.

Ann grew to be a pretty, typical suburban teenager—the scars on her face disappearing to a thin line—an excellent student and an adept housekeeper and cook, capable of meeting the needs of the household during her parents' absence.

Proceedings for her legal adoption were begun in 1961 and court-approved Aug. 15, the same year, shortly after her 17th birthday.

It was a year of decision for Ann: Marriage, career or college? The News had placed $5,000 in escrow for her college education. She rejected that opportunity, preferring early marriage, motherhood and a life of domesticity.

On Aug. 15, 1964, Ann, 20, was married to Harry Dong, 26, an aircraft mechanic and former student at Nassau Community College. She respected ancient China traditions. Following the ceremony she was escorted to the home of her new in-laws, Mr. and Mrs. Chung Dong, where she prepared and served tea as a dutiful daughter-in-law and shared with the Canton-born Dongs the traditional cake and Chinese dumplings served in syrup which her mother-in-law had cooked. She was then given a monetary gift in a red envelope for luck.

Frank Chisari's life has been blessed with good luck and happiness. The closing of the Brooklyn Navy Yard threatened a change in his good fortune. But even that turned into greater success. Temporarily unemployed, he found a job in Florida where he is now working—at a higher salary—as a project engineer at the U.S. Naval Training Device Center at Orlando.

He owns a rambling, nine-room-house—fully wired for hi-fi which is also piped into his enclosed swimming pool—located five minutes from his office. His pride is the rock garden he built in front of his home which took first prize in a community competition.

The two children who made up his family when he found Ann—John, then 2, and Adeline, 5, have thrived. Both have married and each has a child.

The Chisari-Dong families have staked out a piece of Florida as their private, happy world.

Ann and her husband started the exodus from New York four years ago. They live in Cape Canaveral. Her in-laws have their home in the same garden-type development. Various relatives of the Dongs have settled in nearby communities.

Ann's husband is the manager of the Hong Kong House, a family-owned venture at Cocoa Beach which is beginning to show signs of success. Ann's devotion to Antoinette Chisari, her foster-mother, is intense. Living an hour's drive away she spends every Monday at the Chisari home.

The happiest event in Frank Chisari's life since 1949 was Ann's adoption of a year-old baby, Kevin Frank, last November. The baby fills her life and completes the circle that began 20 years ago on a railroad track in war-strained Yunnan province, south China.

Frank sums up the years spanning Manhattan, China and Florida: "You must understand my childhood life. It lacked a great deal of the normal love and affection a youngster needs for happiness. It was something I always wanted, yearned for. With my family—and now Ann's adopted son—I have more than found the love and affection that was lost to me as a child."

CUBA LIBRE?

The ideal assignment for the truly professional reporter is the story that contains some measure of excitement, that tests his skills, that promises to make front-page news and rekindles within him the enthusiasm without which he cannot properly function.

All he asks of such an assignment is that it be different from the last one and the one before that. And the more challenging the assignment, the greater the satisfaction when the job is done.

"Inside Cuba's Total War," the expose of the Batista regime that was to win Joe Martin and Phil Santora a Pulitzer prize for distinguished international reporting, contained not only the basic elements of excitement, difficulty and variety, but was loaded down with a few extras—spies, foreign intrigue, a high degree of personal danger, secret meetings with revolutionaries.

How does an assignment like this get off the ground? Where does it start?

This one was born when Martin, in Havana to do a series on gambling in December, 1957, had a chat with a Cuban liberal who passionately denounced the Batista regime. The Cuban told of the atrocities being committed by the government, of the men and women rebels who were murdered in the streets of the outwardly gay capital.

He said that Batista was in power only through the sufferance of the U.S. State Department, that when the protective umbrella was removed Batista would fall from power.

Weeks later, Martin received a call from his informant, by this time a refugee in Mexico City. The Cuban said he was sending a list of names, phone numbers and addresses to check out.

After conferences with the then special features editor, the late Tenold R. Sunde, and editor Richard Clarke, it was decided to bring in Santora, who at the time was on a story in upstate New York.

Martin and Santora complemented each other perfectly. Both were able, shrewd, hard-bitten graduates of the police beat. Martin had won a reputation as a great reporter. Santora's reportorial skills were overshadowed by his considerable talents as a writer.

They knew and respected each other and they wasted no time checking out the list supplied by the Cuban refugee. Those in the New York area were questioned and found to be sincere, passionate patriots but ill-informed.

Martin and Santora folded their list, now cut to 15, and went to Miami to check out the rest. Instead of registering at a plush hotel, they stayed at one on Flagler St., a hotel where many of the refugees from the Batista regime lived. And that was where the action was supposed to be.

Saturday, a bright, sunny day in late March, (1958) was the blastoff. But by that evening, the two reporters had gotten precisely nowhere. One of the names of the list was that of a doctor who was alarmed at the prospect of giving information. He knew nothing, he said. Nothing.

The second was another of those passionate patriots who really knew very little. Struck out again.

But nearby there were posters in front of the Flagler Theater announcing a memorial service for a young Cuban hero, Pelayo Cuervo, an Orthodox Party president who had been killed by Batista's men.

On Sunday morning, Martin and Santora visited the Flagler Theater. There, sandwiched between advertisements for a girlie show, was a picture of Cuervo. Little boys scampered about, collecting funds for Fidel Castro, then in hiding in Oriente Province and plotting his 26th of July movement against the Batista regime.

Dr. Roberto Agramonte and Dr. Manuel Bisbe addressed the group. It was typical of other rallies—with poorly-dressed Cubans being pressured into giving until it hurt by sharply-dressed characters who kept shouting that Fidel was a combination of Tom Mix, Robin Hood, the Lone Ranger and George Patton.

Away from the emotional atmosphere of the meeting, Martin and Santora had a quiet drink and decided that not only would they be in danger of getting doctored information, but that they couldn't buy Castro.

It wasn't a final decision as yet, they cautiously told each other, but the day's work could be set aside and re-examined at a later date in the light of future developments.

By Monday evening, nine names had been crossed off the list and the two reporters were becoming a trifle edgy. By Tuesday night, the list had been reduced to one. Then Wednesday.

This one had an unlisted telephone number. He lived in the Cocoanut Grove section of Miami. Martin and Santora looked at each other. This was the end of the road, or—if a miracle occurred—the start of the real investigation and the real story.

They were tired and they were discouraged, but there was no question of what they had to do. They hopped into a cab, with Martin checking airlines schedules as they rode. The cab driver pulled up on Darwin St. There was no such number, he said.

Santora got out and rang a doorbell and was told that Darwin St. breaks in two, that the other section goes off at a tangent from another street.

A few minutes later, they arrived at a dun-colored stucco house. They told the cabbie to wait a minute and knocked on the door. A chunky Cuban in khaki shorts and a sports shirt came to the door and Martin and Santora went through the routine.

Or at least they started the routine. They mentioned the man who had given them the list.

"Come in," said the man in the shorts. Let's call him Luis. He teaches now and maybe he doesn't want his name mentioned.

The cab drove off and the two reporters walked into a house decorated with paintings and prints. Luis explained that he spoke little English, but that his wife—who was teaching English to Cubans—would be home soon.

But in that first 10 minutes, the reporters knew they had come to the right place. The miracle was about to happen.

They knew it because good reporters can feel a story. The short hairs stand up on the backs of their necks. They feel it in the seat of their pants.

There was something about this man Luis that rang true. He had authority and dignity and sincerity. He was soft-spoken but his words, spoken in halting English before his wife came home, convinced The News team that they had hit pay dirt. Santora took the cover off the typewriter. He likes to take notes on a portable whenever possible.

Luis had been a publisher, it was learned, whose town house and farm had been confiscated by the Batista government. But he was not a Castro man. Neither was he behind any of the other groups fighting to gain control of Cuba. He was a patriot, but he was logical enough to realize that there was no immediate hope for his country.

The stories came out—of torture and death, of rape and enforced prostitution. But it would be wrong, Luis said, to base a series of articles on his word alone. He would bring in other refugees, men of standing in the Cuban community, men who would tell the truth as it was.

He added that he would supply the names of contacts within Batista's stronghold when the Miami investigation was finished.

Then came long sessions at the typewriter. Most of the men who came to the house spoke no English, or very little. Luis' wife patiently sat at the kitchen table and translated, sometimes for 16 and 18 hours at a stretch.

Occasionally, she would serve thick, strong Cuban coffee. Martin and

Santora would send out for food, reluctant to stop the machine while it was producing.

But even Luis was not infallible. One night, as Martin and Santora alternated taking notes on the portable, they patiently listened to three young men give a highly-colorful story of how they had escaped, how they were planning to return, etc.

Good reporters are equipped with an early warning system that is all their own. Occasionally, the two reporters would exchange uneasy glances. The story didn't ring true.

At 1 a.m., as the pages of notes piled up, the spokesman for the trio suddenly stopped and said in heavily-accented English, "I like you."

"I like you, too," said Santora politely.

"I trust you," said the Cuban.

"I trust you too," said Santora, lying in his teeth.

"Now I tell you the right story," said the Cuban placidly.

Martin resisted the impulse to wrap the typewriter around the informant's neck and the session began all over again. The sun was up when they left.

The two reporters had not been told by Luis that his life was in danger. They knew he had a gun; a great many Cubans have weapons in their homes. On the third day, they showed up at the house on Darwin St. and found that a would-be assassin had pegged a shot at Luis from a car parked in front of the house.

It was nothing, shrugged Luis. A bad shot that one. Let's get on with important business.

Things didn't always dovetail. There were Cubans who were reluctant to talk to Americans, even though Luis had vouched for their integrity.

On several occasions, there was stubborn silence. Martin would open the act by hammering mercilessly at the reluctant witness. When he had reached the shouting stage, Santora would angrily shout, "Dammit, Joe, that's enough. You can't insult my friends. Go out, take a walk and cool off."

Joe would go out on the front porch, light a cigaret and sit down. He knew what was coming. Inside, Santora would be purring apologies. "You must forgive us, senora, for having created this disturbance in your home. Mr. Martin is overwrought. He seeks only to help, but he's Irish and they don't have our Latin ways."

Then he would turn to the Cuban who had been questioned so futilely and smile disarmingly. Outside, Martin would smile to himself as the portable began to clatter once more. The production line had hurdled another obstacle.

There were 250 pages of notes in the bank when Luis, more excited than at any time during the week of interviews, announced that the grapevine had told him the revolt against Batista might come off any day, that if Martin and Santora wanted to get the story into The News they might have to hurry.

The two reporters refused to be panicked into submitting a story that was only half-finished. They asked for a list of names in Cuba—a request that led to one of their most difficult jobs.

Luis said that a list might be confiscated by the dread secret police, the SIM, and that the lives of the men listed would undoubtedly be forfeit.

Santora, who is gifted with a trick memory, calmly suggested he memorize the names, addresses and telephone numbers. There were 28 in all and it took a full day to commit them to memory.

Martin, precise as usual, suggested they make up a code and send it to Sunde in New York in the event a revolt broke out while they were in Cuba and they were unable to get stories out of the country.

The code was based on requests for money (what else?). "Urgently need" meant an island-wide revolt. "Please cable" would mean that the army was going over to Castro. Different sums of money meant that Batista was killed, that he had been arrested, etc.

Havana was a gay, charming city in early April of 1958. But Santora and Martin saw little of the glamor. They were only too aware that they were not tourists, that they were two foreigners gathering material from groups plotting to overthrow the government.

And they had no illusions as to what might happen if their mission was uncovered. Accidents often occurred to people who got nosy about the Batista government.

They registered at the Sierra Biltmore, a couple of blocks from the presidential palace. It was dusk and they went out to have their first meal. But first, they stopped at Sloppy Joe's, almost across the street, and had a couple to keep the corpuscles active.

It was after 9 p.m. and they were merely sightseeing when they found they weren't alone. Curiously, it was Santora—who can barely see across the street—who first noticed that a Cuban in a well-cut gray suit was following them.

"He stops when we do and walks when we walk," he said. "I saw his reflection in a store-front window across the street."

"You like to walk?" asked Martin.

Santora nodded. The two walked rapidly, not too rapidly for this would create suspicion, but fast enough to tire out a man wearing tight Cuban shoes.

For over three hours, they strode through Havana's twisted streets. Finally, they sat down on the seawall of the Malecon and rested.

"When we get up," said Martin. "He won't be able to take a step. Those shoes are tight and his feet will swell."

He was right.

After that first episode, which was in the way of a little light-hearted experiment, the two reporters developed other tricks. They would walk together for a few blocks and then quickly separate and go in opposite directions.

If the tail followed Martin, then Santora would meet the contact. And vice versa.

They knew the telephones couldn't be trusted. Whenever possible, they walked to their destination, or used an outside phone—and even then used terse, non-committal phrases containing the code word, "Casino."

It was becoming a sort of game now, and reporters like to play games—even when their necks are the stakes.

The game palled somewhat when they found they had to lug their notes with them to keep them from falling into the hands of Batista's boys. They had found that their rooms were searched each day. Thin strips of scotch tape, stuck to the bottoms of the bureau drawers, were found broken—a sure sign.

On their third day, a young man in sunglasses rapped on the door to one of the rooms and said that he represented Chomon, leader of a band in the Sierra Escambray. He was taking his life in his hands but he had come to deliver a message in person.

Martin and Santora were more than careful that night. When they were convinced they had ducked the last of three tails, they met their man in the gloom of the local cathedral. He was a photographer for La Bohemia and he had hundreds of photos of the outrages committed by Batista. He would deliver them within a couple of days, he said.

He did—but Martin and Santora had to find a hiding place for their notes and photos now. They packed them carefully and gave them to an Embassy attache for safe-keeping.

The attache, an FBI agent, said he would keep the package in his home until it was needed. He didn't ask what was in it. Maybe he knew and maybe he just had a suspicion, but the seals later showed he had not tampered with the manila envelope.

What Martin and Santora didn't tell him was that there were copies of the notes and some of the pictures and these were hidden out in Vedado Beach with a friend of News columnist Bob Sylvester.

It was on their way back from the beach that the two reporters had their first encounter with Batista's SIM. Their cab was forced to the shoulder of the road and two of the secret police, their machine guns poised for action, got out and walked over.

"Americanos," chorused Martin and Santora. The members of the Cuban gestapo asked for the reporters' identity cards and the two newsmen produced their visitors' permits, phoney letters of introduction to Batista, everything but their bowling scores.

The secret police looked the papers over carefully, pretending they could read English, then grunted and it was all over.

In between "meets," the two newsmen played the part of tourists to the hilt. Santora played roulette in the casinos, while Martin renewed acquaintances with some of the gambling element.

The story was rounding out now, nearly complete. Another day, a couple of meetings with the publisher of a Cuban magazine, and it was nearly done.

They packed their photos and notes in a suitcase beneath some cheap souvenirs, some loud Cuban sports shirts and the tourists' allotment of rum and went to the airport.

There were anxious moments there when they had to wait for almost three hours while the airport rode out a near-hurricane. There were even more anxious moments in the air. The plane was held up by storms and two hours out of Havana still had not landed at Miami.

The two reporters looked at each other. Words were unnecessary. Each knew that if the plane headed back to Havana, customs inspectors there might look through their luggage.

And they knew what would happen if the photos and notes were discovered. It could mean imprisonment or even something more permanent.

But their luck held out. Back in their hotel, they called the home office. Then they had dinner and sat down to discuss the material they had collected. Curiously, despite the voluminous notes, each segment of the series fell into place.

There was some work to be cleaned up in the Miami area. Martin stayed behind and covered a Mata Hari angle, that of a former actress who had been found guilty by a kangaroo court of exiled rebels and had been threatened with death.

Santora went back to New York. Within hours after his arrival, he had talked to managing editor Shand, Sunde and Clarke. They agreed on ten articles and Santora sat down to write what he later said was the "easiest series I ever did in my life."

This was the lead of the first article:

"Tortured, enslaved Cuba is teetering on the brink of the bloodiest revolution in its strife-ripped history, with most of the crocodile-shaped island's population awaiting the call to death or liberation with almost cheerful fatalism.

"The Cubans hope the outside world will understand.

"They want others to understand, for instance, that when a young girl is raped by a police chief while his grinning cops hold back the heartbroken father, the day of reckoning can include no mercy.

"That the police official who produced a bullet-riddled body and sneered, 'There's the answer to your habeas corpus!' cannot be dealt with in the ordinary way.

"These are merely random atrocities committed in the name of President Fulgencio Batista . . . ."

There were no embellishments. The simple facts were enough. But Santora wrote them with an underlying, fiery passion that reflected his feelings and those of Martin.

Page by page, the indictment of the Batista regime flowed from the typewriter. There was no praise for Castro, nor even for Chomon. Castro, the newsmen were convinced, was hardly the answer to Cuba's problem.

The facts, inexorably documented, checked and rechecked, were basic, Batista ruled by death and terror. He was allied with the bigger U.S. mobsters.

The rebels, risking their lives, relied on sabotage as their major weapon. Martin and Santora had seen caches of arms and explosives. They had also seen that mere children were used by Castro in planting some of these explosives. An old Communist trick.

There was the economic rape of a rich island; Batista had stashed away over $300,000,000 in Swiss banks.

Close to 20,000 words flowed out of Santora's typewriter, and Martin would snatch each sheet and look it over to double-check the facts.

The first of the ten-part, double-bylined series appeared on April 7, 1958, and the impact was tremendous. Mail poured in, the switchboard was jammed with calls. Washington even sent men to try—with no luck—to pry the source of the information from Martin and Santora.

When the announcement of the Pulitzer award was made on May 4 the next year, Martin was taking a day off and Santora was working on a story in a Trappist monastery in Piffard, N.Y. They were ordered to come into the office "for a big celebration" but both refused. Each expressed astonishment, although probably in their heart-of-hearts they had been expecting it all along.

Santora claims he went into the chapel at the monastery and said a prayer of thanks. It is a matter of record, though, that he finished his assignment there four days later.

* * *

The Santora-Martin Pulitzer prize was the latest—although one hopes not the last—of such awards coming to The News and it had a story-book quality. Other Pulitzers were won by Reuben Maury, the editorial writer; C. D. Batchelor, the editorial cartoonist, and the entire photographic staff (of which mention is made elsewhere).

Martin, who has participated in many major stories for The News, is an ingrained cynic. "I was a high school dropout," he says, "and a sort of juvenile delinquent, which suited me admirably for this kind of work." Actually he is a born reporter, an omniverous reader whose self-tailored education would be more than a match for some of the horn-rimmed summa cum laudes from the Ivy League.

In the early '30s he submitted contributions to John Chapman's column, "Mainly About Manhattan," and later wrote that he would like a job as an office boy. Chapman arranged it and he has been a member of the staff ever since except for a leave of absence during which he served as deputy police commissioner in charge of public relations.

Santora likes to identify himself as "the only pool hustler who ever got a degree from the Sorbonne." Among other things, he has been an athlete, a mathematical whiz who did research for books on political government, a Marymount professor—and a pool hustler. In his high school year book, the class prophet wrote "1950—Phil Santora will be a feature writer on a New York newspaper." The class prophet was Santora.

* * *

First Newsman to win a Pulitzer was Clarence Daniel Batchelor, who picked it up for an anti-war cartoon (shown elsewhere in these pages) which was published April 25, 1936. When the award was announced a year later, there was consternation as well as joy in The News city room. The first edition had already gone to press and a frantic search for the original drawing was fruitless. (Only reproductions had been submitted to the jury judging the cartoons.) No one answered the phone at Batch's Connecticut home. Finally a cut was made from the issue in which the cartoon had appeared but the quality was far inferior to one that might have been made from the drawing itself.

The mystery was solved the next day. Bill White, the picture editor, to whom Batch submitted his cartoon each day for a check on the spelling—artists being notoriously poor spellers—had been so lavish in his praise of this one that Batch had made him a present of the original a few days later. It had been framed and was hanging on a wall of the White home. Bill naturally returned it to Batch, who sent him a copy in color to take its place.

Batch, a debonair genius who promptly eschewed bachelorhood whenever it was thrust upon him, as it has been several times, was born in Kansas, grew up in Osage City, attended the Chicago Art Institute and arrived in New York in 1912. Patterson hired him 20 years later because he admired a half-page of human-interest drawings that Batch had been doing for the Post.

When automobile fatalities became a matter of national concern in 1937, Batch suggested a series of safe-driving cartoons showing how a driver can get himself killed, with the title "Inviting the Undertaker." The first appeared that July and they continued every Monday without a break until Sept. 9, 1968, when the final one appeared. It was No. 1306.

Warren King was hired in 1955 to ease Batch's work load and is now chief editorial cartoonist. Batch, still dapper as ever with broad-brimmed hat, cane and boutonaire, is 81 and looks half that age.

Rube Maury, who also sports a cane and swings along at the same young-man-in-a-hurry pace that distinguished him from the start, won his Pulitzer prize in 1941 for distinguished editorial writing the previous year.

In 1935 Patterson decided it was time to break the traditional taboo on the subject of venereal disease. He assigned Carl Warren to do a series, specifying the dangers of syphilis and gonorrhea and using other terms equally strange to newspaper readers. The series won a Pulitzer mention for constructive journalism.

Warren had earned a degree at the Medill School of Journalism and had worked for the Chicago Tribune before becoming city editor of the Detroit Mirror and was transferred to The News when the Mirror folded. He conducted many campaigns for The News, some of which were issued later as books. His "Modern News Reporting" was a textbook in more than 300 colleges and was revised twice. For 20 years—until it was disbanded in 1962—Warren was chief of the crew which turned out an hourly, round-the-clock news program for radio broadcasting and he wrote a textbook on writing for radio that was well received. He retired in 1963 and died in 1966.

Neal Patterson, who won a Silurian award with Joe Martin and photographer Bill Wallace for his part in the rescue of a Chinese orphan (told in another chapter), was for years one of the bulwarks of the rewrite staff. He was its dean when he retired in 1966. Henry Lee, who came to The News in 1946 after serving on the World-Telegram and contributing to many national magazines, is the present star of rewrite, with close competition from two other veterans—Harry Schlegel, who came in 1944 also after a year with the World-Telegram, and Arthur Mulligan, who joined The News as a copy boy in 1936.

TODAY AND TOMORROW

The outsider's first impression is bigness. The height of the building. The extent of the floors. The masses of machinery, the truck fleets. The floors of people. Yet the News building is only part of the picture. There is another plant, garage, newsprint terminal in Brooklyn. There are a dozen borough and suburban editorial and circulation branches, correspondents in all major cities in the United States and a score abroad plus hundreds of stringers; and a half dozen advertising offices outside of New York.

The second impression might be of informality. The anonymity of shirtsleeves, common to editors and bookkeepers. The guy with the sports jacket is probably a deliveryman, compositor, pressman. The mod youth is a copy boy or messenger. The mini-skirted girl may be a typist, receptionist, punch card operator or movie reviewer. And the age assortment is wide. Jobs have long tenure. Retirement has been largely optional. Harry Bailey, a composing room foreman, set type in the Mail composing room for the June 26, 1919, issue, came to The News in 1924 and is completing his 45th year with the paper. Ben Gross, television and radio columnist, has been with the paper 44 years. Promotions come generally from the inside, keep the same people on The News a long time. Yet there is a growing proportion of young people. In the paper's 50th year, there are more than 5,400 full-time and several thousand part-time employes.

And as the outsider gets inside, he becomes aware of competence. Planned order, focused effort, close timing. The only noise is from the machinery.

* * *

News management is a seasoned team. On March 18, 1969, F. M. Flynn completed his 40th year with The News. He has been president since 1947, publisher since 1955.

W. H. (Tex) James joined The News as assistant to the business manager after his graduation from the Massachusetts Institute of Technology in 1940. He served in the Army Ordnance Division during World War II, attained the rank of captain. Since 1946 he has been successively administrative assistant to the business manager, assistant business manager, assistant to the publisher, acting circulation director, after the retirement of William Welkowitz, from May, '62, to August, '63; vice president for sales in December, '64, and executive vice president since August, '65.

Valfrid E. Palmer, currently business manager, is an MIT graduate, served as a navy jet pilot during Korean war, came to The News as administrative assistant to Tex James (then assistant business manager), supervised a three-year conversion and replacement of presses, and in 1957 acted as coordinator during the building program and construction of the 18-story wing. He was named assistant to the general manager in May, 1962, and became business manager in December, 1964.

James P. Hewitt, assistant business manager, is a relative newcomer. With an M.A. from Fordham and three years of public school teaching behind him, Hewitt came to The News as superintendent of the gravure plant in 1965.

Francis R. Walsh who became production manager in 1969 started with The News as a junior pressman in 1940; was subsequently foreman and pressroom superintendent; advanced to mechanical superintendent in October, '67.

James J. Lynch, treasurer, is a graduate of Princeton and took graduate work in finance at Northwestern. He served with a number of accountancy firms before joining the Chicago Tribune. He was transferred to New York in 1941, took time out during World War II to serve with an armored unit in Europe, became assistant auditor in 1953, auditor and controller in 1955.

Robert J. Rohrbach is the paper's controller. He was graduated from Notre Dame in 1932, with a Ph.D. in foreign commerce. After some time spent with the Chrysler Corporation, he joined the accounting department of the Chicago Tribune in 1938; served with the navy in the Pacific in World War II, attaining the rank of commander. He was transferred from the Tribune to The News in July, '52, as assistant controller, was advanced to controller in October, '63.

Jack E. Underwood, circulation manager, is another comparative newcomer. With The News since October, '64, he was formerly circulation director of the Los Angeles Times. One of his principal concerns has been the organization of the city and suburban home delivery.

John F. Herrick, advertising director since 1968, joined The News merchandising staff in 1931. During World War II navy duty, he served in the Pacific, attaining the rank of lieutenant commander. He returned to the paper in 1945, became western advertising manager with headquarters in Chicago in 1952. Seven years later he came back to New York. In 1963 he was appointed advertising manager.

Second in command in advertising is Edward F. Kroepke, advertising sales manager, who joined The News in 1935 and subsequently handled automotive linage. He served in the war for three years as the skipper of a sub chaser and engineering officer of a destroyer escort in the South

Pacific. Discharged as a lieutenant in 1945, he returned to the paper, concentrated on department store accounts and became manager of that division in 1956. He was made assistant advertising manager in 1963.

* * *

It became apparent in 1963 that industrial relations were not only a vital part of the newspaper's development but would become increasingly important as The News continued to grow. Consequently Walter K. Graham, an expert in the field, was brought in to fill the newly created post of director of industrial relations.

Graham, who had been vice president for industrial relations at Clark Bros. Co. at Olean, N.Y., since 1955, assumed his new duties that October. Since then he has been coordinating the activities of Manager of Personnel Relations Alfred H. Savage and Manager of Labor Relations Helmut J. Kracke.

A graduate of Georgia Tech, where he earned a B.S. degree in mechanical engineering in 1933, Graham also has taken graduate studies in management, business administration and industrial relations at Massachusetts Institute of Technology.

* * *

The editorial department in 1969 has more than 600 people, with 270 of those hired since 1960 still present. There were more hired in that period, and The News would have liked them to stay, but other publishers are willing to pay a premium for News experience.

Bob Shand, the late executive editor of The News, once said that the principal requirement for a good picture newspaper is 50 absolutely dedicated and experienced photographers determined to get the most telling, significant, different pictures.

There are 51 on this paper today. Some of them ride around in the 10 News cars, with drivers tuned in on police calls and in contact with the office. Some catch planes on special assignments to any place on the globe that news pictures are to be made. Some pose celebrities in the color studio. And their efforts are supplemented by wirephotos from all over the world.

* * *

The traditional progress from copy boy to reporter has changed. The reporter trainee has a bachelor's degree in something and starts at $143 a week. There are still copy boys but most of them are working their way through college.

And the photographer trainee today is a pretty sophisticated type who has been using cameras and making pictures while he was growing up. The developer and printer in the dark room is a technician with a training all his own.

Confrontation. National guardsmen hold hecklers at bay during racial disorders in Newark, N.J. This was scene in Springfield Ave. on third day of the disturbances, which resulted in a score of deaths, hundreds of injuries. Date was July 14, 1967. Photographer, Mel Finkelstein.

Chicago melee. Police battle demonstrators during 1968 Democratic national convention. This clash occurred outside Hilton Hotel on Aug. 28. Photographer, Ed Molinari.

TURMOIL IN THE STREETS

Racial and anti-Vietnam war demonstrations flared in many urban centers during the summers of 1967 and 1968. News cameramen recorded some of the violence.

Desecration. In the Sheep Meadow of New York's Central Park, anti-war demonstrators burn Stars and Stripes on April 18, 1967. Photographer, Leonard Detrick.

The News composing room has more than 800 regular employees. These men and women operate linotypes, photo-composition equipment and other auxiliary machinery. The complete operation requires a staff of more than 60 foremen and supervisors covering a 24-hour day seven days a week.

The big volume of news copy goes to the composing room between 3 and 5 p.m. A copy cutter cuts the copy into portions and distributes them to linotypers. Makeup men see to it that all the pieces come together with the proper headline, which was written to fit, marked for size by the copy desk.

The linotypes are constantly being updated or replaced and supported by the most modern electronic composing equipment.

* * *

Photoengraving has slightly more than 80 men on three shifts and can produce a finished halftone engraving ready for mat molding in as little as 30 minutes. Color comics are printed in four colors direct from chrome-plated quarter-inch zinc engravings which are secured to the rotary presses in the Brooklyn plant.

* * *

The gravure engraving plant in Brooklyn produces printing cyclinders for both color and monotone and has a staff of more than 80.

The two-page forms of type go to the sterotype department. Molds of a paper-mache composition are pressed down over the double-page type forms, dried in ovens, passed to the molding rooms. The mold is put into a cylinder which is flooded with hot type metal, cut to size and released. After inspection it is marked with a page number and slides along a roller conveyor to the pressroom.

Mats for the Brooklyn pressroom are taken there in mat cars or motorcycles and cast there. Between 90 and 100 stereotypers are employed in the two plants. Either plant may turn out as many as 4,000 plates (two pages per plate) a night.

The quality of the mold and the cast determines the quality of the actual printing surface. Quality and standards of the printed product in The News are high.

* * *

The silvery semi-circular casts slide down to the pressroom, travel by roller conveyor to the presses. Flyboys (apprentices) take the casts off the conveyor for their press units. The pressmen lock them to the cylinders. When a unit is fully plated, they wait for the start button. The start is signalled by a low rumble that rises to a roar, and assembled folded papers wedged in the spring wire conveyors are carried in a ribbon stream down to the mail room. Manhattan has 62 black units, Brooklyn 63, plus 33 gravure units and 16 color comic letterpress units. The 1930 black press units have been twice replaced. These presses transfer more than 13,000,000 pounds of ink (includes black and white, comic and roto) to 330,000 tons of newsprint in the course of a year. During the spring and fall peak advertising periods, the black and white press capacity is 356,000 copies of 192-page products per hour. Sunday comic and roto sections are printed during three shift operations the week before issue date; Sunday black and white sections (several sections) are printed two days prior to the issue. This complex production requires complicated planning and close controls.

* * *

Down in the first floor mailroom, papers stream down long narrow conveyors through tying, bundling and counting machines. Mailers slap orange paper wrappers, already addressed, on top of each pile. The bundles for out of town shipment are collected on movable tables.

* * *

Delivery is more difficult than it was 30 years ago when the population was city-centered. The spread to the suburbs burns up more truck tires, takes more time, requires the presses to roll earlier. City outlets have shrunk. The Broadway to Spuyten Duyvil route that once served 118 outlets now has fewer than 90. The older news dealers die and their more privileged offspring find more lucrative occupations. The spread of after dark crime has also closed many outlets.

To reach readers in outlying boroughs and suburbs, The News in recent years has been promoting home delivery to supplant the newsstand and the newsboy. In 1969, The News had in excess of 180,000 home delivered circulation daily, 250,000 Sunday.

* * *

To help cope with its immensely complicated payroll, accounting, production, circulation, advertising and distribution problems, The News has installed an elaborate computer system. Sophisticated programs are already on paper which will assist the executive, plant manager, group supervisor, employee, and eventually provide The News reader with an improved product geared to his changing requirements.

* * *

Operating two printing plants, two garages, and a newsprint terminal may not be the ultimate in efficiency or economy. Demands for more production capacity influenced The News management in 1965 in its decision to purchase a 24-acre tract on Long Island across from E. 35th St., Manhattan. The site is unofficially named Newspoint. It would accomodate water and rail delivery of newsprint direct from the mill and provide sufficient ground area for concentrating newsprint storage, production and garage space in a single location. Planning for this site is under study.

The News' impact on the public, the popular liking and long patronage come in no small measure from the personal contacts that have been a part of its program. A letter, a voice on the phone, a pretty receptionist, a visit, offset the impersonality of a business and improve its image.

If 50 years affords any index, The News of tomorrow will continue to be the peoples' paper, changing as people change, adapting to their needs, their interests, their educational level. It may be printed electronically, some form of facsimile, or televised visual recording. It will be of its time.

But it will not abandon its credo, as announced in its first issue: "This newspaper will always be free and independent. It will have no entangling alliance with any class whatever—for class feeling is always antagonistic to the interests of the whole people."

The News has always been a good place to work, above average rewarding, an equal opportunity employer before the term was known. It promises to be an even better place to work in the future, more exciting, more absorbing, more rewarding—not only for writers, picture makers and editors, but for specialists, marketing planners, systems engineers, computer programmers, Ph.D.s and M.B.A.s. As its complexities increase, so will its opportunities—for the young, the gifted, the adventurous, and the people-oriented—beyond and above the ordinary.

INDEX